THE RELIGION OF PHILOSOPHERS

THE RELIGION *of* PHILOSOPHERS

By

JAMES H. DUNHAM

Dean Emeritus
College of Liberal Arts and Sciences
Temple University

Essay Index Reprint Series

BOOKS FOR LIBRARIES PRESS
FREEPORT, NEW YORK

Copyright, 1947, Temple University

Reprinted 1969 by arrangement with
University of Pennsylvania Press

STANDARD BOOK NUMBER:

8369-1059-1

LIBRARY OF CONGRESS CATALOG CARD NUMBER:

78-80386

PRINTED IN THE UNITED STATES OF AMERICA

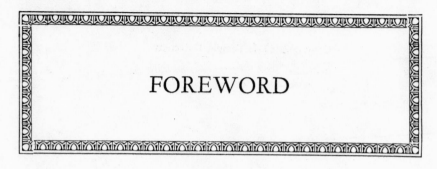

FOREWORD

It is an enticing subject that we have attempted to unfold in the chapters of this book. Every student of philosophy, soon or late, is obliged to consider its ramified implications. What do we mean by universal Substance? Does it exist as an objective reality, or is its concept the only fact we can logically deal with? If we maintain that it has independent existence, how can we investigate its attributes? What sort of intellectual activity can grapple with a reality that is not presented, point by point, to the senses of the body? Then, how can so subtle a power have been developed in a mind which seems wholly governed by its reactions to a sensuous environment? These are some of the questions facing the honest investigator. They have a right to be asked, and they have a right to demand a careful answer. The strictures upon them by the Logical Positivist and their contemptuous rejection by certain physical scientists cannot remove them from their place in the currents of human thought. Philosophy retorts to such criticisms by studiously examining each successive question, in the endeavor to obtain an intelligible answer.

We invite the candid reader to join in this exhilarating exercise.

J. H. D.

Philadelphia
May 1947

CONTENTS

I: INTRODUCTION

No ATTEMPT is made in these studies to place the capital subject under the binding terms of a logical definition. If that were done, we should be obliged, in many cases, either to abridge or to expand the framework within which each thinker develops his particular program. Such a procedure might also force us to exclude at least one of the historic figures from the list, thereby eliminating certain considerations that have a right to appear in an analysis of a philosophical system. The purpose of the work is to record, in some detail, the methods pursued in assembling the materials appertaining to the problem, in pointing out their relations to other problems in the field of human experience, in showing how such materials should be thoroughly "screened" before they are finally accepted, and in determining whether or not they can supply the principles entering into an adequate solution. In every case the master will speak for himself. It should be understood, however, that he is not summoned to defend his opinions in face of a hostile court nor to be a witness against some unpopular precept. This is not a judicial tribunal where evidence is to be weighed pro and con in order to arrive at a credible verdict. Comparisons will be made with other thinkers, and justiciable issues will be discussed with candor and discretion. In some instances it may appear that the interpretation by the expositor follows a path tangential to what is commonly approved. Here, let it be remembered, we are trying to unfold the basic ideas embodied in the texts transmitted to us. We have set up, we said, no categorical standard to which every man's treatment of the subject must be made to conform. Religion is not defined except as the thinker defines it for himself. That a concept like this has an indefinite number of gleaming facets, each significant in itself but by no means comprehending the whole, is proven by the difference of views exhibited here. Because the subject is so wide, so diversified, so compelling in its every feature, the individual philosopher may dwell on one phase at the beginning of his study and another later, the result being that an expounder of his system is bewildered by the wealth of his treasures and knows not which to accept as the heart of the golden store.

Still another qualification must be carefully observed. No competent critic will deny that the concept of religion necessarily splits into two categories, the substantive principles which are polarized about the idea of the revered object, and the manner of applying them in the private behavior of the worshipper or in the public institutions of the state. Theory and practice are not conflicting terms, although at times it seems difficult to reconcile one with the other. Philosophy has its roots in principles and hesitates to shape the external forms in which its counsels may be expressed. We have therefore confined our studies to the didactic issues at stake, leaving personal sentiments to take their place in an organized biography of the philosopher. Yet in certain cases the religious emotions are so close to the controlling ideas that they cannot well be separated. This is true in the attitude of Spinoza and Kant, and notably in the inquiries of Augustine. It has its repercussions in the career of Auguste Comte, perhaps by virtue of his peculiar temperament, specifically because of the engrossing incident which occurred between the production of his two major works. However, while emotional states make an enduring imprint upon the sternest intellect, the task of a philosopher in writing upon religious themes is to state his thought with exactness and logical regularity without—at the moment—allowing his private experiences to influence, in the slightest degree, the nature of his intellectual decisions. The physical scientist knows full well that no obtrusive element of body or mind can be permitted to interfere with the several situations of his experiment. The student of jurisprudence is aware that every disabling condition such as private prejudice or the favor of the group must be resolutely barred, if he is to formulate accurately a theory of social justice. In both cases it is necessary to adopt an objective posture; otherwise the validity of their conclusions will be seriously impaired. At the same time, in the philosophy of religion there is so close a connection between the statement of principle and the sequence of appropriate deeds, that a divorce between them, other than momentary, is out of the question; religion when not backed by behavior is held to be infertile and even unreal. Yet because it is a natural organ of human experience religion has as good a right as science or law to stand apart from its concrete embodiment and study the concepts which later will be crystallized in a system of doctrine and even in a historical institution. This is what the men appearing in this book have done—ten thinkers of the western world, from many ages and diverse stocks, who offer us the fruits of their labors. They do not stand alone; many distinguished preceptors could be added; but they will serve to reflect the unflagging interest of the human race in a subject than which none higher can be conceived.

But there is still another restriction to our theme that must be noted. If we decline to frame a definition of religion at the beginning of our survey, we shall at the end of the study of each type refuse to place its author under some established rubric which could make his relation to other thinkers precise and certain. Theology has adopted such terms as theism, deism, pantheism, atheism, and the like; it has gained nothing but controversy, ill-feeling, and reproach. Philosophy will not use such designations; its habits of analysis are different. Thus the charge laid against Spinoza: first that he was an atheist, then—by way of softening the accusation—that he was a pantheist, has no critical value whatsoever. For apart from the animus implied in the charge, the terms represent a wholly different approach to the study of divinity. The theologian accepts the existence of deity as a fixed integer of thought, and then proceeds to expound the essential attributes involved. Philosophy, on the contrary, studies the problem in the light of developing experience, slowly, steadily, cumulatively, building its judgmental structure until the idea of God is finally reached. Because of this variation in approach it is futile to use the same term for the purpose of defining the same concept. But this is not the only difficulty we are forced to meet; a greater one emerges when we attempt to examine one of the cardinal attributes of the theistic deity, namely, personality. Merely to ascribe intelligence and will without stating *how* God knows or *how* he acts, leaves the mind of the average believer in a state of confusion. Does the divine thought proceed by the same logical rules as man's thought? Or, are the decisive actions of God based on the same type of motive as that which controls man's conduct? To answer that God's thought and action are infinite, while man's are finite, is not constructive. This would simply lead us to infer that personality may reach from finitude to infinity. How is that possible in the light of certain sheer delinquencies inherent in man's constitution—a sudden break in the continuity of personal identity, the overriding of the serenity of temperament by some dominant impulse? Further, if the traits resident in human personality were magnified to an infinite degree, would they not lose their definitional content and thus assume a different meaning when applied to God? A brief critique like this can at least uncover the enormous hazards we are obliged to overcome if we seek to transfer the units of thought in philosophy to a wholly dissimilar situation in theology. In the same way precisely, when the terms are reversed, shall we find ourselves in confusion if we disregard the rules of logical procedure and try to use in philosophy the concepts or designations that may be justified in another sphere of investigation?

With these preliminary matters settled, we advance to the main questions that must engage the attention of philosophers. The first one is fundamental: What is the specific activity of mind by which a study of the high themes of religion can be carried on? It does not embrace the emotional reactions such as awe or curiosity, although a certain fervency of feeling will steal into the most abstract forms of logical scrutiny. Obviously, the elementary habits of direct apprehension are of no value here. Sense-perception collects the data for the objects of sight and touch, but cursory experience, however far extended, cannot change the complexion of the image communicated by the organs of the body. Even Epicurus must introduce a special and supplementary principle if he is to make his perceptions of the atomic gods effective. Nor can the intramental function of the fancy change the revelations of the senses into conceits wholly unrelated to the matter and motions of nature. Again, if we take one further step and lift our thought to the level of coördinate judgments, where universal ideas are the sole instruments of reason, we are still shadowed by the objective situations from which the substance of the judgments has been derived. There remains but one other agency which philosophy has repeatedly toyed with but never fully admitted to its confidence. Pure reason, says Plato, intuition, says Spinoza, has command of ideas which lie outside the range of accredited perceptions; these penetrate into the heart of truth. The genius of Kant plays upon the subtleties of the suggestion, in an effort to regularize the conceptions of God, immortality, and freedom versus mechanical necessity. For Plato intuition is a kind of superordinated logic; for Spinoza, it has an aesthetic value in that it can conceive the principles intrinsic to the divine existence and at the same time unveil the solitary idea that makes it supreme. For Kant the argument ends in the recognition that while the reality of God cannot be established by scientific proof, we can at least think and act *as if* we had gained the end desired. In short, knowledge of God can be only schematic; the content of truth must be filled by what religious sentiment ordinarily calls faith. Hence, whatever be the type of argument set up by the individual thinker, he is in duty bound to accept a kind of rescript such as the one we have just indicated. He is not at liberty to cite the deliverances of a theological creed in support either of his assumptions or his conclusions. Logic, not extraneous authority, must be his only guide.

Presupposing that we have found a procedure for conducting this high inquiry, we next ask, What are the essential points in the problem which must be determined before we can hope to obtain a full understanding of the concept of divinity? They may be conveniently grouped under two heads, the analytic and the synthetic. The former studies the physical universe where man has his dwelling-place; the latter examines the intellectual and emotional resources of the human spirit, properties that are said to make it possible for us to frame the image of God in our own nature. We may begin our inspection at either point, suiting the task to the temperament of the immediate inquirer. If we take the first we shall be led eventually to look upon divinity as the creative mind whose works must be thoroughly analyzed in our quest of its master attributes. If we begin our studies at the second point, we shall endeavor from the very outset to synthesize thought and action in a drama whose dénouement can be nothing other than the union of our souls with the delectable beauty of the supreme spirit. The mystic and the modern idealist have chosen the latter course, arguing that only thus can we be prepared later to undertake a sympathetic exploration of nature's mysteries, the objective expressions of eternal truths.

However, the historic method has been to treat the first subject first, and then to advance to a study of the second. It was in this manner that the Socratic school attempted to carry out its commission. Its founder heard the voice of the Delphic oracle, Know thyself, and at once presented its terms as a bold challenge to the public teachings of contemporary Sophists. Gorgias and Thrasymachus laid the emphasis solely on the uncurbed impulses of the soul: Man acts according to the dictates of taste or inclination, under the rule that might alone makes right; that is, law is always the exercise of the instruments of physical superiority. To this thesis Socrates and his disciples retorted: Ultimate control lies in the judgments of the reason; if man is to emancipate himself from the grip of time and sense, he must make an exhaustive study of the forces of nature as well as of his inherent capacities to meet and conquer them. This is the single and compelling method for the satisfactory settlement of his social problems, for the erection and maintenance of the civil state, and for establishing enduring peace between commonwealths having common but often conflicting interests. But this is not the end of man's quest, he soon passes beyond the purlieus of sight and touch and enters the wider areas of scientific investigation. Here the concept of causality thrusts its fangs into the fancy of the observer, eliciting new and complex questions which must be faithfully studied. Finally, the crowning problem which the Ionian philosophers tried to solve by the simple artifice of a corporeal source—air, fire or water— remained to test the genius of more mature thinkers. Power, aboriginal, primeval power, cannot reside in the fighting Zeus of Homeric legend or in the shadowy indeterminate substance of Anaximander. Instead, the new science glimpsed the presence of a supreme authority conceived at first as embodied in the unbroken universe and then, under the influence of the oriental cults, in an extra-mural deity whose substance was universal and whose power without limit. At length appeared the definitive concept, God, eternal being, triune in nature, linking heaven and earth in his glowing majesty, the incarnation of wisdom and love in a human person who lived and died for the redemption of mankind from its sin. After a revelation such as this, supreme substance could no longer be identified with the structure of a mechanical universe; the debate was joined on an issue of major importance—Is God immanent in the natural universe or is he transcendent in his essence and glory? The Stoics who found a spermatic reason in the forces of the visible world were now faced by a steadily growing company of thinkers, with strong convictions and pioneering zeal, who expounded the doctrine that God is completely separate from the world, that he created its offices and its diversified agencies by the "word of his power," and that he has the authority to intervene in the affairs of the world by virtue of his creative rights. So impressive was the argument in favor of the new theory and so cogent its appeal to the emotions of men through such documents as Augustine's *City of God*, that the principle of transcendence—new to the western intellect—became not only a capital tenet in the belief of the established religion (A. D. 325) but also the first point in the Alexandrian philosophy organized under the tuition of Plotinus (A. D. 204–270). Thereafter the Greek concept of material substance receded into the background of European thought, appearing at intervals only when some masterful soul like Tilesio defied the papal ban and accepted nature as the one existing thing, or when Giordano Bruno, in an ecstasy of sentimental fervor, found God (even though temporarily) in the expanse of an infinite universe. Likewise Gassendi in the Cartesian era, and a multitude of scientific inquirers in the ensuing centuries, declined to go beyond the confines of visible matter in quest of a controlling power. The tale which men in this book will tell reveals both the scope of their vision and the independence of their conclusions. Whatever be their individual solutions, it is plain that some of them have found their answers to the primary question, *what God is*, by following the line of scientific investigation just as far as science could go, then turning to philosophy for guidance in the ultimate decisions to be made.

But there is another approach to the problem, as was said. This time we deliberately put to one side the study of the images of sense and turn to an examination of the meaning and destiny of the human spirit. That was the position of certain thinkers in the Stoic tradition. They felt most keenly their own weakness when confronted with the portents of the physical world. Likewise they were reduced to the verge of despair when they noted the painful inequalities in the social groups and could fashion no remedy to cure or abate them. Even men so highly placed as Aurelius on the imperial throne could not escape the feeling of private impotence, when they compared the might of universal reason with their own puny efforts to copy it. On the other hand, the approach of Augustine to the problem was different, profoundly different. He began with the admission that the human race in the person of the first man had voluntarily, or at any rate spontaneously, sinned against the Lord of heaven and earth and could not release itself from its mortal captivity. For the Stoic it was inherent weakness, for the Christian it was deliberate choice which made the soul's imprisonment hopeless. But what human ingenuity could not do, divine benevolence did—it broke the fetters of bondage by an act of grace unexampled in the history of the world, the death of the divine son. By this transaction the essential nobility of human personality was proclaimed, a type of value never suspected by the mind of Greece. The new philosophy thus conceived recognized the meaning of rational judgment as a function of behavior, but passed beyond that to a coördinating principle which had in it something like a spiritual implication. Plato hinted at such a principle in the *Philebus* dialogue: The essence of character is not emotional gratification or logical acumen but goodness, the rounded whole of the moral self, a fact which received its final formulation, said Augustine, when the man of Galilee breathed his spirit into the living church. From this time forth the new idea of personality passed into the currency of European thought and left its mark upon every code of ethics and divinity in every century.

The statement just made may be verified by a study of some of the arguments examined in this volume. It is not by a circuitous or arbitrary route that the concept of morality has entered even the lofty reaches of the cosmic philosophy. The history of Greece has no record of such an attempt. Her teachers often constructed a parallel between the steady operations of bodies in the natural world and the balance between opposing forces in the world of society; further than that they did not go. Modern man, however, has not hesitated, as we find in the *Monadology* of Leibniz, to make the principles of morals run concomitantly with the mechanics of physical nature. We may urge, in extenuation of his claim, that Leibniz was concerned to expand unduly the conception of moral values or that he deliberately changed the meaning of the term or that he sought to escape from the confusion of his fantastic dithyrambic by citing the confirmatory article of the Christian creed and forcing it into a situation where it did not belong. However, a more capacious thinker in the next century possessed himself of the same idea, not for the purpose of celebrating the excellence of nature's movements but in order to bring to a focus the supreme attributes of deity. To a reader acquainted with the vernacular of the scriptures such an application of the term *moral* might seem normal and quite appropriate. No doubt it represents an enormous change from the logical rigor of the Greek conception. The change can only be accounted for on the ground that personality has now been invested with a new and qualitatively exalted meaning through the influence of the Christian religion. Still we are obliged to admit that Kant has framed his own chromatic pattern of the idea, and we do not in any way suggest that he followed the Pauline precedent when he described divine essence as fundamentally and irretrievably moral. Theology may prefer to sum up God's beatitude by the concept of holiness, thus separating him from his creations as if he existed in unapproachable and stately solitude. Kant, by using the other term, placed him emphatically on a level where his subjects could understand his communications and begin to feel a kinship with his spirit. There is no attempt in this introductory paragraph to decide whether the philosopher holds God to be a regulative conceit of the reason or whether he accepts the actual existence of the deity.

These are two notable efforts in the modern period to sublimate the principle of the moral good first as a necessary integer in the fabric of the universe, and then as the consummatory element in the divine nature, so far as human ingenuity can conceive and formulate its essential meaning.

Facing these theories and completely canceling their validity stands a new and disruptive reading of the idea of personality. It was propounded by Auguste Comte in 1830 in the first volume of his *Positive Philosophy*. By that time the mighty forces of the French Revolution had begun to ebb. Reason, that is, metaphysical truth, was no longer enthroned as the divinity that could shape the ends of human conduct and determine infallibly its destiny. As a practical measure Comte submitted to Guizot, the minister of education, a proposal to establish a university foundation for the study of the history of the sciences. If the history of philosophy required four chairs of instruction for the demonstration of the fancies and unfounded mythologies of human speculation, surely one chair could be devoted to the study of the records of experimental research and its significant conclusions. Particularly was such a survey needed in the field of religious thought. Historical analysis shows that there have been two controlling causes in the organization of its concepts. On the one side appeared the concrete symbols embodied in the classical tradition and in the structure of the Christian church. Here independent figures stood out solitary and alone amid the confused endeavors to frame and interpret the basic instincts of the soul. The figure of Zeus and the figure of Jesus bodied forth the concept of lordship over men's sentiments and expectations. Reverence for an individuated divinity was the single article of belief. But philosophy was not content with so cavalier a decision. It envisaged a change in the point of view which would enable men to define the logical grounds for every doctrine they espoused. It insisted that every item of religious behavior should be carefully examined, so that contradictory ideas might not coexist in the same metaphysical system. The elaborate inquiries of Plato in the *Timaeus* and the *Sophist* were matched by the intricate dialectic of Athanasius, both tending to release religion from the toils of an objective ritual and to concentrate its interests on the proud dogmas of a systematic philosophy. In the Latin church the long line of Scholastics succeeded in shutting up its spiritual hopes within the confines of an infallible creed, signed, sealed and delivered by the edicts of the Roman Curia.

But in neither source of religious authority has the call for the scientific analysis of the actual materials of faith been heard. Indeed, science as an empirical quest has never been cultivated by the officials of the church; in most cases it has been deliberately ignored or haughtily disputed or ruthlessly rejected. Roger Bacon, Copernicus, Galileo are witnesses to the unwavering hostility of its authoritative representatives. In England where scientific procedure was not hampered by the church's antagonism, William Harvey in 1628 announced the discovery of the circulation of the blood, a theory which destroyed the claims of the old Galenian hypothesis. It was Descartes, a resident of the free state of the Netherlands, who acknowledged in his *Methode,* published in 1637, the revolutionary importance of the discovery—"the course of the blood in the body is nothing more or less than a kind of perpetual motion in a circle." No similar advance was made in the study of human psychology. The Roman church has never organized an impartial study of the constitutive factors in the human personality. It gave no heed to the results of Descartes' and Spinoza's study of the power and scope of emotions in men's experience, always affirming that Thomas Aquinas has settled its theorems in that department of thought, and further examination would be unnecessary. In the face of such obstructive tactics, no scientific analysis of human conduct could be pursued. For these reasons Comte concluded that the time had come when a strong effort must be made to obtain a detailed, exact, and authentic knowledge of how men acted, by instinct or deliberate decision, in their relations to one another. Society must become the official laboratory for the "proper study of mankind." Humanity, in the large, must no longer remain an abstract conception, distilled from the observation of a multitude of individual expressions; it must be studied as a succinct and independent personality, endowed with all the qualities of its visible segments and incorporating the distinguishing maxim of the Positive creed, *vivre autrui,* live for others. When the examination is complete it will be found, he argued, that the ancient objects of religious veneration can no longer enjoy the patronage of the scientific mind; instead, humanity will occupy the seat of spiritual authority and will embody as no other divinity could the beauty and pervasiveness of the moral reason. The argument of Comte with a suitable rebuttal will appear in the final chapter of this book.

II: PLATO

In examining the religious ideas of any thinker we must bear in mind two separate facts, (1) the habitual notions inherited from many generations, and (2) the specific teachings drawn from his immediate environment. The first of these included for Plato the ordinary mythological concepts still current among the group though largely rejected or at least discounted by the educated classes. Piety consisted in the recognition of the laws of society imbedded in the acts of public worship as well as in the behavior of daily life. Men are pious because they obey the civil laws. Socrates had criticized this judgment on the ground that obedience to law was the test of just action, not of religious regularity. All pious men are just, but not all just men are pious. The field of behavior is different for the two types of thought. It should be remembered that *Vox populi* is not necessarily *Vox Dei;* submission to the laws of men is not the same as obedience to divine commands. Plato met the same sentiments that Socrates had vigorously combatted. He saw Socrates convicted by the public assembly for teaching doctrines contrary to the body of religious thought as held by the influential leaders. It has been suggested[1] that Socrates had adopted the tenets of Pythagoreanism and since Pythagoreanism was the religion of Thebes and Thebes the historic enemy of Athens, Socrates became automatically the enemy of his own state and should therefore be condemned. The facts in the case are obscure and must not be accepted as proving the contention of the critic. The one point that is plain is this:—Socrates was *persona non grata* to the ruling class who used the cloak of religion as the excuse for securing his conviction at the hands of the assembly. In short, religion had become the instrument of the government for working its own will. The ignorance of the masses brought success to its projects within the range of normal expectation. This was possible because of two fixed principles, first, that religious dogmas are unchangeable and secondly, that the state has the right to compel citizens to accept and practice all authorized religious customs.

It was against this attitude that the philosophers lifted up their voices in protest. Xenophanes had criticized the procedure in the 6th century B. C.

[1] By A. E. Taylor, *Varia Socratica* (Oxford: J. Parker & Co., 1911), p. 30.

He made a thorough examination of current religious concepts and in every instance found them faulty. He regarded the gods of Greece as inventions of the mind; they had no existence apart from human fancy. This may be proven in two ways; first, the character of the accepted divinities possessed the very traits which distinguish the behavior of mankind. They are plural, not single; they originate in time, are begotten in human fashion, and though they perish as men do, seem to represent persistent types of thought and action. Zeus is the perfect picture of the earthly tyrant and Hera the Xanthippe of a nobler mien. Secondly, different races construct their gods according to their own pattern. The Ethiopians make them swarthy and snub-nosed while the Thracians conceive of them as having blue eyes and red hair. Furthermore, if the gods actually exist man can have no intercourse with them; some genius might hit upon the truth about them, but if he did he could never verify its terms. The criticism hinges upon the general principle that religion is a personal experience and must vary with the ideas of different persons and different ages.

That Plato is in complete agreement with this argument is attested by his bitter attack upon the treatment of the theme by the recognized poets of Greece. Any doctrine that conceives of God as possessing the properties of human intelligence is regarded by him as wholly unsatisfactory. He denies, for example, the validity of the thesis that God can be the author both of good and evil. The words of Aeschylus are impious: "God plants guilt among men when he desires utterly to destroy a house." Plato is equally firm in his judgment that the current idea of a god who can change himself into any shape for ulterior purposes, is wrong and must be excluded from the creed of the state. Furthermore, God is falsely represented by Homer when he describes Zeus as sending a deceptive dream to Agamemnon.[2] In his stern invective Plato *seems* to be criticizing the art and intellectual concepts of the poets; in reality he is seeking to undermine the superstitions of his generation, and in this effort he is at one with a multitude of later thinkers who have boldly challenged the spurious dogmas of an uncritical age and attempted to destroy them.

But Plato's attitude was not merely destructive; he entered into the spirit of the Eleatic philosophy and aimed to interpret its concepts in terms of religious thought. The world, said Parmenides, is One, a unity not a multiplicity; it is true Being, the supreme Reality, uncreated, indivisible, immovable, complete in itself. Motion exists within the whole, to be sure, but the Whole possesses the essence of divinity; it is God himself. Such was the fascinating theme that made its appeal to the mind of Plato. He could not assent to the crude suggestion that God was synonymous with matter; matter was not, for him, the ultimate attribute of reality. Parmenides had

[2] *Republic*, 372–73.

some premonition of the value of mind as the expression of reality, as is attested by his saying that "it is the same thing to think and to be." This seems to mean that ultimate reality may be studied from two standpoints, first, its corporate relations which are understood by means of the five senses and the intellectual categories, in short, by the implements of science; and secondly, its principles of action which are the laws of universal substance. Plato develops the latter suggestion because he detected there the correct solution to the problem of reality. What is the law of universal substance? What is the place of "thought" in the constitution of the world? Thought and matter are obviously not the same; the body of man is one thing, his mind is another. The contact of the senses with matter is one fact, the mind's examination of the data of consciousness is another. Plato has made the difference clear; he offers the first logical explanation of the relation of precept and concept in the history of human speculation. We shall not be far from the truth when we say that one of the reasons for constructing his theory of Ideas lay in his desire to understand the universal attributes of reality. It is clear, then, that religion for Plato, does not concern itself with the particularistic forms of religious expression as found in the list of Greek divinities, but with the broad comprehensive questions of fundamental law.

We may pause a moment to examine the suggestion of a recent writer,[3] who regards Plato's distinction between belief and knowledge as the key to his solution of the problem now under review. Belief or opinion deals only with the objects of the observable world, with its changing forms and ofttimes uncertain properties. Knowledge, on the other hand, excludes the images of the sensible consciousness from its consideration and studies only the relations of universal ideas. Between the two mental facts there can be no contradiction, as we ourselves shall argue in the sequel, because they move on different though frequently parallel planes. In the sphere of religion Plato makes the absence of the contradiction very plain. He uses two sets of terms to describe the two independent subjects of discourse. In the one case the figures of mythology belong to the world of sense, even though they are never actually incorporated in the data of perception. These figures are endowed with all the qualities that organic bodies, especially the body of man, possess. The qualities are single and particular; they are applied to objects whose identity is thought to be guaranteed by the coördinates of time and space. Such individuals are called "gods" or divinities; "their reciprocal relations, their friendships and enmities, their internecine wars, the development of their empires in heaven and under the earth, all this belongs to the world of becoming and is com-

[3] Hugo Perls, "Savoir et la foi religieuse dans l'œuvre de Platon," *Mercure de France*, CCLXXXI (Jan. 1, 1938), 5–23.

pletely closed to scientific inquiry which aims only at pure knowledge." [4]
The only thing the Greek could say of them is that he *believed* they existed and that they behaved in the indicated manner. Positive proof for
both these statements was out of the question.

Over against this expression of belief is the unhesitating conviction of
the man who knows. Here we have to do not with the fluid data of experience, some of which are confused, dim, infrequently repeated and
when repeated, difficult to relate to previous perceived situations; not with
images which memory recasts into scarcely identifiable forms; here we
have to do with the logical values of universal principles, the elements
of pure reflective thought, ideas *as* ideas, all empirical and sensible integu-
ments having been removed from view. "The separation of the two parts
of the world," the author goes on, "is theoretically executed with uncompromising rigor." [5] In the second segment of the world we are faced by
the more comprehensive idea, the idea of the divine (*theion*), God, embodying the "highest perfection of ideas, the immortality and the eternity
of their essence." [6] The terms now used have the same etymological derivation but not the same meaning; we have passed from the realm of perception and imagination where the "gods" dwell to the realm of reflection
inhabited only by ideas. Between these two groups there is no conflict, for
they never meet. Such terms—*conflict* and *meet*—are strictly metaphorical,
as we shall later discover. In the particular instance before us, Plato takes
steps to show that the descriptive images of current religious speech are
in no respect the basis of his theory of religion. For that reason he emphatically declines to interpret the myths—his own creations—which represent the activities of superhuman agencies. "If like scientific men I did
not believe them, I certainly should not be unreasonable," he makes
Socrates say in *Phaedrus* (229C). But his refusal to interpret them is not
based on the existence of a contradiction in the two types of expression.
The fancies of the poet are sufficient for the purpose involved; they
present an artistic setting for the Homeric story and at the same time
support the conventional religious faith by tropes and pictures which the
common mind can understand. A government can easily administer the
precepts of a concrete religious creed. But such fancies cannot be made
a substitute for a scientific theory of religion. They must not be used when
they yield wrong implications as to moral behavior, even though ceremonial
adherence to them is ideologically correct and hence sanctioned by political
authority. Furthermore, the instructed man, especially the founder of a
commonwealth, has no opinion or obligation whatsoever in this province; [7]
it is not his official duty to fabricate or stand sponsor for the objects of
a religious cult. If this proposition is true, its inverse is also true, namely,

[4] *Ibid.*, p. 19.   [5] *Ibid.*, p. 18.   [6] *Ibid.*, p. 18.   [7] *Republic,* 427B.

that organized religion is in no position to dictate the subjects of philosophical research nor predict the results it must ultimately reach. Surely
—again in the realm of morals—religion "cannot pretend by its sacrifices,
prayers and formulas to effect a satisfactory reparation for the commission
of unjust deeds." [8] The meaning of justice can be determined only by the
canons of moral science and the sanctions against the violation in the
civil state, only by the accredited officers of government. Plato urgently
insists that the two orders of thought—belief and reflection—be completely
divorced and that each be allowed to follow its own rules of procedure.
The making of this demand marks an epoch in the history of man's intellectual development. For one thing it means that natural science must
stop its ears to the siren cries of some of its mentors, who advise it to
escape from the level of empirical investigation and enter the purlieus
of logical speculation. Plato stands in the road with a drawn sword. He
lets us know that physics, for example, must conduct its operations solely
in the domain of probable induction, that is, as subject to the changes of a
fluctuating experience; since each new discovery is likely to bend appreciably the curve of scientific law. [9] Logic, on the other hand, is fixed and
real and its values are determined by unchanging canons. Scientific
method has revealed the inadequacy of many of religion's external rites;
philosophy will now, under the guidance of the Platonic principle, purify
religious creeds, ennoble their concepts, and fashion ideals of behavior
that will conform in every respect to the underlying principles of love
and honor and fidelity.

This fresh study of the subject of the French writer confirms the conclusion already reached that Plato drew a sharp line of demarkation
between the established interpretation of religion and his own. It goes a
step further: it enables us to see that the conventional forms of ritual may
be safely left in the hands of the public, provided they are not allowed to
invade the field of moral decision and create inaccurate impressions there.
In general it suggests, too, the mode of approach in the construction of
a scientific theory of religion, namely, that it must begin with an examination of the governing ideas, not a mere appreciation of historical sentiments. In this manner, images and emotional reactions disappear from view
and sound metaphysical formulas take their place. The first question,
therefore is— What does Plato mean by Ideas?

TRADITIONAL INTERPRETATION OF HIS THEORY

The traditional but erroneous treatment of Plato's doctrine begins with
Aristotle. He recognized the contribution which Socrates had made to the
new logic of the Greeks, when he peremptorily rejected the thesis of

[8] *Republic*, 366A.   [9] *Timaeus*, 29C.

Protagoras that knowledge depends upon perception and upon nothing else. To know an object, Socrates argued, is to probe into its several properties and determine why and how they combine to fix its permanent meaning. These properties when thoroughly understood become the concepts by means of which true and valid judgments can be made about the object. But they cannot be understood except by a sustained and painstaking comparison with other objects of the same kind. The concept or idea is thus made the symbol of the essential qualities which we may justly attribute to the given thing. Plato adopted the method and proceeded to emphasize the sovereign character of every Idea. He distinguished between the symbolized quality and the substantive object in which it appeared. The idea is single, whole and unchangeable; the objects to which it may be applied have no guaranteed existence but may perish with the suns. It is obvious, then, that we must separate the ideas from their empirical situations. Ideas can be analyzed only by the rules of deductive logic; things, which are concrete individuals, only by instruments of measure—at least in the world of sense—when they present their data to the mind through the organs of perception. There is, then, a natural not an artificial divorce between the image and its idea. It is at this point that Aristotle enters his protest. It is true, he argues, that every individual contains two distinguishable elements, its matter and form, the one physical, and the other logical. They must be studied by different sciences but neither element can be withdrawn from the whole of the individual, except at the cost of its immediate dissolution. Plato, he charges, is guilty of serious indiscretion; for he not merely separates the generic idea from its object, saying that there is both a concrete man, Socrates, and a man-in-himself, that is, the essential principle of manhood; [10] but he also attributes to the idea of man an independent existence; it is an individual of another sort,[11] an individual "without matter," as he puts it,[12] and therefore a rival for the name and prestige of Substance itself. The criticism which Aristotle lays down is no doubt a fundamental one:—Are Plato's Ideas simply universal concepts signifying the properties of concrete and observable things; or are they also particular individuals on a different level of reality, which for the most part correspond to sensible objects but may, in certain cases, contain qualities never realized in the physical world? It must be admitted that Plato sometimes speaks of ideas as though they were *supersensible* entities, true and eternal substances. Therefore Zeller is constrained to remark that for Plato "true beauty is not in any living creature in earth or heaven but remains in its purity eternally for itself and by itself, in one form, unmoved by the changes of that which participates in it. The ideas are prototypes of Being; all *things* are copies

---

[10] *Metaphysics*, 1040a9, 997b5.　　[11] *Ibid.*, 1086a34.　　[12] *Ibid.*, 1032b14.

from them." [13] Zeller like many other commentators has been deceived by
the witchery of metaphors and similes. He seems inclined to accept at
face-value the lofty poetry with which Plato has adorned his scientific discussions. Thus, the theory of reminiscence detailed in the *Meno* and
Phaedo, seems to him to confirm the truth of his contention. Why does the
soul recognize the values of such concepts as equality in mathematics,
likeness and unlikeness in logic, goodness in ethics and beauty in aesthetics,
if not because it has glimpsed the "eternal sensibles" in a higher realm and
brought them as recollected ideas into the experience of the active mind?
Nature is beautiful, man is good; for they participate in the universal concepts of beauty and goodness. Aristotle did not understand that ideas are
the necessary conditions of intelligent behavior; they are, as Stewart says,
"ways in which we *must* or *ought* to think and act on the occasion of the
presentation of objects and opportunities in this world of sense-impressions.
These ways of thinking are *ours*—it is *in us,* not in the 'external world,'
that they are to be looked for. 'Equality' and 'Justice' stand for *rules*
which the intellectual and moral nature of man is bound to follow in the
exercise of its functions—in this sensible world, it is to be noted, not in a
supersensible world." [14]

But Aristotle is not yet finished with his interpretation. If ideas be real
things, they must be associated with one another, precisely as substances
in the physical world are intrinsically and necessarily related.[15] We cannot, however, apply the same categories—quality, quantity, causality—as
we do in the sensible world. The connections of ideas are logical and the
order of the ideas is fixed. If the ideas correspond to concrete general terms,
the order will be that of classification; man is an animal, animal is sentient,
sentient is organic, and so on till the highest substance is reached. If the
ideas are abstract, we must distinguish the terms which belong to the
separate sciences, mathematical terms to physics, ideas of growth to biology, justice to ethics, and so through the list. A hierarchy of ideas is thus
organized culminating in the idea of the *Ens Realissimum,* complete and
indestructible Being. What is the Idea which we may accept as the formal
and final Cause of all other ideas, the ultimate principle which can give
meaning to any particular concept we select for examination? The name
which Plato gives in the sixth book of the *Republic* is the idea of the
Good. Such an idea appears in the usages of scientific analysis as well as
in everyday experience. Thus the function or good of the eye is to *see;* the
function of the eye is therefore the *reason* for the development of that
organ. Generalizing upon this fact we may say that the world itself was
brought into being for the specific purpose of expressing the supreme idea

[13] Zeller, *Plato and the Older Academy,* p. 241.
[14] J. A. Stewart, *Plato's Doctrine of Ideas,* pp. 43, 44.   [15] *Metaphysics,* 990b25.

of order and harmony. According to this interpretation Good and Reality are equivalent terms, the one represents the principle, the other the actuality of substance. Good is the cause of truth, says Plato; but "it is not only the author of knowledge in respect to all things known; it is also the author of their being and essence."[16] Again, in the *Timaeus* (59E) he affirms that God created the world because of his own intrinsic goodness, thus confiding to the processes of nature his own attributes of power and wisdom. Just here, however, there emerges a conflict in the testimony which the traditionalists find it extremely hard to remove. The *Timaeus* (28AB) says explicitly that ideas are eternal and are separate from God; they are "patterns" (*paradeigmata*) on the basis of which the objective world is created by God through the agency of his demiurge. The testimony of the *Republic* (X, 597) is different; it maintains that God makes all reality, including the idea; hence, natural objects and the creations of the artist are real only because they embody ideas that have sprung from the mind of Deity. Certain modern expositors have tried to remove the contradiction by arguing that Platonic ideas are the "thoughts" of God, and while they have been produced by him, they nevertheless are different in essence from him and may therefore be regarded as independent individuals.[17] The same difficulty was keenly felt by Plotinus and he reached a solution much more majestic than any proposed since his day. He assumes the existence of Deity, whereas only ideas were accounted *real* in Plato's conception. God has one positive attribute, the Good, and all negative attributes such as Parmenides ascribed to his universe were disregarded. The problem before him was, how to relate the other elements of being to the original One. The divine *nature* could obviously never be communicated to finite creatures. But divine power could be and was communicated through the single medium suitable to the divine nature, namely, Ideas or Logoi. Ideas, then, become separable substances capable of expressing the wealth of logical judgments we have already summarized. Such ideas are not created by God, they *emanate* from his character and eventually invest the souls of human beings and all other creatures with powers and virtues common to their respective functions. The contradiction noted in the traditional interpretation of Plato's doctrine is thus avoided. The sublimity of God is unsullied, and matter is endowed with the qualities of reason including truth, goodness and beauty.

Plotinus, we know, escaped the difficulty which literal interpreters of Plato could not evade. He boldly faced the situation and accepted the existence of God as an elementary assumption. *They* could not follow this course, since they began their studies with an examination of a different kind of reality, that is, observable substance. Substance can be

---

[16] *Republic*, pp. 508, 509.   [17] Stewart, *op. cit.*, p. 102.

known only through its properties, and properties are understood through the judgmental relation of ideas. Ideas for Plato are logical principles applied to objects or events. This is also the customary meaning of the ideas in all civilized languages. Knowledge is acquired by the use of such well-constructed instruments; truth is established only when concepts have been carefully defined and their contents determined by sound empirical methods. Of these facts both Plato and Aristotle were certain. It is true that each concept occupies its own place in the meaning of a given object; for example, justice is a term that presupposes an organized state with a stable government, a system of laws scientifically drawn together with punitive and commendatory sanctions. Justice is thus studied as a constituent item in an extended series of logical terms. It has an existence by itself in the sense that its meaning is fixed in the mind of the group, and a man of average intelligence can identify the term when it is applied to a moral situation. From this point of view Aristotle was right in speaking of Plato's ideas as having individual existence. His error lay in supposing that the reality of the idea of justice was on the same level as the reality of the character and conduct of the man to which the term justice was applied. Justice and just action are incommensurable terms; they are correlative but not commensurable. The common mind has no difficulty in ordinary cases. The Greeks did not ostracize the concept Justice; they excluded the man who bore the name of *just,* which his fellow-citizens had voluntarily bestowed upon him. In short, no one attempts to hypostatize the idea of justice; it remains an idea, and can never be converted into an observable fact.

There is just one Concept where men are tempted to make such conversion; that is the highest of all ideas, named by Plato the Good. The Good, he says, is the "author of knowledge, of truth, of logical exactness"; it is also the "author of the being or essence of things." [18] What did he mean? If Good is the consummatory principle in thought, may it not also be the ultimate and supervisory Cause? Aristotle is not free from this tendency; in the early part of the *Metaphysics* (983a8) he writes: "God is thought to be among the causes of all things and to be a first principle." The issue is clear and must be clearly settled:—Does Aristotle mean that God, divinity, is a logical principle by means of which all the questions relating to substance will be satisfactorily explained? or, on the other hand, does he mean that God is a supreme Being by whose external power natural laws come into operation, whether in the physical world or in the mind of man? Both of these concepts cannot be true at the same time. The traditional theory maintains that Plato deliberately converted the Idea of Good into an objectively subsisting and operating Cause. Zeller refuses

[18] *Republic,* 509B.

to "see in all this only a conscious adaptation of his language to the popular religious notions"; [19] he argues that Plato was marking out his own line of theological doctrine. Plato was persuaded that a master mind, God's mind, the objective equivalent of the Good, was at work determining the constitution and movements of the universe; and this fact agreed in every detail with the theory of an hypostatized Good. But the fallacy still remains; it cannot be removed by the arbitrary assumption of God's existence; that means really a new beginning to the argument. The conclusion that Plato arrived at was that there existed a logical principle of the Good; further than that he could not honestly go nor should we permit Aristotle to drive him further. Our decision should rather be that Plato does not need an additional assumption; the foundations of his religious creed are already laid in his deduction of the comprehensive concept. This we shall endeavor to prove in the course of our constructive argument.[20]

But granting for a moment that the interpretation of Aristotle is correct, we must inspect two practical inferences that appear to follow. The first concerns the nature of the world in which we live. The picture which Plato presents in the *Timaeus* (28-30) has all the charm of the poet's fancy. Matter is already in existence, the "dark backward and abysm of time." Some expositors have regarded his original substance as the indeterminate substratum conceived by Plato as Anaximander conceived it. Here matter has no specific weight, shape or color; it is capable of taking all forms; that is to say, it is "formless," bereft of order, without motion. Forms are imprinted on it by the demiurge, the agent of Deity. Thereupon the Cosmos appears having all the properties and relations of the visible world. This means that the universe is not eternal; it is fashioned by decree and in the "best possible manner." The literal reading of the dialogue brings these results. If Aristotle accepted them at face value, he forgot to examine the kind of reasoning that Plato is following. For Plato distinctly states that it is *belief* not scientific method to which the narrator has appealed. Since we cannot obtain the elementary facts in the case, we are obliged to fall back upon "probabilities," which are sufficient for present purposes.[21] This logical attitude becomes even more evident when we pass to Plato's study of the universe as a whole. Form exists here as well as in the individual parts; hence the world must have a soul and at the behest of Deity the world becomes an organism, the macrocosm in which man dwells as a microcosm. The world-soul like its prototype, the Idea, is incorporeal but unlike the Idea it is not eternal; it has been created, though the narrator is dubious as to whether it may be destroyed. It cannot be the efficient cause,

[19] *Op. cit.*, p. 289.
[20] The argument is based on the dialogues of Plato up to but not including the *Laws*.
[21] *Timaeus*, 29C.

the starter and director of motion, for as Aristotle points out,[22] it is represented as having been generated together with the world itself. But the world-soul is the formal cause; it is coeval with order and is perhaps its original pattern.[23] It is also the final cause, the embodiment of harmony and proportion as between the material elements in the world which are regarded as secondary causes,—fire, earth, air, water,[24] and which God has ordained for the working out of his ultimate designs in nature. Many of the passages in the dialogue sound like the teleological arguments for the existence of God as found in English treatises of the 18th century. But, as we shall see, the elaborate demonstrations bearing on the subjects of physics and physiology are examples of Plato's scientific erudition rather than rescripts of his theological faith. Creation as religious doctrine has no place in his theory; hence, any comparisons with the early chapters of Genesis is vain.

The second deduction is that God is the guide and conservator of human purposes whether in the individual person or the group. This conclusion is naturally drawn from the definition laid down in the Second Book of the *Republic* (279A). Plato himself affirms that he has the right to use "moulds" or categories of thought in this science just as jurists do in the formulation of a legal system. He therefore unfolds the two capital attributes,—God is complete and unitary or unchanging. God is *good,* as Plotinus repeated at a later time. He has no pathological reactions, he is not touched by the feelings of pleasure or pain, he knows nothing of the sordid moral traits, envy, jealousy, vindictiveness, which appear in the Homeric poems. But the term *good* does not bear the universal logical values accredited to it in the Sixth Book; there it has no opposite, it rules supreme; here it is antithetical to *evil* and this evil clearly involves the unfavorable things that afflict the life and fortunes of man. Since God is good his dealings with man necessarily inure to their wellbeing. The evils they suffer have other causes; what the causes are Plato declines to say. Hence events in nature that seem to be retributory and measures in the social community that undoubtedly are so, must be traced to other sources. The goodness of God is expressed in his providential or "calculating" care for his votaries.[25] The just man alone is pleasing to him, and virtue is defined as "growing as much like God as man is permitted to do." [26] It may even be that divine goodness has devised a heavenly "pattern" of moral beauty akin to the other ideal forms. Plainly, the literal reading of these passages makes his doctrine of providence utterly unlike that of the Stoics. There the supervisory principle is a physical law, a Spermatic Logos whose activity unites the conflicting forces of a body in a steady harmony. There is no freedom

---

[22] *Metaphysics*, 1072a. [23] *Timaeus*, 30A. [24] *Ibid.*, 32BC.
[25] Cf. Zeller, *op. cit.*, p. 498. [26] *Republic*, X, 613A.

for man in the Stoic's world, there is nothing but unresisting obedience as strong as the force of gravity, as unceasing as the flow of blood in a healthy body. Yet somehow the theory of Stoicism draws its primary impulse from the Platonic discourses. Later we may see how to account for the historical connections.

The second attribute, divine unity or changelessness, is a property not unfamiliar to the student of early Greek philosophy. Parmenides applied it to the universe which to him was divine substance. Democritus defines the properties of the atom, the minimal unity of matter, by the same term. Even Heraclitus did not despise the concept of stability; for amid the eternal flux of bodies he recognized the presence of a Law of change. May not Plato follow the same usage? With him, however, it is the idea which is fixed. Yet if the idea of divine substance is converted into substance itself, must not the ultimate concept of permanence be preserved? Certainly, under these conditions Deity can exhibit none of the strange and diversified forms commonly attributed to the ancestral gods. Hence, in the passage already cited, Plato argues that divine action can be changed neither by external compulsion nor by voluntary choice. He uses the dialectical method made famous by Zeno, the Eleatic. Change means passing to a better or worse form, to a more just or an unjust form, to a more beautiful or an ugly form. But God cannot pass to a better since he is already supremely excellent. If he passes by his own consent to an inferior status, what inducement can be offered? Can he be constrained to compromise his unimpeachable veracity? If so, how? Human judgment does not sacrifice its sacred vows for any sentiment be it never so plausible. Shall Deity be otherwise influenced? Could ignorance induce him to change? That would be a contradictory conceit. Could he change by fear of his enemies or from the withering folly of his friends? "God is a being of perfect simplicity and truth both in word and in deed; he changes not in himself nor does he impose deceit on his creatures." [27] The theory here suggested is intriguing; it eliminates the objectionable elements of the old faith; its very abstractions make us feel that Aristotle may have right, at least in part, on his side. Certainly, great ideas, summing up the qualities of Being, do lend themselves to individualization. In the light of these facts may not Plato have anticipated the method of Plotinus? Philosophy does not deal with the crude images of primitive religion. If we strip off the trimmings, including the preposterous negations of the Eleatic speculation, we could at least retain the concepts of the Good and Unity, just as the Neo-Platonists did. The theory will then be monistic in its original design, while from the secret depths of Being stream forth "powers," namely, Ideas which find their concrete expressions in the souls of the

[27] *Republic*, 382E.

world and of man. There we rest the case until our own theory has been unfolded.

We have surveyed the interpretation of Plato's religious system which has claimed the largest number of adherents from the time of Aristotle. This we deem to be wrong. Some of the arguments against it have already been advanced; others will appear as we proceed. The best way to prove the falsity of one thesis is to set up another which can account more scientifically for the facts under review. We shall therefore attempt to establish the following propositions: that Plato's ideas are logical concepts by means of which truth is reached and established; that the idea of the Good is the fundamental principle required for the satisfactory demonstration of every scientific truth; that the idea of the Good is not identifiable with the concept of Deity wholly separate from the universe; that, finally, religion is an endeavor to understand the world of law, order and harmony which necessarily includes the habits and destiny of man.

Ideas Are Logical Concepts

It is admitted on all sides that ideas stand for universal truths, that they refer to a definite area of application and that they are permanently valid. We shall treat them as logical concepts, that is, scientific instruments for acquiring knowledge. They belong to the system of thinking developed by every normal mind. Hence the thesis that the Platonic ideas are strictly separate from their objects is a subtle myth engendered by Aristotle for reasons unknown to us. Ideas and mental images do not represent two distinct and unrelatable realities; they are part and parcel of the same intelligent process. In order to reach its final form every idea must pass through "four stages of intelligence," as Nettleship said, and these four stages are embodied in the Divided Line graphically presented to us in the Sixth Book of the *Republic* (509–511). The first part of the Line contains every experience dealing directly with imagination; the second part everything dealing with the intelligible or conceptual facts of thought. No idea, whatever its character, can become explicit in the mind of the observer except after passing through the alembic of perception. The sensory image gives us immediate connection with the object; it is a reflection of the properties therein discovered. The image, however, cannot stand by itself; when the second percept presents a similar content, it is affiliated with the first by the impulse of memory, and we have a "notion," called tentatively a belief or opinion. No comparison could be made between the two data, memory-image and new percept, if the mind did not have the capacity to recall its first experience. We now derive the elementary meaning, *eidos*, as Plato names it. It goes without saying that the suggestion of a mythological prior career eloquently described by the author of the *Phaedo*, has no value in a scientific analysis of experience. Up to this point we have the two factors, a perceived image and a belief in its meaning developed in the mind after a comparison of the content of similar images. There is no hard and fast separation between the two; there is a steady growth in the mind's appreciation of the significance of the given object.

So far Plato has examined the sensible part of the Divided Line. It is now time to translate the "steady" image into a permanent idea. Ideas are different from notions in that their content is established by the use of logical rules. Notions belong to common speech; they embody habitual modes of behavior in a particular community; they often record the gathered sentiments of many generations. Yet no one has hitherto undertaken to make a sustained analysis of their content; hence no one is in a position to say whether their content is strictly veracious. All that is known is that such conceits or fancies have served useful purposes. Their meanings may readily vary with the change of conditions; "they shift backwards and forwards and seem to be without rational judgment." [28] The idea moves on a different level; it aims at and procures a settled connotation. How is this content determined? that is, how can the "shifting" notion be resolved into a serene and self-contained idea? The third section of the line gives the answer: —we are to proceed by the use of hypotheses. All scientific thought follows this order. Geometry fashions its elementary axioms, the structural concepts of figure, angle, parallel lines, together with the familiar corollaries that issue necessarily from these assumptions. The first principle is taken as true, it is the major premise in the projected argument. But care must be exercised in framing the initial judgment; Aristotle thought of it as "prior knowledge." But it is assumed knowledge, simply because we have no way of proving its value through the medium of a more fundamental postulate. One point is sure: it cannot be a haphazard connection of ideas. Every judgment has a subject and a predicate, and both of these must be drawn from the same field of inquiry. The subject is the concept to be explained; it is alleged to have some sort of reality and that reality is tested by the kind of ideas appearing in the predicate of the judgment. These ideas belong *naturally* together—either by laws of the objective sciences or by the canons of the normative sciences. They will "participate" in the subject; that is to say, the meaning of the subject implies the concepts registered in the predicate. "Man is a rational animal," "man is not immortal" are two propositions in one of which the predicate agrees with the subject, in the other it does not. Various types of relation exist between subject and predicate when

[28] *Republic,* **VI**, 508E.

they are compatible; likeness and unlikeness, sameness and difference, motion and rest, if applied to physical objects.

But comparison does not stop at this point; the next step takes up the connection between judgments. How are judgments related when we desire to find their logical values, which is another way of saying, when we desire to determine what new judgment results as soon as we start to combine them? The essence of all reasoning is inference. Plato reverts to mathematics for his example. The interior angles of a triangle are equal to two right angles. The argument requires no demonstration from empirical observation; we now know that no such demonstration is available. Every time we enter the field of experiment our efforts are frustrated. If however we keep to the settled principles of geometry, the fact that a straight line cutting two parallel lines, makes the alternate internal angles equal, opens the direct path to the conclusion embodied in the theorem. The truth deduced does not lie on the surface of the given judgments, but out of their proper union a new and unerring judgment results.[29] This is the essence of deductive logic, the most powerful single instrument for distilling truth that the mind of man has ever conceived. Yet even this does not satisfy the organizing genius of a Plato. He seeks a combining form of unexceptionable strength—a fit instrument [30] for investigation of every subject under the sun, the "first principle of the whole" [31] by which all discovered truth may be summarized. This idea cannot be an hypothesis, for hypotheses belong to particular sciences, and they pass always to lower levels of thought, that is, to ideas which are to be classified under the higher ideas. There can be but one idea possessing such powers, and we propose to call that idea the Good. It will not be reached by dialectical judgments, it will be reached only by a sort of divine intuition, the exercise of the pure reason. Here at last we have linked our fortunes with a unity that never can be destroyed.

The Meaning of the Good

Why should we be so careful in our analysis of Plato's method, if we intend merely to isolate the final principle as the key to his religious system? We answer that for one thing it gives us a chance to refute the claims of Aristotle that Plato has endowed his ideas with a type of reality which removes them completely from the field of experience. Every idea is now shown to have a natural history; it is born in the sensum, nurtured in the imagination, reared to maturity by the laws of logic, and taught to bind its members into a common whole by the concept of the Good. In the light of this official statement the arguments of his pupil lose their significance. For another thing it enables us to indicate that for Plato God is a divine

[29] *Republic*, 511.　　　[30] *hikanon*, cf. *Phaedo*, 101E.　　　[31] *Republic*, 511B.

aspect, an adjectival quality of substance, not an independent and direc-tive substance in a different sphere of reality. The *aperçu* of M. Perls is full of insight:—"The divine is the expression of the highest quality of ideas; it signifies the stability and immutability of Being. From this divine prop-erty derives the invisible God which like the personification of the divine is a valuable ingredient of the Platonic doctrine." [32] The adjective *divine* appears frequently in Plato's works as the synonym for *extraordinary, most distinguished, chiefest;* at the same time when he wishes to refer to the most comprehensive substance he uses the same term: "the philosopher who converses with the divine and universal does, by his converse, become part of the divine and universal order, so far as his own nature permits." [33] There is a chasm set between the human and the divine; man may approach but he cannot cross it. Still we should not fail to note that the distinction is drawn between qualitative differences, not between concrete individuals. It is with this opinion of Plato's in mind that we proceed to an examination of the idea which he adopts as the consummatory principle of his religious system.[34]

It belongs to the genius of Plato to select the most significant item in the subject under review and determine its relation to the whole. The principle of the Good, he says, is like the sun or light in the reception of the visual image. Before his time psychology had isolated only two of the three elements involved in the scientific analysis of sight. Democritus insisted upon the office of the efflux drawn from the external object and changed in some of its properties in its passage from the object to the eye. Anaxag-oras studied the organ of vision and concluded that it, too, has an impor-tant duty to discharge—it demanded that the color of the given object should be changed into the opposite color as found in the eye itself. There is a third element, says Plato, without which neither the eye nor the colored object can produce the image; light is the bond that unites the two and light is no "ignoble thing." Light is the child of the sun; the moon and stars offer but dim images to our vision; the sun makes every object plain and distinct. The analogy to the acquisition of knowledge is striking. The mind, with its array of categories on the one side, the powers and relations of nature on the other—how shall these be joined in an indissoluble union? Logic with its series of scientific laws, the formulas of the individual disci-plines, geometry, physics, biology,—these are insufficient to establish the claims of authoritative truth. They make mistakes either by assuming the wrong premises or by gathering inadequate or wrong data to support the hypothesis. As the sun alone, on Plato's analogy, can supply the rays of light that being reflected from the body's surface impinge ultimately upon the retinal structures of the eye, so the idea of Good alone can detect the

[32] Perls, *loc. cit.*, p. 17.   [33] *Republic*, 500D.   [34] *Ibid.*, pp. 533–34.

inner meaning of every concept and fix that meaning irrevocably. It determines the content and value of a single truth and of truth in general; it must also be regarded as the source of reality itself. We are concerned at present with the logical principle and must now unfold its significance.[35]

The word *good* in a civilized language connotes the property, single or manifold, without which the object indicated could not be what it is. Such a statement is vague and not very illuminating but it contains an important idea, namely, that experience has associated with the object at least one mode of action which enables the observer to identify it at the next moment of inspection. Aristotle used the term, *ergon* [36] to represent the function of the object, strictly speaking, the complex qualities which distinguish it from other objects.[37] This is also Plato's approach. He selects the faculty of sight for especial comment in the *Timaeus* (47); "greater good never has been or ever will be given by the gods to mortal man." Sight is the faculty that invented number, developed the conception of time, and started an inquiry into the "nature of the whole." The knowledge of the eye is therefore not complete when we have examined its mechanism with the thousand details therein comprised; we are obliged to study its function, an element not discernible to sight or touch, a fact determined only by logical reasoning. It is to this element, the function of the organ, that Plato attaches the term *Good*. Without it the instrument of sight has no meaning; the function is the *eidos* of the object, that characteristic idea which forever differentiates it from every other object in heaven or earth. In particular, as we should say, it distinguished it from the fabricated model of the optician's parlor or the physiologist's laboratory.[38] Therefore, the answer to the everyday question, What is this good for? is found in the specific function of the object and in nothing else. Citing the language of logic we should say that the Good is the specific quality, the *differentia*, which is the inseparable second point in every definition. Thus, while Plato's peroration in the Sixth Book of the Republic seems to remove it wholly from the common level of experience and invest it with an almost impenetrable aura, he has only thereby affirmed its universal authority.

The same principle appears in the common transactions of human life. The biological word may now be exchanged for a more definitory term, *purpose*. What is the criterion by which we may determine whether the fundamental purposes of character have been realized? Two measures— nature and custom—are proposed in the "Gorgias" both of which Plato rejects. Nature, he argues, is undisciplined might and custom is unexamined habit; neither one of them can become the basis of rational character. There is, to be sure, a *good* appertaining to the body's preservation and

[35] *Republic,* 508–09.
[37] *Nicomachean Ethics,* I, 6.

[36] The *erg* of modern physics.
[38] Cf. *Republic,* X, 596–97.

growth; a man is required by a sort of instinct, to satisfy his normal appetites, hunger, sex, defense against enemies. But he has another good imposed
by the reflective faculty, a good which has no biological equivalent. This
good is not definable in terms of physical feelings, although both pleasure
and pain may help us to understand its value. Feeling is a necessary element
in all experience but it can never be the standard by which the property of a
given course of action is judged. What, for example, should be the attitude
of the man who has committed an unjust act and has not been punished
for it? Shall he regard himself as happy and be so regarded by his neighbors? Is he to be esteemed happier than the man who has committed the
same kind of act and been subject to civil or social penalty? Finally, are
both these men happier than the man who has strictly abided by the terms
of the law and committed no offense against it? How shall we settle the
case? We can settle it only by accepting a "measure." Polus contends that
the measure is the amount of feeling engendered by the given action.
Socrates objects that feeling is only a part of experience and not the initi-
ating part. Reason demands that the invisible rights of the Self should be
respected; hence, not pleasure but virtue is the expression of the true good
of the soul.[39] Furthermore, the self is an organized whole, like the civil
state; it is composed of three coöperating factors, impulse, emotion or spirit
and reflection, though the second is probably a variant of the third. This is
precisely the argument of Bishop Butler when he defines the role of conscience in modern ethical theory. Like constitutional law in the state, the
moral law, Virtue, in the individual conduct is the prescriptive power of
action; it is the *eidos* of the agent, his function in the construction of a
moral self.[40]

Thus far the Good has been examined as an attributive factor, the logical
thought which leads us to a full and sure appreciation of a concrete situation. Eventually it will be applied to the reality of the universe and its
composite parts. We must therefore come to closer grips with the principle
under review. In the *Republic* (VI., 511), the idea of the Good is, as we said,
an intuition of reason which somehow closes up all the gaps in our thinking.
Yet its meaning is still somewhat vague and must be examined anew. Plato
does so in the *Philebus* dialogue (21E), his latest scientific contribution to
the subject. The question before him again is—What is the good? The
question has had two solid answers—by Aristippus, pleasure is the Good;
by the historical Socrates, knowledge is the Good. Pleasure we have already
found to be but a small fraction of human experience. Is intellectual speculation the dominant purpose of man? "Would you consent to live your life

[39] *Gorgias*, 468 sq.
[40] *Sermons*, III in *Works of Bishop Butler*. Edited by W. E. Gladstone (Oxford: Clarendon
Press, 1897); *Republic*, 435 sq., 473.

with reason and wisdom and universal memory, but wholly bereft of pleasure small and great, and also pain and every other possible feeling?" Feeling and reflection are complementary parts of one whole; neither can be taken as the exclusive purpose of man. Nor in the wider sphere of the world can their equivalents, change and order, be each, for itself, the commending term in its series. Feeling as change and reason as order are instrumental agents, powers, values which express the intrinsic meaning of the whole, called again here, the Good. This perfect idea cannot be either of the other two, since they are subordinate in the logical system; it must be the property of the *Summum Genus* which can have no superordinated genus but must be explained by itself.

What, then, will be the content of the Good? It has something of the quality of wisdom, rational understanding, truth, that which is uniform for all. Harmony of motives and harmony of mechanical motions—these are the desiderata in the field of objective scientific research or in the formation of rational behavior. In science men attempt to reduce the phenomena in a given field to a common physical law as incorporated in a single equation. In human society the citizens aim at the formulation of a common code of legal statutes. The principle of harmony checks the flow of feeling and gives regularity to our experience both in the observations of nature and the development of social aspirations. To this must be added a second concept, namely, symmetry. It is obvious that pleasure cannot satisfy this requirement; for feeling is by its very nature unsteady, liable to ebullient expression or to frigid rigidity; while intellect holds to a single idea until some discovery stamps it as inadequate and in need of correction. A physical world that moved its bodies with alternations of wild excitement and inert stagnation would invite degeneration and chaos. A society which librated from one theory of government to its opposite—regimentation or wide-open license—would end its course in a new cyclical collapse, in accordance with the expectations of some cynical Spengler. In either sphere of action, each parallel to the other, there is the same demand for symmetry, balance, the pendulum-swing of equal lengths, the operation of the law of compensation. This law is closely related to the first, but with a difference. In the one we think strictly of the thing itself, in the other we seek to determine its relation to other things. The form of the symmetry will differ in different groups, for example, in non-organic and organic wholes. The orbital turn of the planet about its sun is a type of motion utterly diverse from the passage of the living "gene" from its primitive type—the paramecium—to the complex orders of the primates. But the end of nature's evolution can be nothing more or less than a Cosmos in which equilibrium is an indefeasible law. Furthermore, in the social areas symmetry is harder to attain and still harder to support. The economic process known but dimly to Plato's age is to our age its most complicated problem. Tell us how we may reconcile the conflicting wills of industrialist and laborer, and you will help us to stabilize the social balance now desperately out of plumb. Finally, the Good will have the quality of truth, meaning that we may put together the elements of the Good into a unitary whole which the rational mind can comprehend. This is not the case in the study of pleasures; we can determine the physiological rules governing their action; but to predict when pleasures will come, how intense they will be, what general effects their operation will have upon the future career of the agent—these are matters beyond the ken of man, all experiments to the contrary notwithstanding. It is not even the case with scientific hypotheses; they may result in a measurable advance of knowledge in the projected field or they may not. They may release a new form of physical power, as when the *Kathodenstrahlen* prepared the way for the discovery of the Roentgen ray. No one can foretell the probable course of inquiry. What the human mind needs is a sort of intuitive look at the total values of scientific thought or moral ambitions; the idea of the Good provides it. "In this argument," says Plato, "the claims both of pleasure and intelligence to be the principle of Good have been disproved; they have both failed in self-sufficiency and in the ability to express themselves in adequate terms." [41]

The Good as the Metaphysical Expression of Deity

It is obvious from the preceding argument that an intelligible world is the only kind that Plato can conceive as possible. The contrary was strongly and persistently urged by some of the acutest thinkers of his day, and a battle royal or, as he says, a "war of gods and giants" was in progress between the Materialists and the Idealists, *Formists*, as he named them.[42] Matter, said the one, is the sole reality, because you can hold it between your hands and break it into bits. Yet they admitted that the living being has a soul which itself is something real; the motion of the body by the inward principle would prove that. Again, they agreed that the soul may be just or unjust, and that it becomes the one or the other by the presence of the corresponding trait in the soul. Hence, virtue or vice must be an independently real thing. Are such traits visible or invisible? If invisible or bodiless things are real as well as the visible, what element do they have in common? Is it not a kind of *power*, which means ability to evoke a response in one's neighbor or to find one's neighbor evoking a response in us? If this be true, have we not come upon evidence to prove that the fundamental ideas of "same" and "other," "motion" and "rest," are plainly recognized even by the men who at first acknowledged the exist-

[41] *Philebus*, 67A; see also 60 sq. [42] *Sophist*, 246 sq.

ence of only one type of being? One further point: looking at the variety
of individuals upon the earth, shall we hold that nature produced them
by some "spontaneous cause" without intelligence or that they came from
a divine source bearing the stamp of reason and scientific understanding?[43] The first was mere opinion found in common speech; the second
might suggest the activity of a extramundane producer or else the presence of an objective teleological power exhibited throughout the entire
visible world? Did Plato mean that the universe is the scene of structural
design, the creative work of a superhuman artificer? Let us examine the
suggestion for a moment.

The origin of the observable world was a familiar topic in the early
speculations of Greece. It was associated with the quest for a primary
substance from which the four known elements could be derived; when
not embellished with the fancies of the poet, it was part and parcel of the
inquiry into the meaning of all physical phenomena. It is obvious from
our sources that the religious aspect of the question had never been explored. The first hint of theological values is found in Xenophanes' poem
on "Nature":—

> God is one, greatest among divinities and humans;
> As a complete Whole he sees, he thinks, he hears,
> By the force of reason he controls all things without labor;
> Even in the same place he rests, motion excluded,
> Wholly improper is it for him to roam hither and yon.

Since Plato has drawn heavily upon Eleatic conceits for his cardinal ideas,
it is fair to assume that standing before the cryptic utterances of Anaximander and the lofty formulas of Parmenides, he could not hesitate in
his choice. The choice is confirmed by the adroit argument of the
Timaeus. We may concede, as Professor Cornford holds [44] that Plato
introduced the concept of a Creator God for the first time in Greek
philosophy. The route he followed to reach this end is extremely ingen-
ious. Not Plato himself but a stranger purporting to come from Locri, a
student of the Pythagorean tradition, a distinguished astronomer,
Timaeus, recites the fable of creation. Certain cautionary declarations
appear in the text; for example, God did not fabricate the world by his
own hand but through a pre-Plotinic intermediary called the demiurge
and the designs adopted by him and faithfully copied, were timeless in
essence and unchangeable in form. Furthermore, there is a conflict between metaphors used in the story of creation; now it is a creator who
exercises the power,[45] again it is the father of the world, forestalling the

---

[43] *Ibid.*, 265C.   [44] F. M. Cornford, *Plato's Cosmology*, p. 34.
[45] In this account he is *poet* or maker.

biological figure which is introduced later in the dialogue.[46] Finally, it is indicated in many passages that the account of creation submitted for Socrates' audition, has none of the earmarks of a logical demonstration but lies only within the range of "probability." Nor is the argument of the *Timaeus* in any way paralleled by similar discussions in the other writings of Plato. The discussion of the subject in the *Sophist* (265C) has to do with the nature of the world as it now exists, not as to its solitary beginning or its possible evolution from an antecedent material chaos. No doubt the subject was discussed often and long, after Plato's decease; there is a possibility that two opinions as to his actual teaching existed in the Academy. One thing is certain, that Plato's nephew, Xenocrates, was firm in his avowal that Plato did not teach the creation of the world "in time," that he used the term merely for "convenience in exposition," and finally that he was concerned with the study of physical phenomena in their due and proper order, "things logically *first,* then things scientifically associated with them." [47] The judgment of Aristotle is therefore wrong and the literal interpretation of the passage in the *Timaeus* a false statement of Plato's position.[48] Over and beyond these technical points is the unmistakable fact that the author's theory of causality applies wholly to the operations of the external world, and that he, like Kant, would stoutly resist its transfer to the field of transcendental reality. In the same manner his doctrine of the Good concerns man's use of the laws of logic in trying to estimate the meaning of experience. Therefore, nothing stands in the way of our rejecting the concept of an extramundane Deity as an element in Plato's philosophy. Plato was not a monotheist; such a theory was unknown in his day. The only divinities he considered were connected with the forms and motions of the physical world. We may then eliminate the word deity and substitute the word "divine."

By virtue of the conclusion now reached we are in a position to say that Plato's theory of religion was based solely upon his study of the universe. Like all objects within its embrace the universe is composed of two elements, matter and form. These denote the two sets of causes which must be rigidly distinguished. Material and efficient causes refer to the one, formal and final causes to the other. Matter is associated with motions that derive of necessity from other sources; it is "destitute of reason" and can produce results only "by chance and without orderly sequence." [49] It is extremely doubtful whether *necessity*—a word fre-

---

[46] M. B. Foster, "Christian Theology and the Modern Science of Nature," *Mind* (new series), XLIV (1935), 444.

[47] Ritter & Preller, *Historia Philosophiae Graecae,* Sec. 330; A. E. Taylor, *Plato,* 442 sq.

[48] *Physics,* 251b17.   [49] *Timaeus,* 46E.

quently found in the dialogue—has any of the implications assigned by us to the modern term, *mechanical law*. Plato exemplified his notion of brute force by this word; it appears to mean that the directive character of reason has been wholly removed; as though the chemist might analyze his elementary units separately, never asking how they could be compounded into a body, and how, when so compounded, bodies might at length be associated into a system. It is here that the second group of causes enter and that the concept of law is affirmed. Law cannot exist unless scientific reflection has assessed the values of the empirical facts. Plato is sure that the qualities of reason belong intrinsically to the nature of the world. He chides Anaxagoras for introducing the term, *reason*, to account for motion and then converting it into a defense of the discredited doctrine of materialism. But the word itself is ambiguous, and Plato does not always make his meaning clear. The world may be rational in one of two senses. It may be conceived as a subjective conscious mind, somewhat in the form of the panpsychic theory. Such an interpretation envisages a teleological behavior not unlike that of man's; it wills and then acts in accordance with the decision reached. If the world were a "great organism," its movements could be described in these terms. But Plato rejects any notion like that; to him it would be petty and jejune. Teleology in his view must be objective, never subjective; for "rational" means not endowed with the power to think but with the capacity of *being thought*. The universe is an intelligible object; it can be contemplated and understood by an intelligent mind like man's, but it is not itself a mind. There is a "good" in the total world; it cannot be divorced from the principle and fact of motion; being universal the Good comprehends not the broken arcs of movement nor even the majestic swing of the heavens but rather the essence of motion, motion considered in itself, its power to establish order and generate harmony. It is this principle, the Good, which contains the ideas of "same" and "other", "like" and "unlike"; together they make an indissoluble unity which constitutes the meaning of the world, that is, its divine character.

The order of the world, then, is teleological, not mechanical. Modern science has used the concept in depicting the organization of the living being. "How should it be thought strange," says Professor Henderson, "to find in the inorganic world something slightly analogous to that which is already recognized in the organic?" Hydrogen, carbon and oxygen make up a "unique ensemble of properties each of which is itself unique." The meteorological cycle is determined by this peculiar relation; if waters accumulating upon the earth flow into the sea, then are dissolved into vapors and finally under certain conditions of heat and pressure are emptied again upon the earth,—this is a sequence which can only be understood as a fixed teleological order. We can explain each change by the laws of physical power, but order and harmony have an aesthetic quality which cannot be accounted for by them.[50] Heraclitus saw in the flux of bodies a tendency to repetition which he called a logos, or law. Plato sought for a concept which exhibited not the regular sequence of individual bodies but the solid and firm order of the Whole. This is divine "goodness," which is both universal and eternal, two attributes that have their respective expressions in the functions of time and space. Time in an "eternal essence"; [51] it cannot be limited to days, months and years, the natural divisions of time which seem to be "moving images everlasting" but are in reality figures of the mind reflecting the fleeting pictures of the senses. Time is a continuum, it has no beginning, it can have no end; "it never was nor ever will be, since it is now all at once." [52] It is therefore the sure signature of never-ending existence and forbids us to describe its processes as past, present or future. Its divinity is registered in the stately and unceasing movements of the heavens. But its eternity is also registered in the rational mind. Time is collateral with thought; ideas cannot succeed one another without the assent of time; they cannot be transmitted to inheriting generations except by the collaboration of time. Nature and thought abide side by side throughout the ages because of the ministry of time.

Scarcely less significant is the office of space. Space is the objective form of universality; it denotes connectedness, continuity, expansiveness, —a unified whole, the receptacle of all Becoming.[53] Without space the multiplied "planes" of independent bodies would have no "home," no abiding place.[54] Space makes impossible the irrational voids of the Democritean system. Plato does not say so in explicit terms but it is easy to conjecture how repugnant to his genius would be the concept of a million unfilled areas in the universe; it would seriously mar the harmony of the world and in particular would destroy the perfection of form which he has visualized as a geometrical sphere. To be sure, space itself is not discernible by the senses; the sphere is a constructed, not an observed, figure. Still, it is an indispensable element in our analysis of nature and ultimately in our estimate of the meaning of the divine. Timaeus, skilled in mathematics, says that Space cannot be a form, *eidos*, like the idea of a triangle; there is nothing with which space can be compared; hence, a scientific concept cannot be obtained.[55] That, however, does not prevent us from framing a totalitarian synthesis such as we make of a picture or

[50] L. J. Henderson, *Order of Nature* (Cambridge: Harvard Press, 1917), Chap. X.
[51] *Timaeus*, 37E.
[52] Cf. Parmenides, frag. 8, l.5, in J. Burnet, *Early Greek Philosophy* (2nd ed.; London: Adam and Charles Black, 1908), 199.
[53] *Timaeus*, 49A.   [54] *Ibid.*, 52B.   [55] *Ibid.*, 52–53.

of a single illustrative diagram, here assumed to be a sphere, the most complete figure in the geometer's studio. We pass then from the analysis of the parts to an aesthetic appreciation of the whole. This implies that divine substance is not an aggregate of individual bodies, limited motions, or separate purposes; it is the order of the world spacially harmonized, changeless in its forms, and eternal in its course. These are the attributes that express the nature of divinity; these are the ideas upon which Plato's theory of religion rests.

It follows from the foregoing reflections that systematic theology, in Plato's eyes, has an intimate connection with the content of the natural sciences. In the presented universe there is a real Whole which organizes and coördinates the infinitely diversified parts composing it. The parts are bound together by the laws of time and space: that is the testimony of science; they contribute inevitably to the significance of Reality itself: that is the deduction of philosophy. Substance is not bare uniformity as Parmenides conceived it, a single Object interpreted by such negative terms as uncreated, unchanging, indecomposable, complete. Nor is it an unending series of abstract numbers with the allegorical meanings attributed to them by the Pythagoreans. The cosmos, as Plato paints it, is the seat of harmonic motions and resembles the "mysterious universe" of the modern scientist. The salient point is that the Whole is dynamic, a directive power which penetrates every element in its structure. Leibniz catches up the same strain and endows his world with a myriad of individuated monads which are centres of incorruptible power and distributed throughout space with scientific precision. The sum of these monads is itself a Monad, called *God* when logic dictates the final word, but *divine* Creator when he bethinks himself of the church's creed. The Idealist today perpetuates some of Plato's grandeur though it is diluted by a shadowy mysticism. Says Josiah Royce:—"*Many* is the Absolute, because in the inter-relationships of the contrasted expressions of a single Will lies the only opportunity for the embodiment of wholeness of life. . . . Individuals are all expressions of the Absolute in so far as they are many; just because when One is individual, every aspect and element of its self-expression is unique."[56] In an earlier passage he exclaims:—"The Absolute for us must be a self-representative ordered system or *kette* (chain) of purposes fulfilled, and the ordered system in question must be infinite . . . yet not only infinite but determinate and not only form but a life."[57] Royce attempts to apply to the universal Real the activating principles of the independent moral agent. Plato makes no such attempt in his writings. Reason, intelligibility, not moral will is the essence of the

[56] Josiah Royce, *The World and the Individual* (New York: Macmillan, 1901), II, 336.
[57] *Ibid.*, I, 545.

world. It is true that the Stoics could easily affix a moral value to the harmony and order detected in the firmament and commend such attributes as behavior patterns to the social group. But Royce's theory meets Plato's in at least one point—the universe is not a collection of pluralistic bits; it exhibits the dynamic co-activity of the Whole. Pious speculation might soon take another step and remove God altogether from the sphere of judgmental apprehension, as Plotinus did; then reason and soul and the intelligible world would be distilled as successive "emanations" from the original and unknown Being. But this is sheer fancy, and Plato indulges neither in fancy nor in metaphysical dialectics. The universe has the only possible contour of divinity and with that he is content.

There is one further aspect of the divine nature that should be mentioned, an attribute implied in what was said about the Whole. The thinkers of Periclean Greece held strongly to the postulate that *being* and *one* are the same, that substance necessarily involves the property which in present day Idealism is called individuality. The insistence on unity was due in part to their dread of the idea of non-being, a concept which actually made its appearance in their time with the rise of the Democritean theory of matter. If substance possesses an inviolable solidarity, then no leaks or vacua, no breaks or unfilled spaces may be supposed to exist in the universe. Plato regards this principle as vital both to the logical procedure and to religious thought; there must be unity in discourse and there must be unity in substance. Logic attains unity by the apprehension of the idea of the Good; this is clear from his argument in the *Republic* which we have already examined. That Plato did thus identify the One and the Good is attested by the report of Aristotle in his lectures on Metaphysics (1091b13). Likewise, in reality itself the principle of unity will be found, and this he demonstrates by the biological concept of the soul. The soul, he argues, is the Form or chief Idea of the individual, and constitutes its essential meaning. Form may be defined by answering satisfactorily the following question:—Does the soul exist, is it forever the same with itself, and is it different from every other conceivable form? The meaning of any object which we desire to understand, will be derived from such a threefold analysis. Thus the content of a sensory image includes, first, the isolation of the common property later called the genus, next, the determination of the differential concept belonging to the particular species, and finally, the union of both in a single object which is the individual under observation.

It is analysis like this which Plato calls upon his *Alter Ego* in the *Timaeus* (35 sq.) to carry out in every detail. The World-Soul is composed of three distinguishable elements, existence, sameness, difference. The object to be contemplated is the universe; it exists; no argument is required to prove its reality. Reason, its essential Form, has but one attribute, a transcendental property, the Good which never changes. Again, the World-Soul is to be distinguished not from other World-Souls for none exist, but—like every other object of aesthetic worth—from its own constituent parts which when taken together establish the beauty and harmony of the Whole. Here we have the final proof of Unity for the Object of pious adoration. Plato's world is like the Phidian statue of Athena. Speaking in terms of philosophical science, the final cause expressed in the aspirations of the artist is the aesthetic judgment of beauty, the formal cause which embraces the wealth of Athena's godlike splendor —her wisdom, her authority, her affection for the City, her embodiment of its ideals, its national hopes, its diversity of interests—is the specific quality; while the concrete image standing calm and unattached in the central cella of the Parthenon, is the finished work of art combining the two in a memorable creation of genius. Here is unity if aesthetic unity ever existed; here is supreme unity in an unfabricated world. Obviously for Plato nature is not an "empty indefinite phrase"; he agrees in that with Hegel. The scientific analyst who measures its spaces, weighs its bodies and ultimately converts its laws into symbolic equations, what has he left but a set of empty phrases? An abstract quantum like that Plato's world is not; rather is it a "full concrete," as Hegel argues every aesthetic object must be, a world furnished with divine thoughts and lovely contours, not a "concrete universal" which seems to be the name of Hegel's Deity. It has the individuality which the German philosopher required; it also has a reality which his doctrine could not appropriate. If this be the correct interpretation of Plato's doctrine, as I believe it to be, then God cannot be *soul* in the anthropological sense of the word,— which, as Hardie says, would be "as much myth as is the origin of the world in time." [58] He is the quintessence of everything real in the observable and intelligible universe.

Man and the Universe

Plato's religious system is intimately associated with his scientific creed of that fact there can be no reasonable doubt. Now in the consideration of either aspect of human thought it is essential that we know the nature of the individual who endeavors to pursue his studies as a man of science or a man of religion. Our aim, however, is not to discover the attitude or views of a particular person but rather the intellectual capacities which enable him to analyze and understand the phenomena presented. It is especially necessary to know the nature of the soul when we are examining

[58] *Study of Plato*, p. 154.

the concepts of religion; because, for one thing, historical theology has always connected a certain theory of Deity with the persistence of the soul after death. And even if the pragmatic thinker eliminates such a certitude, since it can have no form of empirical proof supporting it, he will be inclined to second the proposal of Martineau who defines religion as "the believer's worship of Supreme Mind and Will, directing the universe and holding moral relations with human life." [59] The two concepts, God and man, are effectually united, and it were a vain effort on our part to separate them. Plato makes no such effort; indeed, his purpose is fixed: he intends to use the rational principle, regarded as preeminently man's, as the basis of his interpretation of the world of reality. He is therefore obliged to examine the mental functions of the human being. Unfortunately his doctrine is cast in the mould of metaphor and myth and it is with great difficulty that we can disentangle the guiding threads. We know for a fact that he divided the individual man into two parts, soul and body, analytically not spacially discerned. Aristotle had a grave suspicion that the "parts" were spacially distinguished; but he could not establish his claim.[60] The relation of the soul to its body was never carefully stated by Plato, and as a result two theories of its nature have grown up. The first assumes that the soul is a distinct substance capable of pursuing its course apart from its physical encasement. It may have existed before the birth of body, it may continue its course after the body's decease. But when the union of the two is effected, the soul takes control of all personal activities, including the operations of the sense-organs. Hence, Socrates does not sit because his limbs are joined by ligaments, he does not speak because a "concatenation of sounds" issues automatically from his lips; he sits, because his mind commands, he speaks by free election of thought. The early Greek fancies were wrong; everyday experience attests the truth of the statement just made.

The other theory is more subtle. Man is an individual like every other individual in the world. He has two aspects, Form and Matter; the Form is the soul which represents his normal functions or purposes. Some purposes seem to be strictly animal, such as impulses, imagination and the emotional states. Others are intellectual and find their expression in the second part of the Divided Line. The former impressions are in constant flux, the latter tend to preserve their identity, in what manner Plato does not say. I shall suggest a solution presently. One point is plain—there is no divorce of soul from body; man is a single personality with impulses and emotions distinguished from intelligence but ultimately directed by its ideas. In a famous passage in the *Republic* (VI., 339 sq.) he debates

[59] J. Martineau, *Study of Religion* (Oxford: Clarendon Press, 1900), I, 15.
[60] *De Anima*, IV, 13A.

the question whether desire and emotion are different aspects of the soul. Is there a real difference between them or is emotion merely a second type of feeling now sublimated, so to say, by the mind's judgment on its contents? Take, for instance, the case of the indignant man. Is such an explosive sentiment just another exhibition of the grosser visceral feelings, or,—because we do not expend our anger on the man who justly redresses a wrong even though we suffer personally in the process,—are the emotional excitations so closely allied to the decisions of moral reason that the feeling-charges seem to disappear altogether? Plato certainly teaches that the desiderative and the "logistic" soul must be distinguished; is there still a "third function" called the "spirited" element? The argument seems to end with the identification of desire and emotion, because these are determined in value by the feelings entailed in either case. This, however, does not disturb the right of command exercised by reason over the so-called "lower" nature. It is true that Plato does not state the emotional demands as fully as Spinoza; it is self-control more than courage that, he intimates, requires the attention of the soul. But both thinkers agree that reason is the "sovereign form" of man, his "guiding genius" which at length must be appraised as the "gift of heaven." [61]

The real difference between the two theories lies in the structural nature of soul. The former springs directly from the religious tenets then in vogue at Athens. The gods of Greece though endowed with many human traits, have their own substance which is not subject to decay. In like manner the soul of man though "nailed" to a body sure to be destroyed in time, is simple in nature and therefore itself indecomposable. Furthermore, the human soul is disciplined and refined by the pursuit of moral ideals, justice, veracity and reverence, and cannot lose its identity without impairing their intrinsic value. Again, life which is the counterpart of soul, is the opposite of death; both cannot exist at the same time in the same individual; if one is denied the other must be affirmed. Hence, were bodily life the only property of the soul, it would be futile to hold that it could still exist after the breath had left the body. The independent reality of soul must be acknowledged. But the argument of Plato in the *Phaedo* (107B) does not establish the existence of soul; it guarantees the right of the logical mind to say that of two contradictory judgments, one must be true. Logic can assure us that the idea of *ensouledness* or *livingness*, is opposite to the idea of death; it cannot prove that the subject of a given proposition, the soul, has an unalterable reality of its own. At any rate the argument as an exercise in logic was a failure; inductive proof was the only solution, and it could not be obtained. What Plato did in a later dialogue was to divide the activities of man from

[61] *Timaeus,* 90A.

another angle,—the mortal and immortal; those subject to change and those with universal and therefore permanent value.[62] This distinction actually goes back to the *Phaedo;* for the *cause* of man's action, he avers, resides not in the changes of the physiological organs but in the determination of the mind. The one registers the *conditions* of the action, the other the reasons alleged for its performance. To find the cause we must in every case revert to the *immortal* aspect of the soul—the reflective powers of mind. These alone can give the *meaning* of behavior and may therefore be called the "directive" factors of personality.

Here, then, we detect the analogy between man and the universe in which he lives. Man, says Nicolas of Cusa, is the microcosm and the world the macrocosm. Now an analogy is a mathematical relation, a proportion between terms. As we have already noted, the changes in the physical world are comparable with the changes in man's experience; the settled laws of order and harmony, with the logical regularity of human thinking. Aristotle proposes the thesis that reason comes in from "out-of-doors"; [63] if that were true reason would be immortal in the literal sense. That is not Plato's opinion. Immortal means for him what *eternal* means for Spinoza—the universal application of a given set of ideas. Goodness, beauty, and truth are eternal, because they are universal and abstract names for moral and intellectual properties; such ideas cannot change, it matters not how and where and when they be applied. Thus, Socrates, a man of high reflective powers, gives utterance to sublime judgments on justice, honor and temperance; ideas which by virtue of their universal character can never perish. His reason mirrors the rational capacity of the race; he therefore may pass on to succeeding generations the glowing concepts of his own genius. In time, such ideas become the treasures of thought and the rules of moral conduct. Hence, human reason does not issue from the organic order of the universe; rather, the rational order of the world is the Genus under which all subordinate forms of rational decisions are to be arrayed as specific instances. Reason has eternal logical significance; it is the quality of man, it is the attribute of divinity.

It goes without saying that a scientific exposition like this is the only type of exposition we may justly conceive to be the expression of Plato's mature thought.

[62] *Timaeus,* 69C, 71A.   [63] W. F. Hardie, *op. cit.,* p. 141.

III: ARISTOTLE

It FREQUENTLY happens in the development of philosophy that the ideas conceived by a creative thinker are sifted and organized by a man of systematic temper and reduced by him to a scientific order. It is agreed among all careful readers that this is what Aristotle did for Plato. As a result Plato cannot be faithfully studied without the comments of his pupil. Schelling, the German romanticist, lays down the thesis that history conducts an illuminating dialectic. No thinker can be his own successor; he will be followed by a "system of phases" which will unfold the given ideas in a logical series. The original concepts which Plato incorporated in his dialogues, form the initial stages of the dialectic. They are nullified for a moment by the disappearance of the creator but powerfully reaffirmed by the synthetic genius of Aristotle. There is a body of truth which they held in common, while the manner of approach to many subjects is strikingly different. It is not too much to say that private interests colored the mode of composition although they did not alter the nature of the final judgments. One point is certain, as Schelling thinks, just this—that Aristotle and not another Plato could put the reconciling term to the dialectic. Two results issued from their joint efforts, first, that Socratic thought as defined by Plato with consummate skill was preserved, while its treasures were united in a series of volumes by an expert commentator. Aristotle could not retreat beyond the shadow of his inspired teacher, and at the same time Plato, who might have shone as a star apart, often distills his essential truth upon ensuing ages through the medium of his sympathetic interpreter.

What is it that makes Aristotle a competent advocate of the new ideas? He was eighteen years of age when he entered the Academy at Athens; his mental habits were fixed and he grappled with all phases of the new learning with assiduity and skill. His love of disputation soon made him the "soul of the school," and drew from Plato the epigram that "Aristotle needed the bridle while Xenocrates needed the spur." The promise of youth was amply fulfilled in his later years. Three traits of mind made his career distinguished. He was first of all a man of great erudition, *scholarship* we call it now, and his unimpeded energy carried him through the entire orbit of knowledge as then delimited. Knowledge began with mathematics, and while it is true that he fell behind his preceptor in his grasp of the fundamental laws of that science, he made up for any lack by his proficiency in the study of the laws of human thinking. His frequent complaint that Plato, in his later years, tended to explain the meaning of ideas through the witchery of numbers may indicate his lack of interest in the subject. It may be that his attempt to determine the value of justice as a moral concept by means of the process of proportion is not successful; still, it does not prove that he was "weak" in this particular branch of science. It is true that while he developed a technique in deductive logic which has provided direction and stimulus for the Western mind from his day to our own, his private penchant was for what is now called scientific experimentation. Thus, he submitted to empirical tests many of the conclusions in physiology reached by Plato in the latter part of the *Timaeus*. He knew how to analyze the structure of a living body and relate its activity to its own environment. Modern readers have been astonished at the data adduced without the aid of high-powered microscope or instruments of precision. Nor did he reject the inquiries pursued by men in a simpler era of scientific thought. Empedocles and Heraclitus had something to teach him about the modes of response by animals and the types of change in the wider world. In the arts of inductive logic he adopted the methods already made familiar by Socrates; he did not merely gather a mass of heterogeneous facts; he sought in every case the governing principle. We may admit that he added little to the fund of knowledge in the physical sciences; but at least he laid down the formula that matter is not the principal datum in the natural world, while motion is. This attitude made him a pioneer in the organization of the new science of religion already foreshadowed by his master.

The second trait is the systematizing power of his mind. He appears as a specialist who, moving among the accumulating concepts in the realm of science, can reduce them to logical order and stamp on each its reflective value. His intellect was Kantian in its penetrating vigor; not only can he detect the nucleating ideas, he can unfold their farthest implications. He organized the several departments of thought with unerring accuracy. He did for philosophy what the Roman jurists did for legal judgments. Thus, he put the axioms of the normative science of logic into a workable system which was not disturbed until the time of Darwin. Descartes and Francis Bacon tried to break the tenet of a "fixed class" in thought but failed. When biology discovered an endless progression of changing forms in the organic world and physics pointed out the movement of ionized bodies through unlimited space, class distinctions lost their force as instruments for the acquisition of knowledge. But everyday logic still retains them for the common experience of life but gives them refined forms for the determination of the more intricate types of information. However, the historic worth of his method has been demonstrated in many ways,—here in isolating unsuspected errors of reflection, there in associating independent judgments under a single comprehensive axiom. No man can read at random the *Prior Analytics*—dry as dust to the untutored neophyte—, without being impressed with the many-sided aspects of the logician's mind. Thomas Aquinas and Benedict de Spinoza gladly own him among their most cherished preceptors.

To these traits must be added a third which at first sight might seem to separate him wholly from Plato but which on more adequate evidence links him to the Socratic tradition. In few minds of the highest calibre has the feeling for the objective, the individual, the practical been so acute and pervasive. Aristotle began every study with the concrete and isolated datum of experience. The single physical object, the specific judgment, the behavior of the moral agent, the action of the citizen of the state—these are the details of the problem. Take the concept of justice;—he does not at the start discuss the elaborate program of virtue in which justice is to have its place; he goes at once to the individual centre, the man in the street, the student in the school, and asks what his native and acquired properties are. These must correspond to the type of action which adult society will call just or temperate or courageous. They will therefore at length compose the answer to the question:—What is the fundamental *good* of moral behavior? Aristotle, true to his native feeling, argues that the proper development of virtue depends to some extent upon the possession of external goods— wealth, fame, power, but the prime necessity is the formation of a habit of action. We must acquire a character peculiar to the agent, a Hexis, a determined fixation of temperament based upon natural qualities but disciplined by reflective experience. "The just man becomes just by acting justly" —a convenient phrase, which however does not stand up before the laws of logic. What he demands is a sustained and steady conduct couched not in elegant phraseology but in the form of just deeds. He asserts that no man can develop just character by obedience to native instincts; on that point he is at one with Plato in his notable study in the *Gorgias*. Virtue is not impulsive behavior, it is deliberate decision in difficult circumstances. The mathematical method is the adoption of the mean between extremes, courage as over against cowardice or recklessness. Here, however, exact computation is impossible; and in the case of justice no proportion can be devised—action is just or unjust, and man must choose according to the sentiments of his mind. The deed, the intricate situation, is the object of study both in ethics and in every other scientific pursuit. Aristotle is thus the proponent of objectivity, the formal realist, the standard Hellenist of the period. Emotion and prejudice are excluded, the fancies of the poet and the claims of the rhetorician annulled. When he enters the realm of religious studies, he will carry the same analytical methods with him.

Yet it is an axiom of the scientific inquirer that he must distinguish between the observation of concrete facts and the ascertainment of abstract principles. Logic must be inductive as well as deductive. In the latter sense it must sharpen the instruments of analysis; for example, the principle of same and different, the separation of the one from the many, that is, the universal and particular, the notion that a greater reality, involving the scope of application, belongs to objects of a higher logical class, and finally, the distinction of types of reality which must be dealt with in any scientific inquiry. Some of these will be confined strictly to the needs of the objective sciences; others may be employed either for empirical or ontological research. The latter subject belongs solely to the "divine sciences." Mathematical measurement is here displaced; concepts of universal import are in use. "God," says Aristotle, "is thought to be among the causes of all things, and to be a first principle." [1] It should be noted that the author proposes to treat the object of this science as an individual quite in line with his procedure in the nearer sciences. This he does against the rugged criticism of the physical Monists of his day, and without regard to possible criticism in later eras, such, for instance, as is found in the creed of the Logical Positivists of our day. He was impressed with the importance of organizing a science of substance itself, where the common properties of empirically determined objects will be eliminated. We shall see soon that he approaches the study by way of the laws of physics, at least, in the later discourses. The approach is clearly seen in the twelfth book of the *Metaphysics*, where he describes the movements of the heavenly bodies, names their orbits and spheres, sets up a hypothetical number, 55 in all, and provides a logical place for a First Mover. It may be that this particular passage is not found in the original text of the book; its diction does have a flavor not shared in by the lecture notes that precede and follow it. Furthermore, its subject-matter interrupts the argument dealing with the eminent attributes of divine subsance, especially reason, a property not discernible in the progress of the stars. [2] However that may be, the general purpose of the philosopher is clear; he is bent on proving that the very nature of the physical world is such that it requires the offices of a special science in order to supplement the facts that can be demonstrated by the lower sciences. His words hold him to this course; for the movements of the stars are unceasing and "each movement must be caused by a substance which itself is not in motion, and which is necessarily eternal." [3] The hypothesis he proposes is faulty, and we shall later indicate its fallacies.

[1] *Metaphysics*, 983a8.   [2] W. Jaeger, *Aristotle*, p. 363.   [3] *Metaphysics*, 1073a2, 32–34.

Just now it is our duty to note the author's claim that a superior science is needed to consider the residual data, that is, those elements of the problem which remain unexplained after the laws of physics have been satisfied. Physics, he says, is in its own right a "kind of wisdom" but it is not "of the first kind." Behind its terms and supporting its conclusions stands another type of knowledge where the "inquiry is universal and deals with primary existence." In this field the "natural philosopher" must give way to "a kind of thinker who is above him" and who—despite the lofty character of his subject—is obliged to recognize the value of the logical syllogism as applied to universal principles.[4] Especially must he acquaint himself with the age-old system of Contraries. Scientific speculation in Greece began with it. Opposites like cold and hot, moist and dry, could be reconciled by assuming the existence of a common generic substance called the Indeterminate. The problem grew more complex as men tried to examine the properties of the individual part and its relation to the whole body. Logic entered and distinguished between substance as a unity and its several attributes. Attributes themselves become antithetical,—colors, temperatures, weights;—they must have common factors into which they may be separated, white and black in color, hot and cold in temperature, and so through the list. Furthermore, the same properties make different impressions on different observers at the same moment or different impressions on the same observer at different times. When these speculations approach their limit in the study of the universe itself, then it becomes irresistibly clear that the objective sciences have lost their influence. Physics can determine the scope and meaning of motion in the action of one body on another; it cannot discover the value of the fundamental principle embodied in any kind of motion. Aristotle is faced with the same problem which Kant confronted centuries later. Causality as a law, the "anticipations of experience," the attempt to shift empirical inquiry across the chasm lying between sense and reason, into the transcendental world—all these end in frustration and disappointment. Like Kant he was surrounded by a wide and tempestuous sea, with portentous shapes staring at him on every hand and no sure conclusions within his grasp. Still, he did not hesitate to push on towards the goal of universal truth which mirrored the divine substance of his dreams. He served notice on the dissenting thinkers of his age that Greece's first professional logician was not afraid to entertain as valid, certain judgments which could not be verified by empirical evidence.

We now proceed to examine the meaning of primary subtsance, the principle of motion as embodied in the idea of a Prime Mover, the relation of potential existence to pure actuality, and lastly, the element of reason or thought as set forth in the theory of final causes. These four points consti-

---

[4] *Metaphysics*, 1004a2.

tute the essential factors which—following the classical tradition—belong to the nature of the individual object which in the present argument is the universe itself.

MEANING OF PRIMARY SUBSTANCE

Aristotle begins his analysis with the assumption that every object whatever its intrinsic character or logical status must be studied under two distinguishable heads, Matter and Form. Plato held the same opinion; hence the difference between the men will lie only in the manner of treatment. Matter acts as the basis or substratum of the body, form gives it a steady and specific meaning. The coördinating substance of the world must be approached from the same angle. Some philosophers have alleged that sensible matter alone exists; all other types of existence are creations of the fancy with no root in experience. Thus, Democritus held that the atom—his unitary substance—was strictly material in essence and varied from its fellows solely in shape, position, and order of arrangement. These properties belong to the object and cannot be divorced from it. Do composite bodies possess the same strategic elements? Is the earth with its cycles of heat and cold, its alternations of watery and arid surface, nothing but the coagulation of primitive matter? Is the fiery heat of the sun, its self-directed luminosity, its power to produce change in plant and animal, are these and other conditions nothing but sheer brute force unaffected by the presence of constitutive ideas? To separate matter from ideas is absurd; it is quite as absurd as it is to separate ideas from matter. Plato, says the author, was guilty of the latter error, and he misled the world of thought by his extravagant claims. Ideas are independent natures—Aristotle understood him to say; they inhabit their own sphere of reality and have the particular function of bringing an individual into existence and establishing its inherent meaning.[5] We have already proven that Aristotle was wholly mistaken in his interpretation of Plato's theory. It is true that ideas cannot in their own right influence the movements of stars and planets; they cannot produce a new phenomenon in the heart of nature by the method of genesis and dissolution. Ideas are not separable substances in the sense that they reside in an empyrean remote from the intelligence of man. The plain fact upon which both Plato and Aristotle agree is that ideas and material structures unite to form a single object. This union Plato never denied, and it is this union that Aristotle specifically affirmed. We shall therefore study his version of the matter.

It was evident to him that he was bound to meet certain serious difficulties in his attempt to explain the meaning of elementary substance. Matter is something common to an indefinite series of individuals at the same

[5] *Metaphysics*, Zeta.

time. For this reason matter becomes an ambiguous concept; for it is quite beyond the power of mind to strip every quality from an assumed substratum and still be able to say something about the remaining substance. Thus, the bronze mass which the sculptor uses for moulding his sphere has itself contour, color, weight and pliability all its own; what then is the *material* that underlies the bronze mass? Furthermore, what underlies *that* material? A regress is thus set up which grows ever more dim in qualitative significance until we arrive at what is not a sensible object at all but an undisguised figment of the mind. In fact, as Professor Ross says, "bare matter is not an individual; what an individual must have is some character, and bare matter has none." [6] Such a treatment of the notion of substance is simply inadequate.

There is, however, something in the object which we are entitled to regard as possessing cohesive power. Locke candidly admitted that he could not identify or define it. Still, he could not rid his mind of the concept and every time he obtained a new image of the external object he felt that he must assume a *power* inherent in the object which keeps its qualities together and also enabled it to make a concentrated impact upon the senses. Such a concept seems wholly unscientific and we may well endeavor to eliminate it from our studies. But Aristotle would not allow the term *substratum* to be dropped; he insisted that though we could not perceive it with the eye "there is something common to many things at the same time" and this alone would account for the persistence of attributes. [7] Later, however, his opinion changed; substance is no longer indeterminate matter which—taking on particular form—becomes a gleaming star or grain of sand or living being; substance is the essential character which makes the individual what it is. The accidental properties need to be examined, color, flexibility, taste or smell; it is the generic and specific qualities that fix its meaning. These are not merely logical concepts read into the object by the scientific observer; they are constitutive principles, as for example, the organic, sentient and rational powers united in the nature of man. Under such conditions substance is not an ambiguous term; it is a thing existing in space and time, endowed with attributes that show at once to what class it belongs.

It is clear, from this analysis, that Matter and Form are ingredient and composing elements which cannot be separated by any operative experiment. Aristotle reverts to Plato's use of the organism where function represents precisely what the individual can do. If the function ceases to act the body perishes. If the governing principle is lost the individual is no

---

[6] *Aristotle's Metaphysics*, Vol. I, p. xciv.   [7] *Metaphysics*, 1040b25.

longer the same but something else.[8] He then proceeds to argue that the same method must be followed in examining substantial being which cannot be perceived by the senses. He illustrates the procedure by a kind of existence standing midway between a tangible real, and pure unattached ideas, that is, mathematical concretes like point, line, surface, and solid figures, always present in sensible objects but non-perceptible. Thus, the bronze sphere when it reaches completion in the hands of the moulder, is composed of "intellectual matter" whose meaning cannot be established by empirical tests but only by the laws of Euclidian space.[9] Hence, they cannot have the same kind of individuality that sensible objects possess but are used to set up frontiers between separate objects and to mark the place and limit of each. They contribute, as Ross says, the "pluralizing element to the entire physical world." [10] Without the unseen geometrical distinctions individuals cannot come into existence. In general, space and time without which natural events cannot be scientifically studied, depend on the use of numbers both for the measurement of bodies and the determination of their velocities.

The two kinds of substance just examined have to do directly or indirectly with sensible matter. A third kind differs from both and is characterized by Aristotle as immovable, eternal and separate from matter. These are strong words to bring into a scientific discussion, because they require a new sort of technique. The instruments of vision and touch have no value here; even the rules of the differentiation of individuals are without significance. We turn away from the stream of moving objects to the total view of reality. "It is plain," says the author, "that if the *divine* is present anywhere it is present in things of this sort." The demand is made upon the investigator that he "consider being *as* being itself, both what it is in itself and what attributes belong to it as existing reality." [11] The posture of the thinker now is not that of the prophet or diviner; there is a place for the man of insight in the study of the habitudes of religious thought. In an early work on Philosophy some tattered fragments of which have been preserved, Aristotle argues for the genesis of the belief in the existence of divine power, when "men have glimpsed the whole sky laid out and adorned with stars and the variety of the lights of the moon, now waxing, now waning, and the rising and settings of them all, and their course ratified and immutable to all eternity." [12] But the cosmological argument has a sounder basis in the realistic studies of the man of science. His duty is to search out the primitive causes; he must know what is first and what is derived from a first cause. This implies that we have deter-

[8] *Ibid.*, 1035b3–32.   [9] *Ibid.*, 1036a10, 1077a20.   [10] *Op. cit.*, I, cii.
[11] *Metaphysics*, 1026a20, 32.   [12] W. Jaeger, *op. cit.*, p. 163.

mined what is the precise object whose attributes are to be examined. Certainly, logical predicates cannot be framed until we have fixed upon the subject of the judgment. This is the procedure in all scientific inquiry.

Hence, the object of study must be accepted as *real;* otherwise, no demonstration of its influence on other objects can be carried out. Now universal substance is the object of quest in Aristotle's metaphysics, and he asserts at once that it must be taken as *first* in every meaning of the term. It is first in definition, for, as we have already intimated, it were futile to study a property if there were no individual to which it might be attached. Swiftness refers to a moving body, beauty to a glowing face or sumptuous sunset, thought to a functioning mind in a human being. Again, substance is first in order of knowledge; for we know how to identify the fiery flame as appearing in this place or that and to assess its quantity and quality, only when we have apprehended the object and begun to analyze its parts. Lastly, substance is first in point of time, as when the genus precedes the application of the specific property in our endeavor to unfold the character of the object. The real object like the atom of Democritus is contrasted with the absence of all reality called by him the *void*. It contrasts again, and more vividly, with bodies that appear for a brief moment and then disappear. Recent experiments with the mesotron show that its "life" is less than the trillionth of a second, a quite unintelligible interval of time.[13] The world of Heraclitus was a bewildering world, a welter of changing phenomena,—the passing seasons, the deflected river courses, the growth and decay of organic bodies, the birth and death of human creatures, and the amazing changes in their social habits. In such an unstable existence substance cannot reside; it merely furnishes a background of reality which itself becomes clear and distinct in the revolutions of the heavenly bodies. Thus, substance is present everywhere in the universe, being particularized in this body or that, in this celestial sphere or that, until the full measure of reality is reached in the primary substance. The infinite congeries of independent individuals is in this manner associated irrevocably under a common law, called the law of substance. Physics argues that natural bodies are bound to one another in certain defined relations; metaphysics argues that a universal law governs universal substance and such a law is *divine*.[14]

But substance is not only actual, it is necessary; it is, as Spinoza says, its own cause (sui causa). We have just referred to the presence of law in the realm of physical operations. Sun and stars pursue their appointed orbital motions. Heavy bodies on the earth move towards the centre. Seasons suc-

---

[13] A. H. Compton, "Recent Studies of Cosmic Rays at High Altitudes." A paper read April 24, 1941 in the meetings of the American Philosophical Society.

[14] *Metaphysics*, I, ch. 2.

ceed one another with a precision that can only be construed as determined and unchangeable. Even Heraclitus was obliged to assume a "law of change" to account for the regularity of observed movements.

There are certain minor cases where causality seems to be suspended—abnormal cold in summer, sports on trees, even caprices of the human mind.[15] These are not true cases of chance but rather situations where the full knowledge of cause has not been reached. In complete and primary substance no exceptions are found. For it is dependent on no exterior or coercive factor; it cannot be influenced by physical bodies or their movements, since it is, by nature, wholly separated from corporeal conditions. It is endowed with pure actuality which natural bodies do not and cannot possess, as we shall later see. Aristotle did not have the terms *necessary* and *contingent* which the Scholastic philosophy developed; these draw a sharp line between the conditioned processes of nature and the reality of the highest substance, namely, God. He could see as plainly as Spinoza did, that finite existence presupposes the operation of an unconditioned cause which itself *must* exist. "We exist," says the latter, "either in ourselves or in something else that necessarily exists. Therefore, a being, absolutely infinite, that is, God necessarily exists." [16] The argument is, to be sure, a dialectical conjecture, not a scientific demonstration. It assumes the presence of a universal rule that if an object has no necessary existence in its own right, it will owe its existence to a being which has that right. The argument has been held effective by many of the profound thinkers of the Western World. Yet its fallacies are obvious and cannot be blinked; still it utters the imperious demand of rational intelligence and will not be arbitrarily dismissed.

Nor is this the only ground upon which the powers of substance legally rest. No one can deny that the argument from the principle of sufficient reason is extraordinarily strong in its emotional persuasion if not in its convincing logical weight. There is another point still more penetrating; it springs from the second law of thought, namely, the law of contradiction—that whose non-existence cannot be conceived must exist.[17] Spinoza states the same rule thus: "The existence of Substance must arise solely from its own nature which is nothing other than its essence." [18] Again the argument is familiar to the students of philosophy. That which is complete substance—the *ens realissimum*—must have all possible attributes including existence. If an attribute is canceled its definition is destroyed and the corresponding reality annulled. Time and reflection have exposed the insecurity of this argument, also. For existence is not an attribute but the given object to which attributes are attached. Hence we

[15] *Metaphysics*, 1065a6.   [16] *Ethics*, I, 12; Demonstration.
[17] *Metaphysics*, 1006b32.   [18] *Ethics*, I, 12, Scholium.

must accept the presence of the object before we adduce its properties. Nevertheless the sheer impact of the most commonplace object upon the senses makes it positively real; and the thought of unlimited substance, of which the object is an infinitesimal part, comes to us with such crushing authority that we accept its correlate as incontrovertibly real. Substance *does* exist; if it does not we have denied the validity of the second law of logic.

Finally, substance must be characterized as One. The author is careful to explain what he means by unity.[19] It is one because its continuity is unbroken; it is solid in form much as an artistic object from the hand of the sculptor would be; it is also grounded in a single governing principle. Its relations go back to physics, to aesthetics and to logic. The Pythagoreans attempted to combine the concept of infinity—the endless succession of geometrical units—with the permanent oneness of the physical universe. It is true that the sensible object can be individualized by this method; but what its nature is and what it can do other than occupy its own position in time and space, cannot be deduced by so "simple" an analysis.[20] Again, the bald idea of infinity whether in number or magnitude or duration seems to contradict the prescriptions of ordinary physics which assume that space is complete, hence, a sphere. Nor can unity be defined by solidarity of form; for then we have no organization of the parts into a whole but only a succession of elements, responsible to no fundamental authority, held together by no orderly processes—that is, a *chaos* not a *cosmos*. Thus, the statue is an example of the organic unity of parts adjusted and controlled by the unseen principle of beauty. Proportion and symmetry are engraved upon its surfaces; its unity is the index of creative art passing from the mind of the artist to the plastic matter of the marble. In the movements of nature the same achievements of harmony are found. We are therefore justified in ascribing a symmetry of motion springing from an habitual return of the heavenly bodies in their daily round or their seasonal readjustment. This may not be a definition of unity but it suggests reasons why we may expect to find unity in a complicated situation like the one confronting us.

If neither of the above explanations proves an answer to our question, what gives unity to substance, we may try again, this time not with respect to the observable phenomena but in view of the governing principle of the Whole. Aristotle, we said, conceived of definition or essence as the infallible source of unity in the single individual.[21] It is that which imparts specific meaning to my book, my body, my personality. It will do the same for supreme substance; it will relieve the theory under review of the charge of solitariness or barrenness, a concept from which the Greek mind re-

[19] *Metaphysics*, 1016b32.   [20] *Ibid.*, 987a14.   [21] *Ibid.*, 1030b5.

coiled with instinctive horror, as Plato demonstrated in his *Parmenides*. We shall examine the concept further in our study of pure actuality. At present it suffices to say that unity has a logical value which makes the interpretation of the Socratic school wholly different from the fancies of the physiocrats. Democritus envisaged matter as subject to constraints which were crude and vulgar, holding that atoms fell in a straight line until they were locked in the embrace of arbitrarily constructed hooks and suddenly swept from their course. The new school removes unity from the motion of bodies and places it in the teleological relation of the parts to the whole. This gives a sovereign and *divine* character to substance. Such an article of faith appears in the first book of the *Metaphysics,* and so far as we are aware Aristotle never changed his point of view. In fact, at times he seems to be on the verge of prescribing for his primary substance the quality of a self-sufficient Monad, a substance that has no "windows," that is, no tendency to admit external forces which could in any way impair or destroy its fundamental character. Hence, the independence of substance is complete and its position as a directing force fully established.

MOTION AND THE PRIME MOVER

The recognition of a unitary Substance as over against the multiplicity of individuals in a sensible world, is the first step in the formation of a metaphysical system. A second step must now be taken. "Nature," says Aristotle, "has been defined as the principle of motion and change." [22] If motion cannot be forced to give up its secrets the meaning of nature will go unexplained. It appears, on observation, that all objects in nature are continually passing from a state of potency to a state of actual accomplishment. The end of change we shall examine in the next section; now we are to examine the properties of motion itself. The simplest way to approach the subject is to catalogue the several forms of motion perceivable in nature. They are four in number. The first is qualitative; it consists of the re-arrangement of chemical particles under the influence of normal agents like heat, gravity, and the like. The next is quantitative, illustrated by the growth of plants and animals in size and shape. The most important one is third, a change discernible in every type of action but particularly reflected in the movement of bodies from place to place under the impulse of a coercive force. A fourth kind is expressed in the creation of a new individual, as a house, where the structure is not complete until the last tile has been laid on the roof. In this instance motion seems to be arrested with the erection of the building, inertia being hidden from view and repose substituted for activity. In point of fact motion is never suspended, since deterioration begins even while production goes on. In

[22] *Physics,* II, 11.

certain types of individuals like organisms motion does not begin by itself, when the body starts to move; interior forces,—respiration, circulation of the blood, the digestive process—constitute a continuing series.[23] Hence, the apparently spasmodic or irregular motions on the earth really participate in the steady movements of the whole universe. Indeed, natural forms cannot be conceived without motion; if motion ceases production is at an end; stop the revolution of the heavenly bodies and the world returns to its chaotic condition,—a dread spectre haunting the dreams of many Greek thinkers.

The primacy of geometrical motion is due to the fact that it alone has the capacity of uninterrupted continuity. It is true that an up-and-down movement in sublunary objects implies a change in direction; a stone thrown into the air describes a stunted curve when its primitive energy is exhausted; yet even here the property on which the continuity of motion rests is not excluded; for, as Aristotle remarks, a body "loses its essential character in the process of *spacial* change less than in any other kind of motion." [24] As respects the celestial spheres the rule is infallible; for the "nature of the stars is eternal and is itself a kind of substance; it is also the eternal cause of motion and stands logically prior to the motion of the body moved." [25] It is here that the philosopher introduces his solution for the problems of the stellar world. He expects to prove that motion in general is continuous and everlasting; its principle never lapses. In order to do this he calls to his aid the branch of mathematics next to philosophy in value, namely, astronomy. Science has demonstrated that every aggregate of bodies has its own type of motion; some bodies like planets may have more than one orbital movement. Hence, the total number of motions will be greater than the sum of the stellar systems and for the whole expanse of the heavens will not be less than fifty-five. The natural fact which cannot be disregarded is that each separate motion is independent of every other; it undergoes no alteration in its course, no fluctuation or retardation in its velocity. Each movement is controlled by its own energized substance which is a "divinity" cited by Aristotle as the "spirit of the sphere." Such controlling substance is unchangeable in form, has no magnitude and is bound inexorably to its own motion which must therefore be continuous. But over all these there is one comprehensive Substance, one firmament embracing all stellar systems whose true and final expression is enshrined in the timeless perpetuity of motion. It is hard to discover a single item in this creed which diverges from the theory of Plato; together they register the first attempt of modern Greek thought to clear away the debris of poetic and rhetorical speculations, and build a religious doctrine on the foundations of scientific inquiry.

---

[23] *Ibid.*, 258b7.   [24] *Ibid.*, 261a20.   [25] *Metaphysics*, 1073a34.

But the argument is not yet complete; in fact it is only in its initial stages. We may agree that soluble substances give no sure grounds for the continuance of motion. Democritus recognized this fact and sought to make his atom indestructible. Inertia as found in bodies on the earth loses its inherent power; bodies begin to disintegrate and often disappear. Hence, motion in order to persist requires a property other than mere gravity, some impulse other than its own character in accordance with the commonly observed fact that "everything that is moved must be moved by something." [26] This is the first axiom of physical science, and to it no exception can be taken. Is there also a primary cause which gives the impulse to the totality of being? What is the Prime Mover which Plato and his associates so warmly discussed? It was generally said, and Aristotle agreed, that the human mind revolts against the conception of an infinite regress in causation.[27] Kant certainly rejected the principle; the regress, if any, could only be the indefinite process in experience, which, however, never leads us to a sure conclusion. Aristotle held that thoughtful men declined to go on from one cause to another, from a cause to an effect which in turn became another cause—from one motion to another and thence to a third—without coming to a full stop. The imagination is bewildered and demonstration is never conclusive. The way out of the dilemma is to posit the existence of a stationary Cause, a mover itself unmoved. The logical compass is thus neatly boxed—the unmoved Mover, God; the moved that also moves others, namely, the spheres of heaven; bodies that are moved but do not move others—all things on the earth; and finally, the Earth itself unmoved and never moving others. Logic is not always justified of her children; here the system of permutations is complete; nothing can be added to or taken away from the given series. But the primary question remains—Does the system explain what it aims to explain? How, for instance, can it explain that there will be an originating cause of motion when motion and the universe in which it operates are both eternal? Aristotle's conviction on the latter point is clear, though his argument, long and involved as it is, may not stir conviction in other minds. "The heavens as a whole," he writes, "neither came into being nor admits of dissolution; it is one and eternal, with no end or beginning of its total duration." [28] Time and motion belong of right to the universe and participate in all its attributes. If this be true what part can an independent Cause play in a world already formed? Deists may permit their God to create and organize a cosmos and, departing, leave it to its own devices throughout the length of days. Such a theory can be understood even though it could not be scientifically demonstrated. But to insist that

[26] *Physics*, VII, 1.   [27] *Ibid.*, 242a26.   [28] *De Caelo*, Book II, Chap. 1.

motion is coeval with the world and yet relies for its continuity upon a power which had nothing to do with its production, lays too heavy a demand upon the intelligence of the philosophical thinker. Logic may include such an idea in its system but common sense will not.

Still, this interpretation has attracted a number of important names to its support. Zeller has boldly separated motion from its Prime Mover and given a distinct ontological status to each. The Prime Mover is a transcendent substance untouched by matter or quantitative dimensions; it is pure Energy, it is untrammeled Thought, which directs the activities of the natural universe from its centre to its periphery.[29] The logical contradiction seems to carry no weight with him; the case of the unoriginated Mover is so necessary a factor in Aristotle's theory that we need not quibble over a difficulty that may be only apparent, when finally analyzed. Moreover, in his general acceptance of Aristotle's theory Zeller is joined by another Continental scholar, Werner Jaeger, who maintains that Aristotle reconstructed his theory of the Prime Mover when doubts as to the validity of the argument pressed upon him in later life. However, the fundamental principle was not abandoned; he only tried to draw the line sharply between physics as a science and the hyper-empirical elements which had engaged his attention in his less mature thought. Theophrastus, his pupil, held that the entire subject of divine substance belonged to the realm of metaphysical inquiry and could not be decided by the ordinary laws of logic. Professor Ross also says that it is "exclusively as a first mover that a God is necessary to his system." Aristotle had failed to determine the scientific meaning of motion, and now had to face the question as to how a non-physical agency, implemented by the urge of desire, could possibly direct motion within the confines of a sensible world. Yet Ross continues the erroneous method of his fellow-commentators in interpreting literally the language of the author thereby introducing certain difficulties which have no place in the original problem. He admits that the contradiction exposed above actually exists; however, since Aristotle has transferred the status of the Cause to the level of transcendent reality, we do not seem under any obligation to consider the logical relations further. In this judgment Ross is undoubtedly wrong.

If Thomas of Aquino had not interposed his great learning and wide influence we might very well ask whether the matter would not long ago have been consigned to the limbo of forgotten issues. There are strong reasons for believing that modern scholarship would have defined Aristotle's thesis more impartially if it had not been embarrassed by a theological bias. Thomas needed a vigorous and effective argument for the existence of God. He rejected Anselm's proof that the idea of a Being

---

[29] E. Zeller, *Aristotle*, I, 393.

"than whom a greater cannot be thought" is present in the mind and requires a correlate in the world of Reality. But ideas may represent mere
persuasive fancies and to convert one into a metaphysical Being is an extremely dangerous proceeding. There are dogmas such as the Trinity which
only faith can master; others like the existence of God demand the full
measure of scientific analysis. "Our intellect is led from sensible analogies
to the divine knowledge that God exists." [30] Thomas was deeply impressed with the proof which he thought was formulated by Aristotle.
The objection we have examined was without foundation in his view, because he declined to accept the principle that the universe is uncreated. On
the other hand, he believed the world was created in time, motion began
with creation, and God as the first Cause is the one creative force. The
argument is plain:—Everything that is moved must be moved by something; this is the invariable law. Then, the mover must itself be moved
or not moved. If it *is* moved it is but another link in the regress of motion;
if it is *not* moved, then we are obliged to admit the existence of an unmoved Cause capable of inaugurating motion and charting its course. Two
points are thus clear:—no motion can go on to infinity, and no action can
be taken without a cause. This is the orthodox cosmological argument;
it belongs to the creedal statements of the church. Are we to regard it as
the authentic theory of Aristotle or is there another formula better
qualified to express his thought? Kant in his memorable *Critique* has
exposed the fallacies; we need not rehearse them here. In view of the logical contradiction which Aristotle would certainly understand and try
to avoid, it is wise to seek another way out. This we shall now attempt
to do.

The question is simple:—Did Aristotle wish us to interpret his *prime
mover* as an autonomous substance separate from the world and endowed
with attributes such as Theism is wont to ascribe to its Deity? Or, did he
intend to follow the manner of Plato and study the universe from the point
of view of its totality? Divinity is not creative genius but directive harmony.
Both men took substance as they found it and endeavored to understand
both its particular and universal implications. The prime mover is not a
supersensible Being with conscious apprehension but no material form,
a causal power which could somehow insinuate its intelligence into the
changing sequences of nature. That would be an adaptation of the physicist's conception of cause which Aristotle flatly refused to introduce into
the "divine Science." [31] The key to his definition of causality is given in
the eleventh book of the *Metaphysics*. There are, he urges, certain specific
principles governing the action of any set of bodies or the orbits of such
bodies in relation to one another. These principles are called laws or as

[30] *Summa contra Gentiles*, Book I, Chap, 3.   [31] *Metaphysics*, 982a10 sq.

the Greeks say "genera." Every physical action operates under a prescriptive law and repeated observations enable us to determine the mathematical meaning of the law. But over and above particular laws—circular
motion, weight of body, self-starting power of the organism—there is another law, the *law of motion* itself. This law is entirely distinct from the
subordinate laws and deals not with body but with the meaning of movement. As a law it is not subject to change; as a superior law it bears the
imprint of universal application; it does not prescribe a single form of
movement. Aristotle calls it the "first and imperative" principle (*arche*)
and he applies this principle directly and unreservedly to *God*. That is
to say, he removed it wholly from association with the complex of natural
bodies or even with the revolutions of the spheres. Emulating the example
of Plato again he defines the principle as the "best" in the universe, in
other words, the logical superordinate of the entire series of genera, the
synthetic attribute which unites all motile energies into a common whole.[32]
Zeller stoutly resists this interpretation, as though he knew Aristotle's
intention better than the writer himself did. He complains that the phrase,
"first and imperative principle," proves nothing except that God as supreme independent substance postulates "unity of aim to the whole world";
for since he has already instituted the "all-governing motion of the first
sphere," he must be regarded as responsible for the presence and maintenance of order in the universe at large.[33]

But by this very admission Zeller opens the way for a scientific definition of causality. In the history of philosophical thought two meanings
have been adopted. Bruno taught us to distinguish carefully between the
originating cause and principle of activity or *causa immanens*. St. Thomas,
as we have seen, expressly excluded the concept of an uncreated world,
thereby conceding that his approach to the subject was not the same as
Aristotle's. God, says Thomas, is the maker of the world, its matter and
its motion. The Prime Mover, says Aristotle, is the "principle of motion."
Both affirm that the Cause is immaterial, without extension, without magnitude. Do they define these terms in the same unequivocal sense? For
Thomas they signified a Being whose nature was spiritual, who was endowed with intelligence and will; who could therefore communicate
with the spirits of men, as he did through chosen representatives. Did
Aristotle give them a distinctly theistic value such as this? Cause means
two things, we said, an originating power or a property within the world
which, when understood, explains all the habitudes and actions of the
world. Bruno would probably not carry his definition as far as Aristotle
did. But he appears at times to deny the official postulate of the church,—
God is the Cause of matter and motion. Instead, he saw in God the im-

[32] *Metaphysics*, 1064a30.   [33] Zeller, *op. cit.*, I, 411.

manent principle by which intelligent minds could interpret satisfactorily the several problems of existence.

It is in this manner that we are forced to construe the statements of the Greek. The principle of motion includes all those attributes that are ordinarily ascribed to the divine substance. It is immaterial, for it cannot be measured; it is unmoved, since it is quite without the property of gravity; it is separate from individual bodies or orbital systems, hence, not identifiable with any internal *force*. The term *principle* has sometimes been made equivalent to existence, as when Berkeley speaks of the human self as a "thinking, active principle." [34] Principle may also be compared with the spirit which is said to reside in certain liquors or with virtue which gives strength to certain organic bodies. Aristotle's definition has no esoteric quality such as these. Nor is it a pale reflection of the *anima mundi* which caught the imagination of many ancient thinkers. Soul and motion, for both Plato and Aristotle, anticipate the significance of reason and in the *Metaphysics* suggest the function of desire which we shall examine later. But the *principle* of motion has nothing to do with either the willing of a result or the attempt to produce it. Motion does not create bodies nor does it determine their direction or course. The function of motion is to weld the several systems of the world into a symmetrical whole, thereby proving that order issues from motion and from no other source. Obviously, space cannot of itself produce either equilibrium or steadiness; it is not an element in physical nature but a concept of the observing mind. Hence, it reveals and evaluates the sensible forms of regularity where each point in the given figure bears a necessary relation to every other. When we survey a landscape with intent gaze we plot the position of the trees in the foreground and their composite group against the contour of the hills beyond. Here order is spatial and discrete, silent and at rest. But reflection shows that motion has preceded the momentary calm, in the growth of the trees, in the corrugation of the hills by beating rain and gushing waters. We are reminded of Bergson's celebrated analysis of order. He assumes the existence of two distinct kinds, automatic and willed, the one embodied in the fixed curves of a geometrical system, the other in generative purposes of a living individual. Space is the key to the first, time to the other. They appear to be contradictory in form; yet on inspection we find that what we at first glance took to be disorder is only another type of order having a different origin. It should be remembered that geometrical composition is a process of mind, no more integral to nature than space itself. Consider, for example, the huge deposits of matter spread by sudden avalanche in monstrous confusion upon the high mountain pass. They seem to the casual eye like

[34] *Hylas* (Reprint ed.; Chicago: The Open Court Publishing Co., 1913), Sec. 95.

the impudent sweepings of a human giant as he takes his way from peak to peak, down the steep wooded mountain sides which in an instant are denuded of their agelong growths. There is no order here, we say, there is sheer and irreparable devastation. We are wrong; there is order in lines and solids; in this case it is strictly mechanical, obeying in every detail the law of the parallelogram of forces. But the ancients, Bergson argues, did not ask "why nature submits to law, but why nature is ordered according to genera or kinds." [35] They thought in terms of logic. Thus, time for Plato was a separate genus with its divisions into past, present and future; motion has its types fixed and unchangeable, as we have seen, all of them subsumed under the same generic principle.

The classes of living bodies, on the other hand, have their own rules of order. It is, we said, a willed order, an order provided not by a physical arbiter which lays its inflexible behests upon plastic matter in the manner of the political autocrat, but by the directive *entelechy* which eventually sets up new and unfamiliar kinds of motion. Aristotle uses a striking analogy which, whether intended or not, actually expresses the difference between automatic and willed order. He suggests that the "good" of the army is subserved by the operation of two forces; the first is the instinct for common action as resident in the soldiery itself, and the second is the authority of the leader. Order is achieved by perpetual discipline, so that the movements of the army seems to partake of a sort of mechanical coördination, sometimes so perfect that even the beating of the waves on the rocks could not surpass it in precision of movement and uniformity of step. There is also the vital impact of the general's presence at the head of his troops. His influence permeates every column, sounds in every command, gleams in streaming banners, and makes possible the ultimate triumph of the cause.[36] Order is the first law of nature and no expositor has emphasized its value more than Aristotle.

If the cosmological argument adopts the same fact as certain evidence for the existence of a theistic Deity, no less does the Greek employ the fact to determine what he means by the first and highest principle in reality. He supports the value of the principle by holding that no element in the world is without some connection with the fundamental principle of order. The oft quoted maxim confirms his opinion—"God and nature do nothing in vain." [37] Even Zeller admits that in this passage the term God refers to the "divine force which governs nature whose relation to the first cause of motion is left undetermined." [38] In his view, if a term is found in physics it means one thing, if in metaphysics, it has an alto-

---

[35] H. Bergson, *Creative Evolution*. Trans. by A. Mitchell. (New York: Henry Holt, 1911), Chap. II.

[36] *Metaphysics*, 1075a12.　　[37] *De Caelo*, 271a33.　　[38] E. Zeller, *Aritsotle*, I, 401, note 1.

gether different connotation. Such a confusion will be avoided in the present instance, if we remember that *principle* signifies one thing only, namely, the fundamental meaning of an event, relation or object. The function of God is to preserve the order whether automatic or willed in every part of nature. Thus, if two motions of equal strength confront one another, either there will be no motion, no perpetuated force, or one of them will dominate the other, neutralizing its power and absorbing its inner properties. Here order is strictly automatic; nothing can be misused or lost or disregarded. If the order is willed, that is, subject to a defined purpose, things are lost or disregarded in human affairs, at least, they seem to be so treated. In the economy of nature, however, there is no lost motion, no lost impulse, and no misused purposes. Aristotle's conviction that natural order is never changed, is so well-placed that he cannot do other than identify it with God himself. Furthermore, he feels himself in a position where he can recommend the serenity of motion to the mind of man as the true pattern of moral behavior. Stoicism could offer no better aim.[39]

POTENCY AND ACTUALITY

We have now examined two attempts of Aristotle to discover the contents of the divine science. He first studied the meaning of substance and concluded that all material constituents must be eliminated from the definition and its nature expressed in pure Form. He then selected the most significant property of the natural world, Motion, and decided that its essential cause must be an internal principle whose qualities would be best represented in an unchanging order. In each instance, however, he found himself unable to fix upon a universal formula which could both sum up the laws embodied in the physical processes and at the same time fashion an independent unity parallel to Plato's idea of the Good. It became clear to him that the concept of substance by itself and without defining attributes could not satisfy the terms of the problem. Hence, he was forced at length to adopt the category of intellectual causes; pregnant suggestions issued at once from this procedure. For one thing he saw the value of certain words which Plato selected from the welter of speculative terminology, clothed with distinctive meaning, and handed on to his successor for fuller development. Two of these were Potency and Actuality; can it be that we have here the expressive signs of the wanted Reality? Aristotle resolved to test their values with such an end in view.

The terms cited imply that every object has two kinds of existence,— what it is at the moment of perception and what it may become under the operation of specified causes. He assumes that a body wholly potential

[39] *Nicomachean Ethics,* 1178b28.

does not and cannot exist; Anaximander sought to isolate such a substratum and failed. On the other hand the changes observable in the natural world appear to have no limit; may the mind venture to predict that potentiality sometime would *fail,* and that nothing would be left but sheer actuality? Has Aristotle reached a solution to the problem in his second study which we have just outlined, namely, that motion never ceases but the principle of motion sets a barrier beyond which motion as a physical phenomenon cannot pass? Now science deals with the individual body and every body has its own peculiar Form which Plato called its *limit;* it must be possible for us to construct in thought the highest conceivable Form which will be described as Pure Actuality. This would correspond to the concept of divinity, a substance which has no "material constituents" but is endowed with ideal attributes alone. Such is the hypothesis which Aristotle offers; can he give it logical standing?

No decisive steps in that direction can be taken until we have found what potential means. Aristotle devotes an illuminating section of the *Metaphysics* (IX.) to an examination of the subject. It is admitted without a dissenting voice that in any given object matter is the seat of potentiality and Form or the complex of attributive properties is its actuality. There are two types of potency; the first he calls "innate," since it belongs to the structure of the body, the second he calls "rational," because it is susceptible of change in accordance with the nature of the vital system. Aristotle selects his examples from the science of human physiology. If we inspect any of the organs of sensation, say, the eye, we find that it is so carefully moulded by the forces of nature that it is capable of responding to an external stimulus in a manner that reflects the position and behavior of the body at the moment of contact. For the sense-organ is like a combustible body; the combustible body does not take fire by itself; "it requires a stimulus which has the power of starting ignition." Likewise the organ of vision has a constitutional capacity which waits upon the presence of a suitable agent to elicit its particular kind of response. As Plato had already pointed out, if light did not bathe the eye with its evocative splendor, sight would continue to be an unstirred potency, never a set of glowing images. Actuality, thus, is "kinetic" vision, the sole sensory function inherent in the structure of the eye. It is the one purpose which gives meaning to the object, it is, as Aristotle would say, the eye's *entelechy.*[40] For this reason the behavior of the sense-organ is always the same, assuming that the structural composition is normal and complete.

There is another form of the potential where the results obtained are not always of the same sort; indeed, in some cases they may actually contradict one another. Thus, the human eye is a member of a complicated

[40] *De Anima,* 417a7; 418b7.

nervous system, playing its role as a prescribed medium of communication with the outer world. Its specific entelechy, its settled purpose, is to determine the values of colors which are received from the surface of a body by the vibration of light-rays. However, experience as crystallized in habit adds new and more comprehensive functions. Hence, the reactions of the visual organ in childhood seem to be extremely simple as compared with the responses it exhibits in later years. At this point the organic body reveals a determinate superiority over the inorganic. The latter, for example, a piece of iron, may be altered from cold to hot, from hot to cold, or from large to small, from small to large; its potencies seem limited enough. True, it may be subjected to excessive heat and by incorporating a certain percentage of carbon may be transmuted into a different and artificial substance called steel, a substance notable for its elastic and malleable qualities. Yet no new essential properties have been introduced; its native endowment only acts with greater efficiency; that is the net result of the change. In like manner the structure of the physical eye undergoes no constitutional change; it still *sees*, it does not hear or smell. Yet it has adopted, so to say, a type of response belonging natively to the kinaesthetic sense alone: it can test the value of dimensional reactions, length, area, distance. Here its authority is not exact or decisive, because it is not *at home* in this sort of reaction. In other words its activity here is a learned activity. While Aristotle may not have used such terms as these, it is well known that he understood their purport. He understood also that hearing had acquired the same type of response in the measurement of distance though much less efficiently; men take its reports to be strictly provisional, not authentic. In short, the natural potency for each sense-organ is fixed; other functions are added merely because the organic body adapts its nerve-receptors to some new form of stimulus. This proves conclusively, as Aristotle rightly argues, that the body is a vital system, and its several organs are the instruments by which the system adjusts its needs to the forces supplied by the changing environment. In the evolution of species the elementary organs develop subordinate responses while they retain their native function intact. The eye ascertains the forms of rest and motion, spatial relations, sometimes the determinations of weight, almost always unity as a binding condition for every accepted image; these are derived, not original reactions; they no doubt spring from the tendency of the *sensus communis*, as Aristotle calls it, to combine the various sensations into one single image. Plato interprets such responses as categorical judgments by which knowledge is obtained; [41] Aristotle supposes that the sensa already contain the unifying factor before conceptual judgment begins its work. But howsoever they may be organized they at length induce us to recognize the

[41] *Theaetetus,* 185DE.

image as our own, and they serve two fundamental purposes, first of guarding us against physical harm, and secondly, of aiding us in the establishment of a separate private self. Actuality, thus, is no longer merely a brute reaction; it is the medium through which we can understand our world.[42]

But actuality is even more than a simple individual; it makes clear the universal laws by means of which individuality is defined. The individual involves the presence of one idea and the possibility of another. This would seem to be the meaning of the author's cryptic remark in the *Metaphysics* (1045b10): "everything is unity and the potential and actual are somehow one." The object before us is double: it has one set of attributes at the given moment, it also has the capacity of becoming what at the present time it *is not*. When the new form is assumed, the meaning, perhaps foreshadowed in the first object, will be new and different. The doctrine of potentiality is sometimes regarded as extremely simple—watch the change, and you will know what *actual* and *potential* signify. But the principle is not a simple one. Its meaning is illustrated by the familiar example. This piece of Parian marble contains the lineaments of the divine Hermes; structurally they have no relation to the marble; qualitatively they are utterly foreign to its nature. Actually the block is a segment of the living rock hewn from an ancient quarry; potentially it is one of the immortal monuments of creative genius. For thought, operating as an irresistible cause, has left its seal upon the material substance. So long as the idea lay dormant in the mind of the sculptor it was merely a possible feature of the marble mass. When it sprang to life under the thrusts of the inspired chisel, then it broke its prison-house of silence and uncovered a personality of radiant splendor,—an object of worship, a thing of beauty and a joy forever. Aristotle traces the same sort of metamorphosis in human life. Thus, a child draws his figures in the sand and is stamped as a potential geometer. He *is* a possible scientist, for he belongs to a race which has charted the movements of the stars; and he can, by solid discipline and repeated application, leave the deeds of childhood behind and rise to the level of the expert.[43] The scientific geometer is thus a realized idea, not a potential hint; for the universal idea is the sign and seal of the entelechy. The transition cannot be accomplished in a moment; time and movement are its pre-requisites. The series may be long and complicated but every stage will be marked by a new realization of the foretokened idea. Nature presents innumerable cases of the same principle of change, some concrete like the growth of the acorn into the oak, others abstract like the passage of the sun around the earth; the terminus is always an idea, different from the universal embodied in the preceding individual.

If this be the meaning of actuality when applied to particular objects,

[42] *De Anima*, II, 6.　　　　[43] *Ibid.*, 417a25.

how shall we define it when applied to primary substance itself? So far we have agreed that substance is unitary and that as the essence of motion it is the index of order. Now we are to ask whether divine substance—Nature in all her infinitely varied manifestations, can be described by the term Pure Actuality. Particular and potential situations no longer appear; they are separate parts of the whole and can only be partly understood—that is, understood so far as scientific inquiry will allow us to proceed. Complete actuality will be pure, because all facts pertaining to matter and moving objects are excluded. If, then, we can study the total group of independent objects and motions, study them as a unified whole, we may expect to reach a conclusion pointing to the meaning of substance. Obviously, such a study cannot be made under the auspices of the experimental sciences, as Kant showed decisively in his *Critique*. There we deal with phenomenal cases; here we must deal with the final noumenon, considered now not as a consummate idea but as an existing Thing.

Aristotle attempts to do this in the Twelfth book of the *Metaphysics*. During the course of his argument he creates new difficulties for his readers by the type of language used. The subject provides as severe a test of the understanding as ordinary readers should be called upon to endure. Here he adopts a personalized form of statement in treating of divine substance, whereas in other parts of this book and in all his other works, he deals with abstract principles and only rarely introduces the name of "God." Serious questions are raised at once. Is it true that he is now presenting a type of theological thought in which God is conceived as an independent and transcendent Being? Is Zeller right in his deduction that "the idea of God as self-conscious Intelligence is here for the first time drawn from the principles of philosophy instead of being borrowed from religious notions?" [44] Is the author fabricating a divinity endowed with personal attributes, contemplating his own mind in isolated seclusion, and construed as wholly separate from the world, yet moving it as the object of his thought? Such an interpretation is contrary to any thesis propounded in the Hellenic world. Furthermore, it has little similarity to other dogmas passing under Aristotle's name, except in the very early and somewhat apocryphal fragment entitled *On Philosophy*. Nor is the problem lightened if we assent to Jaeger's conjecture that the present passage is an early production which has been inserted in the book, because it *seems* to belong to the subject under discussion. It may well be that Aristotle experimented with the doctrine in his academic studies but that would not require us to accept the present text as belonging to another era in his thought.

That he should change his language from the abstract to the concrete, would not prove that he has changed his theory completely; it may mean

[44] *Op. cit.,* I, 399 sq.

that Reason is to be viewed from two standpoints, the active and the passive. This was Plato's opinion and we may well assume that Aristotle accepted it for his own argument. A rational or intelligible plan is framed by a rational or intelligent thinker; the thinker identifies himself with the thought; they are one, so far as he is concerned, and they are so regarded by many observers. This simply means that the thinker identifies himself with the object of his thought;—a common practice among the educated Greeks, a recognized practice in modern speculation. Aristotle follows the same identification in studying the universe. He writes:—"That which is capable of receiving the object of thought—the thinker understanding the meaning—is thought; and thought is action when it possesses its object." [45] God is here represented as the holder and communicator of reasonable ideas; this is the personalized form of saying—the world is an intelligible object; it has its own entelechy, and can be understood by a competent thinker. Rational thought then embraces all the attributes belonging to the intelligible object. Aristotle pronounces nature as completely intelligible, when he utters the following words:—"God lives, is eternal, is most good or complete." In fine, God is the symbol of pure reason in its universal application. Zeller quotes, and quotes correctly, Aristotle's remarks in the *De Caelo.*—"The supreme substance has no end beyond itself, because it is the end of everything." [46] The judgment gets its validity not from the assumption that God is above and distinct from nature but because he is identified with the universal course of nature *as its True End*. God is not a Concrete Being existing side by side with the universe; he is the principle and essence of Reality. Hence, he who knows the "thought of God" understands the meaning of nature.

Lest there be the slightest doubt remaining in our mind, let us examine the concept of *reason* as it appears in the soul of man. The text, again, is limited in scope and somewhat obscure in its phrasing; still, it furnishes us with a fair account of what seems to be his authentic doctrine. Notice that as in Plato the soul of man stands in analogical relation to the universe. Aristotle supposes that the passive intellect belongs of necessity to the sensory equipment of the body. The soul is the Form of the body and therefore expresses, as no other element can, the actuality of manhood. On the other hand, the active intellect or reason has no connection with the perishable body. This seems to be strange, for he repeatedly says that no man can think without the use of images, and images pass through the organs of sense, before they can be accepted by the passive intellect. Still, *Nous* is a qualitative form corresponding to nothing in the human body. Hence, as an entelechy it belongs to another level of existence, that is, the cosmic or celestial body.[47] At this point Aristotle himself enters the mys-

---

[45] *Metaphysics*, 1072b22.   [46] *De Caelo*, 268b9.   [47] *De Anima*, II, 7.

teries of a new kind of mythology, or seems so to do. Zaberella argues that God as active Reason guides the reason of man as he guides the "reason" of the spheres. This is a partial anticipation of Berkeley's theory that ideas are themselves inactive and could not in their own right produce an impression on the mind. They must therefore be governed by some force which will necessarily be spiritual, not corporeal. Also, since certain images are forced upon the mind without its consent, we are entitled to think of a Superior Spirit who imprints such ideas upon our minds as well as all ideas or "signs," that is to say, *Laws,* upon the objects of the external world. But Professor Ross rejects the suggestion and proposes one even more bizarre. Aristotle, he thinks, has set up a graduated scale of intelligence beginning with the lower animals and rising through man to the rational intuition of the spheres and ultimately to God as the independent Prime Mover.[48] The mythology in either case is subtle but not convincing. It reminds us of Leibniz' chain of monads from the grain of sand to the Enveloping Monad which is God, all plotted in a fixed ascending order on the ordinate curve drawn between the two abscissae.

There is a far more natural solution to the problem in a return to the Greek system of logic. Aristotle's tendency, as already noted, is to place all objects in "fixed classes," with a generic or chief attribute and differential kinds under it. Reason as a property of primary substance is the generic term. Every form of lawful action in the universe is a specific instance of the universal reason. Reason or active intellect in man is not a separate agent derived from a "peculiar influence of the celestial body which is the special region of Form in the Cosmos," as Grote asserts.[49] That would be merely another variation of the ontological myth which we have rejected. Human reason is not an independent faculty in the soul, coördinate with perception and memory; it is the judgmental activity of mind, comparing and analyzing ideas which are to embrace the meaning of an object or event. We may therefore here call the intellect *active,* that is, man's mind as making a judgment. Thus, reason is never concrete in its utterances; it deals only with universals; hence, Aristotle speaks of it as "immortal and everlasting." In short, reason is a term in logic not in psychology and its deliverances have an unimpeachable authority. Socrates as a sensible object perishes, but Socrates in his system of ideas abides.[50] Likewise, the universe as intelligible substance never changes; its meaning is complete and everlasting.

REASON AND THE IDEA OF THE GOOD

The unfolding of divine science proceeds apace. Three points are now clear, that substance is unitary, that as the "principle" of motion it guar-

---

[48] *Aristotle,* pp. 182–83.   [49] *Aristotle,* p. 487.   [50] *De Anima,* II, 2, 5; III, 7.

antees order, and thirdly, that as a whole it is rationally discernible. This means that Plato and now Aristotle categorically exclude the thesis of Democritus that the world is a congeries of atomic bodies infinitesimally small, yet the primitive source of matter, life and consciousness. While Aristotle begins his study of nature with the analysis of potency whose chief index is motion, he ends it by isolating the consummatory Form which he entitles the Good. To this we now give attention.

He lays down at once the epistemological rule that "there can be no thought without an object of thought"; moreover, since behavior springs from the gratification of desires, the object of thought must also be sought among the things desired. Aristotle is again the operating psychologist. For what is the *good* but the final cause which directs the choice of action? The formal cause furnishes the type of object we are seeking; the *final* cause presents the grounds for selecting the particular type. Finality is a factor in every situation; to that extent Ross is justified in speaking of Aristotle's theory as a "thoroughgoing teleology." [51] Spinoza has no hesitation in affirming that every object, no matter what its properties, "endeavors to persist in its own existence." Aristotle reflects the same principle in his study of subhuman species; he finds there a "natural good" over and above the particular impulses which specific orders of organisms develop. It is a scientific fact that such a ruling purpose is a powerful aid to the fulfilment of organic needs both for animals and for men. To this we must add the supplementary fact that pleasure attends the gratification of every desire and in the case of moral behavior plays an important role as an original incentive to action. Hence, at times desire and its satisfaction are so closely joined as to be indistinguishable. It is for this reason that Spinoza classifies desire and pleasure as two collateral types of emotion which seem to embrace the whole range of action beginning with the assertion of the original purpose and culminating in the attainment of the affective results. "We endeavor," he says, "to bring about whatsoever we deem to be conducive to pleasure." [52] Neither Spinoza nor Aristotle is inclined to espouse the raw doctrine of Utilitarianism, namely, that the sole object of moral conduct is the production of an excess of pleasurable feelings. Purpose and pleasure are defined respectively as the governing motive and its natural effect; even in Aristotle pleasure never appears as the single and definitive end of man's behavior. The principle of the Good is the necessary element in the determination of moral values. [53]

Does the logical idea of the Good have a place in our study of the universe at large? The answer of the philosopher is unambiguous:—"on this very principle depends the constitution of the heavens and of nature

---

[51] *Aristotle's Metaphysics*, I, cli.   [52] *Ethics*, III, 28.

[53] For a recent study of Aristotle's theory, see L. Robin, *La Morale Antique*, p. 145.

itself. Furthermore, its course of action is such as would be equivalent to the best we can ever enjoy, which we can only enjoy for a brief interval. For that which is Good is always in this perfect state, which we cannot be, since its actuality embodies also its pleasure, that is, its complete and final actualization." [54] The language is characterized by Aristotle's condensed mode of writing; nevertheless, two propositions are clear, first, that all movements in the universe are obedient to a comprehensive law, the law of attraction, and secondly, that in all the movements of nature an invariable harmony prevails. Here again we should be warned not to yield too readily to a beguiling anthropomorphic phraseology. God is not an elaborated and highly potentiated Zeus, with the habits and behavior befitting the demeanor of an exalted human being. On the other hand that is total which is divine, and the only way to comprehend the idea of totality is through the reflective judgment.

There is a tendency in the universe which enables bodies to move in certain appropriate orbits. This tendency which has the form of a dynamic power is called the principle of motion. Its force is attractive, but we must be on our guard against identifying it with Newton's familiar equation. If that theory had been understood it could have applied only to bodies in their orbital movements; it would have nothing to do with the subjects discussed in the divine science. The attraction of molar or molecular masses meant nothing to the Greek; his only theory was that every object had its own potential qualities which press towards their realization in a new individual Form. This was, as he says, the "object of desire," and in its full meaning this was the attractive principle no object in the world could fail to seek. Thus, fire ascends to the upper air, water follows its course to lower levels; a heavy body falls towards the centre of the earth, air—a light body—evaporates when rarefied, turns to liquid substance when condensed. [55] Change cannot take place except through the law of attraction, and this attraction must also reflect—by way of anticipation—the new form of body which is to be actualized. Preeminently is this true of the motions of the heavenly bodies. There is no change of structure, there is incessant change in their spatial positions. Using the Aristotelian nomenclature they "desire" to perform the appropriate revolutions of the spheres, some returning every day in the same circular orbit, others executing divergent movements in accordance with the demands of their own character. Nature does not work "consciously," as man does but the evidence of her inspired purpose is unmistakable. Indeed, the creative artist himself in his studio does his task by a kind of unreflective spontaneity, so completely is he caught in the sweep of his magicianlike fancy. Deliberation and volitional initiative seem to have disappeared; he works

[54] *Metaphysics*, 1072b10–25.　　　　[55] *Ibid.*, 1032a15 sq.

like a selective machine. In the same way Arsitotle esteems the universe t
be something other than a physical mechanism; it is the expression of d•
siderative thought. He derides the suggestion that love, a material forc
is the controlling energy in the world, as Empedocles taught. That woul
make physical and rational determinations quite the same. It would als
introduce an antithetical influence, hate or strife, which would lead t
internal disorders and eventual dissolution of the whole. But Aristot
excludes brute force as the primeval source of the world's motions; r•
tional law must rule and law has the imperishable form of an Idea. As i
the civil state so in the cosmic order one principle alone can hold sway.

We therefore turn to the second thesis that concentration of princip•
means harmony of movement. Aristotle connects the concept of harmon
with the psychological fact of pleasure; the opposite is pain. In human b•
havior a feeling-item is a necessary factor. Desire cannot be understoc
apart from the termination of the impulse in agreeable or disagreeab•
emotions. Pleasure and pain exist side by side in the subject's private exp•
rience, in the management of the social group, in the development of
biological series. They cannot exist side by side in a systematic univers
Pain is momentary in duration, acute in intensity, penetrating in its i•
fluence. Pleasure is general, constructive, persuasive; when it becom•
dominant in the mind of the individual or the habits of the group, it di•
appears from consciousness and is no longer commented on. Thus, heal•
is emotional equilibrium, not merely a term in the lexicon of physiology;
is the sign of the normal functioning of mind and body. Pleasure elat•
pain disturbs; hence, pain must be excluded as an undesirable interlope•
In the perfect universe pain cannot be a constituent element; in the be•
possible world, says Leibniz, only evils that depend on contingency a•
admitted; and they are temporary and provisional and are the means l•
which the total good is attained. In Aristotle's universe there are no di•
harmonies. He argued that evil could exist only as a resident law of ma•
ter; and nature gives no evidence of that.[57] Moral evil and organic pa•
are not really evils; they are bad as momentary experiences, but they •
not affect in any way the fundamental character of the world. If evil d•
exist nature could not have a single end; its supreme entelechy would l•
destroyed. In the world there are different grades of reality and differe•
scales of achievements. The economy of nature is not unlike the mena•
of a household. Freemen are members of it and have a limited range
undirected action. Slaves are accommodated in the group but their duti•
are strictly ordered. Domestic animals are in the compound; they are ke•
under surveillance and have nothing to do with determining the modes •
action in the house. All activities are subject to the rule of the paterfamili•

[56] *Ibid.*, 1075b1 sq.   [57] *Physics*, I, 9.

ho alone can decide what is "the good of the whole." [58] The parable is ot exact but it is suggestive. It informs us that contradictory processes annot exist in the universe; if they did chaos would ensue. The plain fact ; that even in sublunary movements conflicts are neutralized, contrary endencies resolved and enduring harmony instituted. If this be true of hysical relations, it should also be true of social behavior. The welter in ociety and nature as exhibited by Heraclitus is reduced by Aristotle to rder and equilibrium. Virtue and happiness are attainable goals in human onduct. How? By a study of the theoretical sciences where order is de- ned and analyzed. Logic having found its rules perfectly embodied in 1e motions of the heavens will impose them successfully on the intelligence f the individual and the group.

The testimony of the philosopher is clear and unhesitating: there is a eleological principle in nature. In what sense is this true? It cannot be rue in the sense that divine power, working from without, has woven a eliberate design throughout the "structure and history" of the world. The heory of the eternity of substance forbids the claim. Let us allow that 1ere is a distinction between permanent existence as seen in the stars and he generative process as seen in earthly things, a process which takes them ar beyond the bounds of their "originative cause." Are stellar problems ne thing and mundane problems another? Do men and animals and lants have no enduring substance? Are these to be conceived merely as ndependent units in the flowing tide of generation? Is it not also the ict that each has its own *genus* which is its particular form of perpetuity, nd that its genus is as rigidly fixed as the genus of sun and star? If genera re determined elements in nature, whether in the heavens or on the earth, 1en no justifiable distinction can be made between them, and design can e interpreted only in terms of genera, which we have found to be the Iellenic word for laws. Again, teleology cannot be defined as the quest f individuals for an "appropriate end." If the quest be *conscious* it would onflict with the rule of necessity which requires the potential to pass into 1e actual in accordance with a determinate law. If the quest be *unconscious* 1en, as Ross has to admit, teleology would lose its meaning; for such a ituation "implies a purpose which is not a purpose in any mind, hence ot a purpose at all." [59] Ross holds that Aristotle "did not feel the difficulty f the argument," and therefore continued to define teleology in this way. f that be so, we shall here and now try to save him from his blunder. Iowever, we do not intend to charge him with presenting a fallacious rgument; we shall adopt the one and only definition of purpose which ill put a suitable capstone to his interpretation of the Good.

Teleology is an element in logic; it was so for Plato and there is no good

[58] *Metaphysics*, 1075a20.   [59] *Op. cit.*, I, clii.

ground for denying that Aristotle agreed with him in this particular. In our study of the arguments of both men we have again and again come upon the assumption that the world of nature is an intelligible world. Reason does not reside in the mind of a supervisory but separate substance; that would demand a type of theistic speculation quite foreign to the intellectual temper of the age. In the judgment of its thinkers reason is a body of logical law whenever a mind like man's endeavors to analyze the nature of mechanical action and the total meaning of its forms. The working basis is always a logical class: "the logical genus," says our philosopher, "appears more substantial than the species, and the universal more substantial than the particular." [60] This implies that the world could only be understood by the use of the superordinated system of logical ideas at the head of which solitary and superb stands the idea of the Good. It is this principle which inquires into the meaning of every attribute and every relation characteristic of a given object or event. It must also stand as the unifying factor in our survey of the universe. Specifically, Good fixes upon the one concept or property which makes the given object different from every other; it emphasizes as well the community of ideas between the species in a single genus. When these two principles are united the meaning of the species is complete.[61] Finally, we reach the conception which carries no idea above it, a consummatory principle which eliminates the difference between genus and species, and this becomes to us the essence of reality, the summum genus of the logical quest.

It was this method that Kant used in his first *Critique,* as he described the operation of the noumenal mind in its efforts to understand the world of reality. There is the homogeneous or unitary system in the universe corresponding to the logical law of unity. It is a transcendental law for which no empirical evidence is available but without which knowledge of the total world is impossible. "For," he exclaims, "how could reason in its logical application presume to treat the diversity of powers which we see in nature as simply a disguised unity, and to deduce it as far as possible from some fundamental power, if it were open to reason to admit equally the diversity of all powers, and to look upon the systematic unity of their derivation as contrary to nature?" [62] The plain fact is that the human mind is never satisfied with the deduction of differential concepts; it insists on discovering a single truth which can combine and explain all subordinate truths. Here logical divisions are overridden; for the sweep of rational thought is progressive and ascending; it discards every conditional idea that it may determine the supreme excellence of thought, and this is identified with God. Analysis will suffice for scientific conclusions, as

[60] *Metaphysics,* 1042a13.   [61] *Ibid.,* 1059a36.
[62] Kant, *Critique of Pure Reason,* M. Mueller's translation (London: Macmillan, 1900), 523.

Kant showed in his development of the conceptual judgment. For the overshadowing truth, however, a final synthesis is needed, such as the intellectual artist might lay upon his logical demonstration. Here we do not discriminate by syllogistic rules; we contemplate the aesthetic Whole, and contemplation ends in complete delight. "God's essential actuality," says Aristotle, "is rapturous life most good and wholly fadeless." The study of the universe is ended: there is nothing more to say.

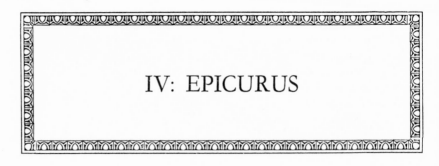

IV: EPICURUS

It is difficult to conceive of a Greek system of thought which has no reference to religious principles. The early inquirers were careful to leave the ordinary beliefs of the group undisturbed, even though they criticized, oftentimes severely, the particular forms in which the beliefs were stated. Xenophanes averred that the tendency of the fancy to clothe divinity with the habits and appearances of our own species should be summarily stopped. If every race created its own gods, worship would be a matter of individual whim which neighboring peoples would not understand or be inclined to accept. Religion was, for primitive man, the single universal concept; it was therefore essential that its terms should be expressed in common forms of thought representing the common needs of the race. Furthermore, in introducing any criticism of a traditional theory, it was imperative that the emotional attitudes of the group should be sympathetically studied. It is a serious mistake to thrust a revolutionary set of ideas upon the attention of orthodox believers, however high the intelligence of the social milieu may be. Anaxagoras was guilty of such a mistake, when he proclaimed that the sun in heaven, to which homage was paid by the Athenian public was in reality a hard mass of fiery substance like unto a red-hot stone observable on the earth. He was at once arrested and thrown into prison, but released later by the good offices of the Chief of State. These two men reflect the attempts of reformers to change the religious point of view of a people, either by universalizing the underlying ideas or by proposing a scientific examination of the ordinary concepts belonging to the religious tradition.

There is a third method which only a master mind like Plato's could follow; we may admit the validity of the ethnic creed for the average man but draw up an esoteric system for the instructed few, expecting that in the course of generations and by due process of education light may break upon the struggling soul of man and confirm it in the knowledge of the truth. Epicurus accepted the pattern laid down by his predecessor; he made no effort to interfere with the religious customs of the city in which he had his abode. Indeed, Diogenes, the chronicler, emphatically states that "his reverent behavior towards the gods was beyond the telling."

Philodemus, a contemporary of Cicero, writes that Epicurus "observed all the religious ceremonies and recommended that others do the same." For this reason he did not escape the charge of insincerity, since the mechanistic tone of his philosophy left no room for faith in invisible deities. He is accused by Cicero of seeking to court the favor of his fellow-citizens by pious pretensions, in order that he might insidiously entice them to adopt his opinions and discard the crudities of their native belief.[1] It is reported, too, that he made a distinct cleavage between duties prescribed by the state and the unreasoned notions of the crowd.[2] We have grounds for thinking that he actually made this distinction, and we have decisive reasons for concluding that he recognized the idea of divinity as a valid concept in systematic thought. It is also clear from abundant evidence that he intended to prove that current notions regarding the nature and powers of the gods, were incompatible with the methods of analysis which scientific thinkers are obliged to use. In particular, he set about demonstrating that the results which the gods were thought to bring about were due wholly to the action of natural forces. How should he proceed to make this proof effective?

He could not, for one thing, deny that so far as his knowledge went, he did not find a single nation or race or tribe which failed to include the concept of divinity in its theory of the world. To be sure, verified information on the subject in his day was limited; the Greek world was small and most travelers who ventured beyond its precincts, were not furnished with the apparatus criticus by which they could judge the value of concepts and customs commonly associated with the name of religion. It is possible, of course, to use the term in entirely different senses. Did the Egyptians whose Book of the Dead was familiar to educated Athenians, give the same definition to religion that the Greeks did? Or, was their religious theory merely a sustained and organized system of reverence for their deceased ancestors? Testimony shows that Epicurus was keenly aware of the change of meaning that has overtaken many of the salient concepts in man's philosophy. Religion is, no doubt, one of the most impressive products of the philosopher's imagination. But fancies, exquisite as they are, may be wrested from their original meaning and made to serve the interests of priest or statesman with the intent to mislead and deceive. It was this fact that turned him from the myths and traditions of popular faith to seek an explanation of religious sentiment in the scientific or semi-scientific corollaries of the Atomic theory.

The psychology of Atomism provided him with the necessary instruments. Fleets of images of every sort swing through the orbits of sensation and have done so for untold generations. Among these images is a

---

[1] *De Natura Deorum*, I, 44.   [2] Cyril Bailey, *The Greek Atomists and Epicurus*, p. 438.

group incessantly repeated which differs explicitly from those derived directly from physical objects. Their form presents a subtlety and refinement which forever excludes any likeness to the concrete surfaces of body whether at rest or in motion. Such images do not reflect the presence of energy that is capable of making impact upon a neighboring image or the object from which it emanates. In fact images or *eidola* like these suggest the existence of beings wholly separate in nature and behavior from those belonging to common experience. This does not imply that a new type of substance has been discovered; it intimates rather that the material atom has been denuded of its hard and gross qualities and now emerges as a divine element acting immediately and unerringly upon the human mind in such a manner as to imprint there the permanent idea of a godlike being. It appears that this idea is distinguished from every other idea in that it is a constant constituent in the thought of the human race; not that it was an innate cognition discernible by every normal mind, as certain later philosophers were prepared to admit. Such an assumption carried with it the implication which Epicurus declined to sanction, namely, that divinity is responsible for the creation and direction of the world,— an idea thoroughly repugnant to his sensitive mind. For if the gods actually fashioned the world and everything therein, they become responsible for all its movements and events,—its earthquakes, volcanic outbursts, its briars and hideous organic monsters, the depravations of moral evil, and finally the sordid maladjustments in human society. To be sure, it may happen that "the greatest evils were visited upon the wicked and the highest benefits bestowed upon the good," but this deduction is the result of a "false hypothesis," indicating that men have constructed their deities in line with their own mode of behavior.[3] The fallacy of the entire argument rests upon the rejection of natural law in accordance with which the economy of the world is sustained. Furthermore, it must be understood that the original concept of the gods contains no information as to their external activity; it simply attests their existence and their intrinsic properties. Lucretius accepts the judgment of his master and disregards the conclusions of theologians: "They observed how the array of the heavens and the various seasons of the year come round in due order and they could not discover by what causes all these came about. Thus their refuge was to leave all in the hands of the gods, and to suppose that by their words all things were done."[4]

Is it conceivable that Epicurus did not see that he himself had fallen into the same error as his opponents? He states categorically that the

---

[3] *Epicurus*, Epis. 124, edit. by Cyril Bailey, 1926—a valuable restoration of the Greek Text, a discerning translation, with copious notes on the important passages.

[4] *De Rerum Natura*, V, 1183 sq.

leaders of Stoicism as well as the defenders of the popular faith had read
into the primitive concept certain facts that did not belong there. But
what did the primitive concept include? It was derived, he said, from the
repeated images that every man receives. He sometimes calls them "visions"
of the gods [5] and he insists that they were acquired by "actual contact" or
by "analogy and composition" [6] to which is added "conscious reasoning,"
before the final judgment is reached. We have here a recital of Kant's
famous formula,—"percepts without concepts are blind, concepts without
percepts are empty." This means that no sensory experience can be enjoyed except by an interpretation of the received content. The analysis of
a flower involves the changes in the retinal structures of the eye and in the
membrane of the olfactory nerve, as well as a classification of the perceived
data under the categories known to the botanist. In this case we accept the
existence of the specimen as an integral part of our environment. In
Epicurus' example we reverse the process and deal first with sensory
images, the impressions sent off by the supposed divinities. These images
are taken up by the attending mind, given a determinate meaning, and
then referred to concrete realities called gods. But there can be no concept
if there be first no impressions. Every concept has its roots in previous
perceptions and in due time becomes the instrument for understanding
forthcoming experiences. In short, the idea of divinity is not a necessary
integer in the order of our thought; it is a deduction from certain notions
that have formed themselves slowly in the imagination of the race. They
do not guarantee the reality of the gods; they merely suggest a method
by which we may approach the study of divinity, without giving us the
slightest reason for affirming the reality of the object corresponding to
our fancy. We may act as if we might affirm the existence of the gods; but
we cannot postulate their reality and then proceed to set forth in detail
their intrinsic characteristics.

But assuming for the sake of argument that there is a typal image visiting our conscious thought different from that yielded by a dimensional
object, we proceed to ask wherein the difference lies. Epicurus says the
image is more subtle, more refined, or as Lucretius [7] reports, "thinner" in
texture. Does he mean that the idea embodied in the image is vague, not
clearly defined, confused in its properties, and therefore not easily reducible
to a logical concept? Or is he attempting to distinguish between a sense-
impression reflecting the existence of the gods and an abstract idea which
expresses the supreme attributes of divinity? In all probability he is describing what he deems to be the essential qualities of a superior being

[5] Cyril Bailey, The Greek Atomists and Epicurus, p. 440.
[6] Diogenes Laertius, The Lives and Habits of Philosophers. Trans. by C. D. Yonge (London:
G. Bell, 1915), X, 32.
[7] Op. cit., V, 148.

which itself is untouched by the laws of natural reaction. We may disregard the fantastic suggestions of shape, food and sex—which are concessions to the prevailing religious pattern—and confine our study to the tradition supported by Cicero [8] that the images did not represent "solid objects" but only intrinsic qualities which, for want of a better word, we may call *spiritual*.

What are the attributes which deity must possess? The Eleatic school asked this question for the first time, and answered it with philosophic insight. Substance, to be divine, must be indivisible, unchanging, timeless and complete. Divinity comprehends the reality of the visible universe; the world as seen and felt is the object of adoration. Such a theory forever excludes the fabricated idols of the market-place. Plato might allow the state to set up its divinities for political ends; but he could not recommend them to the attention and respect of critical observers. The cultured mind required something more than external tokens of religious sentiment, since these merely embody what the human hand has made, they cannot express the universal values of religion. Epicurus knew these facts as well as Plato. Hence, when he removed his gods from the visible scene he took good care to select for them two cardinal qualities, one drawn from metaphysics, the other from the moral habits of mankind. To be gods, his superior beings must possess immortality and serenity of mind.

How could the gods composed of indiscernible atoms be endowed with perpetual and unbroken existence? Physical bodies cannot survive the impact of physical forces. Stones disintegrate under the blows of neighboring bodies or by the chemical re-adjustment of their constituent elements. The human body withers under the heat of the sun or through the fever of disease. Even the strong assertion of will cannot extinguish the breath or still the action of the heart. The testimony of science is undeviating: no body vital or non-vital can resist the tendency to decay. Only two substances, says Epicurus, fail to obey this law—the atom and the void. But says Velleius, Cicero's spokesman for the Greek, one other principle cannot be denied: wherever destruction exists, by its side and contemporary with it and of equivalent potency stands the tendency to preserve the disintegrated elements. This is the principle of Isonomia, equal and uniform distribution. If the power to destroy is universal, the power to reconstruct has no limits. Because the principle is at work incessantly in the natural world, a universe which comprises an infinite number of worlds, how could we set bounds to the intramundane sphere where dwell the everlasting gods?

It is not at all certain that Epicurus pursued the argument in precisely this form. His great expositor, Lucretius,[9] describes the two compensatory

[8] *Op. cit.*, I, 19, 29. [9] *Op. cit.*, II, 569.

forces much in the spirit and mode of Heraclitus. All things are produced, says the Ephesian thinker, by the attunement of opposite tensions. "War is father of all and the king of all, and some he has made gods and some men, some masters and some slaves." Following the same *motif* Lucretius holds that motion which ends in death cannot prevail forever; nor on the other hand can new forms appear without being blocked by the resident forces of nature. "Time contracts," and what men may do or undo can have no lasting value. Epicurus makes it plain that since his gods are wholly removed from the area of physical laws, the modes of genesis and dissolution cannot be reproduced in their community: "the gods are free from all activity and are engaged in no occupations whatsoever." [10] That is to say, natural potencies do not exist in the structure of his gods. Mortality is a painful and inevitable fact in the sphere of organic life; disintegration necessarily takes place in all natural bodies. Can we infer that for Epicurus the definition of substance is not exhausted, when he has finished his analysis of the physical universe? that he envisages the presence of two forms of substance, one that changes, another that does not? Substance as examined by the microscope or in the experimental laboratory is composed of divisible particles each one of which represents electromagnetic charges subject to exact quantitative measurement. The other type of substance has none of these properties; it cannot be weighed or measured or broken into examinable quanta. If the attributes of the two substances be mutually exclusive, how may they be compared? By what right do we say that what happens to the first cannot happen to the second? specifically, that while one perishes, the other survives? The problem is complicated by the fact that Epicurus has already granted a kind of immortality, namely, indissolubility, to the natural atom; for he restricts survival to the atom alone and makes all compound bodies subject to change. In the light of these considerations it is clear that so far he has failed to adduce a satisfactory argument in support of his thesis that the gods are immortal.

Yet, even though there were a hint of reality in the argument, we cannot disregard the preliminary assumption which states that we do not deal directly with the object of our thought but only with the images which are said to have proceeded from it. If that be true then the flood of impressions bearing the same or similar content cannot assure us that the originating object persists in its unchanged character. We might argue in like manner respecting ordinary sense-perceptions: the mountain before us appears to transmit the same image of magnitude and form whenever our eyes rest upon it. But the touch-and-go of common experience flatly contradicts the report. Furthermore, changes of a subtle nature are taking place behind the visible contour as scientific inquiry amply reveals. Hence, even though

[10] Cicero, *op. cit.*, I, 51.

the impression be indefinitely repeated it cannot warrant the deduction that the object observed is imperishable. May we venture to think that uniformity in the substance of images which we take to be *peculiar* enables us to assign to divine beings a perpetuity which natural bodies do not have? The inference is much greater than the known facts will bear, and we are forced to reject it.

Still, the conviction of the school on this point was so strong and so pervasive that we cannot avoid making a brief examination. Cicero relates that the doctrine was espoused with the greatest enthusiasm.[11] An ancient scholiast asserts that "likeness of form" was the key to the interpretation of the nature of the gods. Aetius, a conservative chronicler, reports that Epicurus had erected the quality of similarity into one of the four elements having permanent existence, along with the atom, the void and the universe. Now similarity as a property of substance has nothing to do with the mere sequence of sensory images; the sequence may be rapid, prolonged or infinitely repeated; such facts could not in themselves produce the conviction of continuity. Not a flowing reality like sensation but a sustained property engendered by the mind, is the foundation upon which the doctrine rests. It is this principle—so he thinks—which differentiates the images of the gods from the images stemming from material objects. Granted the validity of his distinction we must then inquire—What is the meaning of Similitude? Is it a quality like the four categories which Kant applied to the data of scientific experiment? Does it refer to size, color, causal relation, or even to a type of logical predication? Epicurus alludes to one comprehensive attribute, serenity of mind, but he does not suggest that it is a necessary factor in the argument for immortality. Obviously what he desires to prove is that the superior beings have an identity of thought not found in the Greek pantheon, where antagonistic habits, functions, moral aims make up an assembly of deities thoroughly repugnant to the critical sense. He assumes that by insisting on the presence of a supreme individuality, which is a never-changing character, he can also count on extending its range of existence beyond the term of natural events where time is an agent. But what he did not take into account was that similarity is a logical principle, conceived by the mind of man and used by him to analyze the data of perception and to determine their meaning. It is a word that is worthless when studying the fundamental basis of reality, that is, a phase of reality other than that represented by the experiments of physics. That being the case, it would have no place in the description of objects such as the Atomic gods which could not be observed by the natural senses of the body.

The positive attribute awarded to the divinities is, we said, perfect seren-

11 *Op. cit.*, I, 19, 49.

ity, a motionless calm, "a peace that passeth understanding," to quote from another classic. No interruption to this calm is possible. It could not come from physical causes; for, separated from the circumambient world by the chasm of space, the laws governing the relations of bodies have no influence upon them. Hence, it is futile for man to appeal to them for help amidst the cataclysms of storm and stress. The divinities did not create the forces of nature and they have no control over their operation. Nor can the supermundane calm be broken by internal struggle; for they are "never troubled, nor do they trouble others." [12] The ancient feuds of Homer's gods are absent from the empyrean of Epicurus. Peace and unanimity of thought reign there, a veritable sublimation of the cordial feelings and friendly intercourse at work in the Garden at Athens. Certainly Prometheus would not have found a satisfactory resting-place in a tranquil scene like this.

We have now assembled the significant points in Epicurus' purported theory of religion. What estimate shall we put upon it? The answer may be made in one of two ways; either he presented it as a scheme of thought which might be taken as a rough substitute for the common belief in myths and images; or he fashioned it as a fictitious conceit with somewhat the same intention, though of a lower order, that led Plato to the composition of his *Timaeus*. In favor of the former interpretation we may cite the succession of mental images which superseded the images carved in wood and stone. The parallel is sufficiently close to make his political contemporaries suppose that he had attempted merely to produce an abstract analysis of the underlying ideas found in the religion of the state. In favor of the second suggestion we may cite the method adopted by Plato: there is a distinction between the prosaic type of worship built about the objects we can see, and the vast superstructure of speculation which explores the reaches of the universe itself and seeks to know man's place therein. In Greece poetic symbolism governs the expressions of philosophic thinking as well as the dramatic treatment of human emotions. If we read the language literally we shall fail to uncover the golden treasures hidden there. A flagrant example of a hermeneutic mistake like that is found in the wilful misunderstanding of Plato's intent in the dialogue just mentioned. What was his purpose in writing this remarkable study of the phenomena of the natural world? Many expositors, especially those belonging to the Christian tradition, have argued that we have here a detailed unfolding, in tropes and figures, of the orthodox dogma of creation. It might seem that the author was intimately acquainted with the text of our early canonical scriptures. It may be said, too, that the writer of the Fourth Gospel found the warrant for his first chapter in Plato's description of the demiurge as the counter-

[12] *Epicurus: the Extant Remains*, p. 138.

part and forerunner of the new *Logos*. It takes but a slight leap of fancy to make Plato the founder of the powerful school which still reigns in the councils of the Christian Church. But the evidence for this tradition is insecure. Plato ascribes the theory to the famous mathematician of Thebes whose name appears in the title of the dialogue. He outlines the thesis proposed by Timaeus and develops a drama of extraordinary complexity and charm. He is careful to keep the interlocutor from committing the blunder which destroyed the value of Anaximander's theory,—that the inchoate mass could by itself produce a cosmic world. He also restrained him from any attempt to lay the divine Hand directly upon coarse and ugly matter and thus frame a universe. But these qualifications do not allow us to hold that Plato is working out his own system. He merely enables Timaeus to construct a world which would not be offensive to the cultivated taste of Greece. Throughout the dialogue there are recurring hints that all this discourse is poetic, not scientific. He tells us again and again that the argument is one of probability, not of philosophic certainty. Throughout the dialogue are heard whispers of another theorem—the world is not created, it always has been; the world must be approached by the principles of logical reasoning, as embodied in Plato's Ideas. Nature is one harmonious Whole; God is Unity and Order and Sublimity. The speculations of Timaeus are good enough for the mathematician of that day but they do not meet the demands of philosophic analysis.

May we venture to believe that the *Timaeus* gave valuable suggestions to a later but less adroit worker in the same craft? Plato was a scientist of the first rank; he was also endowed with unexampled gifts in the art of aesthetic expression; he was further capable of grasping the fundamental principles upon which all speculative thought rests. Epicurus had but a modicum of poetic sensibility; a significant apothegm here and there is the only trace of artistic creation. He had little interest in logic as a method of procedure, and his knowledge of the science of numbers was extremely limited. He had, however, the interest and zest of the modern laboratorian, and though he made no experiments with instruments fabricated by himself he conceived and employed some of the measures adopted by the present-day physicist such as Sir James Jeane who passes from the operating laboratory to a study of the cosmic rays. Being persuaded that sensation is the one source of knowledge Epicurus examines matter in its compound forms for the purpose of discovering its primary elements. Here imagination serves him as it has served the productive scientists of the new world. He probes matter to its core and unveils, as he thinks, the fundamental unit which is the atom. If the atom be basic to all material compounds, it may also be basic, in fancy, to orders of substance that do not strike upon the human eye or awaken response in the human ear. They stand apart from the natural universe. They do not engage in its motions or suffer change as natural bodies do. Here the theology of Timaeus begins to exhibit a resemblance to the conceits of Epicurus. Again we are invited to note that this is not the thesis of Plato, although it appears in dramatized form in one of the majestic creations of the master's pen. Nor need we suppose that the phantasy of gods aloof from nature is the private doctrine of his successor. In neither case is there an endeavor to delude the reader or even to create a poetic illusion that might persuade the unwary reader to accept the judgment of the text as an accredited doctrine.

Two additional resemblances should be considered. The first is that the making of the world is not the province of the divine Power; that special duty, in the *Timaeus* dialogue, is conferred upon the demiurge which does not share the supreme authority of ultimate control. It is this division of functions which enables Plotinus to raise deity above every consideration of rational knowledge, and to create a series of powers reaching down to the formation of the world and man. It is the same mistaken thesis which plagued the early church in its attempt to destroy the influence of the Gnostic emanations upon the doctrine of the Triune God. For Plato divinity is not divorced from the universe; it *is* the universe viewed from the standpoint of the principle of order and harmony. For Epicurus the atom is the essence of power and of perpetuity, and both of these characters are resident in material substance.

The other likeness deals with the appearance of Ideas as the directive factors in the making of the world. Timaeus thinks of them as the blueprint submitted to the demiurge according to which the parts of the world are to be framed. Plato himself, on the other hand, is concerned with a world complete in itself, a world which ever has existed and ever will exist. But this world cannot be known unless we study it first by the rules of scientific analysis and secondly by means of the principle of purposive unity. Here again Epicurus will agree with the authentic formula of Plato —law rules supreme in the revolution of the celestial luminaries and in action of bodies on the earth. There is no law in the realm of the gods; there is *nothing but law* in the realm of nature. Hence, in the final comparison it is the world of Plato not of Timaeus to which the world of Epicurus approximates. At this point the analogy between Timaeus' conception of divinity and that of Epicurus breaks down; for the Timaean god furnishes the rules by which creation is to be realized; but the gods of Epicurus communicate nothing to the natural world except images of themselves conveyed in some mysterious way to the throbbing minds of men. Furthermore, the demiurge insists that his world is organic, it lives and breathes like a gigantic animal and it never perishes. In the Epicurean universe the reign of law is irreversible; it is final; no force of will or matter can change

its course. And yet the new cause of motion which Epicurus reposes in the
"swerve," seems at least to emulate the kind of action which man thinks he
possesses in his private will. We shall return to this subject later.

The proposal we have made is not supported, in so many words, by the
testimony of Epicurus. It would appreciably diminish the influence of
the scheme if it were known to be the rival of a traditional creed; if it
had been submitted as a pure and unvarnished fiction, as Lange suggests
in his History of Materialism, it would have obtained small credence and
might have awakened a feeling of reproach, even disgust, that an accredited leader of Greek thought would stoop to court the attention of
the public by such an undignified device. On the other hand, if it were
recognized as a poetic conceit, a thematic composition, standing in complete antithesis to his own system of philosophy, it could be taken as assurance to a bewildered age that religion is not dead, as some assumed, but
may be reflected both in the language of romance and even more emphatically in the reasonable study of the facts of nature. For Epicurus the gods
are figments of the imagination, ideal patterns, figures in an inconceivable
universe; but as operating powers in a scientific world, they do not exist.
We may therefore reject the strictures of Cicero and award to the philosopher a comfortable seat in the Valhalla of art but not among the masters
of the craft.

What, then, is the essence of Epicurus' religious thought? We shall
argue that it consists in a sure understanding of the laws of the physical
universe and the influence of these laws on human conduct. It will appear,
as we proceed, that while he was inclined to disregard most of the deductions of the Socratic school and to cleave strictly to the bold and naked
dogmas of Democritus, still he could not escape the fascination of the basic
principle espoused by the school—that unity of nature must be supported
by unity of discourse. He had to admit that "accurate knowledge of details" could be acquired only when the general ideas which governed
them had been thoroughly analyzed. To accomplish this end, we do not
need so complicated an instrument as the Aristotelian syllogism. We cannot get at the truth by multiplying abstract prepositions. Knowledge begins with sensation; any other origin is fictitious and void. A major
premise must be subjected to the ordeal of sensory apprehension before
it can be accepted as a valid proposition. What Epicurus specifically set
out to do was to destroy the dogmas upon which current theology was
based. One of these stated that the gods could interpose in the affairs of
human beings, thwart the wishes of recalcitrant worshipers, use the forces
of nature,—lightning, fire and earthquake,—to punish offenders and ter-
rify whole communities with the threat of impending doom. Can such a

thesis be supported by sensible evidence? The only way to answer the question is to examine the elements of the sensory process.

What is sensation? Sensation occurs by the contact of two divergent particles, one representing the stimulating object, the other, the conscious mind of the percipient. The contact may be immediate as in the sense of "touch" or mediate in the passage of the emanation through the circumambient air, as in hearing and sight. With this contact scientific knowledge begins. Since vision is the most valuable instrument for determining a true situation, we must discover its essential function. The other senses give us information bit by bit; but the eye, in its turn, grasps the entire array of emanations at a single glance. Thus, it obtains a complete and, so to say, *mature* image,—a red spot, a fleck of dust in the sunbeam, a flash of light, finally, such composite objects as table, tree, sun,—a totality which cannot be broken, an image whose meaning becomes clear and distinct. The point which Epicurus insists on is that knowledge thus obtained is infallible. The tower seen in the distance is round and small; when we approach it, the object is large and square. Was the first impression incorrect? Have our senses deceived us? No: each image is independently true; it states the facts as we have observed them at a given moment. Time, change of position, alteration in the angle of vision, have intervened between the two responses; the stimulus has in the meantime changed and cannot yield the response first obtained. There is no error; reality has been observed precisely as it was in each case. The rule is universal—knowledge is derived from sensation which itself has a certain power of judgment not unlike that involved in the formation of an idea. This last point we must now examine.

The second criterion to which sound knowledge conforms is before us. Epicurus expressly repudiates the formula of Protagoras:—every sensation stands by itself and accepts no connection with any other. Obviously no permanent information can be procured in that way. Knowledge is always a comparison of perceptual facts. Experience shows that each sensation looks back to another with which it establishes certain points of similarity. When these points are frequently repeated, we form the habit of anticipating them in future sensations. The intrinsic meaning of the original image is thus unfolded. Reality resides in sensation but its interpretation is the work of mind. The peculiar slant of the Epicurean psychology must not be overlooked. The mind is not a single concrete individual inhabiting the human body; it is a congeries of separate atoms operating together to give form to the image; so Epicurus writes in his letter to Herodotus.[13] The semi-critical judgment framed by the senses is supplemented by the presentation of the idea apart from its sensory

[13] *Epicurus: the Extant Remains,* I, Sec. 35.

setting. Conception thus assumes a wider role than sensation; for it ca
deal not merely with perceived objects but also with objects that cannot b
perceived, notably the atom and the void. It is because of the strikin
clearness of such apprehension that we are led to accept as real a type o
existence not subject to sensible observation. If we decline to push expe
rience further than the mere shadows of perception we shall be unable t
understand the nature of the universe. The argument for Epicurus i
conclusive; he does not discard the basic power of sensation; he takes it
elementary facts and builds upon them a system sufficient to account fo
all the phenomena presented. Atoms must be real, for the perpetual divisio
of matter into increasingly smaller bits is unthinkable. The void must b
real, for bodies actually pass from one position to another without let o
hindrance. Since they cannot pass through other bodies, some spaces mus
be empty. If it be objected that empirical evidence does not confirm thi
conclusion, Epicurus answers that if no evidence can be adduced agains
it, it must be taken as true. The validity of the method is open to grav
doubt which can only be cleared away by showing that all ultimate realitie
are intellectual derivatives of the facts already determined by ordinar
sense-perception.

We may now return to the proof for the existence of the gods. The
interfere with the processes of nature, it is said, in order to emphasiz
their authority over the lives and behavior of men. The refutation of thi
doctrine has a strictly modern tone, although the reasons given for it ar
not needed for modern inquirers. "If we were not bothered by our sus
picions about the meaning of the changes in the heavens," he says in hi
Epitome of the Atomic creed, "we should have no need for the science o
Nature." [14] So long as men do not know the laws governing the ele
mentary relations of natural objects, they are prone to adopt a mythica
explanation, with all the anxieties and forebodings attached thereto. Thi
tendency is forever excluded as soon as we can prove that changes in th
physical world are directed by discoverable causes. We are now advise
that natural events take place in one way and only in one; that they coul
not take place in any other way. Therefore there can be no "doubt o
mental perturbation" in regard to any celestial phenomenon; all decision
respecting these are based upon ample evidence and can be "ascertaine
by our intellect as infallibly true." [15] Thus, lightning is produced in severa
different forms and each one of these can be illustrated by verifiable expe
rience. If it be asked why the flash always precedes the clap of thunder th
answer is that "light moves at a higher speed towards us"—a remarkabl
anticipation of the conclusions of an age, where the velocity of light i
measured by the stroke of a second of time.[16] Such scientific reflection

[14] *Ibid.*, Part IV, Sec. 11.   [15] *Ibid.*, p. 51.   [16] *Ibid.*, p. 69.

1ake the Homeric pictures of Jove the Fulminator appear like fairy tales, s they were. It would seem that the social intelligence of Athens had assed from sheer fanaticism which cashiered Anaxagoras with his molten un, to an indulgent posture of tolerance when faced with the plain facts f science as stated by Epicurus. This being true, it is fair to assume that Epicurus intended to set up his system of physics as a direct and adequate ubstitute for the discredited religions of Greece. It is not the last time hat science has offered its fascinating creed to the spiritual suffrage of nankind. Nor is it the last occasion when the reigning faith has fought he new dogma with its mighty arsenal of feeling and prejudice. Epicurus lid not succeed in winning the enthusiastic assent of his age. The weight f the last, though not the most important, criterion in his theory of knowledge, namely, satisfaction with the conclusion of the argument, was too powerful in most instances: men could not release themselves from the ormulas which time and affection had made sacred. Even where logic demanded a change of conviction, emotion kept the religious faith intact. But at least the new science shattered the foundations upon which the argument for the existence of the gods rested, and canceled forever the paralyzing fears springing from the threat of impending punishment.

We are now prepared to survey the composition of the world in which Epicurus is to find the cardinal points of his scientific religion. He begins vith the minimal unit of reality not as Parmenides with the total universe. Yet there is a strange likeness in their procedure. Parmenides, we aid, imposed four characteristics upon his world—it was uncreated, it could not change, it was infinite in extent, and it was complete in structure. The atom of Epicurus possesses the same four properties. The first hinker said, the world is the nucleating source of every part; the second, n reverse, held that every body great or small, in the world, is built from he fundamental seeds called atoms. In both cases, the presence of an indiscernible creative Hand is denied. For Epicurus the following laws are self-evident: that nothing can be created out of nothing, that nothing can be destroyed into nothing, that the universe has been and always will be he same. The indestructibility of matter is thus affirmed. These laws being true, we are not concerned with the problem of the derivation of the world, as were the early inquirers, but with the composition of the world as it stands. In this respect Epicurus follows the lead of Plato. The atom as the basic quantity has size, shape, weight and motion; other properties cannot be discovered. Atoms are never observed by themselves but are assumed to be in coalition with other atoms in every physical body. Compound bodies are related to one another in a definite manner and by prescribed movements. Space is the locale in which bodies move; it is filled, when the body is taken to be at rest, it is empty when bodies pass through it from one point to another. If there were no unfilled spaces, bodies would be stationary and motion impossible. Motion also goes on within a body when it is at rest, for example, the earth which is our residence. The original motion of the atom was downward and was attended with infinite velocity superinduced by the inherent property of gravity which Democritus did not mention. Gravity for the Greek was the tendency to fall, nothing else. It had no relation to the modern concept formulated by Newton: mass attracts mass directly as the product of the two and inversely as the square of the distance between them. Weight in the Epicurean scheme determined the direction of the body but has no effect on speed. Such an effect would appear when bodies fell through a resisting medium but not in the void or, as we say, vacuum. At any rate the property of weight is a scientific fact of immense importance.

But weight was not the only element that determined the direction of the atom: if that were so, atoms would descend in a straight, undeviating path, and as Lucretius says,[17] "no collisions could come to pass, and nature would have brought no authentic body into being." The genius of Epicurus asserts itself once again. He writes to Menoeceus [18] that a destiny as implacable as that would have put the world under tyranny worse than that of the gods who might be placated, thereby causing their tyranny to be less repugnant, supposing it were real. Accordingly he endowed the atom with another quality, the power to "swerve" from the stated direction to another in agreement with its own needs. So important a quality will not be communicated to the concrete body of which the atom is a part; it is a spontaneous act which takes place at the opposite limits of ingredient substance, namely, in the atom and in man. It does not contradict the law of mechanical regularity, nor does it introduce the element of chance, for chance is merely an "uncertain cause," residing secretly in the rigid system of nature. Lucretius adopts the new cause without reservation. Cicero, on the other hand, treats it with scorn and contempt, holding that it is not worthy of a responsible thinker. Many commentators have been puzzled by its forthright character, regarding it as but a sport on the otherwise consistent interpretation of nature. In modern times the brilliant studies of Guyau have revived interest in the doctrine; he believed that Epicurus intended to apply the principle of the swerve to every kind of body in the world. He points to the field of organic life as studded with shining examples of independent changes for which no specific anticipatory causes could have been discovered. Why, then, should not the grandeur and obvious diversification of the inorganic world be charged with the same originating spontaneity? Is it less scientific to seek for novelty in

[17] Op. cit., II, 223.   [18] Epicurus: the Extant Remains, p. 91.

the works of nature than to content oneself with the prediction that each event will follow the precise pattern of its predecessor? [19]

An unexpected answer has been made to these questions by the disclosures of the new physics. The concept of a "swerve" seems to have exercised a witching charm on the metaphysical studies of the group. Sir James Jeane in his *Physics and Philosophy*, published in 1942, traces the progress of research in this department of thought from the age of Newton to the present. The change of base from the theory of absolute motion to that of relative motion has cloven a deep chasm between the old and the new. Science now deals with events, not bodies which entertain unchanging relations to one another. The fourth dimension has been found: time must be considered in determining the work performed by any body. An event is the position of a given quantum at a given moment. What is the constituent property of the quantum? As far back as Lord Kelvin ether as the transmission-medium of light had lost its prestige. The electric-magnetic charge usurped its place. The electron is now the basic atom in nature, it is the unit of physical energy. Niels Bohr, the Danish scientist, appears not to hold the inflexible principle of the Newtonian mechanics to be sacrosanct. He argues that the electron does not vary *progressively* in strength from one time to another but "jumps" from one level of strength to another. This seems to be a modern exposition of the ancient "swerve"; it registers a change not in direction but in inherent energy expressed in the electron's power to emit its specific rays. But how shall we compute the speed of the electron's vibration and its position at a given moment with unfailing precision? The problem was one of great difficulty and appeared to require a new mode of approach. In 1927 Heisenburg introduced the principle of Indeterminacy as a working substitute for the method of mathematical probability. We can obtain the desired results by statistical calculation, not by setting up a system of constants and variables as in the old method. To be sure, we can in no case determine the exact values of a particular factor in the equation; but by continually adding to the number of the tests we shall reach an approximate solution. Is it possible that science no longer goes back to Democritus as its prototype but finds its new theory anticipated by the speculations of Epicurus? And may it be that the principle of contingence in nature as well as in the conduct of man becomes the key to the new scientific religion which dates from the discovery of Epicurus? If this be true, then spontaneity not sheer necessity, the power to create new forms not undisputed mechanism, offers to religion an interesting and trustworthy phenomenon which will make a discreet appeal to certain types of scientific workers.

[19] J. M. Guyau, *La Morale d'Epicure*, Ch. II.

We have thus far contemplated reality in its infinitesimal aspect. The atom seems to have all the properties belonging to the Parmenidean universe, only in microscopic form. But, as we have seen, the atom never exists by itself; it is absorbed into the visible compounds of matter,—grains of sand, nuggets of gold, green boughs of trees, massive hills, meteors, stars, and the untraversable world. We are advised by such portents that the atom is capable of infinite reduplication not once but a myriad times. Cosmic wholes are repeated without end, each complete in itself and each reflecting the original powers of the atom. In the Epicurean system matter is in full command; it produces its forms at will and destroys them when they have done their work. Forms disappear but substance remains. From every angle the sway of the atom is self-sufficient; its omnipotence is fixed; from the sphere of the infinitesimal electron to the wide spaces of the heavens, through the tortuous courses of biological change up to the intellectual achievements of man, its authority is never challenged. On the vast levels of astronomic motion as well as in the smallest cell of a bacterium detected only by the high-powered lens of the biologist, mastery is obtained by the basic unit of substance. If religious theory asks for power, here it is.

What bearing has an exact knowledge of the natural world upon the systematic conduct of our moral life? This is the second problem to which Epicurus addresses his attention. It should be remembered that in the period immediately subtended by his death, the only teachings that struck the public fancy were his moral precepts. Many scholars connected him at once with the men of Cyrene and failed to grasp the nobler sentiments that clustered about the friendly intercourse of his Garden. The passages in his texts setting forth the excellence of bodily pleasures were seized upon with greedy hands, either in order to obtain justification for personal indulgence or to gather evidence which would inevitably condemn his theory in the minds of his insatiable critics. It was not until several generations had passed that the subtler phases of his thought were recognized. Suffice it to say that for a number of centuries after the Roman arms were installed as the controlling power in western society, the Epicurean ethic exercised a profound influence on such capital thinkers as Horace and Maecenas and divided with Stoicism the right to be called one of the prevailing philosophies of the time. In fact, it is fair to argue, with some of the more recent expositors, that many of the key issues in the theory found almost identical expression in the Stoic creed. The Stoic resignation terminating in the Via Aperta, a euphemism for suicide, has some of the cardinal marks of the imperturbability which made the Epicurean motive so persuasive in a social milieu moving swiftly to its final dissolution.

We have already noted that the discovery of the law of cause and effect rids the mind of its tendency to explain unfamiliar events in nature by the interference of imaginary powers. Fear is stilled, the emotions appeased, the heart steadied, and our interest in the knowledge of the world greatly quickened. The gain is substantial but negative; we need an incentive that is positive, and we find it, he thinks, in the very law that has eliminated the sense of dread. This law teaches us that the most important fact in human experience is the feeling of pleasure and pain. Feeling does for conduct what sensation does for thought: we cannot know unless we perceive, and we cannot act except under the impulse of expected delight. Repetition crystallizes the meaning of images, practice touched by the successes of the past unveils the moral values of a given act. There is, however, a sharp difference between them; for truth must be tested by a variety of judgments but good is the simple distinction of pleasure from pain. Still, it is one thing to know in general what kind of action is good; it is quite another to determine whether it is good in the given conditions. We are therefore forced to train our minds how to "grasp the limits of pains and desires." [20] So significant an end can be attained only by long and devoted examination. What method shall be employed to reach the end?

We cannot expect Epicurus to set up a hedonistic calculus such as Bentham devised in the modern period. His study of natural phenomena was not embellished with mathematical experiments; he did not attempt to state the types of mental action in terms of ratio and proportion; he did not even emulate Aristotle by defining justice under the rubric of arithmetical equality, giving an exact *quid pro quo* for each particular deed or by showing how greatly the virtuous action differed from its excess on the one side and its deficiency on the other. Epicurus was content with summoning two principles, drawn again from the operations of nature. Pleasure to be real must be continuous and unbroken; it must always represent a due balance, an Isonomia, between pleasure and pain. Both of them are basic canons in the best systems of Utilitarianism, as we know it. Both of them can be defined—by Epicurus or J. S. Mill—only with reference to the meaning of desire. Even Aristotle admits that while the object of desire was the significant element in behavior, we could never reach an acceptable decision if we were not sure that satisfaction would prevail at the close. In acknowledging the correctness of this opinion Epicurus cautions us that whatever be the nature of the end we seek, it must promote our personal enjoyment or it will be discarded as unworthy of the wise man's ambition.

Cementing the relation of desire and feeling as indissoluble he proceeds

[20] *Epicurus: the Extant Remains,* IV, Sec. 10.

to discuss the relative values of the things men covet in ordinary experience. The letter to Menoeceus gives us a suggestive classification.[21] Desires are of three sorts, those which are natural and necessary, including health, happiness and the perpetuity of life, those which are natural but not necessary, such as the pleasures of sex, and finally, those that are empty or vain "arising from uncritical thinking," the lust for position, preferment, useless money gains. Judging them from the point of view of the affective consciousness, they are either bearers of motion or bearers of rest. To which of these shall we give prior attention, to the yearnings of the energetic body or the aspirations of the placid mind? Do the pleasures derived from their respective sources persist for an extended time or do they fade from the senses after a moment of vivid excitement, leaving behind them nothing but a memory of their fervor and a hope of later renewal? Motion or rest is the ultimate test of the value of our feelings, the titillations of the flesh are violent but shallow, they reign for an engrossing instant, then are gone. But the joyousness of thought is enduring; it falls upon us like the invigorating breath of spring; it is fired by the intercourse of philosophic minds; it issues from the calm inquiry into the principles of law and order in the enveloping universe or through the long history of the human race. The beauties of nature, the majesty of her movements, the ceaseless revolutions of her orbs, the regular return of her seasons, and crowning all this the aspirations of man to master her secrets,—these are the objects upon which our fancy rests, and these the dynamic powers that allay suspicions and generate composure amid the disturbing convulsions of our social life. Continuity of joy is the first criterion in the moral creed.

There is a second test perhaps more stringent than the first, a secure and constructive balance between pleasure and pain. At this point the philosopher harks back to the ancient quality of the Greek mind, *prudence*,[22] which adds to a superior understanding of the principles involved, a keen and accurate knowledge of the time and place and conditions of the act's performance. Prudence furnishes the instrument by which we can fashion and mould the deed to its prescribed purpose. Despite the Epicurean rule that pleasure is always good, it does not follow that pain is always evil. There are "limits" of pain as well as of desires. Pain however intense and tormenting may be endured for a season, if its consequences are known to be agreeable. Or it may have accompanying pleasures which countervail its severity, as when Epicurus on his deathbed suffering excruciating agonies could yet recall the devotion of his friends, almost quenching pain in the transport of delight. Flesh and spirit compete for mastery in moments of crisis and the solemn tranquillity

[21] *Ibid.*, p. 87 sq.   [22] *Ibid.*, p. 91.

of soul has ridden out the storm. In the time of emergency peace will triumph over pain; what will it do in more commonplace circumstances? Take the case of the just man who is disturbed by fear of a ruthless enemy.[23] Fear is the symptom of ill; it engenders a sense of rebuff; it reveals a certain impotence in our nature. Hate or envy or contempt has conspired to invade our personality; we are threatened with injury to body or mind. The wise man will endeavor to meet the situation with serene and confident demeanor. He may be brought to the rack by his opponent but he will not yield his temper to dismay, though the flesh cry out in pain. Or, if the event be not extreme, he may exert himself to reason with his traducer, if by some hap he may convince him of error. One thing he cannot do: he cannot and will not allow pain to dictate the terms of settlement. This is the meaning of the Epicurean equilibrium—a just apportionment of pleasure and pain to the exigencies of human conduct.

But what shall we say of a greater dread which next to the terror raised by the imagined interference of the gods, is the most disturbing thought that ever crosses the mind of man,—the fear of death? The advice of the Master here is explicit and sure. It rests on the primary concepts of the Atomistic creed. "Death," he says to Menoeceus,[24] "is the annihilation of sensation. But all pain and pleasure, all good and evil spring from the operation of the senses. When these cease to act, pain disappears." He argues with great vigor that while we are in life we have no converse with death, and when death supervenes the power of apprehending either its process or effects is taken away. Hence, death is nothing to us, and that very fact makes "this mortal life" radiant with joy. The uncertainty of life, whether short or long, is no concern of ours; we are here to develop the full capacities of our nature, and the shining point in all experience is the attainment of enduring pleasure. Added to these assurances is the further one that the yearning for immortality drops completely from our mind: we live only for the perfecting of our natural ends. In some of these truths Epicurus forestalls the discussions of Spinoza. Each rests his case on the impossibility of avoiding physical dissolution: the laws of nature are inexorable. The one holds that "without an accurate knowledge of the universe we cannot keep our enjoyments unalloyed." [25] The other extols the value of scientific studies especially in their influence on the building of a virtuous character.[26] But Spinoza presents by far the finer interpretation of the meaning of human life; for he teaches that while the individual elements in the natural world, including the body of man, undergo incessant change, yet the total meaning of substance never alters. The loves of human beings in common with all the desiderative energies in the

[23] Diogenes, op. cit., p. 117.   [24] Epicurus: the Extant Remains, p. 85.   [25] Ibid., p. 97.
[26] De Intellectus Emendatione in Chief Works of Spinoza. Trans. by Elwes.

world, are summed up in what he calls "the intellectual love of God." Epicurus may have glimpsed such a fancy in his delineation of the divine calm, but no one in antiquity save an inspired Plato could have brought into infallible conjunction the two principles,—structural uniformity and the functional purpose of thought. From the standpoint of a divine science death is not a hideous spectre which we must fight to destroy; it is an incident in the majestic drama of reality contributing its powers to the new evocation of life. This seems to show that in the theology of certain philosophers the idea of continued personal existence in another state is not a necessary article in the universal creed.

Thus far we have examined the simple reaction of man to his natural environment; it is wholly emotional, since it deals with the physiological reports of pleasure and pain. But Epicurus is not content with organizing a strictly sensuous scheme of moral behavior. It is true that the only external test of action lies in its tendency to subserve the physical interests of the agent. This means that it must yield the exhilarating feeling of pleasure, not the deadening sense of pain. But there is a further function of conscious mind which it would be disastrous to neglect. Epicurus boldly attacks the problem of the will, a problem that has produced more confusion in the study of conduct than any other vexatious concept. He does so because he is faced with two facts, first, the common swerve in the primitive atom offers a fair ground for finding a similar and more pronounced independence in the subtlest of all atoms, the human soul. Secondly, he needed a strong argument for opposing the Stoic theory of determinism, not to say, fatalism which reduced volition to a nullity. If he could prove that coeval with the rise of mechanism in nature, there appeared a free agent which arrives at its own decisions and impresses its own direction on the movements of body, then he could effectively expose the pretensions of his opponents as well as answer finally their derisive objections to his creed.

What evidence may we adduce to show that man can, by concert of forethought, direct his attention to one course of action rather than another? We may inspect the atomic structures that make up what is termed the *mind*. As a composite body the mind cannot be perceived. We can determine its properties solely by analysis. One of them is the ability to fashion a permanent idea out of the congeries of reiterated impressions. Is another property the ability to consider under the same rubric two conflicting courses of conduct and end our examination by choosing one and acting on it? Shall we ground our power to choose in the original right of the atom to move in its own characteristic manner? There seems to be a long stretch between the action of the uncompounded atom and the matured consolidation of a thousand subtle quanta in the independent will of a man. Let us leave the matter in the hands of some master of metaphysics, and proceed to an argument which logic in all its branches will honor and approve.

What evidence can we draw from practical experience to emphasize the presence and potency of freewill? Test the evidence embodied in the moral habits that exhibit the cardinal virtues so dear to the heart of the Greek. A man is not good because he is virtuous, but he can claim an interest in the virtues, since they are always associated with the feelings of joy. Thus to be temperate one is obliged to avoid the extremes of pleasure, and to content himself with the satisfactions that calm the mind. Will is the instrument capable of effecting this result. To be courageous is to face the dangers of life, full of menace, instinct with impending pain, and choose to suffer the agonies of conflict, rather than submit to servitude of mind or condition. Justice is the pledge usually adopted in the communal group, whereby men agree to award kindred advantages to others in order to defend their own.[27] Prudence surveys the possible paths men singly or together may select and then directs every energy to follow one path through to the end, no matter what the cost may be. Friendship, the greatest of the virtues, represents the decision of men to seek intercourse with others of like intelligence; they are brought together in part to obtain private enjoyment from the most prolific source, in part to magnify the abstract principle of spiritual partnership as the corner-stone of all philosophy. Neither end can be realized except by the voluntary and deliberate consent of the individual soul. A social state organized and controlled by these virtues, must be recognized as bearing the imprint of a free and untrammeled electorate. Certainly, when extended to the domain of a modern nation it might well proclaim that the Four Freedoms for which great wars are fought, are already anticipated in the *Principal Doctrines* of the Epicurean epitome. They not only steered the ancient world away from the rigid precepts of the Stoical creed but awakened the hopes which Christian apologists found fulfilled in the teachings of the Church. After slumbering in the decline of faith for a thousand years, they sprang to new vigor and understanding in the restoration of learning and the new birth of thought. Here again, freedom of choice began its sanguine career touching religion, literature, morals, and finally science. When Galileo defied the edicts of the Pope and sturdily espoused the heliocentric theory of the world, he not only proclaimed that he was free to think and speak but that he elected to do so against the most ruthless authority in the European world, the power of the Papacy. This article of belief, written by Epicurus, however

[27] *Ibid.*, p. 103.

much it may have contravened his own scientific formulas, did not contradict his personal conviction that every man has command over his private
thought and decides by his own right what his actions shall be.

A philosophical system closing with the idea of a free and creative will
cannot be far from the type of natural theology which supplanted formal
religion in the eighteenth century of our era.

V: MARCUS AURELIUS

STOICISM is a state of mind rather than a system of philosophy. Its tenets appear in the most divergent forms of cultural development. The type of thought which bears its name sprang from the analytic mind of Greece. Behind it lie the moral energy of Socrates, the constructive metaphysics of Plato, and the scientific imagination of Heraclitus, together with the stern pride of self incarnate in the life and teachings of Antisthenes. Yet the Stoic principles have no exclusive root in the Mediterranean basin. Change their terms, and you may find them again in China or India or in the prophetic heritage of Judah. They embody a form of reaction which Confucius, Buddha and Jeremiah might readily translate into Oriental symbols. They have been studied, revised, and then imbedded in the severe discipline of the Puritan revival. Milton, Cromwell, Cudworth reflect in a variety of ways their enduring worth. The mind of the Stoic knows neither race nor age nor external condition.

Nor does Stoicism appeal to a particular group within the state. The classical examples of its comprehensive influence are Epictetus, the slave in the pit, and Aurelius, the emperor on the throne. Between such extremes we find social types of equal distinctness, Cleanthes, the man of the people, Zeno, the son of a seller of purple, Panaetius, the landed proprietor and Cicero, the Roman senator. These men sought to express their private ideals, they cared nothing for membership in a school. The type is fixed; wherever a master thinker defined his virtue by the infallible laws of nature, men called him a Stoic, admired his unblemished character, praised the boldness of his doctrine, and ended their panegyric by declining to follow his lead. In general, Stoicism enlists its adherents by force of moral interest, not by the deductive arguments of logic. A creed is nothing if it cannot be converted into noble action.

It is therefore appropriate that the "last of the line" should have set down his meditations in writing and addressed them to himself. The value of private reflection has never been better demonstrated than in this Golden Book. There is here no need of artifice or circumlocution, there is no place for dialectic or refined definition. He speaks from the profound recesses of experience, in the midst of the engrossing cares of state, from the environs of the battlefield, out of the distracting intrigues of the court, on the weary paths of travel. In every instance he sits apart from his subjects and looks into the face of truth. Scientific treatises are not born under such conditions; even had he the will to do so, he could not have composed the Organon of an Aristotle. He was not a logician, he was a mystic; he saw a single idea mosaicked in gold and this he committed to imperishable parchment. He thinks as Amiel did, though his syllables have not the finish of the Genevan's. They two communed with themselves, at home with their secret thoughts, unafraid, content. If either had tried to work out a system, he would have smothered his inspirations at birth. Thus, for Marcus, many of the Stoic's conceits are dormant; taken for granted they are unexpressed. Hence, in studying his sporadic remarks we must not disregard the wider reaches of his creed. It would be futile to lift him to his throne and forget the sources from which he sprang. But he permits his mind, as he says, "to view itself, determine itself," in the settlement of each significant problem. The way of life is a philosophy, and philosophy is the first concern of every rational spirit.

Let us understand at the beginning of our study that the philosophy of Aurelius is his religion, and religion is enshrined in the relations which men sustain to the world in which they live. Such relations are not merely physical, they are also moral in form and essence. Hereditary religions have occupied themselves with man's attempts to placate the supervening divinities which are deemed to be unpropitious in their attitudes to mankind. Religion for him is not a set of symbols, nor a sequence of visible ceremonies; it is the choice of moral duties binding its votaries to the supreme Reason which directs the universe. Hence, philosophy which is able to indicate man's true place in the world and to lay before him the imperative obligations which he must try to meet, is not only an authoritative analysis of moral concepts but is the precise expression of the real object of religion, namely, God. We do not mistake the purpose of this writer when we see in his *Meditations* or "Communings with himself," a union of the two groups of ideas ordinarily distinguished as those of religion and morality.[1] While the latter will be much more numerous than the former, not one of them attained its complete definition apart from what Aurelius calls the "governing reason." It may be presumed that reason (*nous*) bears the same meaning with him as with Plato; it has none of the aspects of personality such as positive religions have devised; it cannot be invoked as a superior deity; it has no independent existence; it is not even a co-partnered attribute such as omnipotence or omniscience. It is the logical summation of all the properties of substance of which a

[1] *Meditations*, XII, 26. The references are to the classical text, and to the English translations of Haines, Long, Rendell. In many cases the translations are my own.

universe can be constituted. The God of Spinoza was beyond the ken of the imperial Stoic, but his concepts begin to point in that direction.

THE WORLD WE LIVE IN

The thought of Stoicism has its roots in the movements of the natural world. Mastery of the inner self is an alternate phase of the mastery of nature's forces. This is true in a causal sense; for body comes from body, child from parent, this existing body from that; there is no end to the causal regress, though worlds succeeded one another in an infinite cycle.[2] It is also true in a moral sense, for man's destiny is bound up with the inflexibility of natural law; his "act and word" agree point for point with the changes observable in the courses of nature.[3] The vision of Plato is repeated by the Stoic: there is a universal Good in the revolutions of the spheres; there is also a Good, a dominating interest, in human society. The two aspects of human experience, knowledge of physics and the determination of moral rules, go together; they are never separated. What does nature teach as the basic principles of human behavior?

First, the universe is the prototype of the soul because of its intrinsic unity. This unity stands as the antithesis of change. More than the earlier Stoics Aurelius is impressed by the presence of fluctuating phenomena. Men with the naked eye see diversity, not unity. The world appears to be an arena of conflicting forces; genesis and decay, birth and death, competition and defeat are the tests of strength. The philosopher is strangely moved by the sight; he seeks for the One and he finds the Many. He aims to be governed by the integrating law of reason, and lo! the impressions of sense attract and charm and divert his attention.[4] He has supposed that the world be wrought out of an intractable substratum; he sees it yield to the touch of an invisible power—a plastic medium in the hands of an expert artificer.[5] Indeed, nature seems to take delight, like a vagrant fancy, in eliminating one form and substituting another. The principle of germination is the active principle in her realm; careful of the type, of course, but how unsparing of the individual! Acorn and oak, oak and acorn, man and child, child and man, how ceaselessly they come and go; no regard for the worth of the One but a glorious abandon in the production of the Many.[6]

Nor does nature stop with a particular kind; she destroys one form, a horse, to make another, a tree, and this in turn to generate a man. Nothing seems sacred in her eyes; even human life follows the same disappearing sequence; first the person, Augustus, wife, daughter, kinsmen, friends, then the stock itself, as witness the epitaph on Pompey's tomb. "Last of

[2] *Ibid.*, V, 13.
[5] *Ibid.*, VI, 1.
[3] *Ibid.*, II, 4, 9.
[6] *Ibid.*, IV, 36.
[4] *Ibid.*, VIII, 29.

his line." Surely Heraclitus has wrung the dread secret from nature's heart, "Everything is in flux, nothing remains." Even social institutions erected with exquisite care bear within them the seeds of dissolution. Shall political honor, repute among men, elicit from you extraordinary efforts for success? Fame is a bubble, the plaudits of the crowd are undiscriminating and fickle. In a moment of time all things assume a different cast; the peace of one day is the tumult of another. Neither in mind nor nature is there rest. Marcus wonders how nature could possibly weave a consistent fabric out of these multicolored substances.

Then the inherited creed of Stoicism speaks. Motion, change, individuality exist, that is true; but it is also true that a common denominator has been found. Matter that breaks up into unadjustable parts is not hopelessly discrete; it is pervaded by an intangible energy which is identical with itself. Stoics called it reason, the germinant or spermatic reason; it does for the world what life does for the organic body; it does for the whole of nature what soul does for the whole of man. It provides *tone*, the tension, that which may stretch but will never break.[7] Wherever an individual appears it is the emblem of the operation of reason. The world is a massive individual, as Timaeus had said, presided over by cosmic reason. Men named this reason "Providence"—it makes chance an interloper on the scene. A spermatic system will be at once distinguished from the rule of the atoms. Every atom, says the Epicurean, has its own private property of action called the "swerve," an independent form which carries it whither it wills. The atoms are not necessarily related; it is therefore impossible to predict when they will meet and where. Under such conditions the world we know could not be a universe; it could only be the index of chaos, the complete absence of law.[8] As against this view the Stoic spermatic reason makes the world a consistent whole. It resembles a civil state, the Greek *polis,* where justice or even balance is maintained, no one individual being regarded as a special favorite but all being treated alike. "Death and life, honor and dishonor, pain and pleasure, wealth and poverty, all come by equal lot to all, the good and the bad together, since intrinsically they are neither noble nor endowed with shame." [9] From which it is plain that the traditional theory of the Greeks, a nemesis that pursues the shaken soul even when it has done no specific wrong, or the hopeful dogma of the church—"all things work together for good to those who love God" —have no place in the Stoic's scheme. Providence proclaims that things stand side by side not by accident but by will. It ordains a specific function for every constituent part of the world, the sun to shine, the rain to moisten the earth. Even unconscious sleepers, as Heraclitus held, have their own form of activity.[10] Energy such as this reflects the power of the ruling

7 *Ibid.,* VI, 38.   8 *Ibid.,* IV, 3.   9 *Ibid.,* II, 11.   10 *Ibid.,* VI, 42.

sun; its rays are "actinic," capable of producing profound changes in everything it touches; it is everywhere extended or diffused, yet never exhausted, piercing at times to the hidden particle and irradiating it with light and glory. The world and the individual share in the spermatic influence. What is reason if not God, Zeus, at work in the manifold divisions and motions of the universe? [11]

Clearly, the universal mind is the mode and symbol of the individual mind. We shall see in due time how reason is triumphant over impulse. Here we may establish the similitude between nature and experience. In both, the chaos of change is observable; in both, the momentary impression is contrasted with the power of control; in both, the local and temporary give way ultimately to the sway of the governing Idea.[12] According to Marcus as well as to Plato the natural world is the fecund source of principles which become of mastering value in the field of human conduct. But we must not press the analogy between the two beyond its logical application. The Stoic conception of nature is wholly different from the Christian. Some of its items appear in Spinoza's system, the two properties, feeling and reason, representing extension and thought repectively in his analysis of the universe. The best way to explain the analogy is to recall Aristotle's definition of reason, *nous,* in the psychology of man. *Nous* is the logical genus under which all the various activities of the mind are organized. Reason is not an independent entity, nor even a property, it is the idea which sums up the meaning of human behavior. It survives the death of the body because it belongs to the total principle which governs the entire universe. Reason is thus the key concept in the understanding of the world of nature, for Aristotle and later for the Stoics. Nature is a "living being," every body, every motion, every relation, every event going back to the original impulse, the single perception,[13] which is the true certificate of nature's unity. Especially is this the case in the career of man as a moral agent. Again we may say that for Aurelius as for Plato the natural world is the fecund source of all philosophy.

Again, it is the harmony of nature that furnishes the pattern and incentive for moral behavior. The sun in its orbit has always riveted the gaze of intelligent observers; the hosts of heaven have challenged the admiration of every "watcher." Have they also noted the beauty of form in the minor creations, the "by-products," so to say, of nature's operations, —the drooping ears of corn, the rich colors in the ripening olives, even the foam that drips from the wild boar's mouth? [14] Beauty such as this belongs of right to the particular object; it does not require the praise of man to make it notable. Marcus is not a trained aesthetician as was Plotinus, who defined beauty as the *idea* shining through the physical forms of

11 *Ibid.,* II, 13.   12 *Ibid.,* VII, 17.   13 *Ibid.,* IV, 40.   14 *Ibid.,* III, 2.

nature. But at least he taught that no man could stand before the colo
and imageries of the sunset without identifying himself with its inhere
beauty. Nor could the artist address himself to the divine task of creatin
beauty in marble or sound without sensibly emulating the subtle desig
of nature, her lines and curves, her lights and shades, her modulations ar
pauses, feeling that Art is the universal idea committed sympathetical
to the medium which best expresses its native meaning. True to tl
tradition of his masters the last of the Stoics links aesthetic beauty to mor
grandeur, arguing that beauty is complete in itself and requires no adul
tion from its observers, precisely as virtue melts all actions into a gold
harmony without the addition of expert appraisal.

But the charm of nature is more than aesthetic, it is also teleologic.
Harmony, he affirms, is greatest when action fits the need. Does tl
physical structure of the world reveal so high a truth? Aurelius is in
doubt. "Circumstances," he writes, "may be said to suit each case, just
the mason speaks of fitting squared stones into walls or pyramids; the
is a natural harmony in all things." [15] The mind of the world is soci:
it is not in conflict with itself; the parts necessarily support the who
There is no place for paupers or for excrescences, since these interfere wi
the order of the whole. Men have called certain phenomena by untowa
names, charging that they disrupt the order and destroy the integrity
nature. Particularly is this true in the sphere of moral conduct,—sin, shan
corruption, malice, chagrin. Do not these facts contradict the claim that
this world the means are always suited to the ends? Error, pain, evil, sa
the Epicurean, certainly exist; hence, God, law, and order cannot prev:
The Stoic denies the charge. These are not essential elements in natu
they are mere chips struck off by the skillful artisan while he produces t
articles of craftmanship superb in form and substance. Here lies the mar
of nature's technique that though circumscribed by refractory materials
as well as things that appear to be "corrupt, aging and inutile," she can s
create new and vigorous forms. [17] Is man an exception? Does sin im
that he has been removed from the universal order and cannot be restore
The brutal fact of wrong, injustice, injury, is plain; it cannot be cover
up. But it is not incurable. The tide of optimism runs strong through
the *Meditations*. Confronted with the debaucheries of the city, the devas
tions of the battlefield, the evidences of sullen hate directed even agaii
the emperor himself, still the will to moral victory remains unimpair
The rational impeccability of nature has been driven into his soul; or
triumphs there, it must triumph also in human life. The world we live
is our physical home; it is also the seat of authority for justice and hor
and the attainment of true character under the sway of reason. [18]

[15] *Ibid.,* V, 8.　　[16] As Kant refers to the "stepmotherly" parsimony of nature.
[17] *Aurelius, op. cit.,* VIII, 50.　　[18] *Ibid.,* VI, 1.

Still a third truth is to be considered: nature is fixed in her laws and
there is no appeal from her decisions. Marcus repeats the parable of the
weaver; he weaves his cloth with unceasing application; the hand that
guides the shuttle never loses its grip. Nature is such a workman and her
law is that of necessity. It registers itself in the elementary principle that
nothing comes from nothing and can pass into nothing." [19] Every motion in the universe whether the procession of the stars or the fleeting
images of the mind is controlled by the same necessity. If nothing else,
uniformity of action attests the validity of this great law. No man of
mature years has failed to catch a vision of the "uniform past and the
uniform time to come." [20] The home of man, we have agreed, is not a
fortuitous concourse of atoms; it is the scene of appointed destiny. There
is nothing untoward or evil in the Heraclitean change; change may be
"busy ever" but change is not chance. Dissolution and re-formation follow the sure edict of nature. Change does not connote extinction or impairment of essence or diminution of power; for out of change some new
and unforeseen pattern emerges or some different examples of the original
pattern.[21] The process may be noted on a cosmic scale in the unbroken
regularity of the season, "which keeps the world young" or, as it were,
in the prime (acme) of its strength.[22] Marcus is impressed as Kant was
with the starry heaven above but he is even more impressed with the
changes going on about him in the stone, the wood and the human body.
He sees the faggots kindling into flame and being slowly reduced to ashes,
another kind of change, chemical disintegration, a terrific power upon
the earth. We cannot forget the celebrated passage which he drew from
Epictetus: "What have we but a little soul bearing about with it a lifeless
body"! But if the body changes, so does the soul. The incessant impact
of images upon the mind is a common article of belief both for Epicurean
and Stoic. But, for the Stoic, there is an energy that controls them, the
will implemented by reason. Hence it is not to be taken amiss, if we elect
to change our opinion on a given subject, even submitting in some cases
to the persuasions of our fellowmen. We are entirely free to do so. If mistakes are made don't blame God or the circumambient stars for the dis-
pleasurable effects; we are our own masters. In every instance we must
remember that pleasure is not the aim of moral effort; it is but an incident
of our career. The development of the whole man is the true objective.[23]
It is characteristic that in the Aurelian program necessity and purpose are
inseparably linked. The order of nature is like the "orders" of the physician
it looks to an end. The analogy is not complete; for man may reject the
one, he cannot reject the other. But the "pleasures" of nature and the
operation of "world-laws" are identical; that is to say, the necessary action

[19] *Ibid.*, IV, 4. [20] *Ibid.*, XI, 1. [21] *Ibid.*, VII, 25. [22] *Ibid.*, XII, 23. [23] *Ibid.*, VIII, 10.

of the forces of the world is crowned by the ineffable harmony of all its motions. Again, the parallel between nature and human experience is exact and convincing. This does not imply that Marcus has surrendered the principle of Providence which enables us to forecast the character of impending events; it merely shows that in addition to mechanical law which establishes the unity of action, there is also the idea of beauty which gives to our view of the universe the same impression of wholeness that visits the mind when we study the significance of a work of art.

REASON AND VIRTUE

We are now ready to examine more closely the intellectual faculties by means of which the elements of the world-picture become our intimate possession. It is obvious at once that the human mind is bi-partisan, on the one side reacting to the changes in nature, on the other, claiming an unvarying nexus between its impressions through the efficacy of judgment. Change and regularity are merely processes of mind at work in different directions; Marcus seemed to sense a fact which has become a stock-in-trade in modern thought, especially since the time of Hume. He says specifically in Book III, 11, that inspection of an object, that is, the presented image, does not cease with the gathering of its several modes of representation; we must proceed to a "definition or description of its naked or essential meaning," leaving aside peculiar aspects of the image and dwelling on the basic concept involved. Reason thus becomes the dominant factor in thought; it is judgment, not casual reaction, not momentary passions, that makes decisions possible; it is judgment that gives substance to experience, persisting substance, the principles of action by which unstable feelings can be overcome. In short, moral behavior, the crown of human action, is vain and ineffective without the universal ideas which reason deduces from its imaginative contacts with the outer world. Judgment alone can settle the question whether human life shall be guided by the migrant impulse which if uncontrolled will lead to disaster, or by the rule of right reason which can direct wavering footsteps into paths of honor and truth.

The doctrine of the Stoics does not assume that emotions are radically infected with evil; natural depravity is not a basic article. There is no right or wrong in the constitution of things; such ideas are put there by the thought of man. But if not there in fact they are there in potency. It is the impulsive functions that become the seat of error; if they are not properly directed, that is, if they are allowed to act without let or hindrance, the chances are that the ultimate purposes of the human personality will not be served, and if not protected will suffer serious impairment. This is true not only with impulses having to do with the physical organs but also with feelings such as ambition and anger, that affect the inward habits of the mind.[24] In order to understand the force of the emotional urge, to learn how passion shoots out on every tangent without plan and without check, let us study its operation in the ordinary experiences of the race.

Sensation, memory, feeling and judgment play their part in the responses made by man to objects in his immediate environment. We like this body, and dislike that, we favor the approach of one and resent the approach of another, as though insensible bodies could appreciate the expressions of our affectional nature. But when we enter into relations of beings of our own kind, a new property appears. The subject is not discussed in a systematic manner by the author. He accepts as an axiom of social intercourse that the standard mode of behavior is that which we call good or virtuous. He does not examine the grounds that justify the standard, he merely raises the question whether we can find within the range of experience any better qualities than wisdom, justice, self-control and courage, the four cardinal virtues of the Greek ethic. He flatly affirms that these qualities fulfill the demands of reason, that they meet adequately the moral destiny of man, and that they produce the most genuine satisfaction. The man who has these does not need the adulation of his neighbors; if he has them, the gifts of fortune,—wealth, civic honors, family prestige, or the untempered titillations of physical pleasure,—are of little concern to him. Virtue is thus a good which belongs to men of right thinking, a kind of spiritual *daimon* which has brought all desires into subjection to the rational power of the mind.[25]

If this be the true goal that nature has fixed for human character, why do we allow our fancy to be beguiled by that which is false or ambiguous? Or, why do we crave for objects that are manifestly beyond our reach and neglect the gifts that nature places by our side? In short, why does vice emerge as an aspect of behavior? Is vice merely the antithesis of virtue and therefore we cannot know one without knowing the other? Marcus is not concerned with the logical derivation of the negative of goodness. Experience has taught him the gravity of moral evil, and he stands ready to isolate the causes if he can find them. In Book II, 16, he warns us that wrong, first of all, is done to man himself. The word *Hubris* here used is one of the most domineering in the Greek language. It has two implications: it registers complete withdrawal from the accepted line of conduct, and it states that such withdrawal is violent and intense. The English "wanton" is the nearest approach to a suitable translation, used as Shakespeare used it, to denote a depraved and outcast character. The intimation of the Greek is that when man commits a wrong, he insults his own soul. Marcus compares the deed to an abscess, a malignant growth, a

[24] *Ibid.*, V, 26. [25] *Ibid.*, III, 6.

tumor on the otherwise healthy body. Strong words are these to depict the sin of the heart. St. Paul has nothing more severe in the first chapter of Romans, where the same theme is treated. Note, then, how the wanton spirit operates. It rebels against the laws of nature; it exhibits disgust at certain unusual events,—rain at unpropitious times, earth-tremors that kill or damage; it is perplexed at some untoward happening, which yet follows the necessary law of Cause and Effect. All this is a challenge to the justice of reason and in the Stoic mind a heinous sin.

Again, a hybrid wrong is done when we turn upon a fellowman in anger and resolve to do him hurt. The sear is really on our own person, not on the person of our neighbor. If we could glimpse in advance the distortions of soul to be visited upon ourselves, would we not be stayed in our evil course? There is still another form of malignancy in man's bondage to the fascinations of sensual *pleasure*. It is strange that men endowed with the faculty of reason will allow themselves to be caught by the whims and caprices of the flesh! Once more, if we assume a private disguise and appear to our contemporaries what we really are not, then the hybrid stamp is fixed on face and form: we have done an incalculable wrong to self and society. Finally, if we go through life without an aim—no end to be gained, no lofty motives to be followed, an empty and unspent life, then the nadir of the hybrid sin has been reached, and all is lost,—a vortex of contending forces in life and a hopeless nirvana at death. Sin such as this is a sin against reason, or as the theologian would say, a sin against the Holy Ghost.

What then is the cause of evil? The question has been asked ever since men began to think upon their condition. The Stoics made the distinction which every thoughtful man must make. There are certain evils,—organic pain, loss of goods, mental disturbances,—which have nothing to do with our moral activities. This is the problem of Job, and the answers which his contemporaries made were thoroughly mistaken. Evils of this kind fall upon us, said the Stoics, because we are men not because we are morally depraved. Respecting this fact Aurelius was quite in accord with the ancient patriarch, though he probably did not know that magnificent epic.[26] Every adverse situation can be traced back to its natural causes; therefore, there is no ground for protest or complaint. There are, however, other forms of evil that spring immediately or remotely from the perverse decisions of the mind; for these men are personally responsible, as we have already indicated. The problem now takes a different turn. We are no longer concerned with the origin of evil but with the manner in which it may be removed. The simple device of letting it drop from memory was unsatisfactory. They discussed the method in Aurelius' day; he found it

[26] *Ibid.*, IV, 39.

too simple and hence illogical. What then? Some of the earlier practitioners advocated severe, not to say, harsh measures. Let us "awe the guilty into silence," says Chrysippus; ostracism or unrelenting prosecution was the only way to eliminate evil. Epictetus was more benevolent. He held that authentic justice is tempered with mercy, especially when meted out to our own kinsmen or those in immediate fellowship with us. With this sentiment Marcus agrees. Nature, he thinks, has endowed her human subjects with a rational sense which puts them in relations of mutual regard and obligation. If justice be drastically administered, someone may be injured beyond his desert; then justice hard and merciless turns into injustice, and injustice is an act of impiety committed against the most venerable of all divinities, Reason itself.[27]

But there is a second attitude that must be reckoned with, one that goes back to Socrates himself. It is summed up in one of the great sayings of antiquity: "No man does evil voluntarily." This theme had been the subject for debate in the Academy and other schools for many generations. As paraphrased by Plato it read: Every soul is deprived of truth against its will, and by Marcus, unjust, intemperate, unloving actions are performed against the constraint of the will.[28] The argument sounds paradoxical; it appears to contradict the basic principle of the Stoic creed that nature put will into the human spirit and expected that we should use it in executing the commands of reason. But Socrates approached the problem of moral values from another angle. He not only showed how evil arose but also how it could be mastered. No man was fit to do a moral deed because he had an instinctive urge so to act. Nor could he be a moral agent if he merely followed his neighbor in the customary behavior of the group. Moral action is a prepared action. We are required to know *why* certain types of action are called good, others bad. We must survey the whole field of human thought, feeling, ambitions, hopes and destiny. To put the matter in a nutshell: we cannot discharge the duties of a moral agent unless we know the meaning of human life. Vices private and public have their genesis in the abysmal ignorance of the mind. The shoemaker is a bad workman, if he does not know his art; the physician fails, not because he wishes to harm his patients but because he does not know the technique of his science. We miss the mark in moral endeavor, says Aurelius, not because we will to do so but because we have not fully acquainted ourselves with the purposes of the mind, the usages of the body and congenital relations with our fellowmen.[29] There is no paradox in the Stoic's creed: given the broad knowledge of the facts just cited we cannot but choose one course, the path of honor.

The upshot of the argument is that reason, deliberate judgment, choice

[27] *Ibid.,* IX, 1. [28] *Ibid.,* VII, 63. [29] *Ibid.,* XI, 18.

based upon scientific study, is the one and only antidote to the caprice of passion. The method is Socratic, but its form may be abbreviated. As we have already seen, we must search for the "naked substance" of the object desired, a pure and simple concept which states the appropriate duty for the given occasion. Add to this the injunction that the concept must express the comprehensive interests of the soul, and we have before us the final test of moral excellence. Socrates showed us how to derive the first, for he carried every analysis back to the underlying principle. This he subjected to further scrutiny by many inductive examples, until every possible form of application had been exhausted. Marcus' ardor wanes before such a gigantic task; but he seizes upon the four virtues which Plato has scientifically classified, and asked the consummating question, can the determination of just behavior release a man from his bondage to destructive impulses? Is it true that the victorious soul is a citadel, a "strong point," as military men now say, into which disrupting sensations cannot come? [30] His answer is firm: the prepared soul cannot be taken by the storms of passion or the intrigues of evil men. The rational mind has put itself in sympathy with the eternal verities; it knows what is, what has been, and what is to be.[31] This is clear proof of the unimpeachable superiority of reason over the fluctuating impulses of the soul.

We have up to this moment been engaged in exploring the negative aspects of ethics: how to escape from the sullen forms of evil into which a lapse from the accepted standard of morals has thrown us. We turn now to the positive phase of the subject to which Stoicism has devoted a great deal of attention. Here again the author offers no sustained account of the matter, as Aristotle did. There is, however, no doubt in his mind of what the standard consists; it can be given in a single word—Conformity to Nature. We have already examined the physical principles at stake, unity of structure, harmony of parts and relations and finally the inflexibility of law. Which element of the intellectual life combines them in just proportions? If it can be identified, it will constitute the essential purpose of man's existence and the ultimate goal of his aspiration. This is what the Greeks called the Good. We have already indicated how the operations of the universe and the activities of the soul run on parallel lines. We shall now show in further detail how the properties of the world are also properties of the moral agent.

Marcus warns us that we are not to caption under this head the things that do not come under our private control such as physical functions over which man can exercise no restraint and which in themselves can never be the prime end of his existence.[32] Plato has insisted on the same principle, arguing that unfolding one part of our nature and not the sym-

---

[30] *Ibid.*, VII, 48.   [31] *Ibid.*, VI, 37.   [32] *Ibid.*, V, 15.

metrical whole could never achieve the intended end. He mentions in the *Philebus* two separate and distinct human functions, feeling and intellect, which in his time had been isolated as the chief aim of moral conduct; the former, of course, had been adopted by the school of Epicurus: there is but one objective and scientific test of goodness,—to gain pleasure and avoid pain. Feeling can be subjected to quantitative measurement, and we can therefore make no mistake in judgment. Marcus rejects the method without reservation. For one thing the independence of the moral agent is impaired; for the excitation of pleasure is produced by outside influences—persons, or things, or events—many of which are wholly or in part beyond our control. If the object be withdrawn, pain immediately ensues. It is plain that man's moral stamina cannot be allowed to rest on so insecure a foundation. Moral integrity like aesthetic appreciation belongs to the individual soul. "Everything possessing any kind of beauty is beautiful in its own right; it need not look beyond itself to obtain praise from another." The principle is common to beauty and goodness; anything that interferes with the sovereignty of mind is to be rejected. In this matter Aurelius is adamant: "my neighbor's will is as completely unrelated to me as his breath or his flesh." [33] Duty can never take its color from another's needs; it is true that a certain moral suitability (*kathekon*) suggests that I respond to his call; but the decision must be my own and his pleasure can never wholly shape the contour of my action.

There is still another reason for discarding feeling as the coercive incentive to moral conduct. Feelings vary from man to man, from time to time. What I desire my neighbor may despise; what appeals to me today may be repugnant tomorrow. A recital of all the ambitions that govern men's behavior in a given city may run the full gamut of human endeavor; no two citizens may agree in every point. It will be said that the exuberance of pleasure or the urge to avoid pain is the same in every breast; the objects which claim attention are different. But it cannot be denied that pleasure is inevitably attached to the quest for an end. The conflict between this man and that does not arise from a comparison of the pleasure-units to be won; it stems from the desire to obtain the rights of property in a given object, generally external. Such conflicts are followed by one well-defined result, the experience of pain which men abhor above every other condition. We are driven to the conclusion that the search for a good reckoned in terms of feeling, is bound to be accompanied at some point by the negation of good which is pain. The evidence provided by the common lot of man supports the contention of the Stoic that feeling cannot be the valid standard of behavior; it must be supervised by a superior faculty which can only be reason.

[33] *Ibid.,* VIII, 41, 56.

We return to the *Philebus*. If pleasure fails, then what shall we adopt as the standard of goodness? Another group of thinkers, powerful and keen, has, Plato says, espoused the cause of wisdom. Socrates leads the group, and the Stoics have fallen in line. We shall not have occasion to expound the Platonic view in this discussion, and may therefore state the principle which he selects and let it speak for itself. As is well known Plato was a scientific psychologist. He studied the human personality in its several ramifications. His argument is that we cannot take one function of mind and base on it the structure of moral values; it is the entire man whose interests must be analyzed and appraised. For this reason he finds a place for every expression of mind, including feeling. The standard of conduct under this system may be complex but it is comprehensive, and must be cordially accepted by thinkers who are in search of a final theory of ethics. It will appear that many of Plato's salient conceptions find suitable recognition in every later program.

If wisdom be the compelling fact of the moral consciousness, then the specific aim of moral endeavor will be to produce virtuous action. Moreover, if the framework of nature is to furnish the principles by which conduct shall be guided, we may begin by saying that virtue is the only force which can unify all the functions of the mind, and which, in addition, can draw all men into something like a commonwealth of rationals. We have presented evidence to show the importance of judgment as the instrument for joining all perceptions, feelings, and fancies into a single whole. Peace of mind is possible only under the rubric of a discerning reason. Why? Because it alone can isolate the common principle which governs each new mental experience. Take any distinct emotional set, such as lust in the body or anger in the mind. Each one of these is aware of the presence of a supervisory force, namely, mind. In the case of lust the mastery is much more complete, that is to say, the mind is polarized for the moment, and all possible reflection on the moral implications of the deed is forbidden. In the case of anger, the mind, not the body is directly stirred; to be sure, the face is blanched or reddened, the hand quivers, there is an intestinal shock; still, as Marcus says, the angry man "appears to turn his back on reason with a certain flash of pain and a furtive twinge of conscience." [34] Hence, the riveting sense of manhood is greater in the latter; while in the former the subject has allowed himself to be "unmanned," since he has not only rejected the unifying reason of his own soul but impaired the moral integrity of another. We may follow the individual agent through the diversified involutions of his whole career, and in every instance, if his thought is alert, we shall find the check upon im-

[34] *Ibid.*, II, 10.

pulse, passions, opinion to rest in the capacity of the instructed will to control.

It was sun-clear to the imperial Stoic that while every moral decision must at long last be made by the autonomous mind since morality is fundamentally the business of the individual, still the great majority of our decisions find their locus in the communal life. Inquiry testifies to the profound emotions awakened by our intercourse with our fellows. Marcus has not compiled a catalogue of them as Spinoza did. But his illustrations are so abundant and so telling that we can readily appreciate the influence which he supposes them to exert in the social scene. Take the negative emotions, those that tend to destroy not upbuild, the so-called flexor movements in modern psychology,—vengeance, resentment, retaliation, retribution, intolerance, all instinct with fear and foreboding,—words so infrequently used that they might drop altogether from the Aurelian vocabulary, were they not translated into terms of the cosmic reason. Do not attempt revenge, he counsels, when a wrong is done; instead, consider the point of view that prompted the act. The chances are that if we knew the whole set of circumstances we should be inclined to pity, not chastise the offender, since the commission of wrong is not a forthright act of will. Rational creatures were made for one another; hence, forbearance is a part of justice. Many who spend their lives in bitter hatreds, in suspicions, in uncontrollable enmity—with daggers drawn against the foe, these are really burnt to ashes and cease to be. He urges men to consider the alternative, a reigning providence which is the symbol of reason on the one side and sheer Atomism on the other.[35] Against the sense of vengeance, let us put the persuasions of benevolence which is the sign and seal of a rational world. In the light of teachings such as this we may wonder into what utter ruin the society of the Roman Empire might have fallen, had it not been for the broad-minded altruism of the supreme leader. If we think it over we may yet find an element of truth in the judgment of Edward Gibbon, who when asked what he deemed to be the happiest era in Europe's history, replied, The age of Marcus Aurelius. There is something Christian here, though without the presence of the captivating Christ.[36] Especially is the fact true and inspiring, when we read his glowing words about the virtue of tolerance. Intolerance was a vice common then, common now. It signifies a feeling of resentment that men, in our vicinage, should entertain ideas, pursue customs, develop a type of living contrary to what we hold to have the core of truth. Yet if we oppose them, we interfere with one of the original rights of human reason, namely, to determine its own creed. Furthermore, open defiance cannot change their

[35] *Ibid.*, IV, 3.   [36] *Ibid.*, II, 1.

judgment, a judgment which has resolved upon a course of behavior regarded by them as distinctly to their advantage. Instruction is the only cure, not resentment, not reproach, not criticism. An intolerant attitude defeats its own ends. Make *clear* to them, the master says,—a strong word, the word that Aristotle used to draw the irresistible conclusion of a syllogism,—make the meaning of their course plain and unmistakable; break down the ramparts of self-opinionated certainty; throw in the condiments of loving-kindness. They see the disinterested nature of the argument: you gain nothing, they win all things. The crust of prejudice is hard indeed, if it can remain unbroken by such appeal."[37]

There is still one more instance of the power of virtue to unite antagonistic forces; I refer to the structure of the civil community. Virtue has its duties, here, as well as in the immediate social neighborhood. The Roman point of view in this matter is bound to be different from the dogma of the Greeks. For generations, as Jaeger has contended triumphantly in his *Paideia* the mind of Greece strove to conceive and erect a city-state where the spirit of political unity could be realized, and where, too, the cultural achievements in art, science, philosophy and letters could be finally centered. The purpose was turned into fact, in part at Sparta, in whole at Athens, and the name of Greece became the emblem of harmony, beauty and dignity. But the change long impending became a reality while Aristotle was still alive. The rise of Philip and the decay of Grecian solidarity brought down the great civilization of Attica tumbling into ruins. Then the acquisitive energies of the Roman state began to assert themselves. All Greece fell, all the neighboring East; all the tribes of Franks and Germans came within the purview of the conquering power. The spell of submission descended upon Carthage and Spain. The civil community disappeared, the ambition of empire was projected. The narrowness of the Greek ethic was obliterated. Men began to think in terms of a wider world, not of a political state. Scholars and philosophers no longer had a stationary home; they could take up their residence in the imperial capital for a time, though as yet the empire was there only in name; its aegis followed the march of its victorious legions. Further, a new spiritual force has entered the confines of the state, something unheard of in the centuries agone; its adherents sprang from every race, and from every phratry within the race. Whether the spirit of grace emanating from the Christian gospel penetrated the life and thought of Marcus Aurelius, we do not know. Certain it is that the themes of the Stoics received a new and more spiritualized interpretation from his example. The law of the state was enforced with rigidity, even with violence, and the brunt of its severity fell upon the lowly Christians. Still the appeal of total humanity rings in the Emperor's ears.

[37] *Ibid.*, VI, 27.

Not the provincial hamlet with its loves and hates, not the royal city with its luxury and filth, but the City of the World with Reason as its king and the brotherhood of man as its precept, was the ideal commonwealth of Aurelius. Putting it negatively he says, What is not injurious to the city cannot injure the individual citizen.[38] Or turning the matter about, every private act of dishonesty leaves its sordid impression on the social group. Infidelity is wrong because, as Kant shows with extraordinary effectiveness, it undermines the moral relations between members of the greater community. Thus, at length, Stoicism leaves the purlieus of the town and countryside and enters the "Commonwealth of Rationals," the first scheme of pure philosophy to attain that end.

The second and third factors of virtue, harmony of action and inflexibility of law, have been adequately explained above. These three properties of nature taken together guarantee the validity of the four cardinal virtues of the classical morality. These are the habits of mind that fit into the scheme of nature; nothing else will do. While to the modern thinker the connection between nature and morals is not so close; to the man living in the dawn of European speculation, the connection seemed to be real and authoritative. It appeared to be real, because the gifts of mind thus conferred can never be acquired in too great abundance, and when acquired could not be withdrawn. Excess of economic goods brings suspicion and distrust from our neighbors and ingenerates a tendency to greed in our own mind. Excess in honors leads inevitably to a mood of haughtiness, to contempt for unsuccessful men, and will surely beget hatred in the bosom of others. Sensual pleasures when carried to excess breed mental sloth, moral callousness, and physical disease. But abundance in moral goods never taints the noble temper of the soul, it is the source of continual expansion and brings the mind of man in touch with the universal principle of reason.[39] This is especially true of the virtue of justice; it does not "crowd the self into a corner"; it is the seat of authority, the essence of law, the law which fashions forth the true worth of personality, the law which tells men how they should conceive and treat the objective relations of life. The law of justice cannot be defeated by the transgressions of our neighbors nor by our mistakes in its interpretation. Such law is nature's edict and bears the seal of eternal reason. If justice be thus understood and executed, then virtue is a settled habit of society.[40]

WILL AND DESTINY

The end of moral conduct is virtue, the organ for its attainment is the Will. Will is the executive force of reason, it puts into effect the decisions

[38] *Ibid.,* V, 23.   [39] *Ibid.,* V, 12.   [40] *Ibid.,* XII, 1.

of the intelligent mind. Virtue has the quality of a sovereign, it reveals the rational soul as a fortress, a beetling cliff which meets without flinching the impetuous waves and lulls them into rest. Its rightful domain, we said, no alien influence can enter, a fair anticipation of the windowless monad which Leibniz will present to the modern world. Fire, sword, tyrannical decrees, slander's tongue—nothing can destroy its natural office, nothing can disturb its equilibrium; it is a full-orbed sphere whose circular form cannot be impaired.[41] In no writer of ethics in antiquity does the autonomy of the will appear so firmly fixed; many critics think that Kant was deeply moved by the loftiness of the Stoic temper. The moral will is affected neither by the changes in nature, nor by the variability of the senses, nor by the bitter contentions of men, nor by the vicissitudes of individual fortune. Its authority is twofold: it initiates action by itself and does not wait for outside excitation as the senses do, which are like the marionettes in the pantomime, set dancing by the unseen hand of the operator. Again, it has the power of controlling all tributary experiences, changing impediments into aids, overwhelming critical comments by sheer force of truth, as when wrong motives are imputed or when devotion to duty is construed as artifice to obtain a reputation for charity. It is the token of weakness to be embittered by opposition; on the other hand, to surrender through fright at the possible consequences entailed would destroy the very purposes of moral conduct.[42]

At the same time the human will has the power of neutralizing antithetical influences by *accepting* them. This, however, is not surrender in the abject manner of the slave; it is a constructive attempt to meet what is not subject to our control, with discerning acquiescence. Nature has placed certain offices within our grasp; others she has withdrawn. It is the duty of the philosopher to find out which is which; that is to say, he will comply with what he cannot change, and act with intelligent discretion in matters that clearly come within the range of individual choice, such, for example, as the immediate conditions and events of the neighborhood.[43] It is at this point that the enemies of Stoicism have launched a frontal attack. They complain that any theory which requires men's will to submit unequivocally to the order of nature is a species of fatalism. On the surface the action seems to be deliberate and free; in the final analysis it is an abdication of freedom. No man can pray the classic prayer: "Thy will, O Nature, be my will," without feeling that his submission is constrained, not free. Now we are obliged to admit, with some of its defenders, that freedom is a word which mocks; it has no content, it turns the moral agent into a pale ghostly reflection of nature. It is also true that Marcus had never wholly rid his mind of the charm exercised by the hereditary

[41] *Ibid.*, VIII, 41.   [42] *Ibid.*, XI, 9.   [43] *Ibid.*, VIII, 7.

concept of destiny, fate, the Greek *Heimarmene*. In his philosophical thought it was imbedded close beside the idea of inflexible law. We are an infinitesimally small part of universal substance, we exist in but an infinitesimally brief segment of time, yet we share, though an infinitesimal fragment, in the destiny of the world. In a striking passage he exclaims: "It is needful to agree with what happens to thee, for two reasons; first, it happens directly to thee, was ordained for thee, was woven as Clotho wove it by celestial direction and from the most ancient causes, and secondly, what happens to the individual is causally connected with the harmony and complete fulfilment and divine perpetuity of the universe itself." [44] The idea of destiny, however, is no longer associated with the arbitrary pronouncements of the gods; it is used as Anaxagoras might use the term Logos to denote the necessary relation between bodies in the physical world; or as Plato makes Timaeus cite the term, *Anagke*, unchanging necessity. It seems likely that in the *Meditations* the concept of freedom has a double connotation, willing compliance with an order which we cannot alter—"obedience to the power that sets us right" [45]—and a change of course by our own election. As facts in human experience these two ideas have equal validity: the former recognizes the presence of physical, sometimes moral, forces which we cannot resist; we do not nullify the meaning of the word freedom when we apply it to such cases. The latter is the active form of freedom, the expression of the energies which represent the desires and judgments of the entire man.

If virtue be deliberate conformity with the laws of nature, what, then, is vice? The problem, we have seen, is elusive and difficult. Granted that men's actions are strictly voluntary; granted also that the human will like the will of nature is the expression of reason; how can we account for the presence of moral evil? The answer of the Stoic is categorical; he does not for a moment palter with the thesis of Descartes that error is the indiscriminate extension of the power of will beyond the pale of judgment; he rejects it unreservedly. Error has no place in the organization of the natural world; it is an *appearance* which will be exposed as soon as we apply the method of logical inquiry; it is found only in man's empirical or sensory nature not in his rational judgments. If this be true, what place does will have in the determination of our moral behavior? It is hardly possible to say that Marcus agreed with Spinoza that every mental act was not only the affirmation of judgment but also the expression of will. He was a disciple of the Greek tradition in psychology which had no independent place for the concept of volition. Still, the celebrated definition in Aristotle's Ethics makes choice a deliberate act, following knowledge and succeeded by an organic plan based on established character, a settled

[44] *Ibid.*, V, 8.   [45] *Ibid.*, VIII, 16.

habit of acting. Hence, while the threefold division of faculties may serve in man's study of the external world, when he approaches the study of his relation to his fellows, the element of will is bound to be emphasized. The Stoic undoubtedly accepted this analysis. The judgments of reason tell us what kind of actions men must perform in order to be virtuous; but they do not provide the driving power by which the decision may be put into effect. The will enters to discharge that function. The will, however, is another name for self, the whole man at work, turning concepts into concrete facts of behavior. If, then, the human agent had nothing but a judgmental mind, he could formulate a whole series of moral concepts, luminous and convincing, but he could not exercise the slightest influence upon the evolution of a moral character or the formation of a civil state. All the imperatives and exhortations that Marcus uses would be inept and futile, without the constraining presence of the human will. Vice would not exist as a moral phenomenon, and virtue would be a name unknown. This implies that will is a constitutional factor in the determination of both evil and good; the judgment is responsible for the contents of the act, the will for its ultimate execution.

The office of the will in moral concerns is never so cogently defined as in the dogma of submission. It is enshrined in the epigram—*Anechou kai apechou* (bear and forbear),[46] and is presented in two forms, the attitude of mind and the manner of treatment. The most difficult task a man ever sets for himself is to preserve his moral balance under the crushing weight of adverse social conditions. Natural disabilities strong men can endure; they belong to the order of things. But the contentions of neighbors, even of kin, awaken a feeling that these should have been avoided. They leave in us a residue of irritation, which is allayed only after a bitter struggle. How, then, shall we treat such recurring situations? The answer is—"we must embrace the whole universe in our view," simple as a formula, mind-shaking in its effects. Let us remember that our sufferings are incredibly brief as compared with the aeons of existence of the world itself. All complaints shrivel and die in face of this comparison. An answer like this is a sharp challenge to the aggressive temper of the Roman creed. It stirs the animosity of the Nietzschean mind which cries out for an uncurbed discharge of all native impulses. Narrowly interpreted, it conflicts with the essential principles of the modern ethic, as we shall show. Yet it offers one type of response to the ills which every man is obliged to bear.

The attitude becomes clearer when we learn how its terms are translated into behavior. By word or deed men express their intuitions. Both of these must be sternly checked. Murmur, disgust, recriminations, accusations against gods and men are not the words of the sage. They tell us that we

---

[46] *Ibid.*, V, 33.

have spent our time in criticizing momentary events when we should have invoked the underlying principles of reason.[47] It is not the duty of the Stoic to exhibit the virtue of tenacity when tenacity can serve no useful purpose. On the other hand, the repression of self may be the very virtue by which the public protest against existing wrongs can be best implemented. If we appeal to the universal reason for relief, the appeal should embody not the desire to be freed from immediate dangers but from the grip of fear itself.[48] We shall thus attain a serenity of soul which is grounded in an accurate understanding of the facts, not the unimpassioned aloofness of the skeptic, a bloodless disregard of events and their meanings, but spiritual concentration and sustained courtesy to others like that of Antoninus who lived his life with devotion and met his end with a conscience void of offense.[49]

In one case, however, the instinct of resignation may be otherwise construed. "If the cabin smokes I will take leave of it." [50] The precept of suicide is organic to the Stoic's thought. At first sight it might seem to contravene the rule that nature provides for the execution of her own laws. Yet this is no exception; for my will, as a part of nature, is the master of its own home. Suicide concerns the body only, the soul, the seat of imperishable reason, is untouched. Body is inferior earth, it is not worthy of the soul which *seems* to be its servant but is not. Revolting diseases infest its members, hideous deaths some are called upon to meet; these give evidence of its imperfect structure. If pain becomes intense we need not keep it whole. Indeed, we are in duty bound not to let the mind suffer impairment of function which inevitably entails physical decay, diminished power of attention, less exact discrimination of moral values, growing inability to relate each new decision to the universal precept. One may legitimately complete one's work in life's prime and then disappear.[51] Finally, physical pain and mental agony have no permanent worth; they do not, as some have contended, reflect divine condemnation of human error; they do not belong to the original structure of the world. Hence, if a man takes his life, he does not violate a natural law; [52] rather does he exercise a native right in order to avert needless visitations of pain.[53] In reality, by this act he declares the true significance of death—"dying is one of the salient features of life." Strange that a recent artist, with no claim to philosophic wisdom, and with every wish to prolong his own life, should as the Lusitania sank under the fatal thrust of the enemy's bomb, have been led to exclaim: "Death is the greatest adventure in life."

We may pause for a moment to ask what the great Stoic thought on the subject of immortality. He had no settled opinion; this is clear. The Roman

---

[47] Ibid., V, 5.   [48] Ibid., IX, 40.   [49] Ibid., I, 16.   [50] Ibid., V, 29.   [51] Ibid., III, 1.
[52] A fact which modern jurisprudence has been forced to recognize.   [53] Ibid., II, 11.

critic of the day speculated on the matter to his heart's content, but without avail. One point is certain: the myth of Charon who admitted the distinguished dead to their eternal abode made no appeal to the Latin fancy. Cicero is our witness to that fact. In an unsystematic manner Aurelius explored the several hypotheses. Does the soul sink at death into a coma of unconsciousness where sensation, perception and personal awareness are absent? Such a theory reflected the dread of the percipient mind to descend into a state where conscious thought was excluded. Or, shall we waken in another world with a different sort of intelligence where the intuition of self and the continuance of memory are wholly lost? Worse than either of these, will the soul at death be simply extinguished, its substance gone, its properties forgotten? Or, against this utter ruin, may we entertain a hope that the individual soul will persist for a time like the coat of the weaver in the *Phaedo* dialogue, and then be merged into the rational soul of the world? The issue is blurred, nothing is defined; the best we can do is to follow the lead of Aristotle who argues that as the soul is the logical genus of the body, and as reason is the logical principle of the universe, so each remains as the complete and indestructible Idea by which both man and the world are to be explained. Yet with all the speculation *pro* and *con,* the hope of immortality refuses to be banished: "How can it be that the souls of good men, when they die, shall never again be born but pass out into utter extinction? If it were to be so, be sure that the gods would have made it possible, if there were need for it. If it had been a just state, agreeable to the laws of nature, then nature would have made it so. Therefore, we may conclude that because it is so, if it *actually* is so, it could not have been otherwise." [54] The hope may flare again, here or there, in Latin speculation but to all intents and purposes as a precept of philosophy it was dead!

The Stoic's doctrine is defective in certain important articles. We shall begin with the theory of resignation. This attitude has been assailed as the very reservoir of moral stagnation. The quiet simplicity that crowns the *Meditations* of Aurelius has no place in the arena of human endeavor. Some are inclined to think that the imperial behavior flatly denies the essence of the creed. If submission became a dominant property in the social group then pain and greed and tyranny would have had unchecked sway both in the world of nature and in the social exchange. But resignation, fortunately, is not an elementary mode of thought; it contradicts in principle the rights of human personality. Whenever our rights are invaded or threatened, the authority of the intruder must be challenged. This is not self-assertion in the Gyntian sense, a crude assumption that my

<hr>

[54] *Ibid.,* XII, 5.

interests are to be satisfied, no matter what the consequences to other men's interests may be. This is the claim to equal treatment with all the other agencies of nature or society. We are not required to accept the disagreeable conditions of life in a submissive mood; we are not even obliged to use the offices of kindly remonstrance, as the Quaker formula suggests. The moral sovereign whom Marcus recognizes and approves, may deliberately turn his sword against any and every intruder. Even in the case of pains superinduced by the violation of natural law, it is not a tribute of respect to nature to accept her pangs without protest. The medical sciences have been organized to promote the opposite end. To hold, for example, that disease is a divinely ordained method for redressing the moral balance in society—a dogma preached in Scotland as late as the time of Thomas Carlyle—though not by him—is plainly an inept and fallacious conclusion. So long as such an opinion prevailed science was dumb and pain unconquered. When men refused longer to bow to the superstition, the triumph of modern research began. In short, the aggressive spirit of moral ideas in our day is a decisive rebuttal of the Stoic's claim.

The same procedure is demanded by the critical instinct in the realm of social enterprise. Ignorance is the direct cause of many ills in politics and economics, today. Thus, the attempt in the past to keep the masses of men in a state of servitude by hiding from them their true potentialities and creating a sort of resignation to unavoidable fate, produced a moral callousness in the dominant and ruling class and a serious menace to the stability of the entire community. The history of Russia in the present century is a case in point. Serfdom however disguised by promise or fatuous laws prepared for the degradation and fall of the Czarist state. The servile temper of the German people is another instance of the same inexorable law. Nature turns upon her assailants; she has never counseled submission. The tragic disintegration of Germany now reached (1945) is due, not primarily to a crudely ineffective leadership since 1933, but to the willingness of the state for many generations to accept a program of war as the true index of political greatness. If Marcus had read the laws of nature aright he would have discovered there the eternal principle of compensation. To advise men to be quiet in face of actual or threatened agonies, is to counsel the impossible. Destiny is not a red-handed despot who crushes his victims to earth and then gloats over their discomfiture. Nor is it a machine which can change human agents into non-resisting re-agents. Destiny for man is not apart from mind, it *is* mind, man's intelligent, discriminating mind, the mind which creates and enforces the rules of honor and integrity. The Stoic forgets his strong adherence to the sovereignty of soul. Freedom is in the soul, and it is nine-tenths of the whole man. No one is obliged to accept the present status as final, he can make a brave and, we hope, successful attempt to change it. He fights, at times, against impressive odds; heredity, environment, his private history may stand like formidable obstacles in his path. Still, no normal mind will yield to current disabilities so long as strength of body and vigor of will endure. Certainly, no sagacious thinker will suppose that suicide can be a substitute for a resolute use of all our inherent powers. Suicide is not protest, it is a cavalier confession of failure, and in some cases the signet of cowardice. The man of courage does not shrink from the task of recovery; he is not daunted by defeat, which is but wine to his soul and temper to his blade. He does not admit that the disadvantages of the physical world may obtain also in the sphere of moral endeavor. If that were true, then moral progress would be forbidden; the *status quo* would prevail inevitably; whatever is, *is,* and cannot be changed! This is a creed from which the author of the *Meditations* would wholeheartedly dissent.

The criticism of the Stoic theory should include still another point. Representative men of the school have held that the sage can neutralize the sting of a given objection by adopting it. The proposition is ambiguous and requires examination. It is true that at times philosophical ideas have sought to profit by the momentum of empirical ideas which are antithetically opposed. These last ideas are "in motion," so to say, while the new concepts are slow to awaken the interest of the public. Thus, Plato accepts the principle of change from Heraclitus but converts it into a fact of capital importance in his theory of knowledge. Change is no longer in the material universe but in the universe of thought. Change is diversity, and the logical genus splits into its species, the species into its sub-species, the sub-species into its individual members. The same method is followed many times in the development of the moral code. We select the disagreeable elements in social experience, for example the ravages of war, with its sordid motives, its brutalizing operations, its tendency to generate intrigues between peoples formerly at peace with one another, and with these catastrophic consequences proceed to work out a new definition of justice together with the instruments by which the revised ideals may become permanent possessions of the human race. If this is what the Stoic dogma means, we may welcome the concept of resignation without reserve. If, however, the dogma means that we must match every moral advance with a "bath of blood," we should reject the proposal with all our consolidated strength. The teaching of history is that when a borrowed concept proves fruitful in a new situation, the reason lies not in the immediate value of the added idea but in the importance of the subject which it is intended to support. Certainly, resigning oneself to a situation which is thoroughly distasteful but which we cannot change, is entirely different from the type of submission which we have just considered. The surrender of the Southern Confederacy to the armies of the Union, was a submission forced and not voluntarily accepted; it had its devastating effect upon the morale of the people but it did not alter the tenor of their thought. Nevertheless, the tribulum of pain has shaped some of the most majestic figures in the evolution of the race, and in some cases the advance has been made by bowing deliberately to the unexpected changes. It has been suggested by men like William James that the world itself passes through such changes "groaning and travailling in pain" until a greater unity is reached. The melioristic doctrine is interesting, but it does not convince. In all our discussion it must not be forgotten that resignation is of value, only when it enables the moral agent sternly to meet the duties attached to the program which he has adopted for himself and, so far as opportunity permits, for his immediate associates. To this decision Marcus Aurelius would give his glad assent.

Thus it appears that despite certain defects in their system the proponents of Stoicism had a significant message for the world. They conceived a firm faith in the unity and harmony of the universe as the first article in their religious creed; they held with Plato that men could understand the laws of nature through the intuitions of the rational judgment; they demanded and endeavored to obtain for human beings the same order and steadiness of behavior that were discernible in the processes of nature, and this they called virtue; they distinguished rigidly between the life of impulse and that of reason, contending that while both are from the same source, the former is necessarily subject to the latter; they organized a Commonwealth of Rationals where brotherhood and mutual forbearance would aid in overcoming the tendencies towards moral error; and finally, they taught mankind patience amid the shifts of fortune and the shocks of pain, pointing not to the dissolution of individual units but to the perpetual rule of reason in the universe.

VI: AUGUSTINE

THE most constructive thinker in the early history of the Christian Church was Augustine, Bishop of Hippo, North Africa. He combined in a remarkable way the strong temper of imperial Rome with the mystical currents in certain Oriental religions. His theological thought followed the patterns of Latin jurisprudence which were ultimately expressed in the Pandects of Justinian, a thoroughly articulated system of law with authority lodged in the chief of state. On the other hand his spiritualized conceits received support from the Neo-Platonic speculations, although there the idea of authority vanished in the extreme remoteness of divine Reality. In practical matters one thing for him is clear, namely, that will as the impelling force in God and man has an exact analogy in the administration of the Empire. Furthermore, the Greeks developed their genius in studious reflection, the Latins in the public execution of their decisions. Hence, when the civil dominion crumbled into dust, an ecclesiastical dominion arose with the equivalent virile properties of the Caesars. Augustine is a faithful representative of Rome's inflexible will and unconquerable energy; he founded his philosophy not on an intellectual method such as Aristotle's but on the principle of volition as the executive element in human personality.

Let us notice another trait of mind just as effective, the insistence upon Faith. He elaborated the program laid down by St. Paul, that faith is not merely belief in but submission to another's will, namely, God's. His own adhesion to this formula began in the Garden at Milan where his conversion to Christianity took place. His *Confessions* may exaggerate the intensity of the mental changes but the preparation for the event was entirely normal:—a mother of unusual gifts, with fine aesthetic feelings, genuine devotion to the creed of the church, great affection for the youth and interest in his education; an early manhood passed in provocative surroundings, with well-developed mental powers, some lapses in morals such as were common in that period, but with a mind searching for the elementary truths of reason and for a *Pou Sto* in the midst of the philosophical chaos about him; a sudden turning to spiritual concepts after a momentary embrace of the Manichean heresy, and then a studious analysis of the Alexandrian system—these are the successive moments in the morning of his life. But an intelligence like Augustine's could not remain at anchor in the shallow waters of Persian phantasies or the ambiguities of the Plotinian dogma. He came under the spell of Ambrose of Milan, masterful churchman and stern dialectician and there surrendered to the appeal of Faith, fulfilling the hope of his mother and at length satisfying his own desire for certitude. Augustine was the man whom the new church needed; he could systematize her doctrines, solidify her laws, and bring the scientific temper to bear upon the problems of her practical experience. These three offices he undertook at once. We are not required in this study to assess the value of his interpretation of the Christian creed; our interest lies in the principles of philosophy which he adopted. Some of them naturally took their color from his religious thought, for example, the significance of the human will and its dependence on divine grace. In fact his whole system, we may as well admit, was permeated with the spirit of revealed truth. He is thus the prototype of the eminent ecclesiastic of a later century, Thomas Aquinas, who while he rejected certain aspects of the earlier creed, is really Augustine's representative in the triumph of the papal church.

THE SANCTIONS OF KNOWLEDGE

The first point in his inquiry is the meaning of knowledge, how it is derived and how it is guaranteed. The procedure is Socratic but carried out within the ambit of a new series of ideas. He hears the dictum of the ancient Greek, *Know thyself,* and realizes that wisdom begins with that imperative. Yet his method is different; it is personal, not objective. The contrast is not between a privately discovered truth, hence one that is uncertain in its content, and a truth that is subject to verification by the action of a rational mind, hence universal; it is the coalescence of the two. Truth cannot be reached except as the mind is open to certain extralogical influences which incite the understanding to inspection of the facts involved. For truth is the goal of knowledge and knowledge is the affirmation of the power of the mind to think. Can the soul of man ever arrive at a solid appreciation of its own destiny, of the treasures of the physical world, and finally of the nature and existence of a supreme Being?

Shortly after his conversion and while he was still in the vicinage of Milan he made a careful survey of the attitude of the learned world to these very subjects. In his attack upon the "Academics" written in the year 386 he singles out the two leading schools of thought, the Stoics and Skeptics,[1] and asks them bluntly if they can answer his query respecting the certainty of truth. All his studies with the recognized philosophers

[1] Omitting the Neo-Platonists, for whom he never wholly lost his affection.

had failed to yield satisfactory results. They could not destroy the doubts raised by Zeno who found the basis of knowledge solely in the deliverances of the senses, a feeble reed to rest on. Even when Chrysippus insisted on the use of the ancient categories to give meaning and zest to experience or when Aurelius probed the offices of nature in an effort to establish reason as an operative force in human thinking, doubt still held its ground against all comers. The situation, he reported, became more serious when a formidable body of Skeptics, beginning with Pyrrho and ending with Carneades launched a determined campaign against the entire system of the Aristotelian logic. They seized upon the principle of Zeno that a "thing is understood and perceived as true, when none·of the characteristics of error are found in it," [2] and turned it to good account. But, they argued, there is no knowledge without some notes of error in it; hence, there is no certainty in any given conclusion. Truth is ruled out and argument is futile. Thereupon, Augustine replied that such a discussion refutes itself. The Skeptics pretend to be men of wisdom; yet they deny the possibility of ever attaining accurate knowledge. Check their sullen posture by plying them with such elementary questions as these: *why* does he, the Skeptic, live? *how* does he live? even the shattering query, Does he know that he lives? Further, if he knows nothing he cannot define what knowledge is; thus he contradicts himself when he tells us, he does not know himself or anything else. In fact the very principle by which the Skeptic argues, is a form of logical truth which he accepts, even though he has denied the possibility of all truth. If he is inclined to demur at this kind of rebuttal, he must at least agree that if any judgment may be true or false, he cannot allege its falsity without giving some standing to its opposite, namely, truthfulness. Hence, a disjunctive proposition results, and every disjunctive judgment of the dichotomous form, as this is, is necessarily true. If this fact were rejected, a human being could not tell whether he was a man or an ant, and the very existence of the school of Skeptics would be put in jeopardy at once.

In the face of such destructive potentialities, it is well to state how Augustine proposed to meet the situation. What he wrote in the *Blessed Life,* a work composed at the same time as the one we have just examined, he repeated on many other occasions, notably in the second book of the *Freewill* [3] and in the *Trinity.*[4] He embarks now on the voyage of discovery—Can we find the certainty of truth? The voyage is stormy but the haven is within reach. Certainty of knowledge depends on certainty of

[2] Etienne Gilson, *L'Introduction à l'Etude de St. Augustin*, p. 46.
[3] A. D. 428.
[4] A. D. 400–418. Many of the quotations of Augustine's works are taken from the Schaff's Edition of the "Nicene and Post-Nicene Fathers," English translation.

existence, first for man and then for God. We now come in direct contact
with the argument of Descartes which terminates in the celebrated thesis
—*Cogito ergo sum*. A long and somewhat bitter controversy has emerged
about the original source of that saying. Did Descartes copy it from
Augustine or did they both take it from a common tradition, or is it of
such a nature that, like the primitive customs familiar to anthropologists,
it may have arisen in the same or similar form in almost any cultured
society of the Occident? One fact is undisputed—the analysis of the capacities of the human soul in the two accounts has a likeness in which few
of the salient points are missing. We need not follow the parallel to the
end but interested readers may compare the two works just mentioned
with the second "Meditation" of Descartes. The gist of the argument is
in the question, How does the human being know that he exists? Augustine presents the case by way of a dialectical discussion. The judgment
is valid, but how can it be verified? Is the soul a unit or a multiple? Do
we actually move from one place to another or is motion a mere illusion?
In neither instance is there a clear and distinct idea. But one thing his
respondent states without hesitation,—*he thinks*. That matter being settled,
Augustine can find nothing to contradict it. But, says the Skeptic, suppose
you are deceived; suppose all your pretensions to reality are empty and
vain. What then? Then, he retorts with great and ardent conviction, then
we must exist; for doubt is a form of thought; the very fact of doubt is the
warrant of the actuality of thought. "Even if he doubts, he lives; if he
doubts he remembers why he doubts; if he doubts he wishes to be certain.
Whoever therefore doubts about everything ought not to doubt at all of
these things; which if they were not, he would not be able to doubt of
anything," for he would be without reality of any kind.[5] Gilson has
summed up the situation as follows: "The argument of Augustine is complete, as is attested by his successive points:—the fallacy of the original
Skeptical argument, the incontrovertible evidence for the intelligible nature
of the soul, the firm fact of our consciousness of existence, and the defeat
of the final objection of the Skeptic."[6]

Nor is that the whole story. For all created things are arranged in a
prescribed manner, which Leibniz later adopted in his analysis of nature
—sheer actual being, organic body and the intelligent soul. Man shares
in all of these but he is confident that his true character belongs strictly
to the third. We know things only when we can understand their inherent qualities. How certain are we of the constituent properties of fire
or of any corporeal entity? Since we cannot know them with categorical
exactness, we conclude that they do not belong to us of right. The rule is
that the mind cannot frame the same clear ideas of things not belonging

---

[5] *Trinity*, X, 10.   [6] *Op. cit.*, p. 52.

to its sphere of existence. The image of the fancy is not the same as an idea of reason, as we shall soon see. Hence, the idea is a "kind of true presence" [7] whence all fictitious elements have been removed. The idea is a better substance than the physical image and when we reach the idea of God, it becomes a "kind of likeness of God," although any substance akin to it is not necessarily equal to God's substance. It is true that Augustine does not set the soul in as sharp antithesis to body as Descartes does, which leads the latter to distinguish his use of the famous formula from his predecessor's, while at the same time he denies the charge of plagiarism. Still the main property of soul is the same for both philosophers, namely, conceptual judgment; this will be Augustine's second point in his study of the manner in which knowledge is acquired.

The first point is its relation to the body in which it is lodged. Soul is not coincident with body; for if it were, then it would not be in duty bound to think of it in terms of images conveyed to it by the sense-organs. In his commentary on the book of Genesis Augustine says expressly that the soul does not fill the body as water fills a sponge; on the other hand it gives life to the body through the agency of an immaterial movement; it directs the actions of the body not by the laws of gravity but by the same invisible influence. The marvel is that the soul can receive by perception and hold in memory so great a number of images and of so great variety. The plain fact is that the operation of the senses is, so to say, automatic, in the Greek meaning of the word,—that is, by the instigation of the soul itself. There is here no hint of the intervention of divine power, as the Occasionalist later proposed. Instead, when an external body impinges on the organs of sense, there is an immediate reception of the image by the mind. Here Augustine is also sure that no invisible efflux, as suggested by Democritus, passes from the stimulating body to the body of the observer; nor does the visiting object leave its formal impression upon mind, as the Stoics argued, both suggestions obviously issuing from the contention that body and soul are of the same texture. No; the two substances are distinct and must not be confused. Perception is the result of a conjunction of two causes, the body contributing the image, the soul interpreting its meaning through its own prescriptive laws. But the latter is the supervisory agent, the true "parent" of the image, he says in Book XI of the *Trinity*. For the image becomes a residential element in the memory and if another similar image were never received by the mind the "form and species" of the original could not be effaced. It may be withdrawn for a season, that is, superseded by a multitude of other images, but by main force of will it can be restored to its place whenever occasion requires. The majestic sentences in Book X of the *Confessions* register his profound re-

[7] *Trinity*, X, 15, 16.

spect for this faculty of the human intelligence. It is supplemented by his delineations of the productive imagination, which is able to conjure up "things that were never seen or experienced, either by increasing or decreasing, changing or compounding those images which have not dropped out of its remembrance." [8] Hence, he adopts the principle of Socrates that to "apprehend is not to acquire new ideas but to bring into present view ideas already stored in memory." This does not refer to the hypothesis propounded in the *Phaedo* that the soul is endowed with ideas perceived in a previous existence. For Augustine denied the validity of that theory on the ground that universal ideas have another origin. As against such a suggestion he would endorse the principle which David Hume has stated with great impressiveness, that memory is a major factor in the determination of knowledge.

We have thus far examined the structure of the image and its retention in the mind; we are now ready to examine the second principal point in the acquisition of knowledge, the nature and function of universal ideas. It is probably true to say that up to this point his theory would not differ to any considerable extent from that of an educated observer of our own day, excluding, of course, the fumbling Behaviorist and the pseudo-scientific Gestaltist. From now on, however, the ways of thought will separate. The question before us is, How are universal ideas formed? Such ideas must be distinguished from the concepts which the mind has individually shaped. Every image has its own concept, the seat of its steady qualities, the true expression of its meaning. Such concepts are universal in the sense that when an object in the external world is noted, the appropriate concept rises in the mind to indicate the meaning of the object in the general field of knowledge. But there are broader concepts which have no place in ordinary perception,—number, equality, similarity, motion, beauty, goodness, truth. We cannot call them intuitions brought with us when we enter the sphere of human behavior, as we have just learned. Yet they seem to carry some implications both of the concrete image and the abstract idea. Thus in his study of free will [9] the author distinctly says that the activity of the senses is controlled by an inner sense which joins the contents of the several images into the apprehension of a single individual; this yields the idea of unity. Did he derive the mechanics of the scheme from Aristotle who recognized a sixth sense, an internal energy, which coördinates the delivery of the several senses? He should have known, if he did not, that Plato had already rejected the proposal and substituted for it the principle that when the images reach the ministerium of the mind, they pass beyond the control of sense-action; they are *inside* the jurisdiction of the mind itself. [10] The "common ideas" to which we

[8] *Trinity,* XI, 8.   [9] *Freewill,* II, 10.   [10] *Theaetetus,* 185.

have referred, were the ultimate instruments of thought; they alone could coördinate the essential elements in the concrète concept and establish its place in the whole body of knowledge. Thus, while concepts were universal by virtue of their enumerated applications in daily experience, the ideas were universal because they had been *impressed* on the mind by the agency of superior wisdom; they bear the signature of divine authority.

This is the Augustinian doctrine of Illumination, a conceit suggested by the doctrine of inspiration in the Christian Church. Its service is twofold; it tells us how we must prove the truth of any judgment, it also shows us why we should prefer one judgment rather than another. How, for example, shall we determine what is just in the practical situation before us? It cannot be determined from an examination of the idea of justice as we have found it expressed in historical events. This is the Socratic method, deducing the idea from a group of similar conditions, after an hypothetical definition has been assumed. Such a method may be effective in civil society, where a compromise program has oftentimes to be accepted. Augustine, no doubt, went back to his studies of Neo-Platonist ethics, which divided virtues into two groups, the civil and the ecstatic; the latter could be attained only by men of superlative achievements. He did not, however, suggest that some strange ontological change occurred in the nature of the mind; the Apostles might lay claim to that, the ordinary believer could not. In fact, so Augustine argues, illumination does not deal with the content of the ideas but with their regulative value in discovering the meaning of truth.[11] Like St. Paul in the Epistle to the Romans, he reminds us that even men who have not come under the influence of Christian thinking "rightly praise and rightly blame many things in the moral life of man." They have glimpsed the meaning of certain lofty ideas not excogitated by human genius but found only, he says, in the "book of light which is called truth, from which every righteous law is copied and by which righteous men have pursued their true way of life."[12] All these facts melt at length into one conclusion, that the fundamental laws of thought afford unmistakable evidence of the existence of a supreme Being.

This, then, is the significance of universal ideas. They are necessary, they are immutable, they are eternal. They belong to no particular country, age, or group of men; they belong only to God. They have no resemblance to the Timaean Ideas which exist apart from the divine nature and are used, one by one, by the Demiurge as he creates the world. They are not identical with the Logoi of Plotinus which, emanating from the divine substance bring its energy to bear upon the production of individual souls. They are embodied in Truth which is unitary and all-

[11] Gilson, *op. cit.*, p. 124.   [12] *Trinity*, XIV, 21.

comprehensive, just as in the human sphere virtue is one and all-controlling. Truth is an independent essence, it is God himself; and it is the constituent factor in everything God has created or will create. Small wonder that in the course of time the doctrine of metaphysical Realism becomes the official canon of the church. It must not, however, be assumed that the Augustinian theory of ideas was the permanent statement of the psychology of the church. The theory was challenged by none other than the Angelic Doctor himself, who, steeped in the logical method of Aristotle, rejected this theory without reservation. The mind of man is, indeed, a divine creation and the universal ideas developed there will have ample sanctions behind them. But they must come into possession of the mind through the regular channels of thought, not by some mysterious look upon divine reality. Aristotle taught that while we cannot discover all the essential properties of the sensible world by perceptual observation we can supplement such a process by the "sufficient light," in the words of Thomas, "which falling upon our intellect, gives us full acquaintance with the fundamental laws of judgment." [13] These "preformed seeds," to change the figure of speech, constitute the principles of all scientific knowledge. They are hidden from us, so long as we are without sensible experience, but the power to form them lies indefectibly in the soul. Furthermore, they differ from the usual deductive conclusions largely because they are remoter from actual experience and therefore harder to reach. The time required to grasp their form and assimilate their meaning increases in proportion to the complexity of the thought, but they serve precisely the same purpose as those formulated by Augustine in his theory of Illumination.

THE EXISTENCE OF GOD

Turning then specifically to the question of divine existence we note that Augustine rejects emphatically the system of the Stoics, which has no Deity except what they find in the sensible order of the world. He criticizes the theory of Plotinus on the ground that God is removed so far from the field of human intuition that no real appreciation of his nature can be obtained. There God was a barren and colorless unity, not an Object which human affection could understand and embrace. Clearly the Christian Bishop will be satisfied with nothing less than a Reality whose presence can be verified by due process of thought. Revelation supports the decision by an anticipatory faith, but he insists on amassing the positive proofs before setting in motion the saving offices of religion. The first proof already offered—that universal truths have the sanctions of divine wisdom behind them—is valuable but it is not complete; he seems

[13] E. Gilson, *Philosophy of St. Thomas Aquinas* (Cambridge: Heffer, 1924), p. 230.

to be suspicious of its ultimate validity; it may be that some of the criticisms we have just mentioned lurked within the premises of his argument. Still we should not pass it by without obtaining a correct understanding of its terms. It begins with the thesis that we must have a known and assured reality upon which we can firmly take our stand; this reality is the existence of our own soul arrived at in the manner already indicated. In examining the natural capacities of the soul we find two distinguishable elements, sensation and cogitation. Obviously, the latter is superior, for it can receive the various data of experience, *species,* the Schoolmen called them, and by comparing them with previous images tell precisely what they mean. There is, however, a function still higher than this, a function of mind which separates the concept from its sensory origins and gives it a permanent and universal character. As we have already noted, Augustine called every universal idea an expression of wisdom, a reality over and above the deliverances of the senses. But is there no reality beyond the universal idea? The question is discussed in the second Book of the treatise on *Freewill.* Two answers are given, first, God, then, Truth; finally, they come together in a concrete Reality. Truth is always the subject of a judgment, the registration of a law. Thus, seven and three make ten, they always do; we never say, they *should* make ten; in the sequence of numbers the rule is invariably valid, it is an immutable fact in the sphere of mathematical existences. In like manner, says Augustine, there are immutable rules of wisdom, for example, happiness is certain to come to men of goodwill. Such laws are judgments arrived at by intelligent mind and applied to every situation where the several terms appear. At this point the argument begins to waver. For the idea of God is not a judgment deduced from comparable experience; it is a conception lying ready-made, so to say, in conscious mind; it is said to correspond to an Object beyond any of the types of existence already accepted as real, but unlike them it is necessary, immutable and eternal. How can the Idea of God, because it is present in the mind, be referred to the external Object of which no sensory intuition can be obtained? Or, in the Augustinian system, how can the truth of the universal ideas in the human mind be guaranteed by the power of the divine mind whose existence we cannot establish by any logical argument? The mere fact that we have such ideas would not suggest, of themselves, the Reality of a higher authority justifying their existence, if we did not first have the idea of God. Here we have a preview of the famous Ontological proof which Anselm will expound centuries later, in his *Proslogium* and whose inadequacy Kant will expose in his epoch-making *Critique.* Does the idea of a Supreme Being, the *Ens realissimum,* having all possible attributes, carry with it the idea of necessary existence? This is the central question that must be answered.

But Augustine gives no detailed and convincing answer to this question; in fact, this is not the point he is discussing in the passage cited. He is attempting there to institute a hierarchy of substances terminating in an infinite substance called God. The attempt is not solitary in the history of philosophy; it was adopted, in part, by John Locke when he framed the method by which the human mind could add, point to point, number to number, space to space, magnitude to magnitude and eventually arrive at the concept of infinity. "We have no clear idea of infinity but what carries with it some reflection on, and imitation of, that number and extent of the acts or objects of God's power, wisdom and goodness, which can never be supposed so great or so many which these attributes will not always surmount and exceed, let us multiply them in our thoughts as far as we can." [14] The hierarchy here concerns the divine nature taken by itself; in Augustine it refers to all substances both finite and infinite. But the effort of the imagination is the same: can we proceed from a given set of facts necessarily limited in form, to their final conception, where limits are removed and the majesty of unobstructed substance is opened to our thought? What we must not fail to note is that, for Augustine as for Locke, the reality thus unfolded is a conceit of human fancy, the construct of a cogitative mind, and nothing more. The ontological proof fails in this form as in every other, but the efforts of succeeding ages to reduce it to a logical verity goes on apace, based on the assumption that religion cannot exist without a recognized Object worthy of man's reverence and devotion.

But why should we assume that God exists when the passage from the idea in mind to the external Reality is so difficult to follow? Augustine now returns to the ancient formula that what is universally believed must have an existential basis. It would be an affront to human experience, if we deliberately excluded from acceptance one of its most seasoned judgments. What are the facts respecting the belief in a divine Reality? Careful investigation shows that here and there a man or body of men have steadily maintained an atheistic attitude, even in societies that had developed a high grade of culture. In some cases, as with the Stoics, the existence of Deity is admitted but the properties imputed to it are wholly different from those espoused by the Christian. In other cases the rejection of the idea springs from a deliberate defiance of all superior authority. "The fool hath said in his heart, There is no God," and Holy Writ has added that such a confession has its roots in moral debasement, an utter disregard of the loftier sentiments of human aspirations.[15] Augustine calls such reflection pure fallacy (*aperta insania*), the loss of every principle that constitutes a sane and healthy soul. His conclusion was that every man be-

[14] *Essay*, II, Ch. 19. [15] Psalms, 14, 1.

lieves *naturally* in the Supreme Being. When asked whether he would commit an unbeliever to condign punishment, making no attempt to restore him to grace and honor, he answered that he would instruct him in the teachings of those who personally knew the Lord of Glory as witnessed by their messages in the canonical Scriptures.

However, we are still dealing with a common belief, not a philosophically accredited truth; how can we change the one into the other? When we examine the idea of the *Ens realissimum,* a phrase already in use among Christian scholars in the 4th century, do we find that it includes the predicate of existence? Or may it be treated as any other idea whose indicated object, because it is contingent in character, can only obtain existence when a group of suitable conditions are present? Augustine's answer is explicit; the idea of God cannot be entertained as an article of faith without at the same time affirming his existence. He did not stop to analyze the fallacy in the premise, *if* he saw it. The conception of God without reality is impious and absurd. God must exist or the aspirations of the race would be nullified. But the proof, if proof it be, is not left in an analytical vacuum. The law of contradiction is now supported by the principle of sufficient reason, as Leibniz called it. The judgment is no longer analytic, the predicate repeating what is involved in the definition of the subject; it is synthetic; it reflects the experience of the thinker in his observation of the natural world. Hellenism and Christianity occupy common ground here; they note the order, beauty, purposiveness of nature and agree that a universal cause is at work. But they disagree as to the character of the causal process. For the Greek, motion, an intrinsic and inseparable function of the world, is the sole explanation; a Deity of overwhelming power and wisdom is the fundamental premise of Augustine. He is not content with the unceasing peregrinations of the stars; he yearns for a more intimate knowledge of the principle of harmony which Plato introduced into his world, a principle that Plato seemed to associate with life but really did not. But there is life, there is intelligence, there is goodness in the universe, and these do not derive from incogitative matter; there Locke was right. Virtue is bound up with a summum bonum, a standard of action which could only be found in a world contrived and governed by an intelligent God. All the noble traits which our civilization has developed, especially since the foundation of the Christian Church, bespeak the presence of a benevolent Overseer as powerful as he is good.

These are objective facts and they demand an explanation. It is obvious that the achievements of the human race in virtuous behavior cannot find their cause in civil government, however wise be the statesmanship that guides it; nor in the logic of ethical creeds, whether or not they be supported by the scientific discoveries of the ages; nor in the sheer energy of human personality great as has been its influence in historic emergencies. Thus the cosmological proof in its widest sweep—motion, life, intelligence, morals, social progress—seeks a creative cause adequate to the manifold reality. The judgment, we said, is synthetic, it deals with objective existences; it ushers in the principle of causality which is strictly empirical and ties it to the being of the infinite God. The logical imprecision of the argument may or may not have been patent to the eye of the author; he may or may not have entertained the notion that the original idea of God does not contain the relation of cause and effect; it certainly did not contain the attribute of a complete actual cause as disinguished from the potential causes at work in the objective world. Hence, if the relation of cause and effect be injected, its validity must be proved, and the validity can be guaranteed solely by a preliminary acceptance of the attribute of causality for which, however, no logical support can be adduced. Augustine may have been aware of the difficulty or he may not; one thing is certain that he is not concerned with the rules of logic but with the dictates of commonsense, which reinforced by the revelations of Holy Writ, establish the trustworthiness of the creed that God made the world and all that therein is; hence, he exists!

There is another aspect of the case which, in modern times, Descartes has brought to the notice of the learned world. Was there in the ancient version of the *Ens realissimum* a hint that the name of God contained the essential principle of Power? The Hebrew word, *I am that I am,* might easily bear such an interpretation. The Greek terms for Deity always suggested the right to rule, hence, to exercise force either physical or spiritual. In his First Response to the Objections alleged against his defense of the Ontological proof, he argued that we "can only think God's existence to be possible, if at the same time we have in mind his infinite power; for God can exist only by his own power; hence, we must conclude that he really exists and that he has existed from all eternity." As M. Etienne Gilson [16] remarks, the allegation has a "sybilline" tone; it indicates that power is to be the middle term between existence and perfection; that if we grant infinite power to God as an intrinsic element in his character, existence must at once result. It changes the idea of God from having a static necessity, which belongs to logic, to a dynamic causality which belongs to perfect existential reality. Clearly such an interpretation finds no place in Augustine's discussions; it is far too technical for him. However, if he had been able to envisage the idea of God in a dynamic form like this, he would have clarified his philosophical thought and made the idea of God more effective as an apologetic instrument for the communication

[16] E. Gilson, *Etudes sur le role de la Pensée Medievale dans la Formation de system Cartesien* (Paris: Vrin, 1930), Chaps. 3, 5.

of Christian doctrine to the mind of the learned world. To be sure there are implications in the revised formula which might have startled later theologians. For if God is eternal cause, he is the necessary Cause of himself, *sui causa,* the phrase adopted by Spinoza which brought the maledictions of the church upon his head. The chief difficulty he would have had to face is this: Can cause ever be identical with its effect? Is the universe another name for God? Bruno had no trouble in answering it though with calamitous results; to men of an earlier century it would have meant intellectual agony and possible death.

THE NATURE OF GOD

Given the reality of the divine Being, can we succeed in disentangling the attributes which rightly belong to so comprehensive a nature? The procedure followed by Augustine is adequate for his time. Apparently he did not turn to the Greek fathers for guidance; he did not understand sufficiently well the language in which they wrote; and he unquestionably was out of sympathy with the almost artificial forms in which they clothed their ideas. He himself had given earnest thought to the type of thinking developed on African soil, in which he had deliberately steeped his mind in his earlier studies. He turned to the philosophy of Alexandria for suggestion, not so much for content as for the mode of developing his argument. Hence, it is a fair question to ask, to what extent and in what points, the bishop deliberately used his knowledge of Neo-Platonism in presenting his case in defense of the Christian doctrine. M. Grandgeorge,[17] a careful and conscientious scholar, has examined the many quotations from Porphyry and Plotinus appearing in his authentic writings and answers that there is clear evidence of his sympathetic use of their materials. Besides making the actual citations Augustine also evinces a profound and accurate acquaintance with the general attitude of the school; he established a remarkable series of resemblances between the theories found in the *Enneads* and some of the capital doctrines of the new religion; and finally he paid a glowing tribute to the genius and ability of the Alexandrian thinkers. Since the concept of God stands at the head of the philosophical thought of Plotinus as it does in the dogmas of Christianity, it is proper that we should begin our inquiry at that point. Neither Plotinus nor Augustine tried to work out a complete argument for the existence of God; they simply took the fact for granted. But with the reality of Deity plainly before us we are confronted with the duty of discovering, if we can, his significant attributes. Plotinus seemed doubtful of success at the very start, for he held that God had no properties which the logical categories of the human mind could explain. Augustine, on the other hand, was

[17] *St. Augustin et le Neo-Platonisme.*

not so easily discouraged. He admitted that man had neither the thought nor the language capable of setting forth the "ineffable majesty of the divine character." "We cannot even speak of God; what wonder is it that we cannot comprehend him? for if we could comprehend him he would not be God." [18] The wisest of men like Plato, although they knew not his true essence, could yet envisage the creative genius of God as of the "only God whom the poverty of human speech can by any accommodation understand." [19]

But if we cannot adequately tell what God is we can at least say what he is not. Plotinus was in entire agreement with this principle, since the general Greek tendency was to refer to supreme substance in terms of nega-tion. In a remarkable passage in *Trinity* (V., 2), Augustine enumerates some of the negative properties. We should attempt to contemplate God as "good without quality, great without quantity, creating but not under constraint, dominant but without ordered ranks, sustaining all things but having no existence as they do, everywhere present but not in space, eternal but timeless, producing change but being changeless himself, feeling but without passion—we must think nothing of him that he is not." There is a singular affinity here with the description of Plotinus. Divine unity has nothing to do with spatial conditions; it is not a residuum remaining after all constituent properties have been removed. It could not, there-fore, be explained as a mathematical unity by which Pythagoras begins his number series; nor could it be interpreted as a logical unity following Plato's lead in his system of ideas. What is the One of Plotinus? It is a single and indivisible substance, if substance it be, with which no per-ceptible substance can be compared. It stands at the apex of reality, the first in the immaterial trinity, the others being ideas and souls. Augustine gave sanction at once to this conception of God, a conception that seemed to him unimpeachable. God is one, not many,—"the Lord our God is one Lord." Thus, God is simple, uncomposed, not determinable as man is by specific qualities. Being simple he cannot be divided, that is, he is im-mutable, a conceit to which the author returns again and yet again. "In Thee rest the causes of all unstable, contingent things; but the Origin of things that change, himself remains the same," as he says in his *Confessions* (I., Chap. 6). God is also immutable in his duration; time and dates and intervals are alien to him. Again, he is changeless in his Presence; matter is partly in the heavens, partly on the earth; but wherever God is he is always undivided being,—"the whole is in the heavens and on the earth." Finally God is changeless in his essence which is revealed in its three

---

[18] Augustine. Sermon 117. *Library of the Father: St. Augustine. Homilies of the New Testament* (Oxford: J. H. Parker, 1845), II, 487.
[19] *City of God,* IX, 10.

coördinate aspects or "persons," a sovereign Spirit, a Trinity, and yet a sublime Unity. Compare these observations with the words of Plotinus in the *Enneads* (VI., 5), and the likeness is so close as to make us think that it was designed: "That one principle single in number and identical in thought should be present without a break, is a conception cognate to the intelligence of man. For it says that God who dwells in us and in all things is one and the same God."

Thus far the delineation by both thinkers is negative. The term unity though positive in form is in its implications negative. It places God, the undetermined, the infinite, above the determinate substances of the world, —ideas, souls, and the individualized forms of the created universe. As Grandgeorge says, "All things originate in him and are necessarily impressed with his nature." [20] Here enter the positive characters of Deity. God is *good,* and it is this attribute which is incorporated in the system of the entire universe, both logos and soul and the organized world of things. Let us understand the meaning of the word. Good is a term of capital importance in Greek philosophy. In its simplest form it means the maintenance of the kind to which the object belongs; a good *coin* as the medium of exchange is a piece of money bearing the stamp of a responsible and solvent government; a good *horse* is an animal of sound physical fibre properly trained to do a certain kind of work. A good *man* is not an expert carpenter or efficient executive but a man of sound character and trustworthy deportment. Hence, the chief good, the summum bonum in ethics, is the standard of judgment by which the moral conduct is to be gauged. So Aristotle defined it. But Plato had, before him, attached a deeper significance to the term as we have already noted. [21] The idea of the Good was the consummatory term in logic, the differentia by which every concept was to be judged. In general, the Good is the principle by means of which order and harmony are established in the physical universe and in the thought of man, especially as developed in his civil commonwealth. Plotinus takes Plato's definition and applies it to supreme substance. God puts his Good, that is, his energy into all his emanations, ultimately into the created world. This does not imply that God has the "seeds" of the new order within his own nature; that would make him a party to the material constitution of the world, an unthinkable proposition. No, says Plotinus, God puts his *power* not his essence into his emanations. What can this mean but that the abstract unity of God is really the seat of living, operating, organizing power to be revealed in due time in ways that could be understood and emulated?

Does Augustine hesitate to follow his mentor in this speculative venture? Consult again the volume on the Trinity (VIII., 3), and observe how

---

[20] *Op. cit.,* p. 82.   [21] *Supra,* Ch. II.

he adopts the very wording of the Greek: "This thing is good and that is good; but take away both and fix your eyes on the Good itself, if you can. Then you will behold God, not the good made good by something other than itself, but the Good of all goods. For we cannot know what a good thing is until we have discovered the idea of the Good itself. That which is to be discerned is God, not a particular good, but the Good itself." It is on such a foundation that Augustine rests his teaching respecting the positive attributes of Deity. We may sum it up by saying that Good means the supreme and perfect purposes by which the divine nature is represented to believers. What then must we include in these purposes, and in what manner shall they be expressed?

The joint tradition of Greece and Judah divides the powers of the human mind into three groups, intellect, emotion, and will. Such a trinity of powers reflects the Trinity of the divine essence. It may be that Windelband's conclusion [22] is not far from the mark though it must be taken with some reserve: God is absolute Personality only in the sense that he fulfills the Greek principle of Actuality, the sublimation of the ideas associated with the three functions named. Some of the Church fathers, notably Cyril of Alexandria, assumed that the Trinity of Plotinus and that of the new religion were in substantial agreement. There is, however, at least one point in which they are at sharp variance: the Christian Trinity regards the three persons as consubstantial, the other subordinates the third to the first two. The supreme Personality, God, moves majestically through the entire drama of thought and experience, but the three aspects are carefully distinguished. The divine intellect is the medium of knowledge and knowledge is both universal and particular, although the latter has been contested by some theologians. In Augustine's system God knows the past, the present and the future with complete certitude: his wisdom is commanding and comprehensive. He foreknew, for one thing, the incidence of the Fall though his will gave no causative assent to it. He also knows what souls shall be saved from the moral wreckage of the world. But, says the author, "not in our fashion does he look forward to the future, but in a manner far different from our way of thinking." For in the divine mind time is not a factor, hence foreknowing is not the same as historical prediction. Matters of fact are turned by God into truths of reason. His promises of eternal life to believing souls were uttered before ever the world came into being. All these considerations are embodied in the familiar saying of Jesus: "It is not for you to know the times or the seasons which the Father hath put in his own hands."

If the intellectual powers are subject to no limitations, neither are the

[22] Windelband, *The History of Philosophy.* Trans. by J H. Tufts (New York: Macmillan, 1926), p. 279.

emotional habitudes. The modulus of the Christian revelation is written in the imperishable maxim, God is love. The marvels of that love are exhibited, says Augustine, in the life and death of Jesus of Nazareth. Here heaven and earth are joined, even as the Neo-Platonic trinity united the two in the second hypostasis, the soul, which gives individuality to its object. But the Alexandrian union has nothing comparable to the law of sacrifice which led to redemption. It does provide for a providential oversight in the affairs of men, but the thesis that the captive soul might be ransomed by the divine payment of the bond, was a conceit quite foreign to the uncultured mind. It has been alleged that the Fifth Book of the *Enneads* enshrines the conception that the divine Word, the emanated Logos, was "made flesh," as John represents the incarnation in his Gospel. The exact language is as follows: "The intelligible world possesses a universal power which penetrates everything without exhausting its infinite power. Its ideas are the archetypes, the models of all things, being at the same time the ground and cause of all sensible things." St. Paul's rhapsodical sentences in *Colossians* (Ch. I. 12–15), appear to anticipate the thought and even the verbal forms of Plotinus: "Who [i.e., Christ] is the image of the invisible God, the first-born of every creature. For by him all things were created that are in heaven and in the earth. . . . For it pleased the Father that in him all fulness should dwell." Obviously, the source of much of the Alexandrian speculation is in the inspired writings of the New Testament. Hence, Augustine is not the co-exponent of an inadequate philosophy but, so to say, the official expositor of the Apostolic theme in his own day and generation. It is noteworthy that in the passage just quoted St. Paul is careful to support the metaphysical statement of his creed by a reference to the historical splendor of the cross by which spiritual peace comes to men's hearts and the final reconciliation of heaven and earth is guaranteed. Neo-Platonism has no place for a theme like that; its logic and its ethics require a wholly different solution.

Finally, God is will, always for Augustine the consummatory principle of spiritual energy. The temper of Roman jurisprudence is registered in his discussion of the relations of God and man. The will of God like the will of the state cannot be defeated. "It is true," he says in the *City of God* (p. 480), "that wicked men do many things contrary to the will of God; but so great is his will and power that all things that seem adverse to his power still tend towards those just and good ends which he himself has foreknown." To go one step further: the will of God cannot be changed. The language of Sacred Writ indicating forebearance or repentance on God's part, is merely an accommodation to the reader's limited intelligence. If men cannot detect the execution of his commands, that is not due to the failure or obscuration of God's plans but to the restricted scope of human observation. For the will of God is spiritually communicated by his inward messenger, the third member of the Holy Trinity.

Augustine is not at all clear in his treatment of this important doctrine. The New Testament, itself, does not present in any single passage a synoptic view of the entire problem. It may be that, here again, the Latin Father found himself involved in the intricate dialectics of the Greek inquisitors. For the practical mind of the Latin the office of the Spirit had executive value only. Thus Augustine was profoundly impressed with the record of the Acts of the Apostles when by divine guidance they abandoned their native tongues and spoke in languages hitherto unknown to them. The functions of the Paraclete as detailed in John's Gospel, made direct and conclusive appeal to his legalistic mind: "He will convict the world of sin, of righteousness, and of judgment to come." The third person or hypostasis of the Trinity is the official instrument of the divine will; he stimulates the sense of duty in human hearts and drives them to action. Does the third hypostasis of the Neo-Platonic trinity have kindred functions? Its primary purpose is to awaken in souls a desire for individuality. Plotinus calls it the "soul of the world"; it "runs like a flame" through every embodied soul of whatever grade or rank. It brings intelligible substances, that is, Ideas, into contact with gross and impure matter, the *Hule* of the Greeks, matter as yet untouched by spiritual conceits. But there is no hint in the whole Alexandrian system of the central thought in the Christian creed, man's sin and his need of redemption. Further, there is no effort to lift the third hypostasis from its subsidiary position in the Trinity and make it equal to the other two. To be sure, a mighty controversy raged in the church on this very subject: Did the Spirit proceed from the Father alone or from both the Father and the Son? The Eastern church inclined to the former, the Latin church to the latter. For the Europe of the West the matter was settled in 1054 when the Roman See and all its retainers broke with the Eastern churches, once and for all, by choosing to support the second interpretation. This is today the dogma of the Roman church: it is also the common creed of the Evangelical communions. Had Augustine formed a stable opinion on the subject? It is doubtful; for in his *Faith and the Creed* (Sec. 19–20), he admits that "competent scholars had not yet reached an intelligent conception of what constituted the *proprium* or individuality of the Holy Spirit." But he assumes that the Christian teacher should emphasize the reality of the Trinity, whatever may be the proportional relations of its members.

There are two points where the omnipotent will is completely revealed, first in the creation of the world, and secondly, in the providential treatment of human interests.

The first of these presents a question which has never failed to excite warm debate among speculative thinkers. Two alternatives are always open, either the world had no origin or it was produced in some manner and by some agency. The Milesian pioneers argued that there existed a single causal factor such as water or air from which all others were derived or that an indeterminate substance was already in existence and from its elements by various forms of evolution the present cosmos was constituted. Against both of these Augustine set his face like a flint. The world, he argued, is the product of God's wisdom; it came into being by the word of his power. But he was not concerned to answer the question whether God made the world out of nothing or out of his own spiritual substance; rather was he concerned to silence the objection so often made: Why, at the creation, did God turn from a purely immaterial reality to one where sensible matter appeared with all the sinister influences that flowed from it? The reply is direct and as he thought, cogent. The design of the universe is a reflection of the goodness of the divine nature. Even Plato, he intimated, was convinced that "God could not be rendered more blessed by the novelty of his creation." For divine wisdom "beholds all things without the shadow of a change in his being . . . everything past or future is comprehended in his own stable and eternal present." To these judgments Augustine gives his cordial assent. He also thinks that objects which seem to us inadequate or hurtful have a suitable place in the divine economy, such as drugs that are poisonous when injudiciously used but have medicinal virtue when given at the right time and in the right amounts. We shall return to this matter later.

The second point where the omnipotent will is exerted is what, for religious people, goes under the name of divine providence. Is it true that at certain critical moments in the career of man or nation an influence other than that which is strictly psychical emerges from the confusion of ideas and events, to mark out a new course different from any hitherto pursued? The entire volume of the *City of God* teems with allusions to a theme which may be condensed into a single sentence: "God can never be believed to have left the kingdoms of men, their dominions and their enslavements, outside the laws of his providence" (V., 11). The subject-matter of the book is not organized with the systematic precision of an Aristotle, but all the ingredients of the new dogmatics are present in his record. It is the custom of careful scholars like Dr. Martensen, the Danish theologian, to distinguish sharply between *providentia generalis* and *providentia specialis,* the former conceiving of nature as the primary object of divine activity, the latter exhibiting in the historical progress of the race the various instances of God's protecting care. The *City of God* offers a new and original meaning for the term providence. The tenseness and inflexibility of the Stoic concept disappear from sight;

the fear of an implacable Fate is displaced by the feeling that love and sympathy have now written their ingratiating syllables into the word. Providence means order, regularity, the emblem of a stable and vigorous will. But it also conveys the thoughts and purposes of a benevolent Father. Yet it does not follow that because God has established a certain fixed order for all courses, there is no place for the exercise of the private will of the creature.[23] Human wills are causes and belong to the chain of causes, and God acts always in accordance with the prescribed order. Augustine denounces the theory introduced by the Deists of his day that after God had fabricated the world according to plans he withdrew into eternal silence and left the world to shift for itself. The will of God is sovereign but as Mr. Cochrane aptly says, it is not "Caesarian; it is not physical uniformity, it is not autocratic control." [24] On this subject the conviction of the author was precise: "God's dominion, his providential activity is constitutional, it bespeaks a government that recognises the rights of individuals and intends to base its decrees on the principle of universal benevolence." [25] So much for a providence that is universal.

We must next attempt to ascertain the author's opinion on a more difficult subject: how God exercises his will in particular ways, especially in the development of moral character. There is one case, we may as well admit, where the principle of providence, in the Christian meaning of the term, goes unheeded. Evil men pursue careers abounding in creature comforts, crowned with material success, laureled with social honors; how shall we reconcile our minds to the concept that moral excellence and physical rewards never meet in a suitable equation? In such situations, Augustine thinks, we must regard the triumphs of wicked men as strictly parasitic; they thrive as a growing plant in winter and wither away in the heat of summer. Corrupt minds cannot endure the terrors of defeat, while believers see in such a condition the evidence of divine testing. For life in the body is not the summation of the good man's career, it passes into eternity. This is what Renan in his *History of Israel* calls the solace of weakness; it has been a powerful incentive to perseverance in the slow advance of the Christian faith against bitter and stubborn opposition. It has generated strong characters amid unpropitious circumstances. But whether a process which has had its place in *every* type of civilization should receive the name of providential when it appears in Christian experience, is a question which must be answered by the individual or his particular group. The question is even more vexing if we seek to read the great events of history as separate integers in the unfolding of a divine drama. "The greatness of the Roman Empire is not to be ascribed to chance

---

[23] *City of God*, VII, 30.   [24] *Christianity and Classical Culture*, p. 442.
[25] *City of God*, XII, 26.

or fate but to the joint will of God and man by the necessity of a certain order." [26] In fact all human dominion is directed by the same serene intelligence. The essence of successful government is the acquisition and maintenance of peace. Peace on earth is the conscious and perpetual concern of contributing wills, in the family, in the community, in the civil state, in the intercourse of nations. Both in social contacts and in religious thought there can be peace without frustration; but there cannot be frustration without some elements of peace. War carries in its own bosom the demand for peace, and peace thus entailed will foreshadow a *pax serena,* a permanent state of conformity to law and civil harmony. It is this kind of providence which later theologians termed *immanent,* because its very regularity gives no hint of the secret operation of divine power.

But if divine power was immanent it was also, as Martensen would say, transcendent. In this case the path of history is interrupted suddenly and perhaps completely, as the supernatural Will breaks forth in a commanding manipulation resembling a "flash of lightning which shineth from one part of the heavens to the other." Providence now is a cataclysmic force which overtakes a crumbling civilization and exposes the insufficiency of its resources. It is in this light that Augustine interpreted the critical events of 410 A.D., when Alaric led his hordes of Visigoths against the Imperial city and sacked it. Rome fell, and the doom of its errors and crimes settled upon its broken walls and devastated churches. "And these be the gods," exclaimed the Christian seer, "to whose protecting care the Romans were delighted to entrust their city." [27] Historical ingenuity has been at work for centuries disentangling the causal threads woven together to accomplish this end. Some said that by the Cycle theory the time of Rome's decease was come, and no power in heaven or earth could have thwarted it. Others held that the Christian church had laid its corroding fangs upon the fair culture and sapped its life-blood. In Augustine's view one plain malignant fact explained its collapse—Rome had sinned against the eternal God, sinned grievously, sinned deliberately, when truth was within her gates. "Vengeance is mine, I will repay, saith the Lord." Whether the inquiry of a scientific mind, untouched by the same religious fervor, would arrive at the same conclusion, we shall not venture to decide. "The greatness of Rome" says Gibbon, quoting an ancient writer (Ammianus), "was founded on the rare, and almost incredible, alliance of virtue and fortune. At length, verging towards old age, and sometimes conquering by the terror only of her name, she sought the blessings of ease and tranquillity." The rest is written in her bitter history.

But there is another side to the picture of divine providence, which portrays in letters of golden light a Fact supreme in human history, the revela-

---

[26] *Ibid.,* V, 1.   [27] *Ibid.,* I, 3.

tion of grace in the person and work of the divine Son. The Incarnation is an event of surpassing significance. It takes its place in the economy of nature as a "new form of miracle greater than the miracle of nature itself." It registers its power in the restoration of the soul of man to its pristine glory destroying the inherited guilt of his transgression. It erects in the world a new kind of moral society, a community parallel with the civil state but excelling it in nobility of purpose and strength of character. It does not, however, try to undermine the foundations upon which the social state is built; rather does it seek to turn the political legalities into the order and harmony of a kingdom of love. As God is one, so shall the visible community be one. Before his enraptured vision Augustine descried the resplendent program of man's salvation. Stagnation, recession, then progress will be the changing aspects of the church's life but the governing temper remains the same,—one Lord, one faith, one victory.

THE MEANING OF EVIL

Victory suggests a struggle and struggle means the presence and sinister power of an enemy against which we must throw the weight of our natural and acquired skills. The Scriptural name of the enemy is sin which, in theological language, is revolt against the commands of a superior Being. All philosophical systems recognize the element of evil in the best of worlds. The modern thinker will tell us that there are at least three distinct forms, metaphysical evil, identical with the contingency of the created world; an organic evil, usually referred to as pain; and moral or spiritual evil, divergence from a norm accepted as true. For Augustine the evil of the human heart is by all odds the most significant. What does it denote, what effect does it have upon human behavior, how shall we conquer its insidious influences? These are the questions which he now seeks to answer. We begin with the first.

"Whatever is, is good," says Augustine in his *Confessions* (VII. 12). "Any thing evil whose genesis I have sought is not a substance. For a substance exists and hence is good. And substance is either incorruptible, the highest good, that is, God, or corruptible which, however, could not be corrupted if it were not itself first good." The problem of evil is thus placed squarely before his readers in the year 400, fourteen years after his conversion. It was not his first attempt to analyze and define this concept. Ten years before the crucial event he had submitted himself as an auditor to the instruction of the Manicheans and had endeavored to find an answer to the question, What is evil? The answer he obtained was simple though it raised more doubts than it dispersed. Substance has two forms, positive and negative, the one good, the other evil, distinguished by the terms light and darkness. Each has its autonomous "kingdom" and its accepted head, respectively, God and the Devil, diabolos. Yet the powers of each are so authentic and so inflexible that though their borders may overlap, each may trespass on the other's domain only at serious cost to himself. The difficulties become formidable after the creation of man, who possesses the elements of both in his character. The spiritual and the sensual are continually in conflict, and at times it seemed that the ascetic triumphs of the Manichean saint would bring a blush of shame to the Christian's face who wanted to escape from the sting of sin but could not. It is no doubt true that Mani had borrowed some of his most striking metaphors from the Biblical record, converting them into historical facts. The contest between Christ and Satan in the desert exposes the natural antagonism of the two substances. The conclusion is fixed and final: evil is an actual force in human society whose origin none could discover and whose moral strategy none could defeat. The program of the school rejected with disdain the church's assumption that sin had originated in the free choice of a rational being and could only be eliminated by a divine decree. Manicheanism taught that evil might be discarded by man through the charms of the Gnosis as communicated by the word or example of the elect, though success is always doubtful. No permanent victory has ever been won by either side.

Against the claims of this school Augustine set up two arguments, the first having to do with the definition of evil, the second with its origin in the experience of the race. Evil, says the Bishop, is the privation of good. The nature of created substance cannot be the same as that of divinity itself. Plotinus agreed that the finite could only be the image of the infinite, a shadow, a reflection of immutable substance: "imitation is like the portrait drawn by the painter or the image seen in unperturbed water, the representation of the personal form." The physical universe is a beautiful and brilliant reproduction of the ideal deities, an accurate *eidolon* of the intelligible world. The image can never be the exact equivalent of reality; so Plato argued that the basic Idea is the true substance, its reflection only being found in the concrete object or a work of art. The sensible world cannot have perfection, it is distinctly inferior to eternal reality. Since evil means the absence of the good, it can have no reality of its own. Divine harmony has come into contact with physical necessity, and necessity has pushed the world into the non-rational, or evil. Hence, created substance is the mingling of ideal order and "dark empty space," which is the negation of good and thus the objectification of evil. Whenever ugliness which is the contradiction of the beautiful lifts its sinister figure in nature or art, it is overwhelmed by the effulgence of light, the Idea, streaming through the interstices of the beautiful body. So far Plotinus.

Augustine has written these principles into the articles of his religious creed. He accepts the thesis that created body is a poor copy of its divine original. "All natures have a rank and species of their own. Those that are not eternal are altered for better or worse, to suit the needs and purposes of the objects which they serve." [28] For this reason sensible things which are derived from nothing have a contingency, that is, liability to error, for which the Creator cannot be blamed. For evil is an accident, as Plotinus conceded, a necessary accident in a contingent world; but like the ugly in the perfect picture, it throws a flood of light upon the total scene, being a *foil* which accentuates the environing beauty. Hence, every failure to reach perfection may be attributed to the power of the original Forms, which allows no contingent being to go beyond its allotted numbers, the laws that govern its operations. Such counsel will not only warn us against undue optimism but will also assure us that in times of stress, when evil and malignant influences are abroad in the land, God will still "make the wrath of man to praise him and the remainder of the wrath will he restrain."

But Augustine is not altogether satisfied with this statement of the case; for in his treatise on *Freewill* (III., 9) he makes another analysis of its terms. If evil in the form of suffering is needed to complete the perfection of the universe, must we then conclude that if men were always in a beatific state, there would be a deficiency in its perfection? Given a condition like that how could we justify the punishment of sin, since sin causes suffering and suffering is essential to moral excellence? But someone may reply that it is not the sin but the soul of the sinner that shares in the perfection of the whole. The soul has the capacity to will; if the soul wills to sin, with or without its usual miseries, the order of nature is dishonored but its perfection is not disturbed; which is another proof that evil is an appearance, not a reality. Here, however, we have a different aspect of the problem of evil, namely, the origin of sin in the individual soul by voluntary assent. This brings us to the second challenge which Augustine makes to the Manichean doctrine of evil. Sin is not congenital in the structure of the universe; it had its beginning in the heart of man.

What is the nature of the human soul? We have already studied its intellectual qualities, learning how "it reaches out to the infinity of the divine reason," as it seeks adequate sanctions for its universal ideas. We have observed, too, its emotional reactions in the changing experiences of life. We are now to analyze its power to act, the meaning of will as the executive function in behavior. Like every other creation, the human soul was originally pure, good, untouched by evil. Therefore, its will acted under no restraint except its own. The soul could not be perfect if deprived of this property. It was thus in a position to make its private choice; *it*

---

[28] *City of God,* XII, 5.

could choose evil, a quite impossible conceit for the disciple of Mani. But
why it *should* have chosen evil, instead of good, the author is unable to
state. He recognizes two essential facts, that sin exists in the world and
that sin is always connected with human action. "No alert mind," he
remarks, "could become the servant of lust except by the consent of its own
volition; not by the constraint of a superior or equal, for that would be
inequitable; not by an inferior, which is beyond the bounds of possibility."
Hence, neither civil law nor the illegitimate thrust of the tyrant can drive
a man to sin. Its causes lie in the active choice; but choice cannot proceed
from the physical nature, as the Stoics held, for responsibility has no place
there: it must come only from the determination of will. We have already
alluded to the Augustinian axiom that power is necessarily volitional.
Since man is an independent integer in the created world, he will also be
the centre of power. But if God controls all natural forces through his
providential economy must he not also hold in check the senses and reason
of men? Are we not then obliged to admit that men live under a sort of
"Fate not unlike that incorporated in the system of the Stoics?" [29] No; for
the problem is not the same. Untempered freedom is claimed for the race
only in its initial stages. The first man exercises his liberty of choice and
from that time onward its terms are severely restricted. We must, however, in this argument be careful not to attribute responsibility for the
sinful act to divine authority; that would forever crush the moral qualities
belonging to the human agent, and reduce him to the status of the brute.
Massive books have been printed to prove that divine sovereignty and
human accountability are contradictory ideas. Augustine was sensitive to
the seeming incompatibility; he tried to reconcile them by the dogma that
God had prior knowledge of the Fall but did not give his consent to it,
—a curious deduction which actually limits the sovereign nature of God,
while he is trying to vindicate it. What comes out of the original act of
transgression was that man lost the freedom he was born with and thereafter lived in a state of abject moral turpitude.

But we have not yet finished our study of the question. It is assumed
by every reputable moralist that when the agent makes a decision to act,
he bases it upon certain accredited motives. In this original act we are
dealing with a state of mind in no way comparable to the mental situations with which we are acquainted, although theological writers appear
to make no distinction. Are we to understand that the first parent deliberately chose a deed which he knew to be contrary to established custom and a direct affront to the intelligence of his Maker? Are we to suppose that the undeveloped mind of the race had a clear intuition of the
meaning of goodness, justice, honesty, love, submission to God, and that

[29] *City of God,* V, 9.

by what the French call *malice prepense* set about contradicting every item in the creed? Augustine is quite convinced that no man voluntarily enters upon a path whose goal is misery and discontent; but when he finds man in such a state, he is inclined to say that "if men are miserable by virtue of their choice of sin, we do not imply that they *will* to be miserable but that they are in a state of decision such that even against their will miseries necessarily ensue." [30] M. Grandgeorge points out that Plotinus had adopted a similar view—men act at times contrary to their will, but when they do so act, they accept the act as their own.[31] Obviously, sin under such conditions is a case of spontaneous action, not a deliberate decision of the moral judgment, and it is difficult to understand how and why two important effects should result from it, first, that it should destroy man's power of free action, and secondly that the sinister consequences of the action should be entailed upon the entire race throughout its entire existence.

The dogma is fixed in the mind of Augustine and reflects again his tendency to follow the legal concepts of his age in expounding the themes of religion, here that penalties are attached to the violation of law. It also repeats the edict of the Mosaic code that succeeding generations shall bear the punishment of their fathers' sins. It was made doubly clear to him that corruption was the inescapable heritage of the race:—*non posse non peccare*, not able *not* to sin. The theory of traduction permits, nay, requires it. It was a forbidding picture but it could not be disregarded. The prostrate moral condition of the Empire verified the formula to the letter. It was important that the truth of the dogma should be written in livid characters on the conscious thought of the church. Therefore he undertook a strong and embittered polemic against Pelagius, a quiet but litigious thinker, who had argued before the Eastern synods that sin is not a settled state of mind but a distinct and pragmatic act of will. Every man, he said, was responsible for his own behavior and must accept as his own the recompense for his deed. He denied emphatically that the sin of the first man involved the whole human world in a condition of moral depravation from which only divine grace could extricate it. Each son of Adam, he assumed, could work out his own salvation, though he would be powerfully aided by the example of the crucified Lord. To this presentment the Bishop replied in scorching words. The sin of Adam was an epochal event; it changed the nature of man from one of stainless personality to one steeped irreclaimably in the mire of corruption. His sin is irresistibly communicated to his descendants, not by emulation or mental suggestion but by direct and natural transmission. By some extremists it was supposed that even newborn infants would be caught in this general condemnation,

---

[30] *Freewill*, III, 5. [31] *Op. cit.*, p. 138.

unless they were rescued by the rites of baptism. This invidious legacy carries with it two serious encumbrances,—it produces ignorance of the finer ideals of life, and it turns the mind against any call to repentance.[32] The long and terrifying list of residual effects recorded by the writer staggers the imagination and drives the sinner to despair. From gnawing care, through murder and perfidy, to blasphemy and shameless ambition, the victim is brought to his inevitable doom, while the demons of hell gloat over his miseries. Dante's *Inferno* is almost an Elysian field when compared with the estate of the damned. How Michael Angelo and Jonathan Edwards must have rejoiced to find here an inimitable representation of what they designed to place on canvass or in the solemn sentences of a sermon! Fortunately, later thinkers abandoned the crudities of the dogma, although many of them retained its essential principles.

The objections to the theory from the standpoint of philosophy may be summed up in these words. First, it is based on a mythological story which enshrines certain important moral concepts but offers no reasons why we should regard it as anything more than a dramatic fiction. Secondly, it makes a thoroughly unscientific use of the biological concept of heredity; physical properties are transmitted, not ideas and moral values. Thirdly, it draws a curiously distorted picture of human personality which no trustworthy psychology would approve. Fourthly, it violates a fundamental canon of ethics which declines to shift the responsibility for moral behavior to an unknown and indiscernible progenitor. Finally, it presents an unworthy delineation of a gracious Lord who lays incredibly unjust penalties on inoffensive human beings with no chance of protest from their lips. With these considerations before him the philosopher rejects the dogma once and for all and regrets that it has ever had a place in Christian thought.

REDEMPTION THROUGH GRACE

The presence of habitudes and deeds that contradict the rules of virtue is recognized in all societies that have reached the level of civilized thought. That men have allowed such practices to go unchallenged until the promulgation of the law at Sinai, is a misreading of the facts of history. In a volume entitled *The Dawn of Conscience* [33] Professor Breasted has defended the thesis that the first intimation of the appearance of moral concepts in the Mediterranean area was at the beginning of the second millenium before Christ. Egyptian monuments of that period give clear evidence of the acknowledgment of the rights of inferior classes to be con-

---

[32] *City of God*, XXII, 22.
[33] J. H. Breasted, *The Dawn of Conscience* (New York: Chas. Scribner's Sons, 1934), Chap. 12.

sidered by their superiors in certain social relations. That would be six or seven centuries before the Mosaic law was instituted. He also argued that the formulas inscribed on the temples of Egypt were circulated among the northern Mediterranean peoples, and in some cases were copied *verbatim et literatim* by the writing prophets of the Hebrews. It is a further historical fact that men of great learning and exemplary moral habits were found among the Greeks and later the Romans, and that they not only taught the principles of jusice but also framed their private and public conduct in accordance with their terms. Augustine candidly admits these latter facts but holds that they are not sufficient for salvation. "Vainly do we invoke the examples of Plato and Pythagoras who surpassed all others in wisdom and who declared that true virtues are impressed upon the soul of man by power of the immutable substance of God." [34] These men were just by civil agreement but they were not "just by faith." They did not know the sublime motive which prompts all just action, namely, obedience to divine law;—*non officium sed finis,* not the act but the reason for it, this is the inflexible rule of true morality.

Therefore at the moment of great crisis in human affairs, when the inadequacies of human judgment descended to their lowest point, when those inadequacies congealed into types of obliquity so sinister that even the satiric tongue of a Juvenal could not fashion language capable of expressing it, at that moment a new decision of the divine will is disclosed, like the gracious offer of a monarch when the disabilities of the subjects are beyond private help. The analogy is instructive; St. Paul lived under its spell, so did Augustine. What human resources cannot do, superhuman authority does. The machinery of redemption is, so to say, set in motion. But at the same time and as a strange concomitant with the appearance of grace, a new wedge is driven into the liberty of the race. For, whether the world might like it or not, the question had to be raised: Who should profit by the exercise of divine benignity, all men indiscriminately or a select group of weary souls with an *affinity for holiness?* If the latter, how shall the selection be made? On what principle shall a man be found worthy of complete salvation? "In the doctrine of predestination," says Windelband, "the absolute causality of God suppresses the free will of the individual, who is refused both metaphysical independence and also all spontaneity of action. The individual is determined either *in his nature* to sin or by grace to do the good." [35] The dualism of destiny is firmly fixed: by nature we can do nothing but sin, by grace alone we may attain to holiness. The race is in a quandary: it has its aspirations towards virtue but it cannot tell if it shall ever have a chance to realize them. Men have a constitutional certitude as to their intellectual rights, and yet are com-

[34] *Contra Julianum,* IV, 3.   [35] *Op. cit.,* pp. 276–87.

pletely estopped from pursuing them. To quote Windelband again: "The same man who founded his philosophy upon the full assurance of the conscious mind, who discovered in the will the ground of spiritual personality, found himself forced to adopt a theory of salvation which considers the acts of will as determined either by the fundamental corruption of the heart or by divine and objective grace." It seems to be an unexpected turn in the redemptive process that God could use only his transcendental knowledge, not his will, in man's fall from native innocence, but could summon both divine prescience and the fore-ordaining will to effect the ultimate recovery. Augustine does admit that recognition is given to the type of soul elected to everlasting life: it must have the capacity to understand the truth and obey the impending commands. If that be true, then redemption is not altogether a gratuitous gift, it is awarded only to men who can make good use of it. That they *will* make good use of it, Augustine guarantees by the supplementary rule that once elected no soul can ever again yield to temptation; *non posse peccare,* it is not possible to sin. At this point a sort of freedom returns; for man once elected can chart his own course in the development of moral rectitude and spiritual purity, always effectuating his decisions by the effusion of supernatural grace. Thus, even in the freedom allowed, he is still limited in the actual construction of a safe and celestial character. The Augustinian rule is perfectly plain: not good works, not beautiful deeds, not the display of whole-hearted devotion to the laws of honor and good will, can make any soul elect, the sure recipient of the benisons of eternal life, but the favor of heaven distributed through the offices of the church. This strange doctrine of election has troubled the counsels of Christian communities in every country and in every age; it has precipitated endless debates and many bloody encounters; it has introduced doubt and distress in many a simple mind; it has evoked the distrust of philosophical seekers after truth; it has elicited the bitter recriminations of skeptics, and filled many a timid soul with the terrors of ultimate perdition. It still remains in concrete terms on the statute books of many evangelical bodies but a dead letter in the private creeds of a multitude of sagacious members. Philosophy and science have drawn its fangs and made its terms abortive.

But the intervention of redemptive grace has a wider application; it deals also with the behavior of men in the mass. As we have already intimated, a division has been opened between two conflicting communities, the City of God and the city of the bewildered world.[36] In the one are assembled order, peace, sobriety, neighborliness, and the hope of future felicity; in the other, moral disorders, the subjection of slaves to their masters, cruelty, infidelities especially such as associated with the relation of

[36] *City of God,* XIX, 17.

he sexes. At times it seemed as if Augustine had forestalled the Freudian
heory of psychoanalysis, so often does he charge the indecencies and ir-
egularities of conduct to the failure of men to obey the laws of con-
inence. The effect of his teaching, in this respect, has been singularly un-
ortunate. It has led, for one thing, to the adoption of the rules of celibacy
or the clergy, with all the sordid consequences that have followed from
t. More generally, it has helped to perpetuate the Manichean contention
hat body itself is the seat of corrupt tendencies and that spiritual purity
an be won only by subduing the natural impulses of the sense-organs. But
against such a pessimistic attitude he teaches that nature possesses the
principles of law and order and that these are the peculiar inheritance of
he children of the kingdom. Against the frequent re-appearance of strife,
overweening ambition, and malignant heresies in human society he sets
he offices of the church, its stimulating ritual, and its right to admit men
o salvation by the ordinance of baptism, regarding them as strong and
effective instruments for maintaining peace and promoting concord. Those
who are endowed with her spiritual gifts, no matter what may be their
later derelictions, "shall not die eternally but at one time or another, receive eternal life." [37] Thus, not only single souls but vast communities of
favored peoples, kings and senates, nations and legal systems, face the
opportunity for a radical change in their mental judgments and moral
habitudes, provided they deliberately and with true devotion submit themselves to the sovereign authority of God.

In the changing facets of Augustine's thought we have been forced to
meet the question which we raised at the beginning: how shall we distinguish the ideas of philosophy from the precepts of religious experience?
Religion meant for him precisely what it means for all discriminating
students of the Christian tradition. Two factors have never failed to demand attention—the intuition of the individual mind and the pragmatic
authority of revealed truth. Which of these shall have the greater weight
in the solution of any important problem, the individual inquirer must
determine. In many stages of his spiritual career we can sense the struggle
through which he is passing. No man can suddenly disencumber himself
of all the sentiments which have gathered strength and prestige during
the time of his maturing thought. Thirty-two years were behind the young
crusader when the crucial change occurred, years spent in severe deliberations, in the study of systems of doctrines, in converse with many competent thinkers. He had analyzed the processes of the human intellect,
he had gone deep into the maelstrom of competing emotions, he had
scanned the incentives by which moral action is determined, he had pene-

[37] *Ibid.*, XXI, 27.

trated behind the veil of mystic inspiration, all for the purpose of discovering the principles upon which a scientific religious experience could be founded. It is a notable fact that he had frankly sought a specific creed, a sequence of organized feelings, a concrete object of worship upon which his ideas and solemn obligations could be focussed. "Take and read," said the Voice in the Garden; he took the book and read, and transformation overwhelmed him. Which was the mightier influence, his perception of God or the authority of the canonical Word? These two factors contended for the mastery, but neither ever became the sole arbiter of his destiny. Perhaps, they are the obverse sides of the same shield and neither can obscure the significance of the other.

VII: LEIBNIZ

"The idea of God, according to my view, is innate in all men; for if this notion embodies an idea which actually occurs in our thought, it is a proposition of fact which depends for its verification upon the history of the race." In these words inscribed in the Fourth Book of the *New Essays,* Leibniz registers the fundamental thesis of his religious philosophy. The thesis is not new, for Epicurean and Stoic alike admitted that the human mind tended to express itself in terms of universal concepts. Every universal idea seems to give a certitude which the factual proposition cannot yield. The idea of God was certain and real for the Greek thinker, even though the attributes were coincident with the ideal characters engraved on the forces of nature. To be sure, Leibniz' admission in the passage just quoted seems to make any pronouncement about the reality of God a question of fact to be determined by the universal consent of mankind. But because God, however he may be described, sums up in himself the universal ideas that govern men's thought, Leibniz concludes he is justified in this one instance in making a judgment of fact exactly equivalent to a judgment of reason. Such a need was not felt by Plotinus who merely removed all attributes except complete existence from the formula of supreme Substance, leaving his implicit energies to be expressed by the universal ideas. The reality of God is recovered when Augustine united the solitary splendor of the Neo-Platonic Deity with the moral vigor of the Hebrew Jehovah. This union became the groundwork of the Scholastic theology. Anselm erected upon it his celebrated argument for the existence of God as well as for the structure and operation of the human mind. The argument is changed by Thomas Aquinas to fit the demands of the Aristotelian logic which did not allow the thinker to pass from the mere idea to the embracing reality, but did presuppose from the unceasing motions of the world an all-embracing Cause of them.

Throughout the entire course of speculative inquiry this theme has never lost its ingratiating appeal. "The existence of God," Leibniz continues, "is the truth most easily proven by reason, and its evidence equals, if I am not mistaken, that of a mathematical demonstration." This truth is indeed central to men's belief but the fortunes of the proof have been extremely uneven. When Bruno awoke Europe from its medieval slumbers, he set out to prove that we do not live in the cramped spaces of an Hellenic world but in the sweep of an infinite and dynamic universe. Yet the idea of God remained unchallenged, although the mystic intuitions of the faithful were worn thin by the hard analysis of the new scientific thought. God may be intelligence, he may be will, but how can he be the mediator of love with all its emotional reverberations, when faced by the ruthless agencies of a material mechanism? And how could he exercise providential care over an insignificant portion of the stellar world and over one helpless denizen on a specified planet in it? Bruno made his protest against the anthropomorphism of the church's creed; they threw him into the dungeon, they burned him at the stake; they disregarded his answer when his sentence was pronounced: "Greater perhaps is your fear in pronouncing my sentence than mine in hearing it." If God be the sum of Reality as Bruno taught, he is inestimably more majestic than the Hellenic Divinity or the inexorable God whom the Scholastics worshipped. Under the magic touch of the Italian thinker the physical universe assumed a scope and splendor hitherto unknown; likewise, the divine attributes passed from the restrictions of the creeds to the conception of unity which was bound to make its impression on the new philosophy. Descartes, Spinoza, Leibniz, Berkeley, Hume and Kant enter the lists of distinguished investigators, and in their work the human intellect will mark out new paths in the study of this important subject.

THE NATURE OF SUBSTANCE

We cannot understand the attitude of Leibniz towards the problem of divinity until we have examined his concept of substance. On this question continental thinkers never attained complete agreement. Descartes insisted that substance is double, spirit and matter, each with its appropriate attribute, thought and extension. He was ultimately forced to admit that universal substance could be only one, namely, God; but in the field of common experience we cannot deny the presence of two antithetical principles. Spinoza rejected this conclusion; he found only one substance with an infinite number of attributes, two of which are known. God or nature is both creating cause and thing created. The world of nature is for both thinkers the seat of unchanging law; for one its mechanism is unbroken, for the other its rigors are lighted by the superb expressions of thought mediated through the intelligence of man. Leibniz is convinced that neither analysis is complete; there is a degree of truth in each and by a due revision of the defective parts, he can, he thinks, deduce a system that will be unimpeachable.

He therefore begins with the Cartesian principle that the reality of the world is found in motion and that the quantity of motion is constant. Motion, Descartes argues, is of the very essence of substance, produced by God when substance was engendered. There is motion in the world; experience reveals it and reason accepts it as a necessary accompaniment of substance. Motion is change, and if change exists, there must be an object that changes. But no object can undergo change in its entirety except by reference to an external point which is spatially connected with it. Furthermore, the relation between the object and its neighbor does not remain fixed or static; it alters in succeeding moments of time. All changes in motion, whether of degree or direction, are accomplished by the "ordinary coöperation" of the divine mind. Hence, when we observe a diminution of velocity in a particular body, we are obliged to assume that the motion in an adjacent body has been proportionately increased. Or, if a moving body impinges on a body taken to be at rest, we must suppose a reaction in which the quantity of motion remains unchanged. Again, every body tends to abide in the same condition, motion or rest, until opposed by a body having a greater quantity of motion. Obviously, motion is a positive factor in body and cannot be removed from it by any natural agency.

To all these allegations Leibniz replies that everything moves or tends to move by an inherent property which Epicurus described as weight or gravity, but which Leibniz held to be a veritable force resident in the body. We shall define its terms in a moment. Here it is necessary to observe that motions not belonging to an independent body must be determined by the activity of a perceiving mind. To this result he was driven as soon as he detected the unreality of space. Space cannot be an external container, as Aristotle supposed; it cannot be the natural limits set to adjacent bodies and ultimately to the entire world. "I hold space to be something merely relative, as time is: I hold it to be an *order of coexistences,* as time is an *order of successions.* For space denotes, in terms of possibility, an order of things existing at the same time and considered as existing together, without reference to the particular manner of existing. And when many things are seen together we perceive the same order of things subsisting among themselves." [1] This is his answer to Clarke, who thought with Newton that infinite space is real and must be interpreted as a kind of "sensorium" of the divine mind. Hence, space is the sequence of sense-perceptions culminating in a judgment drawn by the attentive observer. Now, since motion always deals with the relations of spatial bodies, we are compelled by logic to regard it as also determined by a judgment which has detected the forces at work in neighboring bodies. It will thus appear that the total effects will be equal to the combined set of observed causes.

[1] R. Latta, *Leibniz, the Monadology, and Other Philosophical Writings,* p. 102.

Motion, therefore, cannot be calculated by the inspection of different bodies at different times but by the comprehension of the "metaphysical law which expresses the meaning of each several motive force." [2]

There is another deduction subtended immediately by this principle, namely, that Descartes' definition of body as "extended thing" is false and meaningless. If space is unreal, extension, which is another name for space, is unreal. How can that be? Here are Leibniz' words contained in a letter of 1693: "Those who hold that an extended thing is also a substance, transpose the order of the words as well as of the thought. Besides extension we must have an object which is extended; that is to say, a substance which can be repeated or continued in our experience. For extension means nothing but a repeated or a continued multiplication of that which is spread out (before us), a plurality, continuity and coexistence of parts. Consequently it (i. e., extension) is not sufficient to explain the nature of extended or repeated substances, the notion of which is anterior to its repetition." [3] Obviously, body cannot be explained by the simple attribute of extension: it requires at least one other property which can be none other than impenetrability, resistance to desolating motion. We must be careful not to confuse the argument of Leibniz with that of the Atomists. Force in the atom is passive; even the swerve in Epicurus is only a change in the direction of a given motion. Again, the atom is extended, it possesses magnitude, but because it could not be perceived by the senses, its parts could not be detected or analyzed. But since it is extended, it must have *parts,* and must therefore be held to be a compound, which is a logical contradiction. Thus, physical atoms are mere abstractions of thought and, Leibniz thinks, wholly useless as an index to the meaning of matter.

As contrasted with the Epicurean atom Leibniz' force is active. Nature does not depend on the mechanical connection of constituent parts. Every substance has its private tendency to act, its *conatus,* as Spinoza says, an endeavor to preserve its own identity of form and perpetuity of place in the universal system. Force like this, Leibniz asserts, has no need of outside support, providing nothing impedes its true functioning. Such a force is at work in every substance, mineral, plant, animal, human understanding.[4] He affirms that the principles of physics once grounded on mechanical laws must now be interpreted by the *vis viva,* the living force of dynamism. It is this active force which establishes the individuality of substances. The Scholastics said that the individual is the delineation of brute matter; if you separate matter into its physical parts you obtain an individual. No, says Leibniz; an individual is not generated by setting up spatial limits, impenetrable barriers between it and its neighbors. An individual is en-

[2] *Ibid.,* p. 344.   [3] *Ibid.,* p. 28.   [4] J. F. Nourrison, *Leibniz,* p. 208.

dowed with specific characters and cannot be other than it is; it cannot pass into another nor will it allow another to enter its own domain. The individual substance has no windows; it possesses *antitypia,* a property which refuses to let another usurp its functions or impair any of its significant properties. Hence, no two substances can be exactly alike; if they were alike, they would not be two but one. This is the celebrated doctrine of the identity of indiscernibles. The nature of each substance is divinely created and cannot be destroyed except by divine decree. Such individuals are called monads by the author, a term derived from the Greeks importing not sheer singleness of existence but an independent and explicit character. It indicates the *materia prima* of every substance.

The monad, however, does not stand alone; it is supported by a secondary matter which physics calls body. Bodies, as we know them, are not simple structures; they are composed of a multitude of parts, each with its own supervisory monad. Thus, the human body is made up of many organs, which in turn divide into cells, these again into molecular tissues, and so on to the end. The controlling monad in every system is called *entelechy,* a new name for an old concept. It, too, stems from the analytic mind of Greece, and in Aristotle's psychology appears as the factor in experience which enables man to coördinate all his modes of sensation, feeling, and thought in such a manner as to give unity to his behavior and consistency to his judgment. Entelechy signifies the capital purpose in every system by means of which its identity is preserved and its several capabilities developed. It is the entelechy, the primary force of the individual, which registers the changes taking place in our body and which reports the activity of neighboring bodies. These changes are changes in sensations, usually blurred perceptions which, however, may be turned into clear ideas by the proper judgments of thought. It is thus that every motion in the universe, no matter what its velocity, ultimately becomes a phase of our consciousness, some movements being so slight they are recorded merely as *petites perceptions,* too small ever to appear as elements in our scientific apprehension but, together with all the active perceptions, entering into our acquaintance with the world. In this respect, Leibniz opines, the Cartesian psychology is defective; for if the mind loses its power to perceive while it is asleep, as Descartes taught, this is the same as saying that during any unconscious period it does not think.[5] Thus, the first effort of the monad is to perceive.

But its second task is more formidable than that, for it can change the activity of soul from one perception to another. To the casual observer this seems to be but a natural, spontaneous and hence inconsiderable labor. It is in fact a serious duty. The rapid movement of images before the

[5] *Monadology,* Sec. 14.

mental vision is so persistent that sometimes we cannot stop to discern what is actually taking place. Incident to the change is the emergence of a factor not yet mentioned by the author, although Descartes had emphasized it at the very beginning of his study. Appetition which is the change of perceptions is the same as desire or will. Leibniz is not so explicit in his treatment of the subject, probably because in his opinion the first excitation comes by the decree of Deity. Nevertheless the whole area of impulse and emotion is involved in this phase of entelechy's operations. Certainly, the attitude of the mind towards the problems of moral conduct where a deliberate choice must be made between good and evil, is weighted with possibly serious results both in time and eternity. "Souls act according to the law of final causes through appetites, ends, and means." [6] The whole set of man's interests, intellectual, aesthetic and moral is safeguarded by the basal forces of the monadic soul. Can similar remarks be made about entelechies that do not exercise the powers of rational reflection? This query brings us to the notable attempt made by Leibniz to establish the fact of a full and unbroken universe, a principle which he calls the "Law of Continuity."

The charm which mathematics always exerted upon his mind is evident again in his analysis of this significant law. A geometrical line is composed of integral points, a surface of integral lines, a solid of coördinate surfaces. Thus every test of unity which is open to the observer's eye, goes back to the concept of a point. The world of nature is accordingly a concatenation of points. But what kind of points? Not mathematical, for such points are indivisible, in fact they are mere fictions of the mind, that is, attributes applied to substances in order to discover their spatial or temporal relations. Nor can they be physical points, that is, bodies with their parts and members taken as single wholes. Here, again, the limiting case, the Democritean atom, is a concept of the imagaination, and cannot be detected in actual experience. The only choice left is the metaphysical point, the organic monads which when joined together constitute the continuum of the universe.[7] Hence, continuity rests not on numerical repetition which gives no internal distinctions nor upon the adjacency of space and the lapse of time, since we cannot know why God created the world with its present conditions, but solely on the diversified attributes of an organized world.

At this point the structure of the Leibnizean world begins to emerge. It consists of the successive classes of monads which reflect the order of intelligences familiar to the student of psychology from the days of Pythagoras. Starting with the highest we have the monad endowed with noetic reason to which the name of human spirit has been affixed. Next comes

6 *Monadology*, Sec. 79.   7 R. Latta, *op. cit.*, pp. 310–11.

the series whose ruling property is feeling, including the function of memory, applicable to the whole range of organic bodies both animal and plant life. Finally, inorganic bodies, both great and small, exhibiting the analagon of soul but without sense-reaction; these are subject to the same incessant changes as are the souls of men and animals, and thus are never without the element of a new intuition. "Activity," he writes, "is no more inseparable from the soul than from the body. A state of soul without thought and a body wholly at rest, appear to me to be things which are equally contrary to nature and of which there is no instance in the world." [8] The Greek idea of rest is false; it is the limiting case of motion whose velocity has been reduced to the lowest degree. If it were possible to find a physical situation where change was absent or a mental state where perception or noetic judgment was completely suspended, then the law of continuity would fail and the dynamic structure of his system would be destroyed.

But the law stands regnant and unchallenged, he thinks, both on the cosmic scale and within the milieu of each collegiate class. Thus he writes in 1707: "All these different classes of substance whose assemblage constitutes the universe, are, in the thought of God . . . like so many ordinates on a curve whose union does not allow any space for other objects between them; lest that should leave upon them the mark of disorder and imperfection." [9] There are no gaps in the system of the world. Man approaches the lower orders in "germ," and thus through all the subsidiary classes. This can only mean that certain forms of body are not yet realized in nature, e. g., in the field of organic bodies, but may after the lapse of great aeons be developed from forms already in existence. The evolutionary hypothesis in our day has amply fulfilled his conjecture. His assumption is that potential forms must always be "compossible," that is, they must *fit into* the structures already based in the system of nature. If a proposed entelechy should conflict with attributes now rooted in the biological order, it could not be a permanent integer in the group. [10] Whether such additions might appear in the cosmic order we have no means of knowing; Leibniz makes no prediction. But we may be certain that the general sequence of substantial forms will never be interrupted; the Law of Continuity is eternal.

COMMENTS ON THE THEORY OF FORCE

It is proper for us at this point to remark upon the adequacy or inadequacy of the "new" philosophy. We agree that the two principal theories of nature—leaving on one side for the moment all questions of nature's origin—are those of Descartes and Spinoza, atomism being a variation of

[8] *Ibid.*, p. 130, note.   [9] Nourrison, *op. cit.*, p. 230.   [10] Latta, *op. cit.*, p. 340.

the former. The one affirms that "all variety of matter or the divergence of its forms depends on motion." The relation between bodies can be determined with mathematical precision, because each body is causally connected with its neighbor and is bound to it by inflexible law. The chief principle of physical substance is extension, the single property of spiritual substance is thought. Spinoza's theory has little in common with the Cartesian. There is one substance with two attributes known to us, extension and thought. Bodies are not separable objects depending each upon the other through a natural force; they are modes by which universal substance expresses itself to the eye of the observer. Physical laws are merely aspects of nature, thoughts are intellectual representations of substance; neither is real except as it reflects the total form of the universe.

These are the competing doctrines which Leibniz had to face. He rejected the first, because it gave nature nothing but a succession of motions which he believed to be determinations of the mind. He rejected the second, because it denied the reality of the parts of nature. Thus, Spinoza's rule, "All determination is negation"—every time we ascribe certain properties to an object we must remove other properties from it—seemed to Leibniz to lead directly to a nihilistic creed. Therefore, faced on the one side by a theory that had no place for individual power and on the other by a theory that had no place for the individual itself, he resolved to set up a system which would save the individual from extinction and endow it with a character subject to no change by mechanical collision and incapable of being absorbed in a total unity. Did he succeed? The answers are various; let us state and defend one of them.

The gravamen of his philosophy lies in the word force. The term is used to denote every type of monad but particularly that of one branch of physics which he calls dynamics. We may say at the outset that the alternative word which he summons to explain the meaning of force, namely, entelechy, has no appropriateness when we study mere physical relations. Russell suggests that it is possible to distinguish "three broad types of dynamical theory,"—impact as in the Democritean system, an all-pervading fluid, now commonly found in the theory of electricity, and finally, "unextended centres of force with action at a distance." Leibniz should have accepted the third but either because he had a personal animus against Newton, its author, or because he assumed that the monadic force could have no productive influence upon objects other than itself, *whether near or remote,* he denied its scientific value and turned to the second. It is a force *within* that makes every body independent and sovereign. To render the force effective he distinguishes between primitive force which never leaves the body once it has entered it, and derivative force, the impetus, the conatus, of the individual body which in some manner modifies the original force and which is so "distributed among many bodies as to preserve a constant sum." [11]

It is plain from Leibniz' argument that he intends to use the one term, force, to define the meaning of activity both in the mechanical and the psychological spheres. Does the term retain the same connotation in both? Thus, soul is the primary principle of the behavior of the body, it represents in detail its essential qualities, and shows precisely what the body can do. Students of mental phenomena have not hesitated to speak of the searching inquisition of perception, of the tenacity of memory, of the power of thought, of the intensity of emotion and the decisive action of will. All these terms involve the concept of force. If the expression of force is immediately attended by physical changes, then in some cases the action of mind, as for example in the exertion of will, might well be described by the same term. When however pure ideas are said to be endowed with the capacity for producing influential changes in private opinion, then the physical effects are not immediately apparent. It is true that we speak of the dynamic force of personality; but in that case we have regard not so much to impressiveness of the thought as to the effective manner of tone or gesture in which the thought is expressed. We may understand Leibniz' attitude here by reporting what he wrote in a letter to Arnaud, 1687: "One thing *expresses* another when there is a regular relation between what can be said of one thing and what can be said of another. It is thus that a projection in perspective expresses its original; expression is common to all forms or psychical types, and is the genus of which ordinary perception, animal feeling and intellectual knowledge are species." [12] Thus expression is only another name for the principle of activity, and is a peculiarly apt description of his favorite term, entelechy. Furthermore, we are justified in holding that the same term may be applied to the actions of bodies apprehended in the field of dynamics. All three types of theory cited by Russell could be better understood if we spoke of force as a principle or a law, not as a physical energy whose objective influence we are trying to measure. For force is said to be prior to extension, but the monad in which it inheres has no parts, since it has no magntiude, and having no magnitude it can have no shape or any other property belonging to volume. In short, force must be a *mode of explaining body,* not a physical energy governing its actions.

Let us take another step in our criticism. The specific nature of the monad is what Leibniz denominates its "point of view." The significance of the phrase rests upon the connection which the monad sustains to its bodily envelope. There are certain inadequate perceptions flowing through

[11] B. Russell, *A Critical Exposition of the Philosophy of Leibniz,* pp. 93–97.
[12] G. H. Montgomery, *Leibniz, The Discourse on Metaphysics,* p. 210.

the physical senses which must be corrected by the dominent qualities of the monad,—in the case of man by the interpretations of the rational judgment.[13] In the *Theodicée* he tells us that "each soul represents to itself the universe, according to its own point of view; but in this there always continues to be perfect harmony."[14] Hence, the influence which one substance exerts upon another cannot be that of a mechanical cause, as Newton said, for since it is without magnitude the very notion of physical dependence is a misnomer. The only "influence" we can possibly discover is *ideal,* as he says in the *Monadology* (Sec. 51), which in the original text refers to a divine design looking to the creation and regulation of the universe. But removing our survey from so lofty a level, we are surely justified in arguing that the distinction of one monad from another is logical in form, in accordance with Leibniz' formula of contradiction. Each monad has its private character determined in the manner just noted, a complex of generic properties modified by its necessary relations with the rest of the world. Coördinate geomet-y shows that one and the same circle can be represented by an ellipse, a parabola, an hyperbola, another circle, even by a straight line and a point. These figures are wholly unlike, yet they bear an exact relation to another, point by point. The monad reproduces the total world in the same diverse yet harmonious way. Such a theory has value only if force is a term in logic and not the central term in an equation of higher mathematics.[15]

This brings us to the next significant fact that force is the only principle at our disposal by which we can discriminate between Leibniz' classes of monads, since force is another name for the properties resident in the monad. The Greek mind construed the figures and operations of nature under the rubric of fixed and inviolable genera. Thus, Plato defined time, time understood by the intellect, as "the moving image of eternity," but he was careful, also, to resolve it first into its enveloping classes, past, present and future, and then into its natural classes, day, month, seasons and year. Aristotle taught his own generation and many thereafter to divide biological organisms according to their fixed kinds. Strange to say, his divisions persisted until the acceptance of the evolutionary hypothesis. Leibniz following the traditional order obeyed the simple rule of division, namely, that there must be a common basis upon which the selection will rest, in the present instance, the mode of reaction of one body to another, with the differentia as the degree of intensity and distinctness in the impact of each body upon the other; although he did not notice that numerical values never succeed in separating one type of substance from another. And finally, there was the method of complete integration which Kant, in the *Critique of Pure Reason* followed, when he made logic the scientific

[13] *Monadology*, Sec. 57.   [14] Latta, *op. cit.,* p. 249, note.   [15] *Ibid.,* p. 249, note.

instrument for deriving the fundamental principles of thought. In the Leibnizian world every genus, every species, every individual mirrored the universe according to the "perfection" or logical superordination of the particular concept, already reached. The monad with its interior *force,* that is its essential properties, thus receives the certificate of the role it is to play in the drama of existence. If this be true then the "new philosophy" may rank as one of the major triumphs of modern speculation. But then we may ask, How can it be legitimately distinguished from Spinoza's system assuming that nothing existed except the universe itself? For if our criticism is correct, the monads cannot remain as independent "centers of reality" but must be taken strictly as instruments of interpretation, especially showing how the parts are related to the whole. One result would surely follow: it would render nugatory the central dogma of Leibniz' theory to which we now address our attention.

PREËSTABLISHED HARMONY

The theory of Preëstablished Harmony appears in two forms; first it will account for the unfaltering connection between independent substances, and second, it will associate each monad with its corporate attendant, so that together they will confront the other monads as a single integer. The theory marks the culminating effort of the philosopher to construct an impregnable system of reality and is regarded by him as his distinctive contribution to modern thought. He declared that if Descartes had substituted the idea of force for that of motion, where conservation of energy would supplant the constant quantity of motion, then he must have reached the same conclusion.[16]

The following facts have been determined in our study of the monads: they and they alone represent real substance; they exist separately in the system and cannot be affected by outside influences; they have each in itself a fixed character with which they have been endowed by the Creator; the character thus given emerges as a "fulguration" of divine power, not as a single created individual nor as a Plotinic emanation but as a *form* pregnant with possibilities which will be unfolded in succeeding ages.[17] Leibniz, as already noted, was profoundly moved by the revelations of the scientific microscope. They divulged the presence of extremely minute organisms whose bodies and movements were easily studied by the experienced inquirer. One deduction suggested itself to him immediately: no living body is without its congenital cause; neither chaos nor putrefaction can account for its existence. The seed is the source of life, and the seed, to him, was the inconfutable proof of the "preformation" of every organic body. Both its form and matter were ready at hand *before* conception, and by means of

[16] *Monadology,* Sec. 116.   [17] *Ibid.,* Sec. 47.

this natural process were prepared for each succeeding metamorphosis.[18] Leibniz adopted the thesis because it served to confirm his principle, that changes found in the single monad sprang from the primordial character installed in it at birth. There was also an additional principle on which he set great store, that monads are arranged in an unvarying order, an order so closely articulated that at certain points the several genera could scarcely be differentiated from one another. At once the query is raised—How is the order to be forever maintained? Atomism gave its answer by providing a void through which individuals passed to a new adjustment. Spinoza answers by insisting on the unity of substance and the unreality of the separate units. For the former the problem of the association of atoms was wholly insoluble; for the latter there is no problem. Leibniz by a stroke of genius, as he thinks, breaks the logical impasse by proclaiming that every monad mirrors the universe *in its own way*. It is therefore an integer in an unbroken system. The changes that take place are already incorporated in the original creation. The system of monads, deriving from the wisdom and will of God, obtain an initial harmony which cannot be destroyed; it reflects infallibly the basic design upon which the world is built. Monads have intercourse with one another not mechanically but ideally. There is no need for Malebranche's conceit of divine intervention whenever an event takes place in nature's domain —the rising of the sun, the eclipse of the moon, the genesis of a new organism—the initial form of the doctrine of Occasionalism. God, says the new philosophy, fixes the order of the monads at their creation and the order still stands. This is the first phase of the theory of Preëstablished Harmony.

The second phase is of greater interest, since it involves the problem of mind and body, a problem still open to debate. Assuming that mind is the monad of the body, how shall we state their relation to one another? The Cartesian doctrine was simple: two substances, each reacting upon the other, mind having as its specific function the power not to generate motion but to change its direction. This is the interaction theory. The next theory was espoused by Geulincx who affirmed the existence of two substances but held that neither could influence the action of the other. The movement of mind and body was simultaneous, because divine energy entered both at the same time and brought about the respective results. Two clocks originally synchronized must strike the hour at the same instant, no matter how far apart in space they happened to be. Leibniz complained, and rightly, that such an event was a miracle: it could have no meaning for a scientific age. He added with a sly innuendo, that both parts of the human personality, as well as of any other monad and ultimately

18 *Ibid.*, Sec. 74.

of the universe itself, would require constant oversight, lest one might fail the other at a critical moment. Certainly, such a contradiction might occur in the experience of a beleaguered mind. Here the doctrine of Preëstablished Harmony steps in to resolve the difficulties. Concomitance of endeavor by soul and body begins at birth, yes, before birth, indeed at the genesis of the substantial form which terminates in the given individual. It proceeds bilaterally throughout the period of youth, when the soul learns how to receive and interpret its perceptions and control its passions, through the mature years when it determines its relations to the wider world of thought, and finally in face of the exigency of death when it exchanges its present body for a more suitable integument in another sphere. Such a study reveals the complete parallelism between the mechanical causes of nature and the final causes of the mind.[19] At length there opens to our view the union of physical force and moral authority envisaged in the *City of God*.[20] Here Leibniz leaves the level of philosophic inquiry and rises to the lofty heights of poetic fancy. The symbolism is changed; it is now two choirs in distant regions who sing the same choral at the same time, guided by the coercive Power which first put their voices in tune and has never been obliged to intervene, in order to check the pitch or correct a discord. The phantasy is fascinating but ineffective. Let us hear what men have said about it.

To Immanuel Kant the argument was inconclusive. "It is possible," he writes in 1790, "that by his Preëstablished Harmony between body and soul he meant a mutual conformity of two beings entirely independent of one another as regards their nature, and incapable of being brought together by their own forces." [21] Experience, Kant holds, does not exhibit so serious a contradiction. What it does is to give us sensations which are obedient to certain psychical rules. By means of this process the pure reason turns experience into knowledge; that is, it harmonizes successfully the totally different factors of sense and judgment. In general we may affirm that the causality of nature, as expressed in the use of our normal capacities, is paralleled by the free action of the mind by which we interpret the data of the senses in accordance with established laws. If this be the meaning of Leibniz' doctrine as Kant understood it, we may let our mind rest in peace, being confident that it does not touch the essential point in his doctrine and would have been repudiated by him, could he have anticipated such an interpretation. On the other hand, we may be certain that if the revision of the definition of force as we have proposed, making it a logical principle of explanation and not the residual energy in nature, had been accepted, it would have carried with it a sharp re-

---

[19] *Ibid.*, Sec. 79. [20] *Ibid.*, Secs. 85, 86.
[21] Latta, *op. cit.*, pp. 209–11, taken from Kant's own account of his relation to Leibniz.

jection of the concept of a preliminary decree, and the assertion of a
persisting substance which could be examined and interpreted by the
scientific mind, without the necessity of pushing the question of its origin
beyond the bounds of empirical verification.

THE SUPREME MONAD

We have already intimated that Leibniz deliberately placed his Deity
outside the area of the physical universe. He did this no doubt in agreement with the theological belief of the times. Like Descartes he had no
desire to run the risk of conflict with the authorities of his church who
showed a tendency to identify irregularities in religious dogma with possible disloyalty to the political creed. He was by nature a cautious soul
not afraid to accept an opinion which might be contrary to the official
mind but seeking acquaintance with the whole situation before making
his opinion known. Again, it is not at all certain that he had reached the
final stages in his speculations, even in the year 1696 which Nourrison believes the date when his philosophy was finally organized. Some points
were plainly in need of further analysis, as for example, the sovereign
status of the monad, *why* one could not act upon another, *how* if once
given existence nothing but the decree of God could take it away, *whether*
in studying a single monad he was exploring the individual unit or the
universal principle denoted by it. We might clear up some of these points
if we could obtain an exact idea of what he means by Deity, both in
essence and in activity. This is the theme which he develops in the *Theodicée,* his last major work prepared originally for the Queen of Prussia
and intended to be a refutation of Bayle's article in the *Dictionary.* We
shall reverse the usual order of study and let the argument for the existence
of God remain untouched until we have discovered what *kind* of a God
he proposes for our consideration.

He begins with the concept of perfection which is a term in logic rather
than in ethics. In the preface to his book he says: "There is nothing more
perfect than God and nothing more full of charm. In order to be devoted
to him it is sufficient to represent his perfections. These are his attributes
such as our souls seek for in vain but which he possesses without limit.
Thus as human beings we have certain elements of power, knowledge,
goodness, but only in limitations; he has them in their fulness. The idea
of order, symmetry and harmony fascinate us, as we find them expressed
in painting and musical melodies. But God is the quintessence of order,
he protects the symmetrical parts of the world, he produces universal
harmony. Beauty is the expression (épanchement) of his regard." [22] In
the spirit of Scholasticism he says that God embraces within himself a

[22] In Nourrison, *op. cit.,* p. 266.

onceivable reality, both corporeal and spiritual; not that he combines
hem in his primitive substance but that he is the source of all power
wherever found. Monads fall back on him for their structure and meaning. The argument sounds, at times, like the meditations of Plotinus:
God puts his power not his essence into the successive emanations. The
two laws of logic which are to govern our inquiry into the reality of God,
must now be drawn upon in explication of the divine nature. God must
have intellect and will, both of them embodying power, the power of wisdom and goodness, just as the Ideas of Plotinus stood for unactualized
potencies. These same attributes appear again in the constitution of the
monad, perception plus judgment, leading in man to the understanding
of truth and the application of will, "which makes changes in thought or
action according to the supreme principle of Fitness." [23] Leibniz does
what Spinoza did, but which Descartes refused to do—he declares that
knowledge and will are the original attributes of God. The possession
of truth by God, the acquisition of knowledge by man, depend wholly
on the validity of the Law of Contradiction. On the other hand the law of
sufficient Reason governs the choice of that which is best, whether found
in the divine nature or sought by man as a guide to moral conduct. Obviously the philosopher is determined to justify the high esteem in which
wisdom and will are held by the human mind by leading them back irrevocably to the sovereign nature of God. Listen to these words: "For the
understanding of God is the area of eternal truths or of the ideas on which
they depend, and without him there would be nothing real in the potentialities of things, and not only would there be nothing in existence but
nothing would even come within the range of possibilities." [24] Let us
look further into the matter.

The *Monadology* continually underlines the power of God to choose;
but choice presupposes two distinct principles, first, that he is free to
choose and second, that choice is grounded in the adoption of a commanding motive. Freedom, to be sure, is an equivocal term; it may mean
the exclusion of restraint or it may describe an action which is the opposite
of necessity. In the first sense, "God alone is completely free and created
spirits only in proportion as they are superior to their passions." [25] Freedom, however, is never absence of law; it stands as the model for human
behavior under the aegis of the civil state. God himself is bound by law,
the law of eternal truth, and man is also. Action without the direction of
law is sheer license. Hence, it is folly to argue that when God created the
world he was free to produce any compound whatsoever of mechanical
and spiritual forces, either with a fantastic design or no design at all! As
Russell remarks, "No physical world could exist which did not have the

[23] *Monadology*, Sec. 48.   [24] *Ibid.*, Sec. 43.   [25] *New Essays*. Trans. by Langley, p. 179.

elementary properties of space, time and motion." [26] But Leibniz had already safeguarded his theory against this criticism by assuming that "the supreme wisdom of God led him to choose the laws of motion which are the *most fitting,* and more in conformity with abstract or metaphysical reasons." [27]

More significant is the problem involved in the second definition of freedom. Freedom and necessity appear to be contradictory ideas. Kant argued that necessary action belonged to a mechanically organized system, while freedom had to do only with the choice and arrangement of concepts. Thus, the human mind is free to apply any predicates it pleases to the subject of a logical proposition, if the new judgment does not contradict the meaning of the old. Man is free to choose his course of conduct, provided the resulting action does not have an import other than that ordinarily given it in social intercourse. Kant declines to discuss the hypothesis that God will have a similar fund of choices. Spinoza is more forthright in his statement. There is a freedom common to all organic bodies but especially human beings which depends on the amount of knowledge, the degree of scientific accuracy, reached by the individual in his mature experience. The wise man is most free, because he has learned *how* to curb his emotions and *whither* to direct his energies, in the search for a well-defined moral character. Since all parts of nature are modes of divine intelligence on the one side and of efficient cause on the other, the total substance, God, has both complete freedom and complete necessity, at one and the same time. Hence, freedom and necessity cannot contradict one another but together constitute a single being, God, who is most free as he is most necessary.

Clearly Leibniz cannot find a resting-place in either theory. His world is created, not evolved; certainly it is not static, without beginning or possible end. Hence, God must act in accordance with the terms of a perfect character, when he organizes, creates and supports the monadic system. Let us admit that he was free within the limits of the first definition, when he created it. May we say that he is altogether free in his administration of its affairs? The last section of the *Monadology* makes a sharp distinction between the presumptive or antecedent will and his secret, consequent, and decisive will. The former takes into consideration the basic forms which the will of God lays down; the latter gives a decision reached, when all possible actions, some in agreement, some in conflict, have been analyzed, and by a kind of parallelogram of spiritual forces, coördinated to attain the desired end. "A judge wills with an antecedent will that every man should devise a way to live, but wills with a consequent will that the murderer should be hanged." [28] In the first case, the divine

---

[26] *Op. cit.,* p. 68. [27] Latta, *op. cit.,* p. 417. [28] *Ibid.,* p. 270.

will is supremely free; in the second, freedom means "exclusion of restraint," that is, the overriding of all hostile conditions by the resolution to do a particular thing.

We may now proceed to prove that God's choice is freely exercised with a succinct and controlling motive. We are not concerned at the moment with the pattern to be selected but must demonstrate that the choice, when made, shall depend solely on the directing cause, in this case, the element of goodness. The quality of the good has swept the whole gamut of philosophical thought in the progress of the years. In Plato it is the consummate criterion for the acquisition of knowledge; in Plotinus it is the single attribute of Deity, equal to nothing except the principle of unity; for Augustine it is a solid moral quality stripped of its human limitations and wrapping Godhead in the noble conception of a father's love for his children. In Leibniz it bespeaks the decision of a mind preparing itself, so to say, for the epochal event in the total history of reality, namely, the institution of a harmonious universe. Goodness as a supernal property is to be communicated to the created edifice which must reflect metaphysical unity in the order and perfection of its parts. Thus, all types of created things will express the meaning of goodness, whether in the pleasurable stimulation of the body or in the highest form of excellence, the moral character of man. For these reasons the world must be the *best possible world*. Now if God is necessarily good, then, as Russell says, "his acts must necessarily be determined by the motives of the best"; [29] a sentiment which seems to be a true transcript of Leibniz' thought.

At this point we pause again and ask frankly, Is Leibniz or any other thinker justified in ascribing to Deity the same functional processes as those found in the operations of the human mind? It will be said at once that if we do not employ the common symbols of experience, we should be unable to offer any adequate suggestions of the kind of Deity we propose to worship. Justice and mercy, goodness and truth are concepts found in the confessional literature of every religious faith. If we reduce such concepts to abstract terms, we make religion nothing more than the recital of empty formulas wholly without effect upon moral behavior. Still it is our duty as serious inquirers to set a respectable limit to the use of anthropomorphic forms in a theological creed. The point at issue here is this: what right have we to say that God makes choices and in making a choice is guided by an indispensable motive? No scientific student of human behavior will deny that our actions are done through statable causes, called motives, and that these motives spring from the areas of desire within the mind. Ethics as a science recognizes this fact, jurisprudence refers to it repeatedly. Social intercourse makes the smallest de-

[29] *Op. cit.*, p. 37.

cision rest on a dominant incentive. Political diplomacy seeks the underlying reasons for a nation's action. The military system of modern Prussia
has had a single dogma behind it, the ambition to master and direct the
political habitudes of the entire world. The major principle in the drama
of the tragic stage, in Greece and England, is rooted in the same functional
process. May we not turn to God and find in him the same affinity? But
who in the wide range of scientific philosophy is willing to ascribe civil [30]
desires to the majesty of the divine Being? Or who will argue that the
superlative Will cannot act except after it has studied the object of its
action and formulated the reasons upon which action is to be based? The
current of such reasoning is artificial, undeferential, worthless, and should
be abandoned.

We must, however, let Leibniz tell us what shall be the blueprint upon
which the purposes of God are engrossed. He admits he has no cosmogony to offer as the early Greeks did. He intimates that the "received
doctrine is good enough for his purpose especially in his corner of the
world." [31] One settled idea is ascribed to the process of creation, the idea
of Fitness.[32] Fitness is a term used in applying the law of Sufficient Reason.
Truth is of two kinds, the truth of reason and the truth of fact. The
former belongs to the fundamental judgments whose contradictory cannot be conceived, e. g., the non-existence of God. The latter deals with
conditioned objects, things which might have been different, but *are as
they are* because of certain inherent causes. The world might have been
so constructed that life could not have appeared on the earth. Yet given
the eminent goodness of the divine Mind, no other environment than the
actual one could have been provided for the expression of its original
designs. This is not the law of necessity but the principle of Fitness, *con-
venance,* in French, an agreeable adjustment of conditions to meet particular needs. Such is Leibniz' meaning when he writes: "The order of
nature is grounded in the good pleasure (that is, the volitional power) of
God so that he may derive therefrom the superior reasons of grace." The
rule he follows is that all fit things are capable of actualization. "Possible
things," he says in a letter to Bernoulli, "are those which do not involve
a contradiction; actual things are nothing but the possible things which,
all things considered, are the best." This is the familiar doctrine of Optimism. Its argument is a matter of dialectic, and while to the scientific
mind it carries no conviction, yet it has left a profound impression on
certain religious devotees. Its requirements are simple: there are two preliminary judgments, that an infinity of possible worlds is open to the
imagination of the Creator and that his choice is necessarily the best.

---

[30] The word is used with the connotation attached to it in the *Ethics* of Plotinus.
[31] *New Essays*, p. 509.   [32] *Monadology*, Sec. 46.

We have stated the grounds of the choice; it remains to prove that the choice was a complete success. The proof is from experience or from abstract necessity. Experience shows that the one reason for doubting the success of the choice is the presence of evil. There are marked inequalities in the world, especially in human society. But who, Leibniz asks, does not note that in the end this is distinct good, a fact essential to the true welfare of the social group? Obviously, Leibniz is not an adherent of the school that later brought about the French Revolution. Again, disorder exists in nature, and especially in the social state. But who can say that disorder is not really another kind of order hidden from our view but an essential phase of the total harmony of the world? In general, do not the good things in life far outnumber the bad? Such a conclusion can be drawn by a careful comparison of the bad things which are local and the good things which are universal. The same result will be reached when we study the matter from the standpoint of rational necessity. If God had not created the best world he was capable of creating, we should be obliged to say that his power was inferior to his intelligence, a serious limitation to his excellence. Hence we can come to no other decision than this: he chose the best possible plan, in which variety was mingled with the greatest order. This is the climax reached in the *Theodicée*.[33]

The teaching of the philosopher so far has been of a positive cast; there is, however, another aspect that cannot be disregarded, a sinister aspect in the opinion of some commentators, a threat to future felicity, a hint that the created world may not be the *best* world, albeit it may be characterized as the best *possible* world. For the fact that the world is created and not ingenerate, as Spinoza alleged, carries with it certain serious qualifications. There is, for example, the element of *contingency,* dependence, which eliminates for all time the conception of necessary existence. God's being is necessary because his very name implies existence. He is subject to no other being but contains all reality in himself. "God is one and God is sufficient." [34] Language cannot express the full meaning of his character. But language *can* explain the properties of contingent being; logic has the categories with which scientific inquiry can satisfactorily work; it states the forms which created substance will take and the relations to other substances it will assume. All parts of the world small and great are in this system bound by a chain of causes which no single power can break. They stand arranged in a determinate series, each with its endowed character which it alone is able to develop. In the end, every monad is subject to the will of the Creator and may be extinguished by his decree alone. Leibniz cites the principle of inertia in physical bodies; they are forced to persist in a certain line of action until deflected by a

---

[33] Nourrison, *op. cit.,* p. 303.   [34] *Monadology,* Sec. 39.

body of greater energy; but any change in direction is due to the pre-established relations which God has ordained and which no natural power can resist, block or alter.

Contingency is specifically evident in the status of the human monad, enveloped as it is in a body which prevents it from making its perceptions clear and distinct. From one point of view it might appear that the soul of man possesses sovereign authority over its own career, and, as mirroring the world at large, sums up the fundamental powers of all substance. At this point Leibniz might suggest that he has done a definite service to his monads by confining them within the original Harmony; there they are guided by the omniscient Mind.[35] This is all very well in theory but it does not remove them from the primordial conditions under which all created things rest. If man could absorb the potencies of God he, too, would be divine. But experience with its rough preceptorial discipline instructs him that although he is made in the image of God—a kind of "small divinity in his sphere" [36]—he is still a *reflection* of the perfect substance, not a conquering saint in his own right. For contingency is not merely of body but of mind, a radical inability to grasp the meaning of nature despite its imaged glory in our own thought. The first and immediate problem that confronts the inquirer obtains no solution: "It cannot be demonstrated by any argument that bodies actually exist; and nothing prevents some well-ordered dream from appearing to our judgment to be true." [37] If we cannot answer this question, how can we expect to prove categorically that God exists? Furthermore, in a moral crisis involving a conflict of duties how shall we know, with our meager intelligence, what type of action embodies the *fittest* elements of goodness? The task weighs with crushing burden upon the bewildered soul. Contingency exists, it must be surmounted; but—*how?*

THE SALVATION OF MAN AND THE WORLD

The nature and destiny of man was a subject of perpetual interest to the Continental school. We have in a former paragraph discussed the relation of soul and body as viewed by the competing theories of the time. Here we must study one particular phase of human behavior, namely the meaning of will. Descartes concluded that knowledge was strictly a matter of internal thought; perception and memory, acting through the senses may deliver the brute material but judgment alone could determine the meaning of the object observed. This is in the stage of receptivity. In the case of action, whether in reaching truth or making a moral decision, the initiative proceeds from the individual through the instrumentality of the will. Judgment may fix the content of the thought but its truth or

---

[35] *Ibid.*, Secs. 56–60.   [36] *Ibid.*, Sec. 83.   [37] Russell, *op. cit.*, p. 225.

essential value depends on will alone. If the will goes beyond the scientific evidence, there is error; if it trespasses beyond the borders of ascertained goodness, it is sin. Human liberty is a natural endowment and cannot be restrained. Against this theory the Occasionalist such as Geulinox argued that thought and action are simultaneous but that both are inaugurated by divine energy and to all intents and purposes without the consent of the individual. Spinoza also appeared to leave man without freedom to choose. Man, we saw, is a *mode* of universal substance, not an independent figure in the drama. His duty is to follow his purposes, physical and mental, many of which he holds in common with other individuals, all being subject to inflexible law. According to a superficial analysis of this theory man would seem to have no will of his own; he is nothing but the total will of Nature which is God. Leibniz rejects each theory in turn, the first because will is indefinitely extended and therefore makes no deliberate choice; the second, because a "miracle" would be needed to make possible the proposed union of thought and action; the last, because it is the result of "blind necessity," whose other name is fatalism.

What then does Leibniz mean by will? It does not have the same prominence in his mind as in Descartes'. He appears to identify it, though somewhat hazily, with the appetitive function of soul. Under the spur of Locke's *Treatise,* he later studied the effects of human conduct considered from the point of view of the inducements which lead men to perform the particular action. No act can be done, so to speak, in the void: the will which dictates a certain type of behavior without regard to pertinent motives is the will of a brute not of a rational agent. But—let us be sure of this—the mind of man is not a set of balances where competing motives may be of equal strength, no choice therefore being possible. Even in the most exact measurements of physics it is doubtful if such an equilibrium exists. In the ideal world which we know, it does not exist. If there were no other operating cause, the mere caprice of the moment would tip the scales for or against the proposed action; for the mind is a congeries of disconnected ideas or unanalyzed images or random impulses, and any one of these, even when the mind does not note its presence, may make a decision which prolonged deliberation had been unable to render. Leibniz' controversy with Clarke helped to clarify his understanding of the meaning of will and its influence on human activity. But the main question is, When is the will free? Hence, What do we mean by liberty of choice?

Freedom, he says, cannot be defined to be the capacity of acting according as the momentary impulse suggests. The concept of monadic substance forbids; the will is not a part of the secondary matter, that is, the body, where instinctive experiences originate; it belongs to the federal nature of the monad and therefore represents the basic interest of the individual. In the *Discourse on Metaphysics* he selects an illustration from Roman history. Julius Caesar is destined to become the perpetual dictator of the republic and as such will demolish the liberties of its citizens. All this is specifically contained in Caesar's "concept." For the concept includes not merely the generic traits of an individual but the specific features which are to distinguish Julius from his contemporaries. Furthermore, the imprint of character includes the right of a man to make his own choice. While Caesar is forced by circumstances to occupy a place of great power in the Roman state, he made his own way by the exercise of will, when the particular choices went into effect. Character, thus, is not a blueprint laid down at birth, bearing the items in his entire career: the judgments he is to make, the enmities he is to contract, even the small and trivial incidents, the *petites perceptions,* to which we give a mere passing glance or no attention whatsoever. Such experiences are in the character only in germ, but when we observe them in retrospect, we discover how the future is built on the past. Thus from a career already accomplished we may project our vision into the certain future. This is the rational determinism of a scientific creed. Clearly, freedom is not in any way impaired by so firm an adherence to the type of character drawn from our intrinsic qualities. Rather has it manifested the truth of the approved definition, that freedom is governed by law, which is the group of universal ideas resident in the individual mind or established canons current in the civil state. In this conclusion Leibniz is supported by his contemporary, Spinoza (when properly interpreted), and by the educated opinion of the whole civilized world.

There is another implication in the subject of human freedom which is of interest to the theologian if not to the philosopher. Leibniz refers to it in many connections, and we state it merely to complete the record. It is assumed that the universe is organized on the basis of a plan conceived and implemented before its actual creation. The monads are joined to one another by divine decree, each with its own character, its independent function and its inherent right to liberty of thought and action. However, the omniscient Mind, which orders events, knows in advance what will happen in each of several instances. Does this mean that the freedom of the monad is impaired in quality, reduced in scope, even deprived of the power to initiate its own course of conduct? There is a subtle difficulty here and the religious teacher is bound to approach it cautiously. Let us not forget that the term *necessity* has two definitions, the first is categorical, where we apply the law of contradiction, the second is hypothetical, employed invariably in making existential judgments. If we could obtain a full demonstration of the reasons why Caesar crossed the Rubicon, entailing the conclusion that—given the facts as we know them—the event *must* have occurred, then we should prove not that the event was necessary *in itself* but that it embraced a "world of things which God had freely chosen according to a first decree, which is necessary, and a subsequent decree which committed to men the right to do freely what appeared to be for the best." [38] Caesar might have declined to cross the river, since that action was contingent and therefore could have been supplanted by its opposite. What he did, *followed the concept* of his character and was not an infringement on divine order but an exhibition of his own freedom itself ordained by God. Thus human liberty is seen to be a part of the rational constitution of the world; it is contingent since it springs from a fixed character; yet it is spontaneous, because it belongs to the nature of a divine creation, not as Descartes taught, merely to the feeling of the human soul. But then we ask, Is not spontaneity a sort of concealed intuition, not a judgment based upon logical reasoning? If that be true, how does it differ from the behavior of the Cartesian will? Perhaps, this is what Leibniz means when he speaks of the human monad as a "spiritual automaton," which "could regularly produce in it everything that will happen to it, that is to say, all its perceptual appearances or volitional expressions, without the help of any created thing." [39]

At this point emerges a problem which has staggered the logic and sometimes the faith of the serious student. It is true that perceptions *are* obscure and the conclusions drawn from them uncertain or even false. It is also true that by a combination of circumstances, sometimes unforeseen, even unforeseeable, men fall into sin, a moral dereliction which would seem to be contrary to the undergirding principles of the world. But error and sin are not the only forms of evil. Evil exists in triplicate, metaphysical, organic, moral. Evil is the opposite of good, and since good exists in the corresponding forms, we are required to determine how a denial of the three goods has been brought about. Contingency is an "original imperfection" and therefore anterior to the emergence of sin. Whether sin is prior to pain, is a question which science cannot answer. Pleasure and pain are necessary concomitants of sentient action and one cannot exist without the other. It must be then assumed that feelings belong to the nature of nerve-controlled animals. The case of moral declension is more complex. If *good* means the normal functioning of all organic bodies, including man, then the term does not necessarily include the concept of moral values. In this case the term "good" applies only to physiological or psychical activity, not to the matters of honesty, honor, or other virtues. But evil, as Russell says, is in any system of morals, a "positive predi-

[38] Montgomery, *op. cit.*, pp. 20–22.   [39] Latta, *op. cit.*, p. 315.

cate"; [40] therefore it cannot be merely the privation of good. Here Leibniz is not consistent in his analysis of the term. In the *Theodicée* he is inclined to argue for the negative form of the definition; he calls attention to our outraged exclamations against pain, while we let the evidences of sound health of body and mind go unnoticed. Thus he seems to argue that evil, whether pain or sin, is nothing but our failure to maintain the solid reality of thought and action at all times. In that case we could not blame the Creator for discords originating in our own miscalculations. But if good be the positive quality it must belong to man as a primitive endowment; what, then shall we say of evil? If it is also a positive property and if it belongs to man as a natural gift, then the concept of Harmony must either change its definition or be superseded by another term. But Leibniz would consent to neither alternative: three points are clear in his mind, that sin is a moral factor in human behavior, that it is contrary to the canons of divine law, and that it is in need of drastic treatment looking to its ultimate elimination. Once for all he rejects the implication that because sin rests upon the contingency of our nature we must place the blame for it squarely upon an error in the original plan—God made human beings who could not resist temptations. He also rejects the notion that men pursue an "unavoidable delusion," supposing themselves to be good when they are in reality seamed with guilt. [41] Many of his statements on the subject lack vigor or pertinency; "sin is seeking one's good in an imperfect, unenlighted way" [42] or, "sin is an inconvenient lapse into disorder." [43] He does not hesitate to say that there is a break in the divine Harmony and the break is followed by precise and equivalent recompense. Nature adjusts her movements to the violation of her laws. She makes a similar adjustment when the virtue of a good man is recognized. [44] There is a restraining power in the whole system of natural and ideal law; what is it and how shall we determine its purpose?

At this point there is a sudden change in the argument of the philosopher. The semi-scientific attitude disappears; its place is taken by the sentimental outlook of the religious moralist. Even the terminology changes; the universal Monad is no longer an aggregate of coördinated monads but a "perfect state" with a government based on moral principles. The *City of God* stands over against the mechanical rigidity of the physical world. The celebrated title drawn from St. Augustine has assumed a totally different meaning. For the Latin writer it denoted a company of elected souls which faced with stern decision the City of the World, the Roman dominion of greed and brutal servitude. For Leibniz it embraced the ideal interests as contrasted with the efficient causes deployed by the demands

[40] *Op. cit.,* p. 201.   [41] *Ibid.,* p. 199.   [42] Latta, *op. cit.,* p. 269.
[43] *New Essays,* pp. 261, 206.   [44] *Monadology,* Sec. 88.

of physics. The first example of modern Idealism is drafted in this exposition, the forerunner of Kant's *Criticism*, Fichte's *Voluntarism*, and the adroit analyses of Ward and Royce. The primordial order is disturbed by the entry of sin; the right of sin to exist is challenged by the "realm of Grace" which is the seat of final causes in their loftiest form. It would seem that the author had canvassed the whole area of causes in the natural universe and reached the conclusion that harmony could be restored only by a new expression of the constitutive Will; no man could escape from the effect of hereditary sin by his own resources. The "pure love" of God can and will reëstablish the moral equilibrium. Does this imply that redemption proceeds without any effort by the moral agent? By no means: men singly and in communities must work to make the redemptive principle effective in every sphere. While it may be true that the "greatest possible good is compatible with a certain amount of evil," that does not prevent us from rooting out the iniquities that lie directly in our path. We may agree that while "nature is red in tooth and claw," biological evolution proves decisively that progress in the formation of new and higher species is steady and sure. Social progress demands the application of the same rule. Restraint laid upon arrogant offenders, the isolation of pest-ridden areas, even the conquest of the consummate scourge of war, may share in the realization of the ideal of social harmony. Final causes must eventually triumph over corporeal force. Does this contravene in any way the sentiment with which his *Monadology* closes: "It is impossible to make the world better than it is, not only as a whole and in general, but also for ourselves in particular"? If Leibniz means that we cannot add one new element to the structure of the universe, he is right; if he introduces a defeatist note—progress further than a given point is excluded—he is wrong. However, the argument now passes beyond the bounds of scientific verification; we may accept it or not as seems advisable. At least we must admit, it is not a theory that may be casually glimpsed and then discarded.[45]

One critical point, however, cannot be disregarded. Allowing that the teleological concept may serve as a tentative explanation of certain operations in nature, as Kant does in his *Critique of Judgment*, we refuse to apply the principles of moral purpose outside the realm of human behavior. It is a sheer exhibition of anthropomorphism, we said, to ascribe to the divine Will the choice between competing motives such as human experience reveals. Similarly, to speak of a "moral world within the mechanical world" is an antithesis that has no meaning. To be sure, man has a body as well as a soul, but never in his wildest fancies has Leibniz ever defined God as the soul of the world. Plato and the Stoics taught that human

[45] See J. S. Mill's comment, *Three Essays on Religion* (New York: Holt, 1874), p. 40, note.

morals could find authentic rules of conduct in the order of the heavens and in the relation of means to ends on the earth; but they never, except by a permissible hyperbole, substituted human qualities for the laws of nature. Kant is thought by some commentators to have erected an ethico-theological creed which named moral values as the essential attributes of Deity. What he said in his later works on the subject was that religion is the sublimation of moral concepts; we cannot prove the presence of a divine Being, but we must think and act *as if* a supreme prescription were laid upon our moral consciousness.[46] Even the confessions of the Christian Church are careful not to take literally the poetic language of the ancient scriptures. The anger of man is one thing, the "anger" of God is quite another. Hence, when a modern thinker deliberately places the "realm of grace" on an exact parallel with the realm of mechanism, making God the monarch of the one and the architect of the other, he has deliberately severed his relations with the authoritative ideas of philosophy and has no right to demand an acceptance of his views.

THE EXISTENCE OF GOD

The universe is the signature of God and it cannot be accounted for in any way except on the assumption that he exists. There is harmony, there is order in the processes of nature; the monads despite their infinite diversity act together; they act together unceasingly. God is thus not only the institutor of the world, he is its perpetual supporter. All theories that find the energy of creation and sustenance within the world are inadequate and false. Aristotle's criticism of the atomic theory that it offered no cause for the origin of motion or its deflection from its initial course, is misplaced. A supreme power accounts for both and must be presupposed. Aristotle's own doctrine that God is the principle of motion and hence governs the world, is valuable so far as it goes; but it stops short of the final thesis: *God must exist.*

But the argument for his existence is not as simple as this. Thomas Aquinas made the necessary amendment to the Aristotelian creed and gave a complete statement of the cosmological proof. But what would happen to the proof if nature were found to be disjointed and inharmonious in this point or that? The speculations of the Epicureans, modernized, cannot be wholly disregarded. Leibniz admits the presence of disagreeable elements and is driven to a sophism to save the moral nature of his Deity. The created world is limited; hence subject to error. But error cannot be charged against God, the Creator, only against man, the creature; for God did not put his essence into the world, only his power. The difficulties are serious and could not be surmounted if he followed the

[46] Cf. Chap. X, *infra.*

second proof, to its end. He therefore assumes that before the moment of creation a harmony of all possible created objects was established. But the authentic proof for the divine existence rests not upon the visible order of nature but upon the capacity of the human mind and its inherent ideas. We follow here the two laws of logic, contradiction and sufficient reason.

(a) The first may be stated in these terms: that proposition whose opposite cannot be conceived is true. Leibniz examined the ancient arguments and found them faulty. God is defined as the most real Being, having all possible attributes including existence. This is Anselm's proof questioned and rejected by Thomas on the ground that he takes for granted what he intended to prove. No object can have properties assigned to it unless it is first assumed to be real. But Leibniz retorts that the trouble with the proof lies not in an imperfect premise but in a truncated syllogism. The true underlying premise is this: Is the idea of an "all-great or all-perfect being" a possible idea? If it meets a concise contradiction, it is false and no argument can save it. We *can* conceive of substances, empirical objects, which have limitations. Are we sure that the bursting bud will turn into luscious fruit? Are we even sure that the sun will rise tomorrow? On the other hand, is there any observation or reflection which forbids us to think of a Being which necessarily exists? The mind can add length to length, surface to surface, solid to solid and thus construct an infinite universe, Are we in any manner prohibited from doing the same with the idea of God? He sums up the proof in these words: "It is the reality of eternal truth that proves the fact in question." [47]

But the dialectical form of the proof will not deceive the cautious reader. "We have the right to assume the possibility of every being especially that of God, until someone proves the contrary." But our quarrel is not with the use of the law of contradiction but with his attempt to convert an uncontradicted idea into an objective fact. He calls the argument "morally demonstrative"; that, however, is not a determination of logic but a declaration of faith. He should have admitted that universal ideas require not an external force (God himself) to verify them, but an inward principle to bring them into coördination and keep them so. The logical value of an idea of God who *forces* truth upon a concept is very small; yet the regulative value of the simple idea of God is considerable. But Kant had no illusions about the influence of a transcendental logic; it could not translate the idea into its substantial reality; but it could convince the attentive mind that without the idea of a supervisory Intelligence, universal conclusions would have but temporary significance; they could never become permanent principles of thought and action.

We return for a moment to the dictum that we have a sure foundation

[47] *Monadology*, Sec. 45.

for the existence of God in the "reality of eternal truth." Study the words in the 44th section of the *Monadology;*—"For if there is a reality in essences or possibilities, or rather in eternal truths, the reality must be grounded in something existing and actual and consequently in the existence of the necessary Being, in whom essence involves existence, or in whom to be possible is to be actual." Disregarding here the "truths" ordinarily associated with religious theory, we confine our attention to such ideas as Descartes had in mind when he used the same type of argument. Thus, every axiom of geometry is a universal truth; it is "eternal" because in no instance known to us or capable of being conceived by us, can the contradictory be entertained. However, we must not forget that mathematics is a fabricated system; it is a series of judgments laid down as guides to experience; in most cases they will consist of conclusions deduced from practical observations. That such propositions may at some time be radically changed is quite within the range of scientific expectancy. In our own day the familiar rule of the interior angles of a triangle as equal two right angles, no longer holds. We have substituted physical space for ideal space and destroyed its verity. Dare we say that other universal "truths" may not, sooner or later, be subject to the same drastic treatment? Even the categorical certainty of the law of contradiction is challenged now. How can we indicate the presence of the contradictory except by a negative prefix? But as a matter of actual experience how shall we prove that it is a valid rule? Of course, reasoning becomes a hazardous enterprise when we are not sure whether certain predicates can be imposed upon a given subject. But we must face the probability that universal truths are not fixed and unalterable, as they were under the Schoolmen's regime. If we cannot guarantee their validity, how can we build upon them, as Augustine did, an iron-clad proof for the divine existence? This, we are convinced, is the way to criticize the Leibnizean doctrine, not by the dialectical method which Russell uses, namely, to convict the philosopher of arguing that because the human mind knows the eternal truths resident in the divine Mind, it therefore mirrors not only the universe but also the mind of God itself.

(b) The second proof is based on the principle of sufficient reason which may be stated thus:—No fact is real except on grounds requiring it to be so and not otherwise. Leibniz is concerned here with what he calls "truths of fact," judgments that have no necessary universality but which depend for their validity on the exact properties of the sense-data and on the constancy and coherence of experience. He is not concerned with Descartes' contention that the idea of God appearing in the mind must have an adequate cause; that sensation and reflection can produce all other ideas as, for example, substance, motion, duration, even its own

Ego, but cannot be the cause of this; that, therefore, God himself must have planted the idea in our mind. He *is* concerned with establishing, if he can, the meaning and truth of man's common experiences. In order to do this we must explain two sets of facts,—first, the "present and past forms and motions which go to make up the efficient cause of my present writing," and secondly, the modes of thought which represent the basic purposes of living. Why have I expressed myself in precisely this way and not another? The series of events leading to a momentary action is an infinite regress. What is its ultimate cause? Can it be the group of images, emotions, judgments assembled in my mind, or the group of external bodies from which the first impressions were derived? No: the sufficient or *final* cause must be "outside of the series of particular contingent things, however far continued this series might be." [48] In short, it must lie in a "necessary substance in which the variety of particular changes exist only by eminent representation," which seems to mean that God anticipates every form of monadic experience but never entertains the actual images themselves. This is Leibniz' theory. One point, however, is deliberately avoided—he does not prove why the Cause should be *outside* the universe and not within it. As Russell trenchantly remarks: "He might equally well have said that every finite is conditioned by some other finite, but the whole series cannot be conditioned by any existent." [49] In that case he would have identified his system with that of Spinoza and in due time would have been at the mercy of the reigning religious authorities. Actually at this point he changed his concept of God; then, realizing, before it was too late, the seriousness of the issue, by an adroit act of faith he translated the limiting concept, which would be Spinoza's God, into a real substance, and thus severed the cause completely from the world. In his latest thesis he forestalls the doctrine of Berkeley: God controls the activity of the human mind and certifies to the truth of its decisions. But even here he does not disregard or alter the specific character of finite individuals: "the imperfections of all monads depend upon their own nature which is necessarily limited." [50]

By virtue of these two arguments we have uncovered an infallible sanction for the laws of logic and thus made human knowledge subject to full verification. We have also completed a study of the origin and nature of the physical universe by providing a first and adequate Cause, together with the assurance that moral government both in human society and in the total "City of God" shall be perpetually preserved. The soundness of the arguments remained unimpaired, until the last and successful attack upon them was made by the critical method of Immanuel Kant.

[48] *Ibid.*, Sec. 77.   [49] *Op. cit.*, p. 177.   [50] *Monadology*, Sec. 41.

VIII: SPINOZA

IN ATTEMPTING to study the ideas of so versatile a thinker as Spinoza, it is required of us first of all to decide what part of his public writings we intend to examine, and what our attitude should be to the remainder. The orbit of his life was limited: he died at the age of forty-five. His creative work, however, began at an early period when he uncovered some of the flaws in the Cartesian system and then rehearsed in his *Metaphysical Thoughts* what seemed to him to be the vital points in this doctrine. Prior to both of these volumes, but lost to the scrutiny of scholars for more than a century, was his *Short Treatise on God, on Man, and on his Wellbeing,* an elementary analysis of the principal concepts which have made the name and achievements of their author illustrious throughout the world. These works are lodged in the background of his total contributions to philosophy; they envisage the glories that are to be. We are content to leave them in the hands of critical inquirers, while we peer into the unfinished tractate on scientific method, the elaborate study of theological conceits, and finally the crowning monument of his genius to which he gave the simple but enveloping title, The *Ethics*. It was completed in 1675 and made ready for the press; but the grim menace of persecuting hate curbed his will in the crucial hour; and when he carried the precious manuscript to the printers, he was stopped by the warning words that "the theologicans were laying plots against him on every hand," and that publication must be postponed. "The matter grows worse from day to day," he wrote to Oldenburg, "and I know not what I shall do." He did nothing since there was nothing he could do. But undismayed he threw himself into the prosecution of his remaining projects while his physical strength allowed. He died on the 21st day of February, 1677, and a company of distinguished mourners followed him to his sepulture in the neighboring church. In the next autumn the book, for which he literally gave his life, was duly published by his friends but only his bare initials appeared on the title page.

Then the storm broke and the fury of his enemies found speedy utterance. Contempt and contumely were heaped upon his memory. His "hideous hypothesis" was derided and scorned; it was judged to be a threat to every kind of religious truth. His private motives were impugned and his most sublime precepts were held to be tainted with hypocrisy. His teachings on government were rejected as subversive in their implications. Except for the meagre group of partisans who had supported him when living, the judgment of leaders in church, state and school was wholly against him; that judgment persisted for a hundred years, that is, until the mind of Europe awoke to a new sense of independence which was to culminate in the convulsions of the French Revolution. Lessing in Germany caught the first glint of Spinoza's superiority and confessed that here was the earliest suggestion of a rational system of thought in the modern age. Scholars began to explore the intricacies of his doctrine, and by the beginning of the 19th century his name had lost its forbidding color and he was reckoned by impartial critics to be one of the major prophets in the latest renaissance of thought. But even Spinoza himself could not have dreamed of the "splendor with which his work was to shine forth in the newer world after a period of eclipse." [1] Men have now learned to admire the solidity of his analyses, although they may not accept all of his metaphysical conclusions. They have noted, too, the precise equivalence between his moral evaluations and the serenity of his private demeanor. The *Ethics* is a scientific exposition of human emotions and a recitation of the formulas by which they may be controlled; it reflects the highest wisdom that the unaided mind of man has ever reached. It enshrines also the intimate relations between moral standards and religious ideals, and it imposes a solemn obligation upon the cultivated intellect to study the concepts of spirit with the same zeal that we show in investigating the operations of the natural world.

Therefore in seeking to determine the judgments of Spinoza on the highest of all themes, the nature and activity of God, we shall confine our attention largely to that work which, by his own admission, contains the ultimate and definitive statement of his credo. We shall have occasion to refer to the small treatise on method and the larger tractate on practical theology, as well as to certain important letters written to dispel doubts which have arisen in the minds of his correspondents. In the letters he appears as a patient and sympathetic co-laborer in the quest of truth. He does not dictate, nor does he compromise. He invites objections when the point at issue is not clear. He suffers no affront when his opinion is candidly challenged. But in most cases his conclusions are based on premises so inexorably fixed that once they are granted, criticism is resolved into cordial acceptance. It is significant that his friends, without exception, acknowledge the authentic honesty of his argument; they may disagree with the results but they never hint, even in the most indirect manner,

[1] Pollock, *Spinoza: His Life and Philosophy*, p. 37.

that he sought to reach the end in view by logical subterfuge or a piece of spurious reasoning. Few workers in this extremely difficult field have acquired an equal esteem for sincerity among his learned and unbiased contemporaries. Leibniz is the single dissident, and his complaints, when they have value, spring from motives not altogether worthy of his better judgment. This is an item that should not be forgotten when we confront the new and oftimes staggering conceptions imbedded in the theorems of the divine science, as Aristotle called it.

HOW WE CAN KNOW GOD

The problem of knowledge is the first technical question with which the philosopher is obliged to wrestle. Spinoza considers it in detail in the second Part of the *Ethics*. He had already discussed its elementary properties in the earlier treatise (before 1662).[2] It was obvious at once to him that cognition is not a simple process of mind which a neophyte could analyze and understand. After a meticulously careful examination of the data, he marked off three types of objects which are presented to the attentive mind for its consideration. We have not a scrap of information to indicate that he had critically studied the Platonic schedule unfolded in the Sixth Book of the *Republic* and known to scholars as the Divided Line. He did observe in a letter to Boxel, 1674, that the "authority of Plato, Aristotle and Socrates did not carry much weight with him." However, the remark may have been a mere *obiter dictum* struck off without any intention to depreciate the value of their work. What is clear is that Spinoza has hit upon the same three forms of knowledge and named the objects which each form was capable of grasping. We shall, of course, refrain from arguing that because the two thinkers used the same logical method they must perforce develop the same metaphysical system. A comparison with a previous chapter in this volume will disclose the points in which they differ. It is well to recall that logic is a broad and encyclopedic discipline and can be applied to the most diverse philosophical projects.

The first object of knowledge is the particular and concrete *thing* that comes within the view of the active senses. Let us pause for a moment to determine what this individual thing will be. Considered as an object outside the system of the human body, it must not be regarded as detached from its neighbors, existing in splendid isolation, an atomic unit such as Epicurus imagined, "a monad without windows," as Leibniz taught. There is no specifically formed and spatially independent thing in the universe. What the imagination observes through the senses or what the mind entertains as idea, is a necessary integer in the divine nature; it is caused by God and cannot be separated from God. Individuality, then,

2 *Correspondence of Spinoza*. Trans. by A. Wolf, p. 98.

is what we now call a "mental construct" and has no existence of its own. There is only one individual existing in its own right, as we shall soon discover, that is, God. God is complete substance with an infinity of attributes, two of which, thought and extension, can be apprehended by us. We can never envision the whole of substance, we can only know its *modes,* the forms in which natural "objects" make their impact on our bodies, or as Spinoza sometimes says, by which nature expresses itself. The modes of substance, then, are the objects with which human perception has to do.

Now experience follows a fixed and regular pattern symbolized by Spinoza in the formula: "the order and connection of ideas is the same as the order and connection of things." [3] This means that there are two aspects to every perception, first, the sensory reaction, and secondly, the ideational content. The impact of a body from without the human body or a change of structural relations within the human body, generates a new situation which he calls the *ideatum* or image. This belongs to the field of extension and obeys the laws of physiology in every particular. Corresponding to the image is the idea which indicates what the image means. This, in turn, belongs to the field of thought and ultimately becomes subject to the laws of logic. [4] Thus Spinoza separates the two elements joined by Kant in his sense-manifold, where the organic changes supply the *matter,* while the mind through the idea supplies the *form.* The point emphasized by both inquirers is that every perception has two aspects which are not two separate operations but a single operation judged from two standpoints, or as Spinoza says, by the application of two different attributes. It is not essential at this time to examine the details of his theory of knowledge; we may simply note the following events that succeed one another in natural order: the development of the function of memory, the creation of the productive imagination, the synthesis of ideas by means of common terms, such as man, house, animal, or by the more elaborate concepts, time, measure, number, or again by transcendental ideas, being, infinity, indivisibility, and finally, the assumption that man is a self-conscious subject capable of formulating his own intellectual program and of organizing his own moral conduct. In a rather cryptic theorem he writes: "the idea of the mind is united to the mind in the same way as the mind is united to the body." [5] This appears to mean that the mind is a collection of ideas and thus is a concrete whole when engaged in making a specific decision. Hence, the idea we form of our personal identity at a given time is as firm and irrevocable as the idea which we form of the state of our body at one particular moment or the unlimited experiences which we enjoy throughout life. This is

[3] *Ethics,* II, 7.   [4] *Ibid.,* II, 16.   [5] *Ibid.,* II, 21.

Spinoza's method of justifying a man's right to *think;* it does not, however, establish his ability to think *correctly.*[6] Why not? This is the next problem before us.

The answer is at hand. Imagination which is nature's gift to man concerns itself only with the limited corporeal sphere within which the individual subject moves. Experience proves how exceedingly confused our information is respecting our own sensory behavior or the properties of the objects which impinge upon our bodies. We perceive things after the "common order of nature" and as a result are governed by the "fortuitous play of circumstances."[7] Single images are real and exact in themselves; thus, the sun in the heavens appears to the normal eye to be 200 feet from its point of observation. When, however, reason enters and we study the laws of refraction, together with the principle of gravitation, soon to be scientifically calculated by Sir Isaac Newton, that is to say, when we try "to understand the points of agreement, difference and contrast," then the hasty opinion based upon vagrant images is seen to be wholly fallacious and must be discredited. In fact, he goes on, all particular things, the imaginary wholes which sensation has produced, are "contingent and perishable" and cannot yield adequate knowledge.[8] Then Spinoza takes one further step and demands that we follow precisely the same practice in the solution of certain philosophical problems. In the Appendix to Part I of the *Ethics* he denounces the attempts of distinguished theorists to find an "order" in natural phenomena other than that which ensues upon the operation of natural laws. He satirizes the hypothesis that evidences of design in the world express the benevolent regard of the Creator towards his last and most important creation, namely, man. He brings the dogmatist face to face with the question: "If all things follow from the absolutely perfect nature of God, why are there so many unpropitious things in the world, corruption, deformity, confusion, evil and sin?" The critical attitude here followed is quite in line with that adopted by modern science in its solution of the empirical problems of everyday concern. Men allow their imagination which is extremely restricted, to dictate the terms by which the universal laws of nature are to be construed. Imagination is a fragile instrument which must be superseded by the trusted rules of reason. If every type of knowledge has its own object, what shall be the object which invokes the offices of reflection for its true understanding? In the first kind, it was a concrete individual which left its impression on the human body and uncovered a collateral idea in the human mind. Plainly, reason cannot be satisfied with studying a single isolated thing however striking and diversified its properties are. Reason does not perceive in the same way that imagination does; it has, for example, no need for the ex-

<hr>

[6] *Ibid.,* II, 29.   [7] *Ibid.,* II, 29, Scholium.   [8] *Ibid.,* II, 31, Corollary.

ensions of space; for if it depended on these for its knowledge of the human body, it would fail in its quest. It could not even discover the meaning of a single organ like the heart by the exercise of mathematical computation, which is the device by which imagination acts. Furthermore, the function of a given organ of the body, including its tissues and the cells composing the tissues, cannot be discovered by a concrete empirical image.[9] Reflection deals with capacities more subtle than these; it insists upon establishing the relations between separate cells, between cells and tissues, between tissues and the entire organ. Plato places this type of knowledge within the sphere of judgment; he sets a limit to the uses of the imagination; yet while judgment deals with the contents of the image, finding the source of all its basic facts *there*, it alone furnishes the methods by which appropriate ideas are predicated of any given subject in the proposition. There is no doubt that this is also Spinoza's procedure and that he bases his method of scientific inquiry upon it. It is clear that he anticipates, in the large, the celebrated system of Kant who discovers in the mind the constituent instruments of thought, not independent ideas, as Descartes said, but modes of predication, called categories,— quantity, quality, relation and modality. Spinoza in the realistic manner which he always pursued, pitched on the common properties discernible in every object under review, and at once inferred that the mind will have common notions corresponding to the elements of the organic responses.[10] Such notions are the instruments of explanation. He has not submitted a formal list of categories, but if he had done so, the list would certainly have included substance, intelligence, motion and individuality.[11] These he called the "foundations of our rational thinking." They strip from our thought every contingent, partial and time-serving aspect and force us to perceive things "under a certain form of eternity." [12] Did Spinoza propose that such properties should be conceived as passing into the mind through the channels of sensation, as Alexander suggests for some of the basic notions, such as causality? One point in the argument, however, is fixed, namely, that when an idea has been gained through the correct operation of the categorical judgment, such idea is known to the recipient *as a true idea,* an idea whose verity he cannot question, because it involves the "eternal and infinite essence of God." [13] The conclusion of his argument is that knowledge obtained by the prescriptions of reason is wholly and necessarily true and adequate.

However, lest the argument should savor too much the dry formalism of the Schoolmen, we may study for a moment the criteria he used to detect an adequate idea. Descartes furnishes his point of departure. Ideas

[9] *Ibid.,* II, 27, 29.   [10] *Ibid.,* II, 38, Corollary.   [11] *Ibid.,* II, 40, Scholium 1.
[12] *Ibid.,* II, 44, Corollary 2.   [13] *Ibid.,* II, 43, 45.

are true when they are clear and distinct, and under no other conditions. When is an idea clear and when is it distinct? For Spinoza as for Descartes, clearness meant that the object under scrutiny was separated from all other objects of perception or thought and considered on its own merits. This attitude did not imply that the object could be completely insulated from its neighbor, which would obviously be impossible, but that its individual position in the world of things or ideas should be strictly delimited. Thus, the so-called objects of "design" in the physical universe had not been sufficiently segregated, that is, removed from the environment of other objects, namely, human beings, whose "good" they were supposed to promote, in order to enable the observer to make a critical examination of their meaning. The idea, says Spinoza, must always agree with its ideatum; but when the ideatum, image, carries with it as a penumbra the vague forms of adjacent objects, surely no clear perception will result. But this is not all: the idea must also be distinct in presenting its essential properties. If these properties cannot be disengaged from the given object for immediate and separate study, it cannot be understood. Spinoza states the matter succinctly thus: "Who, I ask, can *know* that he understands a thing, unless he first understands it? Or, to put in other terms, who can *know* that he is sure of a thing unless he is first sure of *that thing?* For a true idea is the criterion of truth, and as light uncovers both itself and darkness, so truth is a criterion both of truth (trueness) and falsehood." [14] Recurring to the previous example, we ask on what grounds we can assign the attributes of beauty or order or significant purpose to a universe whose physical edifice is based on the laws of mechanism, not on the postulate of a moral Architect, building for the benefit of his rational creatures. A distinct idea contains only the principles necessarily belonging to the object we are investigating. The introduction of irrelevant materials confuses our thought and makes definition impossible. Hence, when an idea represents its own object without the addition of extraneous matter, and when it expresses fully the inherent properties of the object, then it must be taken as adequate, that is, as true. This is the logic of science and by the precise use of its methods we may understand and appreciate the immediate world in which we live, move and have our being.

But Spinoza is not satisfied even with the second form of knowledge important and convincing as it is. We have indeed been released from the casual and uncertain forms of imaged thought and been taught how to construct the laws by which things are governed and ideas controlled. But we are still bound by the conventions of eye and ear and touch; we can go no further than the eye can reach either by its naked glance or the accentuated sight of the telescope for distance and the microscope for

[14] *Ibid.*, II, 43, Scholium.

inute inspection. Beyond these lies the infinite expanse of Reality, divine
bstance, the only complete and universal Individual. How can such an
bject be known? The subtleties of the imagination are of no consequence
re; the analytical discriminations of the syllogism cannot perform their
stinctive offices. What was Plato's resource when the goal of reason, the
ood, swept within the orbit of his intellectual ken? He did what Spinoza
oposed to do; he left behind him the coercions of logical judgment,—
e axioms, definitions, postulates, theorems of the geometrical order, and
ught by Intuition to grasp the ultimate truth. Spinoza, still tempered by
s Scholastic training, writes: "This kind of knowledge proceeds from an
equate idea of the absolute essence of certain attributes of God, to the
equate knowledge of the essence of things." [15] This is intuitive appre-
nsion, the only way by which man can know God. What does it mean?
Intuition, he argues, is different from logical judgment. A simple prob-
n from arithmetic will point the way. Here is the common proportion—
2::3:x. What is the value of x, and how shall it be determined? The law
proportion is that the product of the means must equal the product
the extremes; hence, x equals 6, since two times three equals six times
e. Thus, the problem is solved by making the general rule the major
emise, and the problem itself, the minor, with the answer as the con-
sion. But, says Spinoza, the mathematicians do not wait for the formal
oof; they see the conclusion at a glance, *uno intuitu,* "going through no
alculating) operation," as he says in the unfinished *Tractate.* Still do
hat he will Spinoza cannot, nor could Descartes, persuade his readers
at intuition and logical judgment are wholly different in method or
sult; the liaison is very close.[16] He would not deny that the mathematician
as acting under the spur of the basic principles hidden in the crevices of
e mind. Nor does he think that philosophers, seeking acquaintance with
e ultimate Individual, would be inclined to exclude the application of
gical laws which prepare him to understand the nature of the Object of
s quest. But we must agree with Spinoza that on the third level of
ought we are concerned with a concrete problem, not with a set of ab-
act formulas. The problem may be of God and his infinitude or—by an
structive parallel—it may be the "eternal" nature of a particular human
dy, "this man or that Man"; in either case, cognition is more sweeping,
ore comprehensive, than in the problems of physics or psychology. Hu-
an character in general, he expressly says, is the "knowledge of the
ion subsisting between mind and the whole of nature." [17] But to the
sential properties of man as a rational animal, we are obliged to add the
ecific traits of the particular man whom we are describing—a Socrates,

[15] *Ibid.,* II, 40, Scholium 2.   [16] *Ibid.,* V, 28.
[17] *De Intellectus Emendatione* in *Chief Works of Spinoza.* Trans. by Elwes, II, 6.

a Caesar, a Confucius. As Kant has trenchantly remarked,[18] the nature of an object thus intuited is far more elaborate than the simple definitional properties that make him a man. The apperception of such an individual is instantaneous, even catastrophic; for it embraces an analysis of his private emotions, his adjustment to his environment, and the full evolution of his habits up to a given moment. Intuitive knowledge such as this is extremely complex, but it qualifies us for the greater task, as Spinoza has oracularly phrased it: "The more we understand particular things, the more do we understand God." [19]

The approach to the appreciation of the total object is through the study of the divine attributes, and every step in the unfolding of their meaning brings us that much nearer to the moment when we may intellectually embrace the supreme power and goodness of God's nature. Then we shall realize that impressive as is the conviction which universal or abstract truth lays upon us, it does not compare in splendor with the warmth of feeling which the intellectual love of God brings with it.[20] It is the difference between sheer formalized truth which excludes every shade of doubt from its judgments, and the "actual essence of some particular thing which we say depends on God." It might almost seem that Spinoza had in mind the concrete scriptural representation of God in the person of Christ. But he admits that knowledge of this sort is rarely acquired. In the early *Treatise* he complains that the things he could apprehend in this manner are very few, and in the *Ethics* he is bold enough to confess that so difficult is the path to its goal that few, indeed, can tread it; again, a hint that the Christian goal, which is the same as his, is reached but by a small company of pilgrims.

THE DIVINE SUBSTANCE

What is the divine Being whose formal properties can be discerned and understood by the intuitive science? Spinoza does not promise a quick and facile answer to this question; he warns his readers that the problem before them is one of great difficulty, and that an attentive and unprejudiced mind is needed to grapple with its terms. We are confronted at once with certain strategic concepts, Substance, God, and Nature. Substance is defined as that which exists in itself and is conceived through itself. Such an idea must be studied from two different angles, what it is and what it can do. It is assumed that the object here envisaged has a real, that is, actual existence which can be guaranteed by nothing other than itself. Its essence implies and demands its existence. There is an element of truth in the Scholastic teaching that Substance as *Ens realissimum* must have reality and

---

[18] *Pure Reason.* Trans. by N. K. Smith, pp. 92 sq. [19] *Ethics,* V, 24.
[20] *Ibid.,* V, 36, Scholium.

its fixed and inseparable property. For Substance is not duplicate, as Descartes originally conceived it, mind and matter, *res cogitans* and *res extensa,* each with its own imperishable quality. Substance is single and embraces the whole realm of reality, Spinoza answers. Therefore, it exists necessarily, since there is no external thing that could be its cause.[21] For this reason intellect can provide no argument through which its existence can be demonstrated. The whole subject lies above and beyond the level of logical inquiry; there is no superior genus under which Substance can be classified. Thus we are obliged to admit that the "existence of Substance as well as its essence is an eternal truth." [22] Spinoza does not state on what authority he bases this claim; but if he follows the tradition of Augustine, an eternal truth is that which is intuitively discerned; it is revealed by the intervention of divine wisdom. In the same connection, also, he insists that existence must be included in the definition of Substance, but this, obviously, was an accommodation to the current use of the term which has certainly moved away from the original meaning prescribed by Aristotle. If we are disturbed by the criticism that Spinoza is guilty of the same fallacy as Anselm and his congeners, a flagrant *petitio principi,* we should remember that the new philosopher has changed completely the form and contour of his Substance. The simple ineffable and transcendent Being of religious thought has been changed into the substantive Universe of which every human being is a modal part. Can there be any question, any doubt, any quivering uncertainty about the *realness* of this Existent? In his subtle and somewhat futile manoeuvres to establish the integrity of Substance, now called God, he seems to come precipitately to the end of a long negative recital—if something necessarily exists is it merely finite? If it were, would it not be more powerful than an infinite Being whose existence seemed to be uncertain? Since that is absurd, are we not faced with the disconcerting disjunction, either nothing exists or God, the infinite Being, exists? Now, does not every witness, ourselves included, protest that it itself exists? And if we do exist, do we exist in our own right or by virtue of the activation of another and greater cause? Since the first of these alternatives is contrary to fact, it follows that God, supreme Substance, exists, and we exist in Him.[23] In all this recital we seem to have a premonition of what a modern poet made articulate in his *Higher Pantheism:*

Speak to Him thou for he hears, and Spirit with Spirit can meet—
Closer is He than breathing, and nearer than hands and feet.

God is law, say the wise; O Soul, and let us rejoice,
For if He thunder by law the thunder is yet his voice.

[21] *Ibid.,* I, 7.   [22] *Ibid.,* I, 8, Scholium 1.   [23] *Ibid.,* I, 8, Scholium 2.

Law is God, say some: no God at all, says the fool;
For all we have power to see is a straight staff bent in the pool.

And the ear of man cannot hear, and the eye of man cannot see;
But if he could see and hear, this Vision—were it not He?

The demands of logic have no standing in this society of intuitiv
thoughts. As Joachim justly argues, the criticism of Kant against the tele
ological argument is valid, so long as we are dealing with one piece o
Reality, that is, an independent and supermundane Deity.[24] If necessar
existence be included in the essence of God, then we have an analytica
judgment where we are not allowed to affirm the subject and deny th
predicate. In such a case, we should of course withhold our assent fron
both parts of the judgment, and then the judgment would fail com
pletely. But such a drastic choice is not open to us, when God is identica
with all Reality; "you cannot refuse to conceive without [at the same time
ceasing to think or doubt or feel, in short, withot ceasing to be." Hence
the uniqueness of God carries with it necessary existence, and no detailec
demonstration of that fact is required.

There is, however, a second angle from which the problem must b
approached. Spinoza states the rule in the early treatise, "Everythin₂
should be conceived either through its own essence or through its proxi
mate causes. If, however, the thing is self-subsistent or, as is usually said
the cause of itself, it then must be understood by its essence only." [25] Her
he introduces a phrase which has been a stumbling-block to many com
mentators. How can a substantial thing be the cause of itself (*sui causa*)
Causation, in scientific language, always presupposes two events whic
follow one another in regular succession. Thus, when an electric curren
was passed through a solution of salt, such as copper sulphate in water
Prof. Whetham, Cambridge University, noted these specific effects: th
bulk of the solution was unaltered except in a measurable rise in tem
perature; the copper plates through which the current passed, dissolvec
away, the copper becoming copper sulphate in the solution; copper wa
deposited on the other plate; and there were distinct changes in concentra
tion, in the vicinity of the two plates or electrodes.[26] The experiment i
typical: the cause is present, it is set in operation, in time, under observabl
conditions, and the effects are carefully detected and tabulated. This i
what we mean by the principle of causation. Three factors are essential,—
the originating substance (or event), the plain results of its activity, anc
the element of time.

The Schoolmen recognized the intimate relation between these factors

[24] *Study of the Ethics of Spinoza*, pp. 54–55.   [25] *Chief Works of Spinoza*, II, 34.
[26] *Encyclopedia Britannica*, 1910, IX, p. 217.

and they called this the *transeunt* cause. But they also made place for another cause, the *immanent* cause whose area of activity is its own peculiar structure, with no reference whatsoever to any other object whether near or remote. It is this second type of cause that Spinoza adopted to explain the nature and function of Deity. It has two forms—as internally operating, it is the cause of everything within the system,[27] as *causa sui* it is the registration of all divine attributes.[28] We must stay within the conclusions already reached, namely, that God is complete Reality forming the permanent habitat of all individual modes, and that everything ascribed to God is accredited to our minds in a *modal* manner. At this point we must make sure that we understand the exact meaning of the phrase when referred to Deity. It does not for one moment suggest the notion that God is the source of his own derivation; such a conception is meaningless and should be discarded. In order to get at the true principle involved critics should consult the findings of Giordano Bruno, the brilliant Italian thinker of the 16th century. His quest, says Robert Adamson,[29] was for unity; where could it be found? Not in a physical world whose centre is always the momentary point of view of any given observer. Not in a philosophical system, since no two men can agree on its essential elements. God, for Bruno, is the centre of unity in the field of Reality; he is the *causa immanens,* the coördinating principle; he is *in* things, yet is distinct from them, as the "Universal is distinct from the particular." Bruno, however, could not divorce his thought from the teachings of the church; he had two theories, as Leibniz after him: one was the absent God, the other the immanent God. Spinoza shattered the confusion and boldly declared that "whatever is, is in God and without him nothing can be or be conceived." [30] You will thus come inevitably upon the inherent "power of action," the expression of cause. Both divine attributes, which the human mind can examine, thought and extension, are characterized by the activity of force. "God's power of thinking," he writes, "is exactly equal to his realized power of action.[31] *Causa sui* is not a dead dogma which metaphysicians might revive as an instrument of interpretation; it is the implementing factor of the divine character which we can neither deny nor disregard; it attests the necessary existence of Deity.[32] The sources of such a power cannot be explored; the effort of a Timaeus to create the world by the operation of such a cause, is a dismal failure. Plato makes that point clear by his severe strictures on the logical validity of the argument. With Plato as with Spinoza, it is not the genesis of power but its activating quality

---

[27] *Ethics,* I, 18.
[29] *Encyclopedia Britannica,* 1910, IV, p. 687.
[31] *Ibid.,* II, 7, Corollary.

[28] *Ibid.,* I, 17, Corollary 2.
[30] *Ethics,* I, 15.
[32] *Ibid.,* I, 20.

that commands the attention of both thinkers. Substance, without power, is inconceivable, and the significance of this conclusion will appear when we study, with Spinoza, the nature of the divine attributes.

THE FORMAL ATTRIBUTES OF GOD

The Reality of divine substance being given, how shall we appraise its formal properties? They are three: God is unitary, he is infinite, he is eternal. Each of these is, so to say, indigenous to its object. It is just as necessary to understand the universal aspects of Being as it is to establish the scientific values of the individual modes. Nor should we assume that Spinoza studies them merely to complete his historical affiliation with the earlier systems. These formal concepts are mighty instruments for helping men to grasp the meaning of Deity as the object of human knowledge. We take the concepts in their order.

God is one, says the author. Here unity has a double implication. It embraces the proposition that "besides God no substance can be granted or conceived." [33] The Christian world is thoroughly familiar with the dogma that God is one, and there is none like him. But this conception stands confronted by the multitude of divinities created and worshipped by the undiscriminating mind of antiquity. Spinoza's argument is different; it is grounded in the assumption that two substances, having the same essential and comprehensive qualities, cannot exist. [34] Thus, God cannot exist in competition with the universe of physical nature. Again, such a type of Divinity as Alexander tries to portray in his *Space, Time, and Deity* is merely the result of a foray into the realm of romantic metaphysics. [35] It awakens no emotional response from a thoughtful inquirer; it is a mere fancy cast upon the waters of speculation, with no logical anchorage, with no compass to guide to a safe and comfortable port. For Spinoza unity is not numerical oneness. Pythagoras early in Greek philosophy saw the difficulty stirring in such a conception. He therefore taught that One was the source of all numbers but itself was *not* a number. It contained all the qualities which would eventually clothe the several segments of the unfolding universe. In a more spiritualized form Plotinus conceived of God as the ineffable Being which discharged its Ideas, *Logoi,* as emanations to be consolidated into souls and at length into the structure of the natural universe. Neither of these theories could satisfy the critical mind of Spinoza. He sought for a unity which could be expressed in an infinitude of forms, all of them tributary to substance as the source from which they sprang.

[33] *Ibid.*, I, 14.   [34] *Ibid.*, I, 5.
[35] Samuel Alexander, *Space, Time, and Diety* (London: Macmillan, 1927), Book IV Chap. 2.

He therefore adopted the concept of Nature and identified it, root and branch, with the consummatory idea of God. In the Preface to the fourth Part of the *Ethics* resisting the ancient conceit that Nature works with an end in view, he stoutly declares that "the eternal and infinite Being which we call God or Nature acts by the same necessity as that by which it exists. The reason or cause by which God or Nature exists and the reason by which he acts are one and the same." Here we observe that the third term, Nature, enters upon the scene. Spinoza is careful to show why he admits it to equal authority with the others. Study Proposition 29 in the first Part: "Nothing in the universe is contingent but everything is determined to exist and to operate in a particular manner by the necessity of the divine nature." Such a formula cannot be understood without a sensitive reference to the Scholastic creed. *Natura naturans* reflects the creative and generating power of God; it enshrines "those attributes of his substance which express his eternal and infinite essence, that is, God insofar as he is considered as a free cause." Obviously freedom is not the sheer antithesis of the mechanical, vise-like determinism of the physical world. God is a free cause by virtue of his powers of thought. *Natura naturata,* on the other hand, is objective in its forms; it includes "everything that follows from the necessity of God's nature or the nature of God's attributes." These forms are not driving ideas but individuated "things," which are "in God and cannot be conceived without God." The scope of objective *Natura* is not limited to the world of physical bodies, it embraces ideas as well, great currents of thought in human society, ideas that make or unmake nations, ideas that produce mighty spiritual upheavals. They all belong to the unitary perfection of divine Substance; God is a complete Whole.

But what is the meaning of the term *whole*? Does it suggest a collection of independent units like the component parts of a democratic army? Does it resemble an intricate machine, each piece contributing its share to the production of power, though it itself is nothing but an extension of the personality of the maker or operator? Or is it an organic whole like a living body which cannot survive except it be in unceasing contact with its appropriate environment? Or, still further, is it such a unity as the human Self, its background a breathing, pulsing body changing with every chance and circumstance, its emotions strong and hardy, its ideas shaped by temperament and experience, a sense of *oneness* coursing through the mind, even when the break with the past is most decisive? These are but distant adumbrations of the truth. Hallett [36] has stated the matter correctly, and I am happy to avail myself of his help: "The infinite and eternal whole must require neither external cause, nor external source of stimulus, nor external object of response; it must be all-inclusive, and for the same reason

[36] *Aeternitas*, p. 147.

it must be self-dependent and self-constituting." Whether Spinoza has
succeeded in establishing such coherence in the universal structure which
he calls God, we shall, perhaps, be able to decide when we have discovered
the meaning of the two attributes which are subject to man's reflective
inquiry.

But we must first examine the other formal properties immediately
associated with the foregoing. What do we imply when we say that God
is infinite, and what, that he is eternal? "Every substance," the text testifies, "is necessarily infinite."[37] "God or substance, consisting of infinite
attributes each of which expresses eternal and infinite essence, necessarily
exists."[38] Here are two instances, where the first word is used—God is
infinite in his totality and in his essential properties. The word is ad-
mittedly troublesome; it cannot be treated by the Aristotelian method of
definition. In a notable letter to his friend Lewis Meyer, 1663, Spinoza
has put the matter to a crucial test: first, the infinite is not a mental image
but a reflective concept; secondly, it is not the same as the indefinite, for the
latter varies between a minimum and a maximum limit; the object or
property is called infinite either because of its constituent nature or because
it forms a regress that passes beyond experience. The term *infinite* carries
the weight of metaphysical authority; it has two reasons attached, the
former will be considered here, the latter in our study of the Modes. The
first reason states that from the causal activity of the divine nature as
"from an unfathomable source flow an infinite number of things in infinite ways."[39] Combining the idea of infinite attributes with the idea of
infinite modes, we have a formal presentation of what Spinoza means by
divine infinitude. But now we need to seek a bill of particulars. We might
be inclined at first glance to expect from Spinoza the assumption of a single
and unitary attribute. Instead of that he gives two, thought and extension,
both of which are known to us; have we any right to suppose that there
are no others, and if there are others, can we put a limit to the number? Is
not Hallett's suggestion reasonable that substance as defined by Spinoza
necessarily transcends the category of number, since the moment we introduce the idea of number we surreptitiously introduce the idea of an external cause?[40] Hallett supports his suggestion by referring to Spinoza's
contention that a definition never includes the extent of its application.
Thus, the idea of man does not contain the concept of ten or twenty of a
hundred persons; in the language of logic, it sets forth the connotation,
not the denotation of the term. The same principle will hold in the explication of the divine attributes; the concept of attribute unfolds the
powers of the divine mind, it says nothing about the number or extent of
such powers. Spinoza draws an analogy from the visible world; "it is far

[37] *Ethics*, I, 8.   [38] *Ibid.*, I, 11.   [39] *Ibid.*, I, 16.   [40] *Aeternitas*, p. 28.

from an absurdity to ascribe several attributes to one substance; for nothing in nature is clearer than that every single being must be conceived under some attributes, and that its reality is in proportion to the number of its attributes expressing necessity, eternity and infinity." [41] In short, God cannot be conceived other than as a "Being endowed with all possible properties fully realized." This conclusion is reinforced by the fact that every attribute is expressed in an infinite number of forms, concrete cases, definite "constellations," as Hallett calls them. Of this fact we have ample evidence in the operation of the two properties with which we are acquainted, the multiplicity of images and the complexity of our logical thought. Here, however, Spinoza's third rule of infinitude reaches its second application, the appearance of the empirical regress, which can best be studied under the attribute of Extension.[42]

What of the other property, Eternity, which every code of religious thought ascribes to its Deity? For the great majority of believers to ask the question is to answer it. Still, as a philosophical problem it merits close attention. Can the idea of eternity be defined? No; but we can reach a tentative understanding of its meaning by observing what it is contrasted with. God as infinite is contrasted with things as finite,—spatiality, quantity, imagination, emotion, all of them contingent, and all excluded from the divine attributes. In the same way we may draw a distinction between the passage of time, on the one side, sheer duration, within which all modes "live and move and have their being," and on the other eternity which Spinoza calls the "infinite enjoyment of existence." It is difficult enough to take in the process of duration, when we compare with it the units of time. For in order to complete the hour we must pass its half, its next quarter, its subsequent eighth, and by such analysis we never reach the end of the hour.[43] It is the ancient problem of Zeno and it is still unsolved, if we proceed by a mathematical count. How much more difficult is it to fashion an abstract conception of eternity? Obviously the element of time has no place here; there is no "when, before, or after" in eternity. When his critics complained that he rendered his universe static by the elimination of time, he answered that God is complete Reality, the universe as a whole; "God never can decree or never could have decreed anything but what is; God did not exist before his decrees and would not exist without them." [44] Nor is eternity equivalent to timelessness, as some theologians have argued; that would merely intimate that it has no kinship with the movements of sense, no converse with the fancies of mind. Bergson is certainly wrong when he charges Spinoza with teaching

---

[41] *Ethics*, I, 10, Scholium.   [42] *Infra*, p. 287.
[43] Letter to L. Meyer, No. XII, in *Correspondence*, p. 115.   [44] *Ethics*, I, 33, Scholium 2.

that "eternity is the indefinite duration of a thing contained in a single moment." [45] For Bergson the flux of things and their forward push, both bearing the emblems of time, constituted the sole permanent reality of which the mind had articulate knowledge. But granting that Spinoza recognized such a process operating in the bosom of nature (as he did), he could not and did not limit the existence of God by any temporal qualifications. The Roman Curia may hold that God is resident in an eternal Present, absorbing the Past and anticipating the Future. To Spinoza such a theory is of doubtful meaning; he desires nothing vague or ambiguous. Both the essence and existence of God are eternal and the element of time is wholly excluded.

Still, he does not propose to leave the idea of eternity in a vacuum. Like Plato he will supply inductive material to illustrate if not to prove the principle he is advocating. He turns first to the movements of the physical world, with their orbital regularity and their undisputed sequence of events. In his theological *Tractate* (Chap. 6), he lays down the following canon: "Since the laws of nature, as we have shown, extend to an infinite range, and are conceived by us under a certain form of eternity, and since nature operates in a fixed and immutable order according to these laws, therefore they signify to us *in a certain manner,* the infinity, eternity, and immutability of God." We are advised by this passage that whatever apologetic value the doctrine of miraculous intervention may have in religious practice, it has none of the authority exercised by the laws of natural phenomena. The conclusions of science are grounded in a long series of carefully guarded experiments, and while they cannot reveal the full meaning of a concrete cosmic individual, like sun and star, no exception can be taken to the results of their demonstrations. The splendid analysis which Newton completed only a few years after Spinoza's death, corroborated in every detail the truth of the words we have just quoted. Whether Sir Isaac knew it or not he set his demonstrations "in a certain manner" under the rubric of the concept of eternity. The phrase, *certain form* (or *species*) *of eternity* means simply that the human intelligence, being restricted in its scope, can never gain complete knowledge of the objects presented to its consideration. Still, when we define the laws by which visible bodies operate, we are also expounding the conceptions which reflect the integral principles of the divine nature. It is with these facts before him that Spinoza makes the startling declaration in the last part of the *Ethics* (V., 29) respecting the human body, the object nearest to our intellectual ken:—"This power of conceiving things under the aspect of eternity belongs to the mind only by virtue of the fact that it can conceive the body under the aspect of eternity." If the human body which

[45] Quoted by Hallett, *op. cit.,* p. 14.

frames the images of nature's treasures, did not communicate its qualities
and relations through the organic senses to a supervisory mind, science
would be a dead and inert discipline, and reason without its needed content. There is thus abundant justification for Spinoza's insistence on the
peculiar normative function of the body which is a necessary part of man.

But there is another phase of human experience which brings the idea
of eternity even more clearly to our view. Men are accustomed to speak
of universal or eternal truths, and Spinoza approves of this phraseology.
The locus classicus is in the second Part of the book, Proposition 44,
corollary: "it belongs to the nature of reason to perceive things under the
form of eternity." In this case we are not dealing with the substantive
laws by which objective things are united to one another. Rather are we
required to turn our thoughts inward, and let them rest upon the properties of reason itself. Why is it that reason can grasp the "necessity of
things" with a commanding and comprehensive decision? It is not because it has made acquaintance with the qualities of light or beauty or
even moral goodness as resident in sun or flower or the soul of man. It is
because it has discovered the law by which the object is established in the
whole field of Reality. In this way, reason brings the mind within the
penumbra of eternity, crowns our thought, so to say, with a certain aspect
of finality. Let us not assume, however, that we have thereby reached
the limits of knowledge. Reason strips our minds of idols left by the
tyranny of custom, the idols of the cave, the forum, the theatre; it has
taught us to judge events and objects in the light of universal precepts. It
has released the mind from the fetters of time, which entails change and
chance, and it has communicated to us the value of eternal truths, irrevocable principles, ideas that persist. One action reason cannot take, as
we have already noted: it cannot seize the total structure of reality in one
glance. Only intuition can do that; which is another way of saying that
only intuition can make man "completely conscious of himself and God." [46]

DIVINE ATTRIBUTES AND MODES

We now stand at the threshold of the Prytaneum of the divine economy,
ready to examine the positive points in Spinoza's creed. The formal and
abstract ideas we have just analyzed constitute the outer façade of the
new conception of substance; we enter, as the Greeks did, the inner sanctuary where the basic principles are guarded. God is one, he is infinite,
he is eternal. Wise men have supported these conceits with unimpeachable
arguments; nor does Spinoza yield to them in the lucidity of his exposition
or the firmness of his confidence in them. But the real substance is not as
yet revealed. So far, there is an impressive parallel with the idioms of

[46] *Ethics*, V, 31, Scholium.

Scripture;—the affirmation of Moses, "I am that I am; I am hath sent me," the ejaculation of Isaiah, "I saw the Lord sitting upon the throne, high and lifted up, and his train filled the temple," the quiet, persuasive voice of St. John, "In the beginning was the Word and the Word was with God and the Word was God." The first two are declamatory, the last has serious and informing content. What Spinoza intends to teach will differ in profound and disruptive details from the message of the Evangel.

The subject he presents is twofold, Attributes and Modes, while the persisting Reality is one, namely, Substance, God. "Whatever is, is in God, and without God, nothing can be or be conceived." [47] Descartes attempts to construct first an independent Deity, then two subordinate substances, soul and body, *res cogitans* and *res extensa,* both contingent in nature and both going back to God as the creating cause. The attempt, says the author of the *Ethics,* was a failure. The attributes do not belong to two distinct and separate objects but to one; they are therefore to be construed as simultaneous aspects of the same substance, without which such substance could not exist. Furthermore, the two properties mentioned by Descartes do not by any means exhaust the thesaurus of the divine essence. The attributes are infinite in kind and in multiplication, as we have already noted. We know but two, Thought and Extension. Some commentators have argued that Thought will be wider in application than any of the others, since God must be conceived as *knowing* himself in every phase of his being. But we have no instruction on this matter, and it is vain to make surmises or offer hypotheses. What we must keep resolutely before the mind is that an attribute expresses the essential nature of Deity, and nothing else can do so.

There is an additional fact to be received and carefully guarded, to wit, that God can be known only by the *modes* or states of substance which in every case bear the imprint of his indestructible essence. [48] What are modes? Clearly, they are not single and detached things huddled together in an indiscriminate mass under the canopy of the capacious universe. Modes have no independent existence; they belong to God and follow necessarily from his infinite substance. The language used by Spinoza is Scholastic and often extremely unattractive. But the meaning is plain. Confining himself to the attributes known to us he distinguishes two kinds of modes, immediate and mediate. Immediate modes are those which appear to sum up all the characteristics of particular or mediate modes,—motion and rest for Extension, infinite Intellect for Thought. Later he added another in the realm of Extension,—*facies totius mundi,* the form of the entire world. [49] The only point common to the immediate modes is they cannot be ob-

---

[47] *Ibid.,* I, 15.   [48] Letter to Schuller, 1675, No. LXIV, in *Correspondence,* p. 306.
[49] *Ethics,* II, 44, Corollary.

served by the senses of the body; they are the distillations of reflective analysis.

The way is now open for the examination of the mediate modes in which his main interest lies, and we take up first those appertaining to the attribute of Extension. In his letter to Lewis Meyer, 1663, he frankly admits that they have a different sort of existence from that of substance. For one thing they cannot be defined as necessarily existing; we can conceive of their losing the right to existence at least in the same form; but we cannot conceive of the dissolution of substance itself. Again, the individual mode cannot be sequestered from its local setting and regarded as an independent body. "By existence I do not mean existence in so far as it can be conceived abstractly and as a certain form of quantity." He is seriously offended by the criticism that his doctrine involves the assumption that the "divine nature is extended substance" and that such an assumption is unworthy of the exalted attributes of Deity. But the criticism has no merit, since it misconceived the meaning of his doctrine. He was dealing not with infinite matter which is subject to measure, division, increase and diminution but with infinite substance whose infinite phases are shot through with the principle of power. He recommends that critics who are impressed by the multiplicity of the grains of sands on the beach or the giant constellations of orbs in the heavens, should take note that these facts are derived from the activity of the imagination. If, contrariwise, such critics should observe the infinite reach of the stellar spaces and the infinite velocity of the heavenly bodies in their orbits, they would discover that it is not the craft of the imagination but the reflective decision of the intellect that has the last word in the determination of the meaning of God. Modes are not divided sections in the substance of the universe; they are forms that appear to the eye or the touch at a given moment, only to be merged again into the total system from which they draw their movement and their strength.

It is at this point that Spinoza insists that we observe the irrevocable dependence of one event upon another, of one discriminated body in its relation to another, of one outburst of power, e. g., the earthquake, as incited and caused by a distinguishable series of physical situations. His words have the ring of finality: "Every individual thing, everything which is finite and has a conditioned existence, cannot exist or be determined to act, unless it be determined for existence by a cause other than itself, which is also finite and has a conditioned existence," [50] and the regress goes on to infinity. A thing is infinite, he wrote to Meyer, when its causal regress passes beyond the bounds of established experience. How then can we suppose the regress to be infinite when we cannot trace its course?

[50] *Ibid.*, I, 28.

Critics have sprung to arms again; they charge him with changing the meaning of the term cause. A cause is a chain of events, each linked indissolubly to its predecessor. Spinoza, it is objected, proposes to destroy the chain and to make God the ultimate Cause from which every motion and thought stems. The same accusation has been laid at the door of modern Idealism. Bradley meets the criticism by denying its validity: "The genuine cause must always be the whole cause, and the whole cause could never be complete until it had taken in the universe"; and this, he exclaims in a footnote, is "impossible." [51] Spinoza is more realistic than this; he finds that every object in the world belongs to a system, from the worm that lives in the blood [52] to the meteor that swims in the ether. Nor does he hesitate to assert that "all things are determined to exist and to operate in a peculiar manner by the necessity of the divine nature." [53] Such a dogma is not fatalism; it is a declaration of faith in the supreme authority of God.

This leads him at length to ask, What part does Thought play in the extraordinary drama now passing before our eyes? The theory he is advocating has as its prerequisite the principle that every event in the extended world, every minute granule of sand, every massive collection of bodies, every complex sequence of motions has an ideal aspect registered in the mind of God; or to put it another way, "all individual things are animated, though in different degrees." [54] He sums up the intent of his theory in these words: "Of everything there is necessarily an idea in the mind of God, of which God is the cause," in the same way as there is an idea of the human body in the human mind. Furthermore, the series of ideas in the divine intellect has the same rigorous order as the succession of events in the extensional world. This suggests that there is an abysmal difference between the human and the divine intellect; as Spinoza says in one of his facetious quips, "there is about as much agreement between them as between the dog-star in the sky and the animal that barks." [55] Hallett has expounded the thesis in a striking sentence: "For Thought implies every other attribute, and is thus a draught of the ineffable essence of *Natura* as creative eternity; but our thought is creative only within its own circuit, and even there only with patience, and derivatively: it waits for the *data* upon which it works." [56] Disregarding the presence of the hypothetical properties and confining our study to the natural world which is our home, let us recite some of the facts which are the common heritage of the race. In the first place, we must say that we "perceive things under a certain form of eternity," not with the supreme effulgence of God, to

[51] F. H. Bradley, *Appearance and Reality* (6th imp., London: George Unwin and Allen, 1916), p. 386.

[52] Letter No. XXXII, *Correspondence*, p. 210.   [53] *Ethics*, I, 29.

[54] *Ibid.*, II, 13, Scholium.   [55] *Ibid.*, I, 17, Scholium.   [56] *Op. cit.*, p. 297.

use Leibniz' familiar word. We are visited by a fleet of passing images which stay not long enough to give us more than a partial acquaintance with their contents. Consequently, the deductions drawn from them, however well articulated, do not bring us to a complete understanding of Reality." [57] Once more, every individual in the system has its own private force or conatus which enables it to retain its status for a time but gives no assurance that its identity will be a permanent possession.[58] Finally, in the development of the human mind, attention must be paid to the power of its attending emotions which are modes of extension and therefore subject to all the laws of nature including specific gravity. Passions are confused ideas, hence, they may be dangerous; but "the mind endeavors to conceive only such things as affirm the power of activity." [59] Each victory over emergent passion gives a new sense of moral freedom and is crystallized in what Spinoza calls "acquiescence" or intellectual contentment.[60] These several points exhibit the limited qualities of the human intellect; at the same time, they indicate emphatically that "the mind's highest good is the knowledge of God and the mind's highest virtue is the knowledge of God." What this consummatory judgment entails we shall consider in the next section.

How, then, does the supreme Intellect differ from the intellect of the human mind? We may pass over the canons that find their place in every religious creed: God's infallible judgment, his unbounded knowledge, the inexorable execution of his will, the inevitable sequences of law,—articles of faith which are celebrated in the glowing periods of the *Ethics* and in the theological *Tractate,* and dwell upon one principle whose value Spinoza claims to have made "clearer than the sun at noonday," the principle of necessity as opposed to the concept of contingency.[61] Divine action is never taken in obedience to some external cause; it follows solely from the necessity of the divine nature. Two theorems clinch the validity of this conclusion: "God's power is identical with his essence" and, "whatever is conceived to be in the power of God necessarily exists." Obviously the thesis that God will do some things according to the terms of a *good* not already realized, is a sheer denial of fact. The doctrine of Final Causes, to which we have already referred, comes under this prohibition. The manner of thought there ascribed to God is but a replica of the common habits of the human mind. "Men do all things for an end, namely, for that which is useful to them, and which they seek." The sequence is fixed—a purpose conceived as valuable and suitable action initiated to reach the end. But the sequence itself is grounded in the principle of contingency: without a purpose there would be no action, without the action the end could not be

[57] *Ethics*, II, 42, Corollary 2.   [58] *Ibid.,* III, 6, 7.   [59] *Ibid.,* III, 54.
[60] *Ibid.,* IV, 53.   [61] *Ibid.,* I, 33, Scholium.

gained. When the concept of final causes is stated in such bald language, the argument which attempts to give it a central place in the divine economy is shaken to its foundation. Certainly, the methods of the absolute intellect are quite at variance with human procedure; not only is the initiation of action determined by the changeless thought of God but its process and ultimate result are never in doubt. Immanuel Kant consumed one-half of his Third Critique in developing the subject, only to arrive at a negative conclusion. Still the fancy persists in certain quarters that the interest of devout believers are deliberately and by fixed design protected by a benevolent Creator, in face of the unblushing facts of experience that "good and evil fortunes fall to the lot of pious and impious alike." They do not understand the serious implication of their theory: it destroys the perfection of Deity; for if God acts towards an end dictated by an alien cause he seeks for something not already possessed and thus risks the impairment of his total power. Does this criticism disturb an honest man's faith in the veracity and benevolent justice of his Maker? The difficulty lies not with Spinoza's criticism nor with the original canon which prescribes its utterance, but with the sinister nature of the theory against which the criticism is leveled. For the common terms, order and confusion, beauty and deformity, good and evil are not ingredient factors in the system of the world; they are conceits which men have framed to express their emotions as they meet the vicissitudes of fortune. Consequently they cannot by any stretch of fancy be used to define the operations of absolute substance. Any attempt to charge God with partiality or neglect of men's rights is merely a kind of crude, reckless anthropomorphism unworthy of scientific notice. In short, the concept of design whether applied to creation or providence is foreign to Spinoza's speculations and must be forthwith disallowed.

THE INTELLECTUAL LOVE OF GOD

In the fifth Part of the *Ethics* we seem to enter a totally different mental climate. The title prefixed is, *The Power of the Intellect or Human Freedom*. Its real purpose is to reconcile the apparent inequities of life with the sovereign activities of God. This can be accomplished in one of two ways, either by proving that the reason of man is inherently eternal, or by showing that in the final conquest of emotion we reach a new spiritual status which Spinoza calls the "intellectual love of God." In either case it is obvious that the laws of logic which have dictated evaluations in physical phenomena, no longer have any weight and must be abandoned. Even the finer feelings, love, joy, honor and esteem which are constructive principles in daily intercourse, seem pale, inadequate and "earthly" when compared with the superior order of ideas presented when we are obliged to contemplate the supreme Object of reverence. Accordingly we are ready to affirm that the "human mind is now part of the infinite Intellect of God," which implies that "God has this or that idea insofar as he constitutes the essence of the human mind." [62] At the same time we must remember that even if the divine mind differs profoundly from the mind of man, the difference does not break the organic link which binds man to Deity.

How then does the finite soul become a real, that is, an eternal existent? We have already discovered that the eternal is unconditionally divorced from the temporal; there is no yesterday, today, or tomorrow in the divine economy. On the other hand, finite thought is bound to the wheel of change, change in time and in place, in emotional reaction, in the nature of opinion; how can the soul put off its mortality, which is the essence of change and assume the garb of uncheckered continuance? We are affiliated with the infinite intelligence of God: we know him and he knows us. When we so speak, we—by some subconscious claim—understand that we refer to but a segment of human experience. The body has a shadowy form of eternity, since through its organic senses alone can we obtain acquaintance with the facts of the natural world. But the *idea* of body, that is, the total congeries of ideas called the mind, is a fixed and indiscerptible conception imbedded in the divine Intellect. Here, however, we must be on our guard, lest we repeat the fallacious assumption of the Greeks; for they frequently based their argument for immortality on the presence in our minds of certain reminiscences of a prior state of existence. "Our bodies," says Spinoza, "have no vestigial trace of such an existence." [63] He might also have reported that no empirical image has ever crossed the mind indicating that we could expect a renewal of our identity after the body's dissolution. But he put all these fancies away, as Kant did, holding that they could not be brought within the confines of concise and significant experience. Immortality as a scientific doctrine is excluded.

Still, Spinoza himself was profoundly affected by the persuasiveness of the "eternal hope," as some have called it. He knew with what tenacity men held to its veraciousness as an article of faith. Hallett has no hesitation in saying that Spinoza "intended to establish the individual eternity of this or that man" but there is considerable doubt as to wheher he succeeded in doing so to his own satisfaction.[64] The one point which up to the present moment he relies on, is that every finite mode is a constituent part of nature. If the mode includes only the generic quality, *humanity,* then immortality in the usual acceptation of the term is ruled out. The new problem is whether the individual man, as a single unit in physical nature, Socrates, Plato, Confucius, persists after death but as only a mode possessing the quality of *being human.* The theorem which the author

[62] *Ibid.,* II, 10, Corollary. [63] *Ibid.,* V, 23, Scholium. [64] *Op. cit.,* p. 75.

lays down is the rule to follow: "there is necessarily in God the idea, which expresses the essence of this or that body under the form of eternity (*sub specie aeternitatis*)." [65] The language is precise; Spinoza does not say the body is in God but the idea of its essential quality, that is to say, the Mind. In the very next theorem he declares that "the human mind cannot be absolutely destroyed with the body but there remains of it something which is eternal." Obviously, the mind does not exist under the aegis of time as does the body; it has the property of duration only when connected with the body. When released therefrom it is free. But free in what manner? As an independent entity, able to work out its own destiny or simply as a logical particular under its persisting genus, here, the idea of mind? Is this what Spinoza means when he says: Not all the mind will be eternal but "only that which appertains to the essence of mind"? What is the abiding part? The imaginative elements will disappear; they include the memory which is regarded only by naive thinkers as the key to true immortality. It must also include the constructive fancy, embodying all the figures that crowd the eschatologies of the church. That which persists must be governed by a "certain eternal necessity," that is, must be subject to definite principles which have universal validity; for example, the strong conviction that "death becomes less hurtful in proportion as the mind's clear and distinct knowledge is greater," a scientific conviction arrived at by the study of the laws of physical growth and decay. There is also a positive facet to be scrutinized, the meaning of substance, which carries with it the "highest acquiescence in God's eternal nature" [66] and which teaches us the ultimate significance of perpetuity. In the light of this knowledge the tragic changes in human fortunes lose their sting and they are superseded by the decisions of a clear-sighted intellect which is akin to the Intellect of God. [67]

It is thus demonstrated that a certain part of the human mind is wrapped in the habiliments of eternity; it is, of course, the most valuable, likest to the pure thought of God himself. Does this embrace the individual souls which Spinoza promised to install in the Valhalla of the Immortals, each with his own signature of triumph? At the very close of his discussion there emerges a possible reservation which might destroy the essential value of the idea itself. Suppose it should happen that the possibility of a future life were completely cancelled: would that alter in any way our attitude toward the duties prescribed by the laws of piety and religion? Some men think that all such duties are merely burdens, signs of moral bondage, from which we shall be released at death. Then we shall be free to follow our own inclinations under our own authority. Such an hy-

---

[65] *Ethics*, V, 22.   [66] *Ibid.*, V, 38, Scholium.   [67] *Ibid.*, V, 39 and Scholium.

pothesis is too puerile to require attention. What does demand attention is
the tendency of religious bodies to frighten their votaries into obedience
to arbitrary rules by the threat of punishment in another life. Spinoza
rejects all heteronomous incentives to moral action, as Kant did. He rests
the structure of moral values strictly on the basis of what is right and
what is wrong, determined by the unhesitant reason of the moral agent.[68]
When this is effected, a supreme contentment ensues; the mind is at rest.
The very fact that he introduces this word of caution proves that the
argument for the soul's eternity is not conclusive. It is true that he insists more than once on the strong appeal which the idea of personal perpetuity makes to strained and timorous hearts: "we feel and evince in experience that we are eternal." But experience is a situation that requires
both body and mind; and if, under the imprint of a physical emotion or
sentiment, we entertain the conceit that we shall persist beyond the grave,
still demonstrations of that sort, even though they are the "eyes of the
mind," as he says in the same connection, are in the last analysis nothing
but conclusions in a body-mind proof, with no support from a purely
metaphysical source. In brief, the proof is pragmatic, beginning with and
terminating in a sentiment whose ultimate truth no logical syllogism
can ever verify.[69]

There is still one aspect of the divine nature that we have not examined;
to this we now give attention. What does Spinoza imply in the unusual
phrase, the "intellectual love of God"? The new concept makes its appearance in the fifth Part of the *Ethics,* the 15th theorem, which is followed
by a galaxy of scintillating passages, some repeating the idea, others ex-
panding it, but all focussed on the capital truth of the union of men's
love with God's. We are moving now on the platform of the third kind
of knowledge; scientific formulas are in retirement, the emotional stresses
and strains of everyday experience gone. Now each action is taken by the
central Self which has plumbed the secret depths of human nature and
laid bare its basic obligations. Coming at long last to the pure attachment
to the Being whose intellectual lordship is already acknowledged, Spinoza
calls this sentiment Love and in its terminal stage, Blessedness. We must
not approach his treatment of the subject in a critical or captious temper;
of one thing we may be sure—Spinoza is not the first important thinker
to use the same vernacular. Plato in *Phaedrus* contributes a dithyrambic
eulogy in praise of the lover of truth, that is, the philosopher. Wisdom is
the subtle amalgam of truth and reality, and the quest of it is the highest
ideal in human life. Spinoza unites these concepts, truth and reality, in a
single term, "the intellectual love of God." Critics have scoffed at the
conjunction—the two ideas have nothing in common. Love is the func-

[68] *Ibid.,* V, 41, Scholium.   [69] *Ibid.,* V, 23, Scholium.

tion of the emotions not of the intelligent mind; no man can *know* his emotions, he merely obeys them and takes the consequences. But Spinoza thinks otherwise. Intellectual love does not disturb the soul as instinctive love does; it does not issue in pain, because we know its sources and its effect; it fills us with supreme satisfaction. Love seeks no return to itself for services rendered; we do not worship God in order to receive preferment here or hereafter. Again, it generates neither envy nor hate, envy towards men nor hate towards God; for when other men are won to the same affection, we find our delight immeasurably increased.[70] Furthermore, love emancipates us from the ordinary constraints of the physical sciences, chiefly because we view every organic reaction in the light of its universal and eternal significance. It thus enables the soul to realize the highest type of human character, as will be attested by the kind of personal gratifications entailed. Finally, love introduces us to a complete understanding of the values of Selfhood, especially in the light of our relation to infinite Substance.[71] Such a status has no historical beginning, since it is already included in God's causative activity, not as though we imagined him to be sensibly present but because we now comprehend how we are embodied in his total nature.[72] The direct deduction from these considerations is the same as that already drawn, namely, that the human mind has unlimited perpetuity, mind in general, not the reason of Socrates or of any other single intellect. Such a conclusion contradicts the judgment of Martineau that by human eternity Spinoza means "a system of intellectual laws expressed in our mode of thinking." [73]

Now returning to the identic phrase, *the intellectual love of God,* we are confronted with a new, perhaps surprising angle to the argument: "God loves himself with an infinite intellectual love." [74] So far as we can discover, this is the first time in the history of accredited philosophy that such a dogmatic averment has been made. Religions both ethnic and positive, notably the Christian creed, have celebrated God's love for his creatures, but no theological dogma has added the rhapsodical corollary incorporated in the words just quoted. Nor is this all; for Spinoza proceeds to say that the "intellectual love of the mind towards God is the very love of God whereby God loves himself." [75] So far as we can judge from these references the subjective love of God is confined primarily to one phase of his essential activity, that is, to his relations with the human intellect interpreted in its universal forms. His meaning is not that man's mind leaves an imperishable imprint upon the divine mind but that man's mind *is* God's mind when viewed from a certain aspect of eternity.[76] Yet

[70] *Ibid.,* V, 20.   [71] *Ibid.,* V, 31, Scholium.   [72] *Ibid.,* V, 32, Corollary, 33, Scholium.
[73] *Study of Spinoza,* p. 295.   [74] *Ethics,* V, 35.   [75] *Ibid.,* V, 36.
[76] Note: It is interesting to compare with Spinoza's treatment, that of Nicolas Berdyaev, a

even here we must not be too restrictive in our interpretation of the divine attributes. For assuming that divine love can be formally stated in terms of the logical judgment, it still lies beyond our apprehension to determine whether other types of being have their residence in the divine economy, and if they do whether they would be affected by the same attribute, Love, and in what manner. Hallett here contributes an important suggestion. The two terms, intellectual and love, register the two independent phases of the divine *Natura*, to wit, *naturans* and *naturata*, the creative and the operative, the world of Thought and the world of designated Modes; "not two separate beings but two asymmmetrically related aspects of the same reality." [77] Now one of the integers in the total sum of nature is the reflective experience of the human mind rendered single and concrete under the inspiration of the intellectual love of God. There may be other spiritual modes in the divine system, such as angelic appearances, still accepted as real by some eminent religious teachers. On this subject Spinoza is completely silent. One principle, however, he accepts without reservation: "God, insofar as he loves himself, loves man, and accordingly the love of God towards man and the intellectual love of the mind towards God are identical." [78] The union between God and man is thus complete and unabridged, and the union is sealed by man's release from the anxieties of the sensuous life and from the terrors of death. Spinoza intimates that this is the one and only way by which the common enemy Fear can be conquered. How much of this program did Spinoza extract from the articles of the Evangelical faith?

We have already noted that love such as this has no beginning and certainly it can have no end. It cannot be ended, because of the interposition of contingent forces that may attempt to destroy the power of love. Love is itself a law of nature and the laws of nature never come into conflict. In physics that fact would be illustrated by the principle of the parallelogram of forces, which shows how two forces when joined, produce another force which embodies the elements of both. Spinoza does not specify how the power of love could not be contradicted by contrary forces of nature. It is possible that he had in mind the persecutions, including the threat of death or actual execution, which the proponents of the true faith have had to suffer. In this instance the forces of nature when applied to human bodies have never extinguished the stern devotion of the martyr.[79] Then he goes further and says that the very *idea* of love cannot

---

distinguished religious critic of present-day Russia. He says in *Freedom and the Spirit* (New York: Chas. Scribner's Sons, 1935), p. 195: "God and man are living personalities whose relationship is intimate to the highest degree and constitutes the concrete drama of love and freedom. Only a symbolic and mythological approach to the relationship between God and man can bring us close to the divine mystery."

[77] *Op. cit.*, p. 146.   [78] *Ethics*, V, 36, Corollary.   [79] *Ibid.*, V, 37, Demonstratium.

be destroyed, even though its proponent may. For ideas must always be differentiated from opinions which belong to time and the changing form of the image. On the other hand ideas are resident in the changeless mind of God.[80] If then the intellectual love of God cannot be canceled either as an Idea or a modal form of experience, it must be regarded as the supreme achievement of the human consciousness, the quintessence of eternity.[81]

It remains to inquire under what rubric the united love of God and man is to be enrolled. Or, perhaps, it is not subordinate to any concept or law. Perhaps, it is the permanently creative power in the universe. We know that Spinoza in his *Metaphysical Thoughts* speaks of God the Father as communicating his eternity to his Son. The metaphor is not interpreted by the author, and we are not in a position to say whether it is an allusion to the Gospel of John or to the cosmogony of the *Timaeus,* or to some other tradition. Suffice it to say that it reflects a thought emerging in the mind of the young metaphysician, and which came to full expression in his final work. Let me quote the illuminating words of Mr. Hallett: "God is not the *causa transiens* of the world but its *causa immanens,* and creation is the infinite manifestations of a being whose essence it is to express himself. Creation is eternal. . . . Creation must explain not merely the emergence of extended and conscious modes from the unity of the attributes of Extension and Thought but the union of these and of all other attributes in the *unica Substantia.* That ultimate unity must, so far as possible, cease to be ineffable." [82] The principle of creativity is basic to the system which Spinoza has framed. It is sun-clear to his readers that the prime attribute in his Deity is neither the power inherent in the operations of the natural world nor the infallible knowledge of future events but the merger of wisdom and authority in the symbol of intellectual Love. Power, indeed, is regnant in the universe but it is not the power measured by magnitude or velocity or electrolytic change. Wisdom imposes its laws upon every phase of intellectual inquiry, but it is not the inquisitive kind which science, by hard and even cruel labor, has extracted from the fibres of corporeal substance. Love as infinitely diversified, deploying its energies in the areas of both matter and spirit, cements the unity of the divine nature, and fashions for the human soul a permanent position in the divine economy.

In the light of the crowning conception which Spinoza has just adduced, are we at liberty to ask the vital question— Does God know himself in the same way as human beings know themselves by virtue of their sense of individual identity? Does Spinoza's God possess a personality in which the distinction is unmistakably made between the thinking subject and the object of thought? Joachim answers in the affirmation: "God, in his

[80] *Ibid.,* V, 34, Scholium.   [81] *Ibid.,* V, 34, Corollary I.   [82] *Op. cit.,* pp. 209, 294.

being as a *res cogitans* is aware of himself and all that flows from himself; and since in thinking or knowing we necessarily know that we know, God is aware of his own thinking." [83] But the question cannot be answered by a simple Yes or No. It is not, indeed, certain that Spinoza proposed the question to himself in this precise form. For the data required for a significant answer to the query are not at hand. In fact, it may be assumed that the author would not consider the question as an appropriate one; since it might end in reducing God to the status of a limited being. Furthermore, the question as framed is not relevant to the problem which he has under consideration. He set out to find a way by which to relate his emotions to the invincible laws of nature. The concept "intellectual Love" satisfied the terms of the problem, and he desired not to go beyond that. He stopped there, and he invited his age to seek redemption in this manner. The road is hard and few find it; but "all things excellent are as difficult as they are rare."

CONCLUSION

The drama of imperial Substance, its infinite and eternal unity, its discernible attributes and their corresponding modes, the consummatory lustre of the idea of intellectual Love, have now been unveiled before our eyes. What shall be the final appraisement of its meaning and of its worth? The appraisement will take the form of an historic estimate of his work by various types of critics.

To Spinoza more than to most of the scholarly figures of the modern world men have sought to attach a distinctive label. He was ranked as an atheist even before his death, a title which merely separated him from the orthodox patterns of the church. The name was inept, vain and untrustworthy, in view of the superb tribute paid to Deity in the concluding sections of the *Ethics*. Recent expositors have approached the subject in more eulogistic manner, seeking to do him honor as a thinker of superlative gifts. They selected a less opprobrious name and called him a pantheist. The term itself is deceptive; it might imply that "God is everything," where the authority of the Thought attribute could easily gain the ascendancy. Or it might be read as "everything is God," where the Extension property would pervade the whole with the deadening weight of materialism. In this sense God would be the aggregate of bodily potencies, and the human soul would be resolved into an endless series of conditioned reflexes with every hint of moral responsibility quenched. If we took the former meaning, then as Pringle-Pattison would say, "persons are merged in the ideal continuum of the infinite Intellect, with the complete extinction of the mind's integrity." [84] Since neither of these variants can be

---

[83] *Op. cit.*, p. 72.   [84] Quoted by Hallett, *op. cit.*, p. 317.

found in Spinoza's writing we may lay aside the inaccurate label and try another.

Was Spinoza a mystic like so many of his ancient race? He had studied the deliverances of the apostle John, as noted in his *Tractate,* and appeared deeply impressed by the concept of divine love expounded there. That the human soul could advance from a fragmentary acquaintance with sensible objects to an appreciation of spiritual love so deep and permeating as to evoke a corresponding love in the divine Intellect, suggests that Spinoza had penetrated the arcanum of mysticism and perhaps toyed with the idea of "transfusion" into God, which is the highest achievement of the religious mystic. However, the epigram of Professor Pattison that in such union "God ceases to be an Object to man and becomes an experience," would, if that be a correct exposition, relieve Spinoza of any association with the mystic's creed. So again, if the French historian Récéjac defines mysticism as the "tendency to draw near to the Absolute in moral union by symbolic means," alluding, no doubt, to external ritual or clairvoyant illumination, or sudden lapses into subliminal ecstasies, as Plotinus did, he introduces fancies which Spinoza did not and could not entertain; for when we rise to full alliance with the Eternal, all moral habits are suspended and meretricious aids are useless. Not interpenetration of spirit but organic federation of mind with Mind, is Spinoza's conception of intellectual Love.

Perhaps, we should abandon the field of symbolism and seek a likeness in the Idealism current today. The only Reality conceivable by human intelligence, is Experience, says F. H. Bradley in *Appearance and Reality. Nature* cannot be absolute, if viewed merely as the concatenation of physical forces; it must always be expressed in terms of law, and laws are abstractions. *Thought* by itself cannot be absolute; for we can only with great effort, if ever, make an idea represent exactly the essence of a concrete object; and what we call truth turns out in the end to be in part erroneous. *Will* has none of the marks of complete potency; it is always joined to thought, and though they at times seem diverse, they both occur in a "process of time," itself an appearance and not incontestable reality. Finally, *Goodness* does not fully enshrine the nature of reality. We are justified in saying that the Absolute is good, though manifesting itself in varying degrees of goodness and badness. Goodness as a quality is confined to a system of ends, usually with a moral tinge, and when we ask, What is the Good? is it pleasure, harmony of effort, self-sacrifice or self-assertion, that is, the realization of Self? the answer is negative. Reality is inscrutable, it is nothing apart from appearances; it belongs to experience, "self-pervading and superior to relations." All this means that "outside of Spirit there is no reality; and the more that anything is Spiritual, so much the more is it veritably real." [85] Can we by hook or crook find in such vague ideas anything that corresponds with the strong and coherent canons which Spinoza has laid down? Spinoza knew what he desired to say and he knew how to say it with firmness and lucidity. No thinker in modern philosophy has opened so noble a vision of moral excellence addressed to the age of scientific inquiry.

Have we any right to assume that many of the notable achievements of the present day do not find their original incentives in the subtle argument of the *Ethics?* Let us examine the thought of one of the distinguished physiologists of our own time. Dr. J. S. Haldane began his scientific studies as a candidate for the certificate in medicine. He soon, however, awoke to the conviction that his task lay not in the practice of the medical arts but in the continued analysis of the functions of the human body. He then came into conflict with the mechanistic interpretation of living objects, which he contended—against the opinion of his many collaborators—did not give a full and precise account of the data under review. In a persuasive brochure entitled, *Mechanism, Life and Personality,* he argued that the presence of mind in the human organism released the organic processes from the dictation of a mechanical principle, and injected a new force which he called Personality. By long experimentation and deep thought, he reached the conclusion embodied in his Gifford Lectures, 1927-28, at the University of Glasgow, under the broad title, *The Sciences and Philosophy.*

"Religion," he said, "has always been in practice a general philosophy of conscious behavior and it has stood for the reality [validity] of the spiritual interpretation." But he rejects many of the principal tenets of the Christian faith, such as the personality of God, the possibility of a supernatural revelation, the distinction of soul and body and the perpetuation of the one without the other. For him God is identical with all substance, which is the basic concept of Spinoza. There is no physical reality outside of God and the benevolent love of God is visible in all the operations of nature, a fact authenticated by the message of the Founder of the church. We derive all our knowledge of the natural world through the achievements of the objective sciences. But there is an abstract world which the mind alone can know, the world of the Spirit, and it is by this Spirit that we come in touch with the supreme Reality. Thus philosophy and science meet in happy converse, together they embrace the total interest which the human mind is capable of cultivating. The scientific interpretation is but a stage in the greater and fuller interpretation. Science foreshadows ultimate reality, it cannot produce it. Hence, the intellecual life would be sharply truncated, if it depended on the results of external science; the

[85] F. H. Bradley, *op. cit.,* p. 500 et sq,

God disclosed would be a mere simulacrum, a picture not the final Reality. Obviously, some such conceit as Spinoza's intellectual love of God was needed to unite the principles of science with the central demands of religion. Is it not incumbent on us to affirm that Haldane was not resting in some sort of Hegelian stupor but had deliberately, or at any rate by indirection, turned to Spinoza as his final authority? This is the best appraisement we can make of the system devised by the young Jewish scholar at the Hague.

IX: DAVID HUME

DAVID HUME belonged to the long line of British thinkers who insisted upon a strict examination of the processes of perception and reflection as preparatory to the study of the world itself. He found himself in partial agreement with the attitude of Descartes who sought to know where certitude could be found, whether in the immediate deliverences of the senses or in the sustained habits of judgment. It is a significant fact that the young Scotchman sojourned for a considerable period in the very town, LaFleche, where Descartes pursued his early studies in logic and the objective sciences. Much of the *Treatise of Human Nature* was composed within its bounds. The major interest of the Continental school, however, lay not in the analysis of the mind but in the problem of substance. Spinoza and Leibniz both accepted the Cartesian principle of clear and distinct ideas as the basis for their philosophical researches; they then passed on to weightier matters such as the relation of individual bodies to one another and to the whole of Nature, the meaning of law, the possibility of purposiveness as a factor of universal moment, the reality of God and his explicit attributes such as extension and thought.

It seems at first glance that we have descended from a lofty pinnacle of contemplation to make contact with secondary questions, when we leave the *Ethics* of Spinoza and open the *Essay* of John Locke. The centre of intellectual gravity has shifted. The *Principia* of Newton seems much nearer the levels of common thought than does the "Intellectual love of God" or the "preestablished harmony" of the universe. The difference lies in the manner of approach. The British temper is largely Aristotelian; it seeks to know objective *things,* not the subtle nexus of abstract propositions. For Newton mass and motion are always associated with their impressions on the senses; or conversely the impressions of the senses must always be subjected to the critical application of mathematical law. Bacon had already insisted that science should have a severe and comprehensive method in order to handle its data successfully. Hobbes retorted that no method of inquiry can be created until man knows how the senses act in registering their mass of impressions. The organization of the sensory system must therefore be thoroughly examined; modern psychology begins with his famous theory of motion.

MIND AND THE FORMATION OF IDEAS

It was at this point that Locke takes up the task. He assumes that scientific data have little worth so long as the mind knows nothing of its own capacities. He at once instituted a search into the genesis and nature of ideas. It was held by Descartes that the source of knowledge is in the mind; "bodies are not, properly speaking, known by the senses or by the faculty of imagination but by the understanding only." [1] Or, to put it in less formal language, we cannot know an object by simply seeing or touching it; sensational acquaintance is not knowledge; we must think about it, "turn it over in our minds," make our ideas "distinct," that is, get the relation of the given idea to many others of the same group. In short, we must uncover the *meaning* of the idea; this is what Locke proposes to do, but in a different manner from that followed by Descartes. The first question he asks is, Where do ideas come from? The Continental thinkers could not release themselves from the tradition that ideas, general, universal ideas, are native to the mind. Locke denies it; he finds no evidence in logic, ethics, or religion for the existence of original and underived ideas. Nor does he find any tendency to construct them without the aid of the senses. This is true even of the idea of God. Locke's discussion is elementary as compared with Hume's; but his conclusion is fixed, namely, that every idea once supposed to be innate, may actually be accounted for through the processes of empirical perception. Thus we obtain the images of shape, size and weight from the sensory data. We compare them, by means of transition, with other images of the object; by such comparison the object assumes a systematic form in our mind which we call its idea. By the operation of the understanding, it ultimately becomes known to us as the same recognizable, unitary thing—the object. Then, we add number to number, magnitude to magnitude, idea to idea, until we reach the complex idea or concept of totality. When finally, experience and imagination refuse to accept new and additive information, we call the Object of our quest God. The idea of divine Being having passed through the crucible of perception and reflection 'must then submit to confirmatory analysis that will establish the reality of the Object itself.

But British thought had not as yet come anywhere near to the philosophical conclusions reached by the inquiries of Hume. Hence, we must pause to consider the achievements of Bishop Berkeley, the second member of the

---

[1] René Descartes, *Meditations* in *The Philosophical Works of Descartes*. Trans. by E. S. Haldane and G. R. T. Ross (Cambridge: University Press, 1911), I, 130.

Empirical school. In his early youth Berkeley had challenged the specific dogma of Locke, that a material substance envelopes the properties of the object and gives unity and solidity to its form. Some of these properties, shape, weight, and motion, said Locke, belong of right to the body and cannot be removed without destroying the body itself. Other qualities are present, so to say, temporarily, having no inherent or constitutive connection with the object but being imposed by the observing mind. Although substance cannot be perceived by any sense-organ it must nevertheless exist as a necessary support to the perceived qualities. At this point Berkeley breaks in upon the argument, which he declared to be contrary to fact. Closer inspection, he avers, shows that all qualities, primary as well as secondary, are appraisements made by the mind. Shape and weight are not imbedded in the body any more than sweetness, heat, or color; they are all ideas fashioned by the judgment. Furthermore, ideas cannot be produced by incogitative matter; there is no kinship between the two types of existence; thought and matter are irrevocably opposed. Ideas must be gained by the activity of spirit, and in no other way. At long last only the supreme Spirit, God, can justify the appearance of the simplest image, the sudden, unbidden sensum, the spontaneous return of memory, the unmediated burst of emotion. It is true that the human mind has attempted to exercise a certain authority over the processes of nature, for example, control of magnetic influences or blending two botanical varieties into a new form. This, indeed, is the triumph of ideas over matter. But more than this, the Spirit of God is the ground of all uniformity in nature. Gravitation, then to the fore in all learned debate, is not an independent force of nature, says the Bishop, it is not a law mechanical and invincible, governing the courses of planets and star; it is the *sign* of the operation of spiritual power, in many but not all parts of the universe. This is the only way to explain the unvarying activities and the "admirable connections" of bodies which appear in our study of the external world. Still further, as a good churchman is bound to do, he asks, What other power except God could introduce those changes into the order of nature which are known as miracles? The fact that our perception of miracles is sporadic, not sustained, does not militate against their reality; they serve a prescribed purpose in the divine economy. The sum of the case, then, is:—substance is of one kind only, spiritual, and the supreme Spirit shapes the motions of the stars as well as the thoughts and feelings of the human heart.

The stage is now set in British philosophy for the advent of its greatest thinker. David Hume was born in Edinburgh in 1711. He sprang from Scottish stock, stern in character and devoted to the cause of the hereditary religion. The atmosphere in which he lived was Calvinistic to its centre;

yet he carried into his mature career scarcely a single idea that had been drilled into his youthful mind by church and university. He was aware early in life that the intellectual method he proposed to follow would eventually bring him into collision with men of orthodox opinions, and that he could not afford to awaken prejudice and incur hostility, while he was making his way into the heart of the subjects he wished to expound. In the adjacent field of ethics his reserve was less pronounced. He discovered that the moral philosophy of the past was "entirely hypothetical" and "depended more on invention than on experience," that men constructed their theories rather by the caprice of "fancy" than by a sympathetic study of human nature. Professor Kemp Smith [2] has demonstrated with great effectiveness in recent days that the starting-point of his philosophy was a study of the moral nature of man rather than the needs of the intellect. In every scientific enterprise prejudice and pride of opinion must be set on one side. Hence, while Hume paid attentive heed to the words of his forerunners, he was not disposed to accept them at face value, certainly not as prescriptive guides for framing his own conclusions. Yet one of their declarations he accepted without hesitation, namely, that knowledge begins and ends with the data of experience: we can know nothing beyond the confines of perception.

The problem of Empiricism now comes to a sharp focus:—How does the mind know the world in which it lives? The emphasis is not on *world* but on *mind*. Locke thought he could solve the problem by distinguishing between primary and secondary ideas. Berkeley assumed that all properties were nothing but ideas in the mind and that while bodies existed independently of mind, their essence consisted solely of the meaning which mind imputed to an object. But what the actual functions of perception, memory, and judgment are, neither made the slightest attempt to understand. This became the task of David Hume and this is his contribution to modern thinking. Certain critics have complained that he laid too great stress on physiological facts and they named his theory *Sensualism*. But sensation is the first step in mental action, not the last. He studied the manner in which the mind acted, by the principles of resemblance, contiguity, and causal connection. For the first time in the whole range of modern thought, an exact analysis of judgmental experience was undertaken.

The first and most pressing question that forced itself upon the attention of the youthful investigator was— How shall we account for the element of necessity obvious in every returning experience? The Continental thinkers answered it succinctly,—necessity lies in objective nature. The answer is categorical but unconvincing. Locke could give no solution ex-

2 *The Philosophy of David Hume.*

cept to say that substance keeps the properties in steady connection; that was all. Berkeley placed the causal principle in the Supreme Spirit and left it there. Hume, on the other hand, argues that the "causal axiom" is framed in the mind by virtue of the constant return of the same situations in sensory experience. Heat and fire are persistently joined as concurrent or sequent images; the one seems to be the cause of the other; hence, eventually we accept the connection as necessary.

The answer to the question thus framed is the key to any successful theory of knowledge. Hume insists that the answer cannot be found in a specific tendency resident in the world of nature, which automatically, so to say, combines two such divergent properties as heat and fire. Cause is not a factor in external phenomena, it belongs only to the region of mind. " 'Tis a common observation," he writes, "that the mind has a great propensity to spread itself on external objects, and to conjoin with them any internal impressions which they occasion and which make their appearance at the same time that these objects discover themselves to the senses." [3] Thus the *vis inertiae* which Newton found in the physical universe would seem to be paralleled by the animal *nisus* which prompts us to find a constant connection between certain given sensations. According to Hume's interpretation, the internal tendency of mind projects its perceived qualities into the object observed, thereby persuading many philosophers that such qualities actually exist in the natural world.[4] The upshot of the argument is that if causality be a real principle, it cannot be found in our environment as an active force but only in the mind as a controlling belief.

We are therefore obliged to ask, what ground have we for believing that a necessary connection subsists between any two or more qualities represented in experience, when we find the same conjunction occurring in succeeding perceptions? We must take it for granted, that each succeeding perception will exhibit similar characteristics to those already given and will therefore have a definite coherence in content; otherwise they cannot be recognized by the perceiving subject. Furthermore, the conjunction must be constant; there must be a proximity of vision and a regularity of return, enabling the mind to grasp the intrinsic values of the qualities involved. But in the judgment of Hume, sequence can never be the same as consequence. Certainly, the mere conjunction of the same properties in a hundred sensory situations does not establish a causative relation between them, of such a sort that in the next kindred perception we may expect precisely the same content. "It is impossible, therefore, that any arguments from experience can prove this resemblance of the past to

---

[3] *Treatise of Human Nature*, Selby-Bigge ed., p. 167.
[4] *Enquiries*, Selby-Bigge ed., Sec. 58, note, 60, note.

the future; since all these arguments are founded on the supposition of that resemblance." [5] For conditions may change radically and the re-appearance of the same sense-data be wholly prohibited. It has been said, and will be said again, that reason has worked out the concept of causality on the basis of an inner principle governing the emergence of each new situation, much as Newton proposed the law of gravitation, after sustained and laborious study of the mathematical relations of our planetary system, with the sun as the centre, holding that such a system could not endure without the presence of a dominant physical force. Hume does not discount the validity of the conclusions reached by such inductive reasoning, but he argues that Nature has also ordained a principle of Attraction in a different sphere of her activity, "a kind of attraction which in the mental world will be found to have as extraordinary effects as in the natural, and to show itself in as many and various forms." The effects of this attraction are transparently clear but the causes are beyond the reach of human intelligence, and "must be resolved into the original qualities of human nature." [6] In short, the association of ideas in the mind is an irresistible and invariable process: this is the way the intelligence of man acts, and we can in no manner depart from its prescribed direction. Because of such natural involvements we are equipped to organize our thought by the systematic laws of logic, which is the final form assumed by custom in its sovereign control of human behavior. Thus the causal principle is not a fortuitous idea introduced into the mental practices of the race but a solid rule, a "natural relation," enabling us to retain intact our old experiences and affiliate them with the new.[7] This is Hume's answer to the question cited above: the same or similar collocation of images will recur at intervals endowed with a causal character, since they represent the unvarying nature of intelligence. It is on this basis alone that we can examine the objects of the physical world and extract from them the laws of their operations. Laws are not in the events but in the observing mind.

Assuming, then, that causality is a fact in human consciousness, not a force resident in the circumambient world, how shall we deal with the problem we are studying in this book, namely, the meaning of God? "If every idea be derived from an impression, the idea of a deity proceeds from the same origin and if no impression either of veneration or reflection implies any force or efficacy 'tis equally impossible to discover or even imagine any such active principle in the diety." [8] This axiom is laid down in a challenge to the thesis of the Cartesians who have decided that "matter cannot be endowed with any efficacious principle, because 'tis impossible to discover in it any such principle." That is to say, nature cannot

---

[5] *Enquiries,* Sec. 32. [6] *Treatise of Human Nature,* pp. 12, 13.
[7] *Ibid.,* p. 94. [8] *Ibid.,* p. 160.

itself communicate motion or produce any of the effects we ascribe
to it. If this be true then surely the same course of reasoning should
determine them to exclude the efficacious principle also from the Supreme
Being. Hume asked them to face the issue squarely and admit that they
cannot obtain an "adequate idea of power or efficacy in any object." The
purpose of the argument at this point is not to prove the non-existence of
Deity nor even to deny his possession of causal powers, accepting his
existence as a reality. Hume attempts merely to show that the idea of God
a conception built up from specific impressions which the fertile
imagination extends from single events, which we may call "divine Volitions," to a generalized form of activity which represents the idea of Power.
There is, however, in such an argument a certain kind of difficulty
which will not escape the notice of the attentive reader. For if the Deity
be considered as "the great and efficacious principle which supplies the
deficiencies of all causes," we should then be confronted with the necessity of making him responsible for all our private volitions, the perverse
and evil as well as the wise and good implications.[9] This is a form of
impiety which no honest thinker will tolerate. We shall avoid completely
the insinuation of such a charge, if we accept the thesis that causality is
a part of our natural mental constitution, a type of thinking which
eventually makes us acquainted with every type of reality. Thus, Hume is
explicit in his belief that the world of nature is governed by forces which
when perceived and understood by the human mind are represented to
the mind as unvarying laws. In a letter addressed to Professor Stewart,
'54, he emphatically says: "I have never asserted so absurd a proposition
that anything might arise without a cause." [10] What he denies is that the
causal axiom" is derived either from intuition or demonstration; rather
does it come from "another source," namely, the subtle activity of the
natural mind. How such activity differs from the process known as intuition, he does not report. In fact, in his general discussion on this somewhat mysterious property he refrains from an exact analysis. If the source
of the causal axiom is a part of the activity of nature, general nature
operating in the thoughts of the mind as in the motions of bodies—then he
assigns to consciousness a function, Cause, which he deliberately denies
the observable world. It is obvious that modern psychologists are in
a state of puzzlement on this question; some of them give up the case and
resort to hypothetical assumptions such as conditioned reflexes. Kant declined to adopt so dull and unillumined a course; he followed the lead of
Hume and spoke of the "schematism of the understanding," another
name for Hume's "activity of nature," as an "art concealed in the depths
of the human soul, whose real modes of activity nature is hardly likely

[9] Ibid., pp. 248–49.   [10] Cf. Smith, The Philosophy of David Hume, p. 413.

ever to allow us to discover." [11] Locke had anticipated both thinkers, speaking of the imagination as a powerful mental faculty, with no limits set to its movements. Having once adopted the principle of necessity he could find no way of putting a curb to its use. In due time its regress will be infinite, and we are obliged to accept the existence of a First Cause as a true and necessary concept. The attitude of Hume in this regard will appear in the sequel.

THE IDEA OF GOD, HOW CONCEIVED

From this time forth we turn our attention to the study of one idea, the idea of God. The field here is extremely broad and we are justified in selecting a single phase of the subject, as Hume actually does, to wit, the methods by which the idea of God as supreme Substance obtains a place in the mind, and the reasons for assuming that God does or does not objectively exist. It is possible, as everybody except the Logical Positivist admits, to examine certain ideas which have no conceivable reality within the bounds of physical phenomena. But with respect to the present idea it is essential that we should be able to assess the value of the historical proofs, in the light of the established laws of human experience, such as we have already discussed. Hume, thus, refers to all the traditional arguments, the idea of God in the mind, the Cause of the order of nature, the evidence of design, and the necessity of moral sanctions. The first two he rejects, the third he accepts in principle but stalls at man's attempts to find unimpeachable instances, and the last he admits tentatively, though with technical reservations.

The conception of a divine being exists as a determinate idea in the intelligence of civilized races. Descartes considered it a real and original fact of thought, placed there by its divine Subject and generable in no other way. Leibniz argued that no such idea could be clear or distinct unless it had first been proven to be a possible idea. Hume replies to both that no idea has ever been entertained whose object could not be considered now as existent, and again, as non-existent. But the idea of God does not occur in the thinking of primitive tribes and hence cannot be a structural ingredient in the aboriginal thought of man. The serious problem facing philosophy is not whether the idea of God carries reality with it, but how the human mind came into possession of the idea. This problem is not one of logic but of psychology. Hume sets out to discover the empirical genesis of the idea of God. In accordance with the principles we have already recorded, the mind can have no knowledge whose content does not appear to the perceiving senses. Every idea is the distilled matter of an impression; it cannot be created by the mind through its own processes.

[11] *Critique of Pure Reason.* Trans. by Smith, p. 183.

Hence, such a concept as *substance* has no aboriginal and simple meaning. Berkeley is quite correct in his opinion that material substance
does not exist. The ball is red, it is heavy, it is round; each of these properties is presented to its respective sense-organ and then determined in its
ideational value by the supervisory judgment. What is it that combines
all qualities into a unified whole? Substance, says Locke; there is no image
of it but it *must* exist. But material substance, in Hume's view, is a collection of properties, not an independent entity. Again, Berkeley who
denies reality of substance in body, finds it in spirit. But, says his critic,
can you obtain a factual impression of mind, intellect, spirit? No, Berkeley
replies, but since spirit is the only *active* thing in the universe, the idea
must exist in the mind of man and in the mind of God. Then Hume
enters his devastating caveat—ideas require no combining substance,
whether matter or mind; they are subject to law, the law of association;
they are associated with one another by their natural quality—red is always red, heavy always heavy. By sequence near or remote, by the efficacy
of cause, the same images follow one another in a sustained order. In
short, we have "no perfect idea of anything but a perception," and "it is
impossible that our idea of a perception and that of an object or external
existence should ever represent what are specifically different from each
other." [12]

Confronted with these facts, says Hume, the "hideous hypothesis"
of Spinoza must be rejected. Spinoza conceives that substance is one, with
two attributes and an infinite number of modes, both physical relations
and logical ideas. Other thinkers have held that matter and mind are
antipodally diverse and can never be joined. Spinoza answers that what
seems to us to be individual objects are merely modifications of the same
reality, conveyed to us by the organs of body and the dialectic of the
mind. Hume retorts, the one and only reality we can detect is the primary
image; if it corresponds to no external object, such an object can never
come within the range of cognition. Now substance, matter or mind, cannot present itself as a clear and distinct image; if it be apprehended at all
it must be by the office of the inner judgment; or, as Hume says in the
Inquiries (Sec. 14), "The idea of God as meaning infinitely intelligent,
wise and good Being arises from reflecting on the operations of our own
mind, and augmenting without limit those qualities of goodness and wisdom." The experience is found in all civilized races. Men study their own
habits of thought, isolate the properties classified as intellectual and moral,
reach their own limits in the pursuit of truth and virtue, having passed
through stages of growth in each field of thought. Finally, by the sweep of
the imagination we conceive of intelligence so great that it cannot be added

[12] *Treatise of Human Nature*, p. 241.

to, goodness so full that it exhausts all contemplated ideals. The conception of *God* thus thrills through man's soul, an idea complex and coördinate, organized in experimental fashion from the judgments of the past, precisely as every other concrete-general or abstract term has been. It is a just and suitable inference from experience and reflection, not a "perfect idea," as Descartes would say; it is a human judgment and cannot by any Cartesian manipulation be transmuted into concrete fact.

So much for the psychological principles at work in the argument. But there is a second avenue of approach that should be carefully traversed. Like every single concept such as energy, power, cause, selfhood, the constituent characters implied in the consummatory idea, God, have unfolded slowly through the vicissitudes of time and experience. Hume has presented the subject with great cogency in his *Natural History of Religion,* published in 1757, six years after the appearance of his first *Enquiry.* He begins with the admission that "the whole frame of nature bespeaks an intelligent author; and no rational enquirer can, after serious reflection, suspend his belief a moment with regard to the primary principles of genuine Theism and Religion." But whether logic can prove the actual existence of Deity is a question to be considered in a different connection. In such a discussion the choice lies between two contradictory hypotheses. Did the human race receive an "effusion of grace," as St. Augustine would say, at the very threshold of its career, which implanted the germ of the notion of a supreme and immutable Deity and allowed it to come to maturity after a long period of gestation? Or, did the race make its debut on the earth without the slightest suspicion of its spiritual destiny, but having aptitudes of mind certain to call for acquaintance with powers other than those of sensible matter? Hume believes that the religious instinct is not on the same level as that of self-preservation or resentment or even gratitude. It is "secondary" in its genesis and depends on other factors that emerge in the slow development of the racial character. We have already agreed that the conception of a superior being is not an immediate intuition but an inference drawn from one or more of the surging images that infest the daily experience. One of these images congealing into belief is the impression of power, e. g., the effect of the impact of an external body upon our own. The tumbling torrent of the river, the crash of the falling tree under the might of the storm, and especially the blinding flash of lightning with the accompanying roar of thunder, all conspire to turn man's minds to objects quite unlike those of common perception. He feels himself in contact with a kind of energy which cannot be discerned by the physical senses. This new concept is supported by the emotion of fear, echoing with horrid reverberations in his brain, bating his breath, exciting his pulses, communicating a deadly chill to his whole nervous system. But experiences like these did not suggest to primitive man the concept of an omnipotent creator, a conceit far beyond his limited mental resources. Instead, he was content to cite the influence of an invisible demon, a spirit of mischief abroad in the land, a concrete individual whose qualities he did not know and whose insidious devices he profoundly feared. In the course of time these phantoms take the shape of personalized divinities, some favoring the people, others inflicting hurt upon them. Oftentimes, as in Greece, one god gained the ascendancy and exercised dominion over his colleagues. Homer has described in eloquent language the kinds of deities which presided over the destinies of Hellas. This extraordinary race of men whose contributions to art and science and philosophy are beyond price, spent their early days in the practice of the most revolting forms of polytheism in human records. Not the slightest hint of a theistic temper is found in even their most cultivated thinkers. In the subtlest examination of natural laws we find no intimation of the refinements of serious religious thought. In their endeavor after a "magnificent simplicity," they run the risk of becoming immersed in a profound mystery which would "destroy the intelligent nature of deity, on which alone any rational worship or adoration can be founded." [13] Anaxagoras and Parmenides and even Plato seem to have passed through the period of purgation but they found it difficult to slough off the mortal coil of mythology, and assume the garments of a pure religious feeling. The end of every revolutionary attempt among the Greeks was the creation of a "limited deity" which could serve the interests of a particular group but not humanity itself.

The shrewd analysis which Hume makes of the character of pagan divinities indicates how inadequately their votaries have understood the meaning of religious truth. The creed which the Greek state adopts has two irreversible articles,—every divinity must possess (1) knowledge and (2) power, the dominant qualities of imperial statesmanship. The quality of moral rectitude is deliberately withheld. Plato recognized its absence; he charged that Homer had extolled shrewdness of intrigue and lust of power, while justice, modesty and sobriety are not required in the behavior of the Sons of Heaven. Hence, Hume exclaims, as an echo of Plato's reproaches;—"The higher the deity is exalted in power and knowledge, the lower is he depressed in goodness and benevolence." [14] The call of religion as well as morals is, as Hume thinks, for a god credited with virtues greater than those attained by human beings; instead of that, we have approval of the archaic rule: *Sunt supremis sua jura,*—the gods have their own laws of behavior, inferior to the moral standards of the cultivated community. The result? simply this: that the gods could have

[13] *Selections from Hume* (New York: Scribners, 1929), p. 272.   [14] *Ibid.,* p. 277.

no interest in the moral excellence of men, and men retaliated by exhibiting no interest in the established religion. Elaborate ceremonials, strange forms of personal sacrifice could not enlist the favor of the Blest. Even in the covenanted faith of the Jews, ignoble traits were ascribed to Yahweh,—jealousy, vengeance, retribution for trivial faults. Also in the pagan traditions superadded to the Catholic faith, similar improprieties have been recorded. But Christianity in its pure program has made moral grandeur the inseparable quality of Deity. Hume was but the precursor of Kant in his insistence on the moral reason as the heart and centre of the divine nature.

Let us examine the subject from still another angle. It is said by certain thinkers that divine energy can be apprehended intuitively, because it is indubitably at work in the world. Hume demands that they submit evidence to that effect. The argument from inward experience must be based upon a direct intellectual contact with the operating force. Malebranche opines that scientific causes such as Newton discerned in the world, do not exist. The true and immediate explanation of every effect in the series of physical events, is not the presence of a distinct and measurable force in nature but of a volition of the supreme Mind, which wills that particular objects would be irrecoverably united with one another. Thus, "Deity is the immediate cause of the union of body and soul, and it is not the organs of sense which being agitated by external objects, produce the images in the mind, but it is a particular volition of the Omnipotent Maker which excites such a sensation in consequence of such a motion in the organ." [15] Nature is so full of God that we are obliged to identify ourselves completely with his will. Hence, the idea of God is literally forced on the conscious mind whether we will or not. This is not a logical deduction, it is a form of empirical intuition.

But the answer of the expert empiricist is ready. The mind of man, says Hume, is too meagerly furnished to obtain the kind of sense-content demanded by this theory; "our line is too short to fathom such abysses." [16] He means that the sensory material thus obtained it too restricted in form and quality and amount to yield the inference that Occasionalism attempts to draw. If the terms of the law of gravitation required twenty years of close mathematical calculation to be finally fixed, how much wider must be the scope of observation and subtler the dialectic that would lead to Malebranche's safe and happy ending? For in addition to the complexity of the logical argument, we must not forget that gravitational force and divine Energy are utterly different concepts; indeed, to apply the Newtonian formula to the multitude of solar systems in the universe, is a task of gigantic proportions and never will be accomplished. How much more

15 *Enquiries*, Sec. 55. 16 *Ibid.*, Sec. 57.

complicated is the work required for any incipient demonstration of the validity of the Occasionalist method! The line, indeed, is far too short. Nor is this the whole story. When we start to arrange the terms of the new experiment, we are confronted by certain unsolved problems—the way in which physical bodies act upon one another, the relation of body and mind, the knowledge of the supreme Being which is something more than a mere "reflection upon our own faculties." Are we in a position to make a reasonable judgment as to the inherent powers of God, or even of his existence? A "voluntary act of the imagination" may yield a tentative answer to these questions, but commonsense never can. The only point we may accept with certainty is that the idea of God's existence has had a natural growth; it was not implanted by some surreptitious agency; but its presence in the mind does warrant us in asking whether a corresponding reality exists.

GOD AND THE IDEA OF CAUSE

The second classical argument for the existence of God depends on the validity of the principle of cause and effect objectively applied. Experiment shows that every event in the physical milieu is caused: it is the effect of a prior event. Motion is produced by a moving body in contact with a body at rest. The value of the "work" done cannot be determined simply by the ensuing situation, that is, the change in the inner qualities of the body immediately affected. Every impact represents the accumulated force of all preceding impulses. A causal series is thus instituted and the chain of causes goes back to the original Cause which cannot be other than God himself. Now the original Cause may be either the total coördinated powers of the universe regarded as a single whole or a being, unique and solitary who has the power and will to create a suitable world such as the one we inhabit. Spinoza or Leibniz will dictate the kind of world required by the causative factors. But there *must* be a supreme Reality. Hume excludes, without reservation, the idea of an immanent Deity; he is not an atheist in any sense; he holds to the traditional thesis of the British community, even though some of its elements are distasteful to him. His business as a philosopher is to determine whether the existence of God can be established by a logical process. If it can, then he is in a position to answer his bitterest critics; if it cannot, then, at least, he can assure himself that he has done his best, thereafter being encouraged to fall back upon the principle of "natural belief," for which no substantive explanation can be given. But he cannot forget the primary conceptions upon which his whole system rests. He is a tried and true empiricist, and for him merely "received" ideas have no logical value.

(a) He will therefore formally isolate and define the concept of Cause.

But he faces at once a serious dilemma: either one thing cannot be th
cause of another thing, except where the ideas (images) of these thing
are constantly connected in experience, or all objects when constantly cor
nected are, on that account, to be regarded as cause and effect. The firs
part of the dilemma is inadequate; in it we actually affirm, by implicatior
that there is no First Cause in the universe, since such a Cause involv
the attribute of power, and no perception of power in any form has eve
been received by the mind of man. This last fact we have already dis
cerned, and repeat it here with fresh emphasis. The second horn of th
dilemma is just as devastating, namely, that whenever external objects ar
connected in experience they must *necessarily* stand in the relation of caus
and effect. If that were true then every event because it follows anothe
would be its formal result,—a plain case of the fallacy of *post hoc erg
propter hoc* (after this, hence the effect of this). No scientific conclusio
can be built on such shaky premises. Here Hume is particularly concerne
not to give any advantage to his opponents, the materialists, that is, thos
who adopt the formula of John Locke that material substance must exi
whether we obtain an impression of it or not; but especially the disciples c
Hobbes, who contended that since motion is the only power we know i
the world, thought must also be motion, for it proceeds by momentar
impulses. But the plain fact is that perception which is the basis of a
thought, is of two kinds, "extended and unextended," that is, ment
images of the physical body and ideas already deduced from previou
images; they cannot be identical but the latter kind will be used to defin
the former. This means that the process of thought is different from th
process of natural movement; and while we cannot isolate or define th
object called soul or establish its perpetuity when the body is destroyed, w
can at least find in moral action a strong argument both for the solidarit
of the soul and its possible future existence. He concludes this part of th
discussion with the remark: "If my philosophy makes no addition to th
arguments for religion, I have at least the satisfaction to think that
takes nothing from them, but that everything remains precisely as b
fore." [17]

What then can we do? Obviously we must keep the meaning of cau
sality within the orbit of the empirical system. The only *things* we kno
are the images which pass through our conscious experience, and imag
which appear in constant conjunction seem to us to maintain a necessar
connection with one another. But we have already discovered that we ca
not "penetrate into the reason of the conjunction." All we are at libert
to agree upon is that the uniformity of experience may be determined t
the presence of a causal factor resident in the external world. We do n

[17] *Treatise of Human Nature*, pp. 248–51, ending of last paragraph.

affirm that such a factor exists, neither do we deny its existence; we only say that so far as our scientific judgment goes, the causal principle is at work only in our mind.

If this be true, the ancient proof for the existence of God by the law of cause and effect, is abruptly blocked. The usual method for refuting the argument is to say that we can determine the causal nexus of physical events from unit to unit in an observable world, but when the series passes beyond the bounds of empirical verification, we are helpless to complete the argument. But in Hume's refutation we do not need to wait for the series to become infinite and thus be out of reach; we are confronted at once by the logical condition that cause is a concept of mind, not an integral force in nature, and the term can be used only with reference to the facts of sensory experience. Let us be sure of Hume's meaning at this point. We have already noted that Hume is extremely careful in phrasing his language when dealing with this extralogical problem. He had been repeatedly accused of removing the incidence of causality wholly from the natural world. He denied the charge in the passage already quoted (p. 219). Here again we are obliged to note that the main question is not the existence of cause, but *how* we can apprehend and appraise it. By an edict of nature the return of the same images with inflexible regularity bears the symbols of necessary connection. Science bases all its inquests upon this cardinal fact. But in the extramundane sphere no such empirical acquaintance is possible. It follows as a matter of course that no attempt to apply the causal maxim can be successful. The idea of a First Cause is, as Kant proved, a mental concept which cannot be handled by the methods of scientific investigation. Hume left the subject where it was; he added nothing to it, and he took nothing away from it. That is to say, he did not deny the existence of God, and he did not disallow any of the divine prerogatives.

But suppose that the second part of the above dilemma (p. 226) were true; suppose that all the objects in the natural world were conjoined and by virtue of that conjunction causally connected. And suppose, also, that the principles of causality might pass beyond men's apprehension so that we could assume the presence of a Universal Cause, as Descartes actually does. Then, in Hume's judgment serious difficulties cross our path. For unless we resort to the absentee doctrine of Deism, as Hume is inclined to do, we are driven to ask certain questions about God's current relation to the created world. "There are many philosophers," says Hume, "who after an exact scrutiny of all the phenomena of nature, conclude that the Whole, considered as a System, is, in every period of its existence, ordered with perfect benevolence; and that the utmost possible happiness will, in the end, result to all created beings, without any mixture of positive or absolute ill or misery." [18] This, for instance, is the opinion of Leibniz, the contemporary of John Locke, in his doctrine of the best possible world. He admits the presence of three kinds of evil, metaphysical evil resulting from the contingent character of the world, organic pain, and the tendency of man to disobey the divine law as written in the operations of nature and the human mind. There is something wrong with the world dating from the moment of its creation. With this conclusion Hume might agree, but he flatly dissents from Leibniz' deduction that the sum of human experiences is in favor of a calm and roseate life, and he denies that the conception of a "best possible world is borne out by the established records of history." Moreover, he took grave exception to the Stoic's dogma that "the ills under which they labored were, in reality, good to the universe" and that when we meditated upon them in the large view, which comprehended the whole system of nature, every event, no matter how tragic or painful, "became an object of joy and exultation." With all the indignation and contempt at his command he rejected the opinion found in many orthodox creeds that the sufferings incurred on the earth will be compensated for in a future life. Hume was a realist and he had no sympathy with the mischievous sentiments of the pious doctrinaire.

He had even less patience with the moralist who affects to believe that evils have no independent qualities of their own but are merely incidental waymarks in the march of human destiny. Nature, he argues, has prescribed that "certain characters, dispositions and actions" will awaken approval in the perceiving soul, while others will produce contrary feelings. The former contribute to the peace and harmony of the social group, the latter to public discord and distrust. It is folly to maintain that "everything is right with regard to the whole," and the qualities which disturb society are, in the main, as beneficial and suitable to the primary intentions of nature as those which more directly promote its happiness and welfare." [19] Can such bizarre and even contradictory speculations carry conviction to a mind which judged the edicts of nature to be wholly exact and proper? To be sure, it is the verdict of history that the brutalities and horrid iniquities of war may so work upon the conscience of survivors as to cause them to right ancient wrongs and set up a system for the prevention of subsequent social crimes. But we should take note that in every case time must intervene between the commission of the deed and the scrupulous reconstruction of the moral system. Hence, atonement, be it never so well conceived and administered, cannot wipe out the stain of the original misdemeanor. The decision of posterity is the same as Hume's —sin is a definite and uncancelable event, it cannot be absorbed into the harmony of the social whole.

[18] *Enquiries*, Sec. 79.   [19] *Ibid.*, Sec. 80.

Hume is not afraid to meet the consequences of his argument in a wider field. He admits that if we eliminate the element of cause in the objective world, we virtually exclude the principle of providence. For providence as it is ordinarily construed means the interference of Deity in the affairs of nature and of man, in order *to work out the particular good of a particular group*. Apart from its philosophical impossibility, that assumption he regards as intrinsically vicious, not to say, blasphemous. The denial of the principle of providence does not explain either the presence of evil or its ultimate conquest. Assuming that God is the "ultimate Author of all our volitions" is he, like the man who fires the mine, to be held "answerable for all the effects and must he bear the blame or acquire the praise which belongs to them?" [20] Or shall we fall back upon the Augustinian theory that God constructs the form and efficacy of the human will but has nothing to do with the type of behavior to be willed? Hume proceeds to analyze the forms that evil takes. There is first, pain, the acute suffering of the body which leads to moral depression and strange volitional activities. Still, pain may be the instrument of intellectual growth and moral discipline; the state has adopted it as a civil sanction. Again, the inexorable laws of nature, if broken, bring disastrous consequences on individuals and the group, on single communities and great and powerful nations. Yet a minute alteration in the brain structure of Caligula might have converted him into a benevolent Trajan.[21] Further: human creatures possess but a minimum of possible power, physical and mental, and thus suffer defeat at the hands of natural forces or by the combined strength of communal clans. Were the individual's capacities substantially enlarged, society might pursue its course in peace and amity. Finally, "inaccurate workmanship" in certain parts of the natural machines induce pain and emotional horror which under a different economy would be entirely avoided. Abolish storms, floods, droughts, earthquakes, war itself, and the change in human experience would be instantaneous.

These are common and indisputable facts. It is vain to say, as Spinoza did, that nature is a system where the question of good and ill does not arise; nature is controlled by law, it is the seat of invincible necessity. Pain and error are mere negations, not solid actualities; they represent the feelings of a particular organic group, not the property of substance itself. To Hume bred in the anthropomorphist tradition of British theology, such a theory is blind to the plainest items of experience. Pain and error are resident factors in every transaction of the social group. If God is responsible for the creation of the universe, he must be responsible for every type of operation within its bounds. There is abundant evidence to give warrant to the judgment that the order of the universe proves an omni-

[20] *Ibid.*, Sec. 78 sq.   [21] *Dialogues*, Ch. XI.

potent mind, that is, a mind whose will is constantly attended with th
obedience of every creature and being.[22] If this be true, then we are con
fronted with a most serious dilemma: Can God be the maker of th
world, its operations, every aspect of its developed structures, every act o
its individual bodies, including the thoughts coursing through their super
visory minds, and not be responsible for the damage inflicted on man b
wind and tempest, the struggles of men for social supremacy, and th
ensuing sorrows, the fires of hate, the disregard of spiritual ideals and th
extinction of moral virtue? Hume recognizes the implications of the d
lemma, and formulates its terms thus: If the actions of the human min
could be "traced up, by a necessary chain, to the Deity," still they could nc
be held to be criminal; for the infinite perfections of God forbid it. If o
the other hand they are held to be criminal, then we must "retract th
attributes of perfection which we ascribe to the Deity," and regard hir
as the author of "guilt and moral turpitude." The first part of the dilemm
can be cleared up, at least in part, by inspecting the nature of our mor:
consciousness, where we find a certain mixed tendency to approve th
good and reprobate the bad. The second part is more difficult; for if Go
is the author of all thought and behavior he must be chargeable wit
producing both the evil and the good. At this point, Hume thinks, w
are faced with a great mystery, and it would be the wisest course to atten
to the common dispositions of life and not venture upon the field c
metaphysical inquiry.[23] So far as he is concerned, the problem of evil re
mains unsolved.

But the course he intends to follow is the one and only course whic
he is entitled to pursue and which in fact he has not pursued in th
previous discussion. This course is laid down in his elementary proposal
to treat empirical data as the sole source of knowledge, and to test th
authority of every judgment on that basis alone. When this course
followed, there is positively no chance to raise the question whether c
not God is the cause of evil, natural or moral. Causal connections arisin
in experience refer to our private actions, never to the activity of the Orij
inal Cause. God cannot then be accused of instituting a created order whos
issues involve organic pain and moral dereliction, and the whole con
plaint of the Epicureans, ancient or modern, can be dismissed as groun(
less. At the same time there is no evidence to support the declaration w
have just quoted. Hence, the argument for the existence of God cann(
depend on the apprehension of any natural forces which leads the min
back to the idea of a supreme creative Intelligence.

(b) There is one further facet of the subject which we must not di
regard; Hume gives it a large place in his thought and in his publishe

[22] *Enquiries,* Sec. 113.   [23] *Ibid.,* Secs. 78–81.

observations. He accepts the thesis of the Deists that no intervention in the order of nature is conceivable. Nature is subject to no change from any source or for any stipulated ends. If he had been acquainted with the theory of biological evolution, he would have been the first to comply with its rule; for the changes involved in the development of species are not changes in nature's explicit law but only in the diversification of its contents. The changes he denies are those which could be superimposed upon the structural constitution of the world. Berkeley had made room for the intrusion of spiritual Might other than that represented by the basic law. Since God had created the world he could reënter the world by a series of events called miracles, in order to give effect to certain purposes not already embodied in the natural processes. Such a conceit was thoroughly repugnant to the scientific outlook of the Scot, who under the tuition of Newton was inclined to transfer his principle of causality from its seat in experience to the cosmic force imbedded in the law of gravitation. Law whether resident in the mind or realized in nature, is exact and irrefragable; no violation of its terms can be admitted.

The evidence against miracles which Hume proposes to adduce is of two kinds; first, no suspension of the laws of nature by any power within or without the universe can be countenanced; and secondly, the rules of logical evidence in support of a change are so precise and comprehensive that the adoption of such evidence as proof of a miracle would demand a miracle in human belief greater than the actual proposed change in the physical world. In fact, Hume avers, the "proof against a miracle, from the nature of the fact, is as entire as any argument from experience can possibly be imagined." [24] We may note two important provisions, first, that the evidence must be drawn from empirical data only, not from a convenient set of presuppositions, and again, that the attitude of the critic will always be negative, to the effect that the established law of nature cannot be disallowed. To be sure, the first of these provisions is itself based on the assumption that natural law is the crystallization of uniform experience, which implies that it is not beyond the scope of physical powers to reveal events not hitherto within the province of perception or fancy. But in a note appended to his chapter of *Miracles*, Hume warns his readers that they must be careful to distinguish "miracles" from events which turn out to be merely extraordinary or unforeseen. A Hindu having never seen ice in his subtropical clime, would account it a miracle, if water should suddenly congeal before his eyes. He could not understand the possible change of atmospheric or geological conditions introducing a phenomenon new to him but entirely in accord with natural law. Miracle, on the other hand, connotes a complete reversal of physical sequences, which, from the reli-

[24] *Ibid.*, Sec. 90.

gious point of view, could only take place under the influence of a divine volition or the interposition of another powerful invisible agent. The religious belief thus stands in direct antithesis to the substance of scientific experience and is a summary challenge to the latter's authority; but at the same time it must be treated by the same principles of reasoning to which every problem in science is subject. Hume answers the challenge in the negative, and this leads him to examine the nature of the evidence required, if we would understand the actual form of all external events. The test of the reality of a miracle will be found in this evidence, and only there.

Let us recognize at once the difference between the event and the evidence for it. The former, we said, is in the natural world, the latter is in the experience—sensory images, interpreting ideas, emotions awakened, final judgment—of the witness. If there is no supporting evidence, there is no miraculous event. What is the character of the evidence? In general, it must arise from a mind capable of arriving at a true logical decision. It must not reflect the bias of a mind in love with the marvelous, or of a mind that could be thrown into confusion by the insistent objections of scientific critics or of a mind that respected the privacy of the action in question and feared the strong glare of deeds not done in a corner. Now since the event under consideration belongs to the sphere of physical phenomena, e. g., rising from the dead, the evidence submitted will be the same as that adduced to prove the existence of any particular causal relation such as turning water into steam, or the reverse of the event instanced, how the living body is changed into an inert and lifeless one. The object must be examined by men who have studied the symptoms of life and the properties of the cadaver, and can distinguish between them. They must be able to use the professional instruments which can detect the beating of the heart, they must be able to affirm that the heart was not beating before the event took place and that it was beating after the event. Again, the witnesses must be men who are trained in the art of making conclusive judgments based on accurate and convincing evidence, not men who come to their work with a preconceived judgment or who allow themselves to be diverted from their task by irrelevant circumstances or by the suspicions or doubts of their collaborators. They must also be men of indubitable moral probity, who know the meaning of truth, and have repute among their fellows as persons capable of finding the truth and having once found it of adhering to its terms, except when contradictory evidence is at hand. By virtue of such stubborn and irresistible requirements, Hume had no hesitation in proclaiming that a reversal of the laws of nature under the rubric of a miracle, was impossible. Professor Orr calls his examination of the matter an "elaborate sophism." [25] He opines

[25] *David Hume*, pp. 215 sq.

that Hume discredits the evidence of Holy Writ by denying it a hearing, after the manner of a dictator, not that of the court of law. Hume would probably answer by saying that no court of law can settle a scientific dispute; the laboratory alone is the seat of authority. But in all his argument on this thorny problem, Hume appears to have in the back of his mind the anterior query: Is the evidential value of the miracle the proper support for demonstrating the truth of the Evangelical doctrine? At this point we ought to note that the primary element in the Christian scheme of revelation is wholly absent from Hume's argument. There is not the slightest hint that a divine purpose, hitherto unannounced, may suddenly emerge upon the platform of human history, promising a new exhibition of divine power in the natural world. Furthermore, there is no hint in any of Hume's works that certain groups of believers have possessed mental endowments beyond those of their neighbors, qualifying them to receive unusual spiritual communications, if these actually occur. In fact, he is by his original assumption obliged to reject all utterances except those mediated through the senses and installed as logical judgments by the ordinary processes of thought.

THE ARGUMENT FROM DESIGN

We turn now to the argument which Hume favored as a possible basis for our knowledge of the divine activity. The argument holds that there are manifold teleological relations in the physical universe and that these can be observed by the organic senses and interpreted in the same way that we construe the meaning of scientific data in any field. Since we are now dealing with the question of origin, we may ask, How could such relations have been developed in a world governed by inflexible law? Two theories have been advanced—and they are the only ones available—the first alleging that the potencies of matter can by themselves produce the harmony and order visible in the celestial sphere, and the adaptation of means to ends found in the smallest of organized bodies on the earth; the second, that the composition of the universe is so exact, diversified and refined as to oblige us to assume the presence of a master intellect operating on the basic substances at hand. The second theory reflects the methods followed in the human economy and we cannot forbear making the analogy complete in every detail. Thus when an object of peculiar value is presented to us for consideration—a building, picture, statue, carpenter's tool, steamship, atomic bomb, we at once agree that it is the handiwork of an agent who possesses the following properties,—a creative imagination, a keen and discerning eye, knowledge of the laws of physics, acquaintance with the concept of purposiveness, and especially the genius to translate the image in the mind into a like form in wood or stone or any other medium of expression. An organizing intelligence stands behind the finished product. Paley's peasant finding the timepiece on the moor, the trained archeologist uncovering the relics of a forgotten past, both are sure of two basic facts, that the maker was a man of mind, and that in making the object he inscribed its purpose on its form. However, when we pass from human fabrications to the construction of a world, we perceive how tenuous and indecisive the analogy is. Still we follow our bent whatever its consequences, and we record our satisfaction in the words of Berkeley: "the constant regularity, order, and concatenation of natural things, the surprising magnificence, beauty and perfection of the larger, and the exquisite contrivance of the smaller parts of the creation, together with the exact harmony and correspondence of the whole." [26] The starry heavens of Kant and the delicate infusoria of Darwin declare the same extraordinary wisdom and relate the same tale of purposive handicraft. These or similar phenomena are the alleged facts that Hume was forced to study, and while he acknowledged, as Kant did later, that they make a profound impression on the reflective thinker, they do not present that degree of conviction which, to his mind, ought to accompany an indisputable truth.

He therefore lays his finger on the difficulties that the honest inquirer must steadfastly face. The first is this: if we affirm the existence of God on the basis of the presence in nature of certain purposive types of objects whose creation would demand the exercise of an exceptional form of intelligence, we have only proved the reality of a Deity with one kind of creative skill. We observe the inspired genius of Zeuxis, the distinguished Greek painter; we reckon him as a plastic artist of the highest competence. [27] May we deduce from this circumstance that he is also sculptor, modeler, or practitioner in other arts, having the same creative skill in each? A deduction like that would be thoroughly illogical. Shall we then venture to reach a similar conclusion with respect to the capacity of the supreme Designer? God can fashion an organic cell of surpassing complexity: can he also finish the amazingly intricate program of the cosmic creation with the same success? For this universal achievement there is no empirical proof. Therefore, all we can hope to establish by this method is that God is limited in his work; we are obliged to depotentiate his essence and to "renounce all claim to infinity in any of the attributes of Deity." For, obviously, if the cause is to be proportioned to its effect, and the effect, as it comes under our observation, can only be limited, then the cause, too, must be nothing other than limited. Furthermore, the danger of an anthropo-

[26] *Principles of Human Knowledge*, in A. C. Fraser, *Selections from Berkeley* (3rd ed., Oxford: Clarendon Press, 1884), Sec. 146.
[27] *Enquiries*, Sec. 105.

morphist interpretation is always present. For we are inevitably attributing to God the attitudes and types of action common to men. But men are not perfectly sure that they have found the exact means by which the end is to be realized; they may, for one thing, be wrong in their understanding of the end to be attained; and, again, they may not have the foresight or power to select the means by which the end could be reached. We may, of course, ascribe to God a complete and infallible wisdom in selecting both the ends and the means, but we cannot at the same time assume that we, with our finite outlook, would ever be in a position to understand fully either the meaning of the end or whether it had been achieved. In short, the use of the analogical method in determining the activity of God, is hazardous in the extreme, as Kant showed with great amplitude of illustration. It did not occur to Hume at this point to give up any attempt to prove the existence of God by empirical or semi-empirical evidence, and to adopt the postulate that the concept of God is the regulative principle through which we may give a just account of the teleological processes which seem to us to belong to certain operations in nature. Like Kant he does not reject the fact of divine existence but up to the present moment he has found no way of establishing it by strictly scientific argument. God is as real to him as an ethnic divinity to a primitive animist, as he confesses in the little book, *The History of Natural Religion.* His principal problem is to bring the reality of God within the range of a probative belief.

Therefore, the next step will be to compare briefly the two theories which have engaged the devout attention of many investigators. Both are based on a common premise, namely, that ultimate substance can be known only by what it produces; or to state it in another form, each event means something which can be apprehended by the examining intelligence.[28] Thus, the motions of bodies are summarized by certain intelligible laws but the same interpretation is not given by the contending theories. Lucretius and St. Paul approach the subject from different angles and obtain different results, the one is semi-scientific, the other strictly religious. The Epicurean proponent argues that the "religious hypothesis must be considered only as a particular method of accounting for the visible phenomena of the universe"; it is only a "conjecture" and should be declared to be such. For if the opponent goes further and holds that God, as supreme Substance, actually produced the atomic structures of the world, then he has deliberately "departed from the method of reasoning attached to the subject, and certainly added something to the attribute of the cause, beyond what appears in the effect."

The Lucretian theory argues on the other hand, that causality exists in the constituent atoms. Atoms are endowed with specific powers and ar-

28 *Ibid.,* Sec. 102 sq.

range themselves mechanically in bodies and groups of bodies in the very patterns now forming the system of the world. Mind has no place or authority in the system; the order and harmony of the parts are fixed by the atoms themselves. To this theory Hume takes strong and immediate exception. It contemplates, he says, an unfinished universe which requires completion at some distant time. Experience proves that mind exists in the world, and apparently Hume is not satisfied with the species of intelligence developed by Lucretius. Take a simple illustration, derived from Plato. Idea and purpose are embedded in every statue carved by the hand of the master. The marble is nothing, the engraving tool is nothing; they are creatures of the physical forces of nature; they are not the true causes of the *Athene* of Phidias or the *Appollo* of Praxiteles. The true cause is in the conception that flamed in the fancy of the artist and ran like a raging fire through the chisel and the marble. If Hume had lived a century later, he could have cited the conclusion of biology, that no man knows truly the organic body who is unaware of the meaning of its function, the principle that encompasses the total behavior of the body, the purpose which is the same as the impulse of self-persistence. Thus, the principle, the function, is a law of life; it is not a conceit of the scientific fancy. The point he actually insists on is that the chemical constituents of a body are not its "universal" elements. They may be decomposed and scattered abroad; the individuating principle remains. The purpose of a particular object, whether statue, organism, or grain of sand, is its universal aspect, which enters into the thought of the observer. But the individual object cannot stand alone, nor does its purpose remain unattached; nature puts its elements into necessary relations, although it does not make the purpose of one part the "rule for another part very wide of the former." [29] The difficulty grows serious when we attempt to carry the entirety of nature back to its authentic source. Here evidence fails us. The pathway is strewn with pitfalls; we should walk warily and with discreet steps, especially since we must resume the use of the method of analogy which has so far proved ineffective.

It is obvious to the critical student that the present proof for the existence of God is a subsidiary phase of the second or cosmological proof. It cannot establish a causal relation between the universe and its Maker; it only suggests that *if* God created the world he put into it certain patterns of thought that reflected his wisdom and benevolence, patterns that correspond in detail to the marks of adaptation exemplified in man's intercourse with his fellows. Analogy, we said, consists in framing a manner of procedure in one field and applying its terms, so far as possible, in another. No analogy can be set up except where elements in each situation have a constant con-

[29] *Dialogues*, II.

junction in our experience.[30] Hence, the argument is really a study of the principle of analogy and not simply the evidence of empirical facts. But Hume agrees that analogical knowledge is probable, never demonstrative; it deals with matters of fact not with the truths of reason. "That which chiefly constitutes probability," says Bishop Butler, "is expressed in the word *likely,* that is, like (analogous to) some truth or true event." [31] Berkeley accepted the term as providing a useful method in philosophy; he applied it first, to the primary acquisition of knowledge—the steady recurrence of images implied a regular recurrence of events in the external world, and secondly, to the detection of design in the natural universe in agreement with the common practice of our own thought. "We should," he says "propose to ourselves nobler views, such as recreate and exalt the mind, with a prospect of beauty, *order,* extent, and variety of natural things; hence, by proper inferences, to enlarge our notions of the grandeur, wisdom, and beneficence of the Creator and lastly, to make the several parts of the creation, so far as in us lies, subservient to the ends they were designed for, God's glory, and the sustentation and comfort of ourselves and fellow-creatures." [32] Here Berkeley puts the argument on a strictly deductive basis, and he aims to reach his conclusion by a "proper inference"; but the empirical method stands squarely against his effort, and he confesses ruefully that we "may extend the analogy too far and thus run into mistakes." [33]

Hume without hesitation agrees with this decision. Specifically he says —referring to the teleological patterns men find in nature—that we must not insert into the supposed cause anything that we cannot wholly verify by experimental tests. It may be that gravitational power contains "the source or spring of order originally within itself as well as mind does." [34] Then, we do not need the conception of a Creator but may blithely accept the mechanical system as having "fallen into the most exquisite arrangement by some known internal cause." Still, even though such results may be demonstrated by the method of "proper inference," there is a lurking resistance to the suggestion in the minds of many inquirers. "Throw several pieces of steel together, without shape and form; they never arrange themselves so as to form a watch. Stone and mortar and wood, without an architect, never construct a house." These effects proceed from a precedent and causative idea; the human mind is not satisfied with any other interpretation, and it does not appear to overstep the bounds of taste or judgment, when it requires us to place amongst the attributes of Deity

[30] *Treatise of Human Nature*, pp. 142, 197.

[31] *Analogy of Religion* in *Works of Bishop Butler*, edited by W. E. Gladstone (Oxford: Clarendon Press, 1897), I, Introduction, Sec. 3.

[32] *Principles of Human Knowledge, op. cit.*, Sec. 109.   [33] *Ibid.*, 108.

[34] *Dialogues*, Pt. II.

—given his existence—the authority to add means to ends in the composition of an enduring world.

But the argument from cause to effect, as pursued by the deductive method, cannot bring us to the point where we confidently affirm the necessary existence of God. Analogy gives probable knowledge, nothing else; we can gain prescriptive knowledge from it only when the terms are exactly equal in meaning, which is impossible if we draw our materials from the operations of the physical world. Shall we do better if we study the issues of moral behavior? Is it possible, for example, to find the "marks of distributive justice in the world"? [35] The proponent of the Lucretian theory puts that question and Hume regards it as pertinent. For the whole problem of justice is a vexed and vexing one. When is retributive justice separable from distributive? Is the one delivered by the state in the civil courts and the other by society in general practice but by no legal statute? To lure the question within the confines of our present discussion: May God step in at critical moments and stop the mad march of the military conqueror or the sly devices of an adroit assassin? May society, by a single coup release from the clutches of a greedy syndicate the economically helpless mass of toiling men and women? Is the unscrupulous dictator the inspired messenger of the Almighty or his ultimate prey? Definitions are needed in every case before a judgment can be rendered. What is justice for one may be regarded as brutal injustice for another. The terms are difficult to define and their applications even more so. Can we devise a system of juridical actions in which violation of law is always supported by appropriate penalties and obedience by splendid vindication? The scheme was proposed on a celestial scale in Grotius' theory of Atonement by governmental, that is, divine decree, but without success. What justification does logic or custom give us for supposing that history is the arena of divine adjudications? Or what right does experience vouchsafe to us for claiming that justice, if not administered in this life, will surely be done in the life to come? Is it true that we have tried to extract from our Cause what does not belong there? Have we, Hume asks in a moment of desperate depression, mistaken completely the connection between cause and effect? May there not be aspects of the Cause which have no expression in the known effects? Hume grows cautious and reserved; he changes the tenor of his query by referring to a possible "singular effect which could not be comprehended under any species"; we could not reduce it by any device to the accepted cause.[36] That would not help us to reach a decision. The one factor that might help, in most cases does help, is the principle of faith on which the final determination of the matter may have to rest. The argument, then, passes from the realm of logic and

[35] *Enquiries,* Sec. 109.   [36] *Ibid.,* Sec. 115.

takes its place as an issue in religious thought. Here again, analogy is a suggestion, it is not a proof.

THE ARGUMENT FROM THE MORAL SENSE

The argument for the existence of God drawn from the presence of a moral sense in man has appeared in virtually every religious theory in the civilized world. Religion and morality are thought to have a natural affinity which accounts for the tendency to explain the one by the other. The connection, however, has never been logically established and must not be taken for granted. We are obliged simply to recognize the possibility of such relation and proceed to show how, historically, it has entered the field of philosophical dogma. Locke set out to prove that moral conduct was based upon the principle of computable happiness and that the rectitude of a given action can be demonstrated with the same accuracy as the theorems of Euclid. But ultimate happiness can be guaranteed only by the authority of a divine Being. For moral actions depend on fundamental laws of thought which when organized into a permanent system would be equivalent to the laws of God. The "measures of right and wrong" have eternal values, once they have been understood by the agent—a difficult thing to do. For Berkeley the problem of finding God in human conscience seemed to have slight significance. In the last two sections of the *Principles,* after discussing at some length the second and third of the classical arguments in the earlier sections, he intimates by a sort of hortatory suggestion that moral virtue and moral duty exhibit fully the purposes of Deity and should be cultivated sedulously by all believers.

Hume approaches the subject with his accustomed analytical skill. It is necessary to determine the function of morals in common experience before we can relate it, even distantly, to the offices of religion. His procedure is essentially Aristotelian. He examines, first, the original endowments of human nature in order to discover whether and how moral distinctions can find a place there. Two facts are perfectly plain in the normal intelligence, first, the ability to receive impressions from the outer world and organize them into rational ideas, and second, the principle of interest or desire which through experience expands into sentiments of beauty or virtue. The one issues from the reflections of the understanding, the other from the flow of emotions; "when you pronounce any character or action to be vicious, you mean nothing but that from the constitution of your nature you have a feeling or sentiment of blame from the contemplation of it." [37] Interest thus advances to the level of appreciation of our repugnance to a certain deed. Reason may dictate what kind of policy should be adopted so that you may procure the sense of approbation, that is,

[37] *Treatise of Human Nature,* p. 469.

pleasure in the act; it cannot furnish the incentive to action. Reason is cool, detached, objective; it deals with images as they come and go; it tells us *if* they represent facts. Sentiment or feeling constitutes the guiding principle by disclosing the values incorporated in our judgments. Scientific analysis can never superinduce the sense of praise or blame. We do not reprimand one age for not understanding the problems of another. Who would censure the Socratic thinkers because they knew nothing of the principles of relativity or the hypothesis of biological evolution? But the humblest scholar in any part of the world and in any age may hold his group responsible for ideas and habits that contravene the rights of human personality. Thus, we condemn Aristotle harshly for defending the terms of chattel slavery, even though it gave to free and gifted men sufficient leisure to pursue their studies in the pure or objective sciences. Hume's ethical creed is clear: "the external performance has no merit; the moral motive is in the quality of the mind projecting the deed." [38]

The sources of moral thinking are then fixed; is the power to make distinctions between moral values also determined? In his earlier treatise Hume lays down the maxim that the "general opinion of mankind has some authority in all cases but in this of morals it is perfectly infallible." [39] It is true, we may agree, that matricide is a crime universally reprehended. But universal disapproval cannot by itself settle the matter apart from the grounds on which the disapproval rests. To be sure, the pressure of public sentiment especially when supported by physical force, can go a long way in compelling obedience to its behests. But mere "performance," says Hume, is not the modulus of virtue; we must study the "quality" of the action if we would come upon its true value. Here emerges the principle of sympathy, humanity, which he assigns to the "original constitution of human nature." By "all the rules of philosophy" we must conclude that the "sentiments of morality and humanity are the same." [40] But even this formula does not bring us to the core of the matter; there is still another factor which decides between the questions of good and bad, right and wrong; the "circumstance of *Utility* in all subjects is the source of praise and approbation." [41] But utility is a term of divers meanings. When cited by Bentham it refers to the outward results of a proposed action, especially those that are determinable by legal process. As used by Plato it covers the fundamental functions of human nature which conspire in developing a moral personality. In Hume it is the only property of mind that reconciles the otherwise conflicting interests of the individual and society. The individual cannot maintain his existence without agreeable affiliation with his fellows; on the other hand, the recognition of individual

[38] *Ibid.*, p. 477, and *Enquiries*, Secs. 234–35.   [39] *Treatise of Human Nature*, p. 552.
[40] *Enquiries*, Sec. 192.   [41] *Ibid.*, p. 188.

rights is the *sine qua non* of civil justice, the ranking quality of the state. If Hume were alive today he could not fail to condemn the Totalitarian dogma—the citizen only for the state, not the state for the citizen.

The presence side by side of these two interests—self-love and benevolence—was a stated canon in the English ethics of the 18th century. Butler and Hume approaching the subject from two different angles, agree upon this formula. Human nature contains the synthesis of the two, and its presence in man's thought must be accounted for. Whence did it come? Anthropology was at the time an immature science; it is mainly so today. But it did not then have before it the researches and generalizations of Darwin; it did not suspect that there was a possibility, perhaps vague and unfruitful, that the moral sense of man had its premonitions in the behavior of the subhuman species. Prince Kropotkin has argued enthusiastically for that thesis though with not much success. The danger of the argument is that we may unintentionally read our human modes of action into the behavior of life on another level. The biological parallels were not laid before savants of Hume's generation. He did, however, undertake a study of the rise of religious concepts, and he argues with a show of plausibility that theism as a basic Christian postulate could be compared with some of the dogmas of nontheistic faiths, and that a sort of genetic relationship could be established between them.[42] But in his major works the traditional thesis remains unaltered. Moral judgment is a resident fact in the nature of man, and reason and feeling are its two forms of expression. "The standard of the one (reason) being founded on the nature of things is eternal and inflexible, even by the will of the Supreme Being; the standard of the other (feeling) arising from the eternal frame and constitution of animals, is ultimately derived from that Supreme Will, which bestowed on each being its peculiar nature and arranged the several classes and orders of existence."[43] There is no systematic attempt in his writings to prove the reality of God by means of the moral reflections of the human mind. The reverse order is used by him. If self-preservation is the first law of nature, it is invested with the authority of divine wisdom; that is, God exists and he must exercise his potency in this manner. Again, if man possesses the ability to distinquish the evil from the good, it is because the universal Mind has already conceived ideals suitable for every possible situation. The religious sanctions which are extremely prominent in Bentham's ethic, are entertained by Hume for a moment but tacitly rejected.[44]

With the negative instances before us, and in spite of the single citation just made, it would appear that Hume was not deeply impressed with the argument which is to bulk large in the energetic presentations of

[42] *Hisory of Natural Religion*, pp. 8, 9.   [43] *Enquiries*, Sec. 246.   [44] *Ibid.*, Sec. 109.

Kant. It may be that Hume's hesitation in his treatment of the third proof brought home to him the subtle inadequacies of the whole discussion. He does not affirm in so many words that the argument from the moral sense was part and parcel of the argument from design; but he always held that the end of virtue was the attainment of approbation both of his own conscience and the conscience of the group, while the means to be used were the essential properties of utility, that is, virtue as embodied in honest thought and just behavior. In short, the theme that never lost its spell was the presence of a fixed order in the structure of the human mind. Hence, his argument is not the proven fact of design leading to the hypothesis of an original Designer, but rather a variation of the Cartesian doctrine—the Idea of God not as a concept which has its necessary objective equivalent, but as a recognized force in human character to be accounted for only on the basis of the reality of God. Here at length we seem to be on solid ground, the ground for constructive faith if not for reasoned judgment—until some new Darwin appears and rejects the primary thesis upon which the entire argument rests.

X: IMMANUEL KANT

IT IS common belief in many circles that religious habits shaped in childhood will exert a powerful influence upon mature judgment in the field of religious theory. Certain classical educators have lifted the belief into an inflexible axiom. Let them have control of a child's mind up to the age of seven and they have no fear what later suggestions can do to change its currents of thought. The emphasis here lies upon the series of religious acts rather than the creedal complex. Still the rule holds good that lessons learned in youth will emerge as guides to future behavior, unless they be confronted by another type of experience more appealing to the riper intelligence.

The test for Immanuel Kant came shortly after his matriculation as a student at the University of Koenigsberg. It was candidly admitted by him that the instruction received in the home under the care of a pious mother and at the preparatory school founded by the Pietistic brothers came into sharp conflict with the broader views of philosophy and science entertained by the members of the learned faculty. Pietism sponsored by Spener and Francke was a revolt against the didactic orthodoxy of the Lutheran communion. The Reformation in upper Germany had rejected the caste system of the Roman clergy, together with its elaborate symbolism in sacrament and ritual, and fixed its attention upon a coördinated set of dogmas to which all the faithful must subscribe. The defenders of this dogmatic structure were the ordained ministers of the church, and these were supported by the civil authorities whose sanctions might be called upon to preserve the purity of doctrine. Kant himself was to feel the weight of political pressure in the latter part of his life.

The new religious surge sometimes called the final stage of the German Reformation, began its course in 1675. It affirmed the judgment that religion is not at base an intellectual movement but a spontaneous expression of emotion. Articles of confessional belief are valuable but they do not represent the essential nature of religion. Nor do they tend to bring the soul into intimate union with the divine Spirit, a contingency which Kant feared as opening the way to fanatical excesses. He was on the other hand strongly attracted by the second element in the Pietist's belief, the demand for purity in motive and conduct. Spener's *Pia Desideria* became the touch-stone of spiritual restoration. Believers are responsible for their brothers' safety; they must share their own moral victories with their neighbors. Not only was it their duty, it was also their right to challenge the careless attitude of members of their own community. They did not note that invasion of the privacy of the religious consciousness might and did awaken resentment and alarm. At this point Kant would dissent emphatically from the habits of the group; for he suspected that if the rules of obedience were enforced in the moral sphere, they could also be applied to the exercise of the speculative judgment. Then conditions existing in the state church would soon be repeated in the evangelical communions. Purity of behavior is a sound article of faith, but inquisitorial methods in discovering lapses in conduct would be contrary to good morals and religious progress.

There was a third point in the new creed to which the philosopher could give unstinted approval. The state church made the breach between clergy and laity so wide and so efficacious that any appeal from the decision of the ruling pastor was null and void at the start. In England the established church followed a more liberal policy. The non-clerical group were allotted certain voting rights and were invested with certain important duties in the administration of the parish functions. Despite the social cleavage evident both in parish and in civil affairs, at the sacramental service the equality of believers was recognized and respected. There was no equal status for believers in the Lutheran church. It was this principle which excited the Pietistic revolt. The Christian priesthood, said Spener, is universal; it belongs to the clergy, it belongs of right also to the laity. The spiritual government of the Gemeinde cannot repose solely in the hands of the former, whether in the formulation of a creed or in the discharge of religious duties in the parish. Tolerance is a tenet of the Christian faith; it is a phase of universal love and the seal of spiritual fellowship. It begins within the confines of the individual parish, it extends its influence to the social group adjacent. It proved that the organization of society on the basis of superior and inferior classes was without scientific or religious warrant. Master and servant, lord and vassal, are terms with no significance in the economy of religion. Pietism was a kind of Teutonic prevision of the French reaction a hundred years later; but it made no enduring appeal to the intellectual classes in Prussia, and while it merged its enthusiasms into the romantic movement of the *Aufklaerung* in the 18th century, it left no permanent impress on the religious habits of Germany.

Such, in brief detail, was the peculiar situation that young Kant had to face at the opening of his academic career. Since we are to study his attitude to the very subject which is central in the Church's thought, it is imperative that we should be well advised as to the substance of the teachings under whose rubric he had been reared. We are now ready to review his treatment of the matter.

THE CONCEPTION OF GOD AS A PROBLEM IN PHILOSOPHY

The first problem to be settled was the method of procedure. Two avenues were open to him, either he could accept the Object of supreme homage as a necessary reality, which was the usual manner of the theologian, or assuming the presence in the human mind of the idea of God, he would take pains to marshall the evidence furnished by logic and psychology, together with the testimony of the natural sciences, in a formal and persistent attempt to establish the existence of an unconditioned Being. The former method had been adopted by Spinoza, although he was careful to organize into a logical unity the attributes which could belong only to such a Being. The Kantian approach was simpler; he took for granted that there was good ground for examining the question as a serious problem in philosophy. As early as 1763 he published a small volume in which the subject was discussed under the title: *The only possible argument for the existence of God,* the last sentence in the book being his apology for undertaking the task: "It is essential that we should be convinced of God's existence but not so essential that we should prove it." It may be noted here that the question of the reality of God was a matter of personal concern at this period in his life. For he asked his former teacher, Pastor Schultz, to sponsor his request for an appointment to the regular faculty of the University. Said the Pietist pastor, "Do you fear God with all your heart?" The answer returned would seem to have been satisfactory, for he received the recommendation but did not obtain the appointment. The argument in the book was this: If the concept of Deity is possible, as it is, then this possibility must have its roots in the reality of such a Being. Leibniz had argued in the same manner, and neither he nor the young tutor detected the serious fallacy underlying the argument. In the first *Critique* Kant made a comprehensive scrutiny of the three classical Proofs, and in the third *Critique* he returned to the teleological proof for further examination. The Proofs are finally rejected as invalid, but in the second *Critique* he manages to find an argument which brought him safely to port. The idea of duty coupled with the truth of the Perfect Good which includes happiness, requires both the perpetuity of the identical existence of the moral agent as well as acceptance of the reality of a divine Being.

In order to understand his approach to the problem we must review for a moment the basic elements in the Critical method. The earlier studies of the philosopher dealt with the facts of the physical universe as they had been recited by Sir Isaac Newton. Cause is a resident force in the body of nature as attested by the proven formula of the law of gravitation. Granted that force exists and is in operation, we are obliged to seek a universal Cause to which physical causes are in subordination. Traditionally this Cause goes under the name of God. The great philosophical systems on the Continent had borrowed the concept from the Scholastics and adopted it as the basis for unity both in nature and logical thought. Hume, however, challenged the truth of the assumption and proceeded to argue that causality, motion, energy are concepts of the mind, not inherent factors in nature. They assume reality only in our thought, and they reach such reality merely because the senses of man have given repeated and continuous images of the same situation, which images in due time obtain an identity of meaning, a concept with an established content. This revolutionary revision of the old conceits Kant accepts as valid. As he says in his *Reflections* (II, 6), these concepts "set forth the conditions under which alone we can apprehend or comprehend the object." Such conditions embrace the mental processes of perception, imagination, and judgment, and these processes with their contents are the only realities that we can know. Scientific analysis pursues this order in every case; it is the one and only way by which knowledge of the external world can be acquired. Time, space and cause are the fruits of judgment not its original source. Thus the four categories which science employs to explain its findings are aspects of thought, they are not realities in the physical world. The second Copernican revolution is now complete: we have discovered the meaning of causality and also the habits of mind by which that meaning is determined.

There is still another feature in the theory demanding attention. Scientific experiment deals with single situations,—this object, that event in time, a given relation between objects or events. An electric charge emitted in a laboratory or on the bosom of the cloud—how can we elicit its specific properties? The charge is visible in a flash of lightening, it is accompanied or (to our hearing) succeeded by the roll of thunder. To the critical observer the charge itself is never fully known. We can measure the intensity of the light, the volume of a detonation, the smashing power of the stroke; but we cannot know the charge itself, the independent momentary *thing*. The mind constructs a noumenon, the *thing as thought,* a limiting concept which gathers up the ideas derived from sensation into a compact whole which is *like* the original object but can never be identical with it.

The problem of knowledge is difficult enough in the field of scientific inquiry; it is forbidding when we attempt to examine objects that never impinge on the areas of perception. The categorical rules, the conditions upon which scientific knowledge rests, do not apply to them. They come to us as concrete ideas for which no images are available. Yet, each idea presents a completed whole which no empirical concept ever reaches. The consummate Idea, God, becomes, in our thought, the instrument by which logical unity in the determination of all knowledge is attained. Even if the laws of logic do not allow us to grant reality to the object envisaged in the idea, still the idea remains as a regulative principle, the concept of a thing, as Kant avers, "which stands at the source of the possibility of all things, and supplies the real condition for their complete determination."[1] To sum up the evidence thus amassed, the scientific concept, e. g., the electric charge, points to a physical situation which we know exists by virtue of the properties detected by force of sense-stimulation; on the other hand, the regulative principle enables us to think and act, *as if* we had formally established the reality of a Supreme Being, though we are aware at the same moment that we can never do so.

Yet with all the evidence gathered against it, men have persisted in defending the thesis that the "absolutely necessary Being" *must* exist. They begin their argument by calling attention to the fact that the objects of scientific value are all contingent in character; they have no permanent existence; they are not endowed with properties which are necessarily enduring. Yet we are confronted on every hand with relations that possess universal values. The triangle *must* be composed of three sides or its reality disappears. The terms of the syllogism having once been legally set up, they *must* lead to an inflexible conclusion. Even the extraordinarily acute mind of Spinoza was deceived by the argument, largely because he assumed the reality of Nature without requiring proof for the same. But Kant insists that there are two distinct meanings written in the word "necessary"; they are radically distinct and must not be confused. A judgment is necessary in its results when its terms have been properly related. Necessity here, is a thought in the mind; it has no reality in the external world; this is illustrated in the universal law of the triangle. If we draw a triangle on paper, we do not give necessary existence to the observable object; we merely state that the pictured object is a triangle, because it obeys the rules prescribed for all triangles, without which the given object could not be a triangle. We are obliged to follow the same line of reasoning in dealing with every judgment presented for consideration. Thus, "God is omnipotent" is a regularly organized proposition submitted for examination. It is, Kant thinks, an "analytical judgment," that is, a judgment which has in the predicate nothing that is not already implied in the subject. One of the assumed attributes of Deity is omnipotence; hence whenever God appears as the subject of the judgment omnipotence appears either named or implied in the predicative statement. If, however, we set up another proposition—"God does not exist," or "There is no God," then the subject is withdrawn and with it every conceivable

[1] *Critique of Pure Reason.* Trans. by N. K. Smith, p. 495.

attribute. If God does not exist, omnipotence is no more essential than any other character. This means that necessity belongs to the form of the judgment, as in any geometrical theorem, for example, that the three interior angles are equal to two right angles. If triangles are impossible, then the laws governing their form and function are also impossible.

But the defense of the ancient proofs takes a different tack. Let us assume, it says, that there is one subject that cannot be removed, because it deals with necessary existence; what should be our treatment of the judgment then? The obvious answer is, that this is the very point we are endeavoring to prove, and it is fallacious to accept it as the basic assumption. However, it will do no harm to examine it. The assumption involves an important question in scientific procedure:—Is existence to be regarded as an attribute which must be treated on a level with the other attributes? If that be true, then the judgment, Kant thinks, is still analytical. But then we have made an unwarranted distinction between existence and reality. This, indeed, is precisely what the protagonists for the argument have done. The *Ens realissimum* contains all the elements of Being including necessary existence; hence, God who is the one necessary Being must exist. It is clear that we never treat other subjects which appear in scientific propositions, in the same way. If that were done the scientist would run into serious difficulties, and in many cases would find his argument completely nullified. The mistake lies in the interpretation we give to the copula in the judgment. The "is" does not point to external existence; it simply reveals the logical relation of the predicate to the subject. When we say—"God is omnipotent," we do not therewith cite a case where the attribute appears in the real world; we merely uncover an essential property. If, however, we remove all attributive forms and put the judgment baldly—"God is," then we have not affirmed real existence, but simply placed the object *God* in direct juxtaposition with our *concept* of it. The concept remains unchanged, whether it be my idea of the object or the real object itself; a hundred thalers in my mind or in my pocket have precisely the same value; the only question is to what extent my financial position has been altered. The upshot of the discussion is this: the mere insertion of the idea of necessary Being into a logical judgment cannot guarantee its objective reality. The idea still remains a possible idea; but a possible idea is an altogether different thing from the idea of a possible Being. We need to be taught a good lesson in logic, namely, that an existential judgment is not the same as an attributive judgment. If we can respect this distinction in our study of religious themes, we shall avoid many dangerous pitfalls.

The second proof for the existence of God is based on the principle of universal causality and is known as the cosmological argument. It constructs a syllogism whose first premise is a universal judgment deriving from the assumption of Leibniz that if contingent existence is given then necessary being as its cause is also given. The second premise contains the assertion, "I at least exist," the human individual being regarded as an integer in the physical universe. Thus is introduced an empirical element which distinguishes this argument from the ontological. When the two premises are combined we arrive at the legitimate conclusion that God exists. The success of this proof is no more satisfactory than its predecessor's. For the empirical premise had nothing to offer in elucidation of the nature of the supreme Reality; it can only repeat the implication of the former proof, namely, that necessary being will be the *Ens realissimum*. If we test this thesis after the manner of the Scholastics we may convert its terms, holding that "Some real beings are necessary beings." But since real beings do not differ from one another in any particulars, it follows that Real Beings are necessary beings; and we are back again at the point where the other proof started, setting up a claim for the truth of the assumption before the argument has begun.

Having finished with this dry and unrealistic refutation Kant attacks the proof from the standpoint of its obvious fallacies. He probes to the heart of the trouble. It is of no concern to him that many of the wisest thinkers of the past have found satisfaction in the argument. Thomas of Aquino ignored the ontological proof as sheer formalism but gloried in the Aristotelian ingenuity of the new one. Poets have sung in praise of the wonders of the world, as Addison in 1712:

> The spacious firmament on high
> With all the blue ethereal sky,
> And spangled heavens, a shining frame,
> Their great Original proclaim.

Nor does Kant falter in his criticism before the solid expectation that he, too, in time would join the company of the elect in their thought that two marvels rivet the attention and faith of mankind, the Starry Heavens above and the Moral Law within. But faith rests on the utility of the claims though reason cannot. First, we observe that the principle of causality is employed in the supersensible field while by the laws of logic it can only be applied to events which are capable of scientific examination. Secondly, it is argued that if a series of successive events be given, each dependent on a prior event, we may assume that there will be an end to the series, and the end will be a necessary First Cause. But if we never find an initial cause in the sensible world, have we the right to infer that it can and *must* be found in another and inscrutable realm? Thirdly, in sensible experience cause has conditions which we can carefully analyze,—

a course which is not open to inquiries on the highest levels. The presence of these errors warns us that any attempt to prove the existence of Necessary Being in the same way that we prove the reality of scientific objects, will fail. But it must be remembered that in the study of the objective sciences we never obtain complete acquaintance with the situation under review. Contingency and necessity are terms that are used in our study of events; they do not belong to the events themselves; thus they are rules for the guidance of thought. The one assures us that we must not cease our efforts until we reach the limits of our examination; the other advises us that we can never obtain all the facts at a given moment and hints that we should keep the way open for further disclosures at the proper time. Such concepts are regulative principles. With regard to the first rule, it is historically true that at least one conclusion of modern physics, made at a particular time, namely, that matter is the original and required basis of all substance, should be taken with great reserve. Here the rule of necessity was applied in an improper manner, with the result that serious objections supported by powerful evidence brought the doctrine pretty close to the edge of disrepute. Yet nothing hinders us from holding that the idea of a Primary Cause is extremely valuable as a coördinating agent in our thinking, and we may treat it *as if* the proof adduced had been shown to be strictly valid.

THE TELEOLOGICAL PROOF

The two arguments thus far examined found their warrant in the coercive concept of the Most Real Being. The lure of fancy and a strong religious belief united both meaning and reality in one idea. The attempt to support the union by an appeal to the facts of experience which teach us that things in the physical world *do* exist and must have an original Cause, was unsuccessful. The empirical element disappeared after the syllogism was set up and was never heard of afterwards. In the meantime thinkers, both ancient and modern, both Greek and Christian, studied the problem whether the sensible world contained individual factors which pointed, with a fair degree of certainty, to the creative activity of supreme Reason. To be sure, contrary opinion was at once at work, warning that if Reason produced the harmonious connections between cause and effect, it must also be held responsible for the malignant forces in the universe. Moreover, the serious student was dwelling on the very issue which Kant in due time raised: can the human mind which detects the evidence of purpose in the world of sense be sure that a divine Intelligence, if it exists, would define purposive relations by the same terms? Nonetheless, the teleological proof became an accepted form of approach to the general problem of supreme Reality. Many workers hailed the new developments in the field of biology as yielding strong corroborative testimony to the conclusions already reached. But the argument needed a thorough and unbiased examination, and this it received at the hands of the professor of philosophy at Koenigsberg, first in the *Critique of Pure Reason,* and later in the *Critique of Judgment.* The appraisal there made is definitive; it will never require to be done again.

Four points in the teleological proof stand squarely before us. First, it is alleged that the world we live in exhibits an "intentional arrangement which is carried out with great wisdom and forms a complete whole, varied in content and unlimited in extent." Secondly, the purposive order is wholly foreign to the nature of the constitutive "things of the world," and could never have been provided or coördinated by them upon the basis of appropriate ends, such ends being prescribed by a governing rational principle in conformity with fixed fundamental ideas. Thirdly, this leads us to postulate the existence of a sublime and wise counsellor (or more than one) which being free and intelligent is capable of making existentially real the preconceived ends. Finally, the operating cause must be unitary; otherwise the reciprocal relations within the universe would be seriously disturbed. This serial judgment is grounded first on the rules of experience used when we deal with physical phenomena, and secondly, on the law of analogy followed when we pass beyond the bounds of sense-perception. Kant makes mention of the great prestige which the proof has enjoyed but argues that this should not prevent us from submitting it to rigid scrutiny. In this respect as in others he is obeying the instructions of his preceptor, David Hume.

We are advised, then, at the start that the logical method of analogy is the only one we can consistently follow. He seems to confine it to the second phase of the argument but it has a place in the first part as well. The method has its limitations and its dangers. In the first place, it is a precarious instrument for determining the scientific facts in the physical world; in the second place, its utility in comparing empirical relations as set up by the human mind with the activities of the divine intelligence, is very low. What situations do we refer to when we say that nature gives evidence of purposive adaptation? It is sheer folly to refer it immediately to individual cases,—that grass is made for oxen and animal meat for man; or that vegetation was produced for the specific purpose of serving as nutriment for animals. Purpose as a principle belongs strictly to organized bodies in the sphere of nature; these we may represent in art but their "organization infinitely surpasses all our faculty of presenting the like by means of art." Furthermore, physical science has no niche for the new concept; this is true even in the study of organized bodies, as we shall see later, but conclusively true of the mechanical forces of the world. Kant refers to the composition of light; there is suggestion of purposiveness here; but science does not hold that the *purpose* of the collection of gases in their respective volumes in the sun is to yield light and heat and actinic power.[2] Professor Henderson, in our day, has suggested that the water cycle is teleological. It begins with the clouds, hovering over the mountains and emptying their contents under certain pressures of temperature and wind-velocity upon the earth. These waters join the river systems of the country and ultimately flow into the ocean. In due time they are returned to their original state by the process of vaporization. The course of this cycle is objectively purposive, not that it demands the interposition of an unknown force beyond scientific observation, but that to our aesthetic sense the repeated return of the elements from one state to another yields a factor which we do not include in the formal definition but which cannot be disregarded by the observer, namely, the idea of harmony. Still, teleology as thus described is a notion of the observing mind, not a principle resident in the fabric of the world. The truth of this deduction becomes clearer, if we substitute the old term for the new. The Deists always spoke of *design,* the intent of rational thought to repeat its ideas in a foreign medium, as the artist puts his designs on canvas or the architect his plans in a noble building. Nature, they said, does not act in this manner, it acts solely by law, that is, by the output of irresistible force.

If the method of analogy refuses to aid us in isolating designs in nature, it fails utterly when we attempt to use it in framing an extra-sensory judgment. We might adopt the scheme of a Timaean demiurge to meet the needs of the problem; but then either we must define the worker as an Architect, trying to make a world out of refractory materials, and in that case we should have to go elsewhere to discover the Creator of the original substance; or we should be obliged to see in the demiurge nothing but a semipersonalized figure of the power of matter, seeking to develop forms that *appear* to be the products of an artistic intelligence for whose existence no positive proof can be adduced. Kant meets the situation squarely in his third *Critique* (Sec. 75). He draws the distinction between two ideas; first, that the production of certain "things of nature" either singly or in combination is possible only on the assumption of a creative cause acting by design; and secondly, that the peculiar conditions of my mind make it necesary for me to conclude that the structure of the present world of nature could have been produced only by a cause working according to design, i. e. by an intelligent Deity. Neither one of these propositions affirms in categorical language the actual reality of the world. The first describes the nature of the Being who would be capable of creating the world, assuming that creation was a real event; the other describes the

2 *Critique of Judgment*, Sec. 66.

properties of the human understanding which can formulate the terms under which creation takes place. Consequently, the principle of purposive action by Deity must be taken to be strictly regulative, it can never be made determinative. For even if we should analyze every situation in the whole of nature, which we cannot do, there would still be the total universe which must be glimpsed at one stroke, an experience which the most ardent supporter of the doctrine of Final Causes would not claim to be possible.

However, the reflective idea is extremely valuable. For one thing, it offers a direct protest against the common scientific formula that matter is the sum and substance of the universe; nothing else exists. For another, it opens the way to the affirmation of a faith that passes beyond the bounds of sensibility and enters the mysteries of another kind of existence. There is still a third deduction that might be made; if the defenders of the proof find themselves hard put to it to answer the broad difficulties they face, they may not be averse to examining again the pertinent points in the first proof. Perhaps that proof is not as "artificial" as they had suspected; perhaps it would be well to ask the question: May not the reality of God stand as a plain guide to faith, even if no logical demonstration is offered; and may it not be accepted as a rock-bound base upon which all our religious aspirations shall be built?

We may pause for a moment to survey the new areas of scientific research which Kant opens in the third *Critique*. His study of the problems of teleology had brought to his attention the sharp difference between living and inert bodies. The difference had been glossed over by Descartes who insisted that all bodies with or without life were mechanically contrived and therefore subject to the same laws. But physiology became an independent science after Descartes' day largely as the result of Harvey's discovery of the circulation of the blood. Organic bodies were now assumed to possess a factor which inert bodies do not have. Science, in the course of time, called it function; Kant applies to it the term *purpose*. Purpose means that the parts of an organized body bear such a relation to the whole that they can be understood only when taken in reference to the whole. This is not true of the inert body; its parts may be removed and may become individual bodies existing by themselves. But the parts of an organism once removed, disappear as correlative parts and dissolve into mere chemical units. The stone is a congeries of smaller stones; the crystal, if broken into bits, repeats in each piece the same geometrical pattern. On the other hand, the parts of an organism are necessary to the whole; the blade of grass with its ribs, color, shape, power of growth, is bruised and decadent, if any of its properties be withdrawn or changed. Because of these conditions, it is proper to say that the parts and the whole are reciprocally cause and effect, that is, end and means. For the purpose or function of the body indicates what kind of an organic body the union of its parts will be. Purpose, therefore, is not a cause in the physical sense; that is, it cannot be examined by the laws of mechanical science, the law, for example, of cohesion. Purpose is a statement of what the several parts can do, once they are arranged in their appropriate order. It indicates also that the parts are dependent one upon the other, and in the full-grown organism neither can exist without the other. Thus, in studying an organic body we may properly use the principle of causality in its two forms, first, the effective cause which controls its structure, and secondly, the final cause or purpose which registers its behavior. Purpose defined in this way entails no reference to an external agency which may have produced it or which now directs its actions.

GOD AND THE MORAL PRINCIPLE IN MAN

The first *Critique* closed with a negative result: the ancient arguments for the existence of God cannot stand the test of modern analysis. It should be borne in mind, however, that the negative conclusion does not carry with it a denial of divine Reality. For in the same work Kant has hinted many times that he was dealing with only one department of human judgment, the theoretical or speculative. But reason is more than reflective, it is also practical, that is, it leads to action. It concerns both the determination of scientific ideals and the realization of moral values. Hitherto we have examined the problems of religion by the methods of conventional logic; now we propose to break away from the saga of the categories and study the actual road men follow in settling upon a course of conduct. It may be that by this route we shall gain a new approach to the age-old query, How may we know that there is a God? The desire to explore this route persists throughout the whole *Critique of Pure Reason* and comes to full expression in the final pages: "A man's moral precept is his maxim and it inevitably draws him to a belief in the existence of God and of the future life." [3] That was then an ardent hope; he now proceeds to turn it into a legitimate truth based on trustworthy evidence.

We must first inspect the nature of the moral agent. It falls necessarily into two distinguishable parts, the empirical and the rational. The first is involved in the sensory mechanisms of the body and functions in accordance with its inherent laws; the other operates by its own principles, the chiefest of which is Freedom. The speculative reason can arrange and classify its ideas, it cannot change their content or interfere with the objects that engendered them. Practical reason is different; it cannot only create its ideas, it can choose the manner by which man acts them out. Desire

[3] Trans. by N. K. Smith, p. 650.

which is rooted in sensation is subject to change, sometimes suddenly, often after long periods of time; and change is evoked by a twist of temperament or by the stimulus of new objects of interest. Judgment is universal in scope and unaffected by desire; it therefore lays down the law for human behavior, it also dictates the form and time of action. But judgment and law are really terms in logic and must be converted into will in order to become effective. At this point, freedom, the sponsor of will, begins to play its part in human conduct. If men were bound by the restraints of nature, there could be no freedom, no choice, no individual initiative. There is, however, solid foundation for my opinion that the action I have just taken could by free election of will have been left undone. I am conscious of my ability to make a deliberate decision, and either to execute its terms at once or withdraw it from public operation for a time. This choice, I assume, belongs to me by right of my sovereign personality. Neither man nor God nor the brute force of nature can wrench it from my grasp. Moral good and human dignity are one and the same and together they form the Good Will.

How shall we determine when and in what manner the will of man shall act? We note at once that the practical judgment is embodied wholly and necessarily in a categorical imperative. The commands of Hedonism are hypothetical—"If you would be happy, act in this or that way." The judgment in that case is contingent; it waits on the definition of happiness, on the instruments of the will at hand to effectuate it, on the conditions of society that may block the successful execution of the deed. The imperative of reason has no such limitations; it speaks with clear conviction and with inflexible expectation. Duty does not move the will by threats or persuasions or sophistical logic. It orders us to act by the precept which we can at the same time will to be or become universal law. It warns us to recognize the existence of human purposes which must be pursued with scrupulous and unfailing respect, no exception being made either for myself or anyone else. These maxims bear the imprint of infallible authority; they are the expressions of an inner conscience of which Bishop Butler said: "If it had the power as it has the manifest authority, it would rule the world." [4]

One further question requires an answer before we take up the specific matter under review. What is the universal and prescriptive end of all moral action? Kant reverts to the decisions of Greece for his reply. Epicurus and the Stoics employ the same terms but reverse their order in the final judgment. Happiness, cautioned the former, is the summum bonum of human conduct, and virtue is one of the means by which it can be acquired. Hence, prudence in the choice of means is the chief concern of a moral

[4] *Sermons, op. cit.*, II, 64.

program. Virtue, thundered the Stoics, is the sum and substance of moral good, while happiness is a state of feeling consequent upon the achievement of virtue but without any influence in fixing its value. Neither of these attitudes is possible for our philosopher. The first is eliminated because pleasure is a strictly physical fact, a feeling which comes and goes according to its laws but cannot aid in forming our moral motives. The other argued that since virtue was the sole good, it necessarily contained happiness already as a part of its character; hence, happiness could not be held to be an effect of virtue. Neither of these formulas correctly states the facts in the case. The immediate good of the soul is the acquisition of virtue; but that does not mean that it is the only good. Common sense and a critical understanding of the processes of nature, both reserve a place for happiness in the scheme of moral conduct. "Happiness," says Kant, "is the condition of a rational being in the world when everything goes in accordance with his wish and will." [5] It involves, therefore, a harmony between his physical nature and the essential principles of the moral law as apprehended by the agent. The plain fact, however, is that man cannot control either his own physical condition or the circumstances in which he is forced to live. How then shall he institute a causal relation between the attainment of moral good or virtue on the one side and pleasure or happiness on the other? No serious student of moral behavior is willing to say that happiness is the ground of virtue. May we reverse the order and affirm that virtue can by its own decree, produce the harmonious state of mind that men are wont to call happiness? We might, he thinks, "presuppose morally right behaviour as its prior condition." [6] In a perfect world both would occupy a coördinate and controlling position. But the world we live in is not perfect; certainly that part of it which has to do with moral motives exhibits no glint of perfection. Hence, we are faced with the antimony of practical reason, precisely as we had to meet a similar antinomy in scientific inquiry: virtue cannot subsist without happiness, but virtue cannot produce happiness. The Epicurean doctrine is wholly false, the Stoics' "not absolutely false, insofar as virtue is considered as a form of causality in the natural world." [7] This brings us to the point where religious problems arise: Is there a future life before us where character may be fully developed? Is there an omnipotent rational Being which can effect a perfect balance between goodness and constitutional harmony?

The first of these problems has to do with the capacity of the moral self, the soul, to reach the status of holiness in its sensible environment. History is explicit in one of its deductions—Society has never presented a

[5] *Critique of Practical Reason*. Trans. by T. K. Abbot, p. 221.   [6] *Ibid.*, p. 207.
[7] *Ibid.*, p. 210.

case of complete virtue (apart from a religious program) and never will. Sin takes its rise in the solicitations of the senses; "they lie in the road." Reason cannot tempt any man to disobedience of its own commands; "a malignant reason is the reason of a devil, not a man." [8] Hence, if the moral agent were solely rational, not at all instinctive, he would infallibly follow the principles of virtue. In that case, however, he would not be a man! Yet with all its errors and mistakes, with its prevarications and heinous sins, human nature holds to the conviction that the moral law must and shall be fulfilled. There is a perfect character that man may create, and the aspirations of the faithful soul cannot be denied. There is, Kant thinks, a steady progress to such a goal. Perhaps, his sense of certitude might be somewhat tempered if he were living in the present age. But progress is measured not by numbered years but by the long stretches of human endeavor. At any rate, it appears that the formation of perfect character cannot be reached during our sensible life, either by successive stages or at one fateful bound. The *summum bonum* becomes an adequate theory only if we assume the perpetual continuance of our personality. This sounds like a defeatist doctrine in the articles of a stern and rigorous philosophy. But for the religious enthusiast, at least, it means that our achievements here can be supported by the expectation of complete holiness, hereafter, together with unalloyed bliss at its realization.

The second problem concerns the vital connection between virtue and happiness. How can we obtain a guaranty that the one shall be invariably followed by the other? We have noted the rigid ruling of the practical reason—duty for duty's sake; no incentive lower than that can be considered by the critical thinker. Still, the terms of the *summum bonum* are fixed and irrevocable: virtue and a harmonious life go hand in hand in moral experience. What cause as yet unstated can bring the two elements together? Such a cause cannot reside in the mechanical laws of nature, that is, in our sensory equipment; it cannot be found in the essential potencies of the will; we are free to act but we are not free to command the discharge of our feelings to suit our own convenience. Thus, we are shut up to one conclusion: there exists a divine power possessed of a supreme intelligence, having "a causality corresponding to moral character," [9] whose control extends both to moral agents (human beings) and to the complex of natural forces. Therefore, we are required by the rules of logic and the needs of the soul to postulate the existence of a supreme rational Cause. Kant is careful to admonish us not to attach to this thesis the meretricious end which Berkeley proposed, viz., the happiness of mankind. Happiness is not the effect of virtue, but it cannot come to any man unless he is *worthy* of receiving it. This means that he has made every

[8] *Ibid.*, p. 325.   [9] *Ibid.*, p. 222.

attempt to carry out the intent of the moral law, the issue of which must be virtuous conduct.

There is no evidence to show that Kant ever seriously questioned the validity of the moral argument. It is true that in his later studies he underscored the operation of the imperative in men's experience rather than its apologetic value as the key to divine existence. In one passage he boldly said that "faith needs merely the idea of God" as guide to good moral demeanor. It does not presume that it can certify to an objective reality of the idea by sheer theoretical speculation.[10] But his readers have not accepted his conclusions with the facility he might have desired. So shrewd and sympathetic a critic as Mr. Webb [11] has singled out the logical flaws in his proof and has not declined to expose them. Accordingly we do not hesitate to lay down the following objections.

In the first place, we deny the right of any scientific student to carry the course of moral development beyond the bounds of the conceptual judgment. The critical method transgresses its own principles when it does so. The history of the race encourages us to look for a progressive growth in moral intuition, one phase of which will be an increased power of mind to grapple with the problems of experience and solve them. But progress in the individual or his group is slow and sporadic, now hesitant, now spurting ahead, retarded by unforeseen conditions, compromised by mistakes, expecting victory when it meets defeat, never reaching the goal which fancy and faith have pictured as its rightful end. In fact, we have the greatest difficulty in maintaining a unity of conscious endeavor, let alone finding the way easy in building a strong coördinated thought and character. We cannot prove, Kant argued in the first *Critique,* that we possess an actual unitary self corresponding to what the Greeks called a Soul; yet we irresistibly draw the conclusion that it *does* exist. If there be doubt in deciding so basic an issue in our present life, shall we try to prove the perpetuity of the Self after death? and if we did prove it, could we ever speak confidently of the nature of that subtended Self? Faith may have its innings here but logic refuses to act.

The second objection deals with the ancient problem of virtue and its associate, happiness. Kant stubbornly insists that they move on two distinct and incombinable planes, judgment and feeling. Feeling may help us to appreciate the moral values of an action but Judgment alone can decide what is good. The theory is based on the triple division of the faculties of mind current in his day. Each faculty has its own purpose and together they constitute the conscious life of the human being. Modern analysis insists upon the unity of mental action with the three aspects ex-

---

[10] *Religion within the Limits of Reason Alone.* Trans. by Greene and Hudson, p. 142, note.
[11] C. C. J. Webb, *Kant's Philosophy of Religion,* Chap. V.

pressed in every act. Thus, moral behavior is the discharge of the desiderative function of mind. It has always an apprehensible end, that which states the nature of the action. It also registers an emotional quality; such a virtue as justice or honor embodied in a particular deed will surely be followed by a sense of satisfaction. Satisfaction settles into a deep feeling of contentment when the conviction of having done one's duty is realized. Happiness as thus defined is the direct result of the normal functioning of the mind; it requires no extra-natural means for its justification. In short, a moral decision like every other judgment of mind is accompanied by an appropriate feeling which serves as a public test of the validity of the given sequence of ideas.

The third objection is more general; it pursues the form adopted by Kant in disposing of the preceding proofs. The moral-sense argument is a variant of the teleological and suffers from the same faults. He categorically denies that happiness can be the purpose and end of the quest for virtue but he assured us that happiness cannot exist in an undisciplined mind; man must be worthy of happiness or he will not attain it. Thus, the consummate good of man involves the two elements in the order just mentioned. The purposive principle is as necessary here as it is in the structure of the human body. But the organization of the living body is not an authoritative guaranty of the reality of a supreme Designer. By the same token, the sense of moral obligation, strong though it be, even if it be distinguished by the presence of unperturbed contentment, cannot point unmistakably to an original and infallible source of holiness and bliss. Faith may teach us *what* duty is; it cannot tell *why* duty exists.

THE MEANING OF CONVERSION

The first problem in any theological discipline is the certification of divine existence. Kant finds the key to its solution in the inescapable judgment of the moral reason. Now every human desire has an appropriate end, that is, an object which we endeavor to possess. Universalizing this proposition we agree that there is a total purpose which embraces the realization of every conceivable purpose and that is named the Final End. What is the Final End? The complete satisfaction in body and mind enjoyed by all who have proved themselves worthy of it because of their moral attainment; the perfect Good guaranteed by an omnipotent Reason, whose decrees are the same as our self-ordained decisions arrived at by the free judgment of mind. Thus, morality leads head on to religion.[12]

It is not to be supposed that the philosopher confined his attention solely to the formal framework of religion during the many years of his produc-

[12] *Religion within the Limits of Reason Alone*, p. 7, note.

tive career. In the second *Critique* and in several smaller works he introduces significant concepts belonging to religious theory and practice. In particular he grapples with the problem of the divine attributes, a subject which has excited the curiosity of thinkers from Xenophanes and Parmenides to the present time. But he does not content himself with citing merely the negative terms; he also emphasizes the positive or moral elements in the divine nature, holiness, blessedness, wisdom, which he will later erect into a new Trinity. What is a fact of record is that in the first *Critique* he began to speak of a moral theology, which at once distinguished his attitude from that of the professional theologians; and in the second, of the solemn relation subsisting between man and his Maker —"for nothing glorifies God more than that which is the most estimable thing in the world, respect for his commands, the observance of the holy duty that the law imposes on us." [13] But the time at length was ripe for a systematic statement of his belief. It appeared at the very moment when the Prussian government, through the Commission charged with the defense of the doctrinal purity of the Lutheran Church began to inquire into the teachings of the university professors. Kant himself came under suspicion. One of the commissioners actually proposed to the King that Kant should be prohibited from lecturing at any time on any subject appertaining to religion. Nevertheless, permission was granted to publish the first section of the book on religion, and while strong representations were made against the later sections, it was finally published in 1793 under the title: *Religion innerhalb der Grenzen der blossen Vernunft* (Religion within the bounds of Reason alone). This work is reckoned by some expositors as a worthy companion-piece of the three *Critiques*. It is his last large, single contribution to philosophy and his only substantial treatise on the subject of religion. It is not to be viewed as a program-book for a new type of religious theory. It has some points in common with St. Augustine's *City of God,* not only in his emphasis on the moral values struggling for expression in human society but also in the subtle fervor with which he expounds his thesis. But it is the work of an independent inquirer, fearless and persistent, and it stands as a monument to his genius as an analytical thinker.

The book opens with the question—What is the moral nature of man, and what is its present status in the world of social action? Opinions differ widely. Almost every race on earth has cultivated the tradition that the Golden Age is in the past; like a dream in the night it has slipped from view and left behind a multitude of woes and miseries. Other observers like Rousseau have adopted a more optimistic outlook: there are brightening skies, beacon lights before our eyes. Man is essentially sound of body,

---

[13] *Critique of Practical Reason.* Trans. by Abbot, p. 228.

capable of meeting the forces of physical might and mastering them; he must also be or become sound of mind since he has passed through his mental childhood and has begun to weigh and solve the elementary problems in natural science. Furthermore, the principles of human conduct are slowly taking shape in his mind; he understands that he is not a single integer in the welter of experience, that he stands associated with uncounted millions of his fellow human beings who seek for moral excellence and expect to reach it. These two theories occupy contradictory attitudes as men face the future: there is no hope, there is nothing but hope.

But there is a third theory which avoids the contradictions of the others. Let us begin with the assumption that in his native endowment man is neither good nor bad, but he may become one or the other by reason of certain maxims which he accepts as the ground for thought and action. Just here, however, let us be sure of one point: we cannot find goodness primarily in the overt act but in the hidden motives of the heart. These are grounded in the original maxim which governs the choice of each particular type of behavior. Here the choice is free and the judgment unaffected by the whims of impulse or the surge of emotions. We must recognize then the presence of two basic maxims, that which reflects the predisposition to good, and that which Kant calls a propensity or tendency to evil. The former is the stronger and should in the end prevail. It is buttressed by three natural functions in the individual,—his physical traits, his ability to think, and his sense of responsibility as a free agent in the community. If these are carefully noted, the maxim of a good character will be thoroughly understood and dutifully obeyed. On the other hand, there is a proclivity to evil rooted in the mind of every human being, whatever be his private endowments or his public achievements. Kant does not state this maxim as the equivalent of natural depravity, original sin, which is to be distinguished from single deeds, unjust, dishonest, impure actions. To do so would shatter the right of free choice which every man holds dear; it would so seriously modify his sense of obligation that he could not tell how far he would be held responsible for the effects of any moral decision. Kant has no doubt of the reality of the evil maxim as a disposition in the soul. Evil is a fact in human history whether imbedded in the cruelties of uncivilized man or in the intrigues of cultivated societies or notoriously, in the persecutions and frauds perpetrated by religious bodies. He passes a stern and uncompromising sentence upon the attempts of one state to conquer another and impose its fetters on vanquished citizens, a procedure which removes not only political liberty but also virtue, aesthetic feeling and the rewards of learning. His words seem almost like a preview of the cataclysm that fell on Europe in 1939 and thereafter engulfed the entire world. Public evil is but another aspect of the propensity

existing in the individual soul. In both cases there are degrees of seriousness, grades of malignity. The first is the common Pauline plaint, "to will
is present with me, but how to perform I know not." The second is that
the intended action, moral in its inception, is prevented from coming to
fruit because of certain sinister internal or external conditions that interfere. The third is the perversity of mind which knows the right but deliberately declines to follow it.

The fact of evil is undisputed. What is its cause and how did it emerge
as a proclivity of human nature? We may disregard the dogma of the
church that man has inherited the tendency from his primordial ancestor.
Such a theory robs him of his intrinsic freedom and unfits him for the
duties of a sovereign moral agent. Of course we may institute a parallel
between Adam's first transgression and the actual thrust of the maxim of
evil into our conscience. While this does not explain the origin of sin, it
may help us to see how to rid ourselves of the tendency to sin. The traditional story in Genesis points to a possible source, the very source that the
Stoics adopted, namely, man's sensuous nature, together with the desires
and lusts that inevitably proceed from it. This, however, involves the impairment of the will and the elimination of choice; it puts man into the
class of automatic re-agents in no way differing from the brute. Nor,
again, can evil be the corruption of our legislative reason; for then reason
could be accused of destroying the very law upon which its authority rests,
and conduct would lose its distinctive meaning. If this explanation were
correct, we should only be pushed back another step, for one should be
obliged to discover how the original corruption in the maxim was produced. We should thus be carried away to the dark and deep abysm of
time whence no determinable answer has ever been drawn. The conclusion forced upon us is that the constitutional source of error is unfathomable, whatever the non-philosophical expositors, such as men of
medicine or of religion, may have to say on the subject.

We return to the *fact* of sin. Two aspects of it must be carefully studied.
The first is that the mind of man willingly accepted the maxim, although
no time can be set for the initial decision. If proof for this is needed, it
is found in the additional fact that when wrongful deeds are suggested to
the mind, they are already colored by the moral quality we have agreed
to call sinful. Every man acts *as if* the present action were his first, that is,
as if he were not already surcharged with a mass of stored-up iniquities.
He is as free now as he was in his earliest youth; despite his previous
transgressions, he is free *now* to perform a truly righteous act. Instead,
he chooses to sin and the choice hinges not on the disqualification incident
to a perverse character but to the dictate of the basic maxim he originally
espoused. In the words of the philosopher, "we cannot inquire into the

temporal character of the deed but solely into its rational character." [14] There is here a touch of the very mythical creativeness found in the story of the Book of Genesis; but there is nothing legendary about the individual misdemeanor itself or about its place in human experience. We may, as Mr. Webb suggests, return to the method of the critical philosophy: we may regard the evil maxim as the noumenal or intelligible structure of sin, and the deed as the phenomenal expression clothed in the terms of empirical behavior. The contradictions between the two aspects of evil are thereby removed; time disappears in the former but is wholly real in the latter. Freedom of action remains unchallenged, and the authority of conscience is sustained. [15]

If, then, man is by voluntary election in bondage to an evil principle, how can he make good his escape? Or, is he bound hand and foot for all his natural life? This is the next item in the religious creed. To these questions one clear and decisive answer is given: man *can* be restored to his native quality of mind, he can be regenerated. The change takes place suddenly, spontaneously, by a kind of internal revolution. Divine help may be needed during the process of recovery, to remove certain hindrances or give a positive lift in the period of crisis, but the original effort is made by the individual agent. Help will come only if he proves himself worthy of receiving it—a typical Kantian statement of the case. Here again the modal factor is beyond our scrutiny, how the change actually takes place. The assurance that the change *can* be made depends on the predisposition incorporated in the original maxim; the expectation that it *will* come hinges strictly upon the motive power of the agent. When a man resolves to do his duty, when he grasps the meaning of the moral law within him, the restoration has already begun. As a positive result there will be a new element in his thought as well as an observable improvement in his external conduct. If the intemperate man abandons his excesses merely to conserve his health, if the dishonest man discontinues his faulty transactions merely to maintain his reputation, clearly the change of posture is not a moral revolution but a simple change of dress for an old form of behavior. No man can deceive his contemporaries; even a child will detect the sham. No: conversion is a single, decisive event registered in the invisible conscience; its epochal implications may not become public for a long term of years. Some religionists who do not understand the process may think it wise to introduce certain seductive methods for gaining divine favor, and thus hasten the outward change. Such subtleties are vain, because they mistake the meaning of conversion. Works of grace which Kant calls a *parerga*—something added by an extraneous agency—cannot produce the desired effect. If we excite the mind to an artificial and

[14] *Religion within the Limits of Reason Alone*, Book I.   [15] *Op. cit.*, p. 107.

ephemeral state of zeal—fanaticism—which he had seen in the Pietist group, "waiting for power from on high," as it is sometimes called, nothing but sharp illusion, a strange mental aberration, excessive stimulation of the nervous system—nothing else, will result. The whole procedure is contrary to the course of moral development; it depends upon a *good* provided by a power outside the soul, which contradicts the meaning of freedom and turns the man into an automaton, when he is by right a self-determining moral agent. The ancient doctrine of justification by faith has been annulled and we have substituted for it a justification by false and ineffectual feeling. Nothing can take the place of a firm resolve made by the man himself to change his ways by first changing his maxim.[16]

THE RELIGIOUS COMMUNITY

We now enter upon an area of inquiry where abstract conceits give way to concrete situations, where moral differences appear as struggles between shadowy personalities, spiritual potencies, and where Deity is no longer cloaked by impassive reason but is cited as the real object of reverent contemplation. The purpose of the author is to sharpen the distinction between the contrary maxims which the judgment of man is obliged to confront. The great moralists of Greece and the Fathers of the church have both named the *summum bonum* (the highest good) to be Virtue, *arete, virtus*. This implies that they expected its acquisition to demand courage of the finest brand. We are now engaged in a conflict of supreme importance in the history of the race. The Stoics mistook the nature of the enemy; they assumed men are fighting again the undisciplined stimuli of the senses. But moral values do not inhere in the appetites of the body or even in the ambitions of the mind; these are natural functions and have their purposes clearly defined. The Apostle in opposing the Stoic concept contended that we are in combat not with physical forces but with "principalities and powers, with spiritual wickedness in high places." The enemy, grim and resolute, is seated in our will, and until he is dislodged and beaten, we cannot reckon that we have gained the victory. We must therefore examine the two antagonists and determine how the campaign is to be waged. They are described in terms that cannot be misunderstood; in the Christian vernacular, they stand opposed to one another as heaven and hell, an antithesis which the Greek mind could not understand.

We look first at the legal claim of the *good* principle to exercise sovereignty over the will of man. The claim is unquestionably involved in the purported end of creation, which is the moral perfection of the rational creature. Moral reason is thus coincident with the nature of God; it is not a created thing, it is his "well-beloved Son." Such an idea is embodied in the

[16] *Religion within the Limits of Reason Alone*, pp. 48–49.

very nature of man, it is his guide and his destiny. Having identified ourselves with the good principle we require no model wrapped in human
habiliments to incite us to the due exercise of our moral rights. Kant pays
tribute to the flawless character of the Man of Galilee but doubts whether
a perfect character, the crystallization of holiness, could ever be given as
a legitimate object of emulation. The single query is, Has man accepted
the challenge of the good principle and sought to mould his conduct by its
standard? There are set and determined hindrances to the realization of
the idea in private experience. The first is the obvious fact that we are
obliged to pursue our moral efforts under the conditions of time and
space. How can we address ourselves to the task of attaining the perfect
holiness of God, when every action shows itself to be defective, and we
have no guaranty that the defect will ever be removed? The answer is
that moral acts are necessarily subject to our private limitations, as, for
example, to the number of persons we may reach by our influence. But, as
we have already seen, the principle at stake is not *in time,* it is timeless, and
every reflection of the principle in our behavior draws us nearer to the
ultimate goal, whose fascinations increase as we observe it more distinctly.
The second difficulty considers the question whether moral happiness
will continue to attend the development of moral character. The answer
is that a comparison of our moral achievements will bring the fact home
to us that we are making substantial progress and need not be discouraged.
The third objection is hypothetical and, as would appear to a mind untouched by the fruitless controversies of the schools, thoroughly untrustworthy and without point: How can we pay our debts for evil deeds done
in our unregenerate years? The question presupposes a system of divine
jurisprudence modeled upon the canons of the Roman law. If the question
is worthy of an answer, we say with Kant that for the converted man, the
program of life is completely changed. What happened before the change,
has no connection with the present form of behavior. The job facing the
moral agent is to obey in every detail the laws of righteousness; that will
meet the situation perfectly.

But we must turn back again to the eternal conflict with the Prince of
evil in the world. The fable, enshrined in many mythologies, pictures him
as having engaged in spiritual rebellion against the authority of the divine
Ruler of the universe. Whereupon he was stricken from his seat in
heaven, and condemned to wander up and down the face of the earth. He
at once proceeded to conquer, if he could, the world of human nature. He
came at length in collision with the supreme expression of goodness in the
person of the Son of God, and by wiles and intrigues with the reigning
powers, brought him to an ignominious end. Disregarding the legendary
elements in the account, Kant proceeds to argue that the evil principle

still threatens the hopes and aspirations of the seekers after holiness. He warns us that selfishness, with its mortifications and sufferings, persists in human society. The mystic veil has been torn from the monster but his works are still at hand—iniquity, perversity, deceit and fraud. These are the evidences of the application of the evil principle in human undertakings. They can be canceled by the adoption of sound moral judgment and fearless moral action. The gates of hell cannot prevail against the man of moral probity. Thus ends the second Book of Kant's significant volume on religion.

The third Book opens with a militant re-iteration of the victory over the evil principle, and goes on to show how the victory is safeguarded by the erection of a new community called the Church. What is the church? what is the nature of the new society whose simple creed is the control of conduct by reason? It is clear, at once, that moral values must be developed within the confines of a political state. The state is founded on constitutional law; that is what differentiates it from a natural state which has no laws, except the desires of the untutored mind. Social unity is impossible unless wayward passions are checked, and only instituted law can do it. The same course must be followed in the private life of man. So long as reason is not recognized as the law of human behavior, impulse will hold sway and a settled character cannot be produced. These two authorities, civil and ethical, run parallel in the execution of their respective ordinances. Neither may encroach on the domain of the other. The civil state cannot attempt to coerce men into sobriety of behavior by restrictive statutes. The attempt will fail, it will not only prevent the creation of virtue, it will make insecure the social fabric by causing mistrust of the whole legal system. Nor should the moral reason attempt directly to influence the administration of civil justice; it should rather teach privately and publicly, the principle of just relations between the social groups. It should not be guilty of such excesses as those committed by men who suppose themselves equipped with a special degree of illumination. There is only one way to avoid all excesses—adopt the concept of a supreme rational Being who organizes the social forces which make for righteousness into a coherent body of workers, the People of God acting exclusively under his commands. Here let one admonition rule: church and state do not stand in opposition to one another; their functions do not conflict; each is able to give counsel to the other, and the time may come when the church needs the police protection of the state. But if the conflict ever comes, there is but one stand to take: "we ought to obey God rather than man." In our day the action of the German pastor (Niemoeller) who defied the edicts of the Leader and suffered for it, is a case in point.

We therefore ask again— What is the church? The answer which Kant gives is definitive: [17] it is the ethical commonwealth ordained and guided by divine legislation; *invisible* as the idea of the union of all the righteous, *visible* as the actual congregation of men holding the same ideals.

Here again we see the schematic movement of the critical philosophy: the principle of piety governing the wide sweep of activity in a specific field, and the individual cases of religious experience subject to empirical observation. Like every other concept it must be interpreted by the four categories of thought. The church is universal in scope and therefore single in structure; it is pure in motive because directed by the moral law; it is free in action since it depends on no code of rules or symbols of outward authority; and finally it is unchangeable in its virtuous character and in its obedience to a common Reason.[18] Such a community cannot have arisen out of historical conditions; for historical religions require the habits of worship, regular and formal, which alone can justify the hopes of members that their devotion will be rewarded. A moral religion demands no statutory law, no priestly intercession, no ecclesiastical system to support its faith. If sacred books are preserved, they must be interpreted by scholars with adequate erudition and a clear understanding of the basic truths.

We must not, however, refuse to trace the gradual incorporation of the sovereign principles of moral right in the objective history of the race. Since Christianity has the greatest affinity to a moral religion, we confine our study to its development. Kant has been subject to severe strictures for his arbitrary treatment of the subject. Troeltsch and others have complained that he had no acute sense of the progress of human thought in the field of religion. In particular, Mr. Webb [19] is inclined to view Kant's recital of the activities of the church as thoroughly unhistorical. For the philosopher seems to think that the externalization of religious sentiments in creed or symbol is impossible; they belong to the inner sanctuary of human reason and resist any analysis such as that given to scientific data. Hence, what goes under the name of religion in social development has often no connection whatsoever with the serious ideas which true believers accept and live by. In fact, the history of Europe is principally a struggle between the religion of formal worship and the religion of moral precepts. The essence of the Christian faith and what makes it a veritable religion is the moral sublimity attaching to its original teachings. It should be remembered that while racially Christianity springs from the Hebrew group, it obtained but few of its key dogmas from the ancient Scriptures, and these were revised in the light of the new mode of thinking. Indeed, the Jewish order was a civil policy, not a religious program. Its ordinances prescribed duties that were strictly external. It knew nothing of the church

[17] *Ibid.*, p. 92.   [18] *Ibid.*, pp. 115 sq.   [19] *Op. cit.*, p. 149.

universal; the Jews were a "peculiar people" and other peoples could not share in the rights and privileges granted to them. In their creed there is not the slightest hint of the idea of a future life, a notion always associated with a religious creed wherever found throughout the world. Hence, the history of the church does not begin with the age of Moses but with the appearance of the Teacher of the Gospel. His public life was short and he left no written record. But his words and observations were collected by his disciples and after due interpretation were ultimately accepted as the canonical text. The interpretation of the text in due time became the major duty of the church. The East and the West disagreed as to the doctrines and their application. Sharp controversies arose between the idea of moral excellence on the one side and the bizarre conceits of monastic particularism, on the other; between the assumption of authority by the papacy in matters both temporal and spiritual and the claim of political control over the church by the Empire. As a result, discord, schism, persecution, fraud appeared in the body of the church. In his survey of the facts Kant could think of no classical utterance more suitable to the case than that of Lucretius [20]—*Tantum religio potuit suadere malorum"* ("Such monstrous evil deeds could religion urge men to commit"). The evil propensity of human nature had challenged again the silent forces of moral conviction and for a time seemed to have defeated them. However, as we have seen, the idea of moral truth is timeless; it may be obscured by the controversies of the age but its universal authority cannot be destroyed.

Faced with the repeated failure of the church to maintain a pure doctrine and an unsullied faith, Kant found himself ready to admit that true religion cannot be attached to an historical institution; it belongs to the experience of the inner reason. Still, it cannot exist by itself; it requires the recognition of a supreme moral Being with the element of mystery surrounding it. We should be extremely careful in our interpretation of this idea. The wonders of nature are not mysterious; they are simply unknown. The free volition of man is not a mystery; we can exercise it by ourselves and share it with others. But the ground of our freedom is beyond our ken and therefore a mystery. Furthermore, the idea of the Supreme Good remains unexplained; how *does* happiness associate itself with virtue by the intervention of a supreme Moral Ruler? Later in the book he writes, in a footnote, that "faith needs merely the idea of God . . . it need not presume that it can certify the objective reality of the idea." [21] This would clear away some of the mystery, for then we should have to do only with an idea, not an existing thing. We could use the idea at once as a regulative principle which being a logical rule will enable us to explore the meaning of our relation to the *summum bonum*.

[20] *Religion within the Limits of Reason Alone*, p. 122.   [21] *Ibid.*, p. 142.

In the given situation, however, we are invited to accept the actual presence of the divine Reason in which our own power of judgment takes its rise. Divine Reason appears to us in a threefold character, as a holy Legislator, a gracious Guardian and a righteous Judge, which the older theologians called the "Economic Trinity." This is not the essential Trinity of the church creeds; it is a sequence of thoughts which moral reason necessarily develops. Here, then, there *is* no mystery; for the ordinary relations in human society are classified under the same three heads, administered by different groups of officials, though in the Christian symbolism they are united in a single Mind. The mystery, if mystery exists, lies in man's own experience. How can we, mere human beings, who are enmeshed in the toils of nature's law be called upon to act with perfect freedom in the determination of our moral conduct? How can we who are bound by the fetters of voluntary assent to the evil principle shake off the corrupt habits of our early life and work out our own salvation under the dictates of moral reason? And, lastly, how can any man convince himself that he, and not someone else, shall be delivered from captivity by a kind of supernal election in which Grace supports his private efforts for release? The answer seems to be: Let each of us remember that Law, moral authority, has another aspect often disguised which we call Love, and that this has been applied to us. *Why* the choice is made remains a profound mystery; it belongs to an inscrutable wisdom and we shall never penetrate its terms.

The fourth and last Book in Kant's treatise considers the elements of true and false service under the dominion of the Good principle. This, as we have already noted, presupposes the foundation of a commonwealth in which all men of good moral report will be enrolled. How shall such a community be instituted? Human wisdom is not adequate to the task; God must be the founder of his own kingdom. This does not imply that human beings will be forced into its membership. The plain expectation is that slowly but surely, throughout the length of the centuries, the church will approximate to a pure rational faith which will no longer require public worship or the administration of the sacraments. If, however, it should happen that the symbols of service are taken to be the sole means of salvation and the clergy assume the authority of being the sole intermediaries between God and man, then the primary purposes of the church will be destroyed and its value to moral agents will wholly cease.

It is fitting that we should study the Christian religion in the light of the considerations just noted. Is Christianity a *natural* religion in the sense that its original concepts can be apprehended by the moral reason without the aid of a transcendental revelation? Let us look at the record. The preachments of Jesus preserved in the Sermon on the Mount move on an extremely high plane of moral speculation. He rejected the principle of obedience to statutory law; he teaches that hate in the heart is equivalent to overt murder, that injury to one's neighbor can be repaired by only equal satisfaction paid to him in person; that revenge must be changed into tolerance; in general, that mere fulfilment of the outward terms of duty will never guarantee the growth of moral purity. The principles of action are summed up in two; love the Lord with all your heart and your neighbor as yourself. The moral program consists in seeking the kingdom of God and his righteousness, with the understanding that in this way all the true ends of moral behavior will be attained. There is nothing in these teachings that does not belong to the intimate interests of the moral reason.

But in addition to the natural truths thus recorded there are other precepts issued in the form of required beliefs, commands based not on the assent of reason but on the facts of history. Here the authority of truth is less obvious. Still there is no good ground for disregarding these commands. Rather should they be treasured as valuable instruments by which the main doctrines, approved by reason, such as sin, recovery, the growth in holiness, may be impressed on the minds of true believers. Yet, while we assent to the significance of the added material, we must steel the affections against the forms of false worship which sometimes takes the name of sacramentalism. The genesis of such a system lies in the mental illusion which substitutes rites, ceremonies and procession, penances, castigations and monkish orgies, for the true exercises of spirit. It is fostered by threats or subtle persuasions, when the person of the priest takes the place of the unseen Ministrant, when sorcery and fetishism are palmed off on unsuspecting worshipers as valid exhibitions of faith. Against these misrepresentations and shams should be placed the concept of Godliness, fear of God as the duty of the subject, Love of God as the duty of the son. The illusory faith of sacramentalism will be superseded by a clear understanding of what is involved in the legitimate "means of grace," such as prayer, fellowship, baptism, and the eucharist, all invested with surpassing beauty when sympathetically interpreted. "By their fruits ye shall know them."

Thus ends the fourth and final Book of the last *Critique*. It is the swan song of the philosopher, an intoned hymn to the divine Reason which makes moral religion the dominant force in human society.

CONCLUSION

Immanuel Kant was in his seventieth year when he published the work we have been examining. His natural life continued for eleven years and during that period he was incessantly busy with the same cluster of ideas that had engaged his attention from his youth. His many notes, reflections and suggestions have now been pieced together and edited by a careful scholar, Professor Adickes, under the title, *Opus Postremum*. The chief interest for us lies in the question— Did any notable changes take place in his views respecting the Idea of God and its relation to human experience, a subject which is bound to make appeal to an acute intelligence as it moves towards the term of life? We may follow the lead of Professor Kemp Smith [22] and select the passages written during his last three years, that is, before 1804.

It is certain that Kant accepted the reality of a divine Being, precisely as he accepted the existence of the thing-in-itself, though logical proof fails in both cases; but such acceptance does not include a statement of the kind of reality he has in mind,—whether an independent substance called God or a determinate idea of the Being called God. Still, his words are generally clear and emphatic, albeit they hark back to the ontological proof which, in his early years, he designated as the only possible one. "The mere Idea of God," he says, "is at the same time a postulate of his existence"; and again, "the thought of him is at the same time belief in him and in his personality." But the reality of an independent substance grows less sure when we hear him saying, "God is the product of our Reason. . . . He is the Ideal of a Substance that we ourselves make." Thus, if we identify him with the Creator of the world, we should be obliged to represent him in accordance with his works. But which works? Shall we make him responsible for the disharmonies in physical nature, for the hollow insincerities of human behavior, on the principle encased in Roman adage, *Homo homini lupus?* His conclusion seems always to be this; "No: God is not a thing outside me, he is my own thought." Yet even this phrasing of the matter is ambiguous, as we shall see in a moment. But we may at least deduce from these remarks that the second and third proofs of divine independent Reality are invalid. "It is not nature in the world that leads to God, e. g., through its beautiful ordering, but reversewise." If we accept the existence of God as a fact we can proceed at once to interpret the glories of nature as evidence of his design and handiwork. But how shall we prove that God exists?

He turns again to the moral argument that God is needed to make effectual the perfect Good, a kind of *Deus ex machina* introduced to do what neither nature nor moral reason can do, namely, unite virtue and serene contentment in the human heart. But the scene is now changed; the dramatic instrument disappears; he does not call upon heaven to help; he returns to the counsel of his old mentor, Hume, who wrote: "The standard of Reason being founded on the nature of things, is eternal and inflexible,

---

[22] *Commentary to Kant's Critique of Pure Reason,* 2nd Edition, pp. 636 sq.

even by the will of the Supreme Being." [23] Kant puts the argument in a new dress: "Being which is capable of holding dominion over all rational beings, in accordance with the laws of Duty, is God." The reality of God is now a deduction from my conviction that "I must so act *as if* I stood under this awful but also at the same time salutary guidance and guaranty." The old regulative principle is again at hand. "I do not postulate the reality of God in the categorical imperative but the obedience of my reason to the law which I deem to be final and hence divine." In a further note his language is even more explicit; he refuses to commit himself to a proposition which neither "empirical concept" nor "metaphysics" will support but holds that "the categorical imperative or the command of Duty is grounded in the Idea of an *Imperantis* (commander) who is all-powerful and holds universal authority, which is strictly *formal*. This is the Idea of God." The imperative is the key to human freedom; it is also the principle by which all experience whether in science or moral conduct can be interpreted. He seems to have in mind the famous passages in the dialectic of the first *Critique,* where logic, by its laws of integration and specification, gives our mind control over the issues of physical nature and moral reason.

Nor is this all; if there is any element now appearing for the first time in his reflections, it will be found in these words: "God is not a Being outside me, but merely a thought in me. God is the morally self-legislative Reason." He goes on; "There is a Being which though distinct from me stands to me in relations of causal efficacy, and which itself free, that is, not dependent on the laws of nature in space and time, inwardly directs me (justifies or condemns) and I, as man, am myself this Being." He says still further: "God must be represented not as a Being outside me but as the highest moral principle in me" . . . "not as a special personality, *substance outside me,* but as a thought in me." What does he mean by these fugitive remarks? Does it appear that he has abandoned the concept of a transcendent reality and resorted to the idea of divine immanence? We know that he was studying anew the philosophical theorems of Spinoza, at the suggestion of his friend, Lichtenberg. Or, has he given thought to the Pietistic conceit of enjoying communion with God *through* the moral reason? Both these suggestions seem so unlike him that we turn from them as futile. There is good ground for arguing that Kant approaches the position taken by Bishop Butler of whose works he was a careful student. "Conscience," says Butler, "is the natural guide assigned us by the Author of our nature." The British thinker would never identify the two concepts, God and moral Reason, as Kant was inclined to do. But the two men are on common ground when they speak of the mainspring

---

[23] *Enquiries,* Sec. 246.

of moral action as a judgment, an assertion of reasoned thought. While Kant describes the idea of God as the "highest principle" in me, Butler esteems conscience to be the actual voice of God in the soul. Such a comparison will help to remove the charge of Immanentalism from Kant's account.

The idea of God remains, for him, a regulative formula which directs our use of the laws of moral rectitude. Furthermore, the value of the idea has been enormously increased, since it puts the divine power, if it exists at all, squarely behind the categorical imperative as the executive aspect of our will. This would appear to make unnecessary any further exegesis of the concept of divine personality. For whatever moral force we might deposit in the nature of Divinity is already at work in our own experience, both with respect to our rights as a moral legislator and to our duties as a member of the Kingdom of Ends. There is nothing in the later meditations of the author that obliges us to regard him as clothing Deity with attributes which he declined to apply in his systematic study of religion.

XI: AUGUSTE COMTE

"WE TIRE of thinking and even of acting; we never tire of loving." With these sententious words Comte begins the second of his major works on the philosophy of Positivism. His purpose is to release the social mind from dependence on the concepts of pure speculation. He feels himself destined by nature to neutralize the baleful influence of the critical theories of Immanuel Kant and his successors. He resents strongly the influence of German thought upon the moral and political posture of eminent Europeans. Yet like Kant he returned for his intellectual progenitor to David Hume, the British Empiricist. With Hume he affirms that the supreme experiences of life are imbedded in conduct, one of the governing motives of which is the desire for happiness. Hence, the test of all virtue is the utility of moral action, and the only possible rational ground for proving the existence of Deity lies in man's capacity to produce virtuous and therefore satisfactory conduct. Comte disputes in part the latter proposition but agrees that it is impossible to conceive of a true society without a balance of feeling on the side of pleasure.

But Comte who was born in 1798 was subject to intellectual conditions much nearer at hand. Some of these were negative, for example, the power of two conspicuous formulas, one in religion, the other in politics,— the scholastic elements in the church and the individualizing tendencies of the French Revolution. He rejected both of these historic attitudes. The speculative arguments of the Schoolmen clashed, he said, with the scientific requirements of modern thought. The individualism of the Revolutionary program denied the fundamental principle on which all philosophy rests, namely, the solidarity of social interests. At the same time the compactness and finesse of the Catholic organization during the Middle Ages were to him a "masterpiece of political sagacity." These cohesive tendencies were checked by the Renaissance, the Reformation, and the rise of the National state. The French upheaval, instead of giving practical demonstration of the avowed principles of Liberty and Equality and Fraternity, destroyed the basic sense of order through the exaltation of the individual. Intellect is primarily divisive; it cannot re-organize shattered habits nor can it gather dissentient minds under one rubric. No abstraction can accomplish a social redintegration, as the efforts of Rousseau proved. What is required is a scientific analysis of the facts of human behavior, and this cannot be obtained without a thorough knowledge of the various sciences involved. Comte thinks of himself as a sort of residuary legatee of the investigations of earlier scholars, though his true prototypes he takes to be Descartes and Leibniz. Not that he accepts their conclusions as binding but that their method, their mental posture, their sweep of imagination, their sense of reality agree completely with his own. J. S. Mill adopts this judgment and adds:—"They (including Comte) were all great scientific thinkers, the most consistent, and often for that reason the most absurd; because they shrank from no consequences however contrary to common sense, to which their premises seemed to lead." [1] Therefore, in determining the tenets of the new philosophy Comte is obliged to establish three propositions, first, that all religious ideas are Positive, that is, scientifically derived, secondly, that the several sciences necessarily culminate in the science of sociology which Comte himself founded, and thirdly, that sociology must interpret all its data in the light of the laws of moral behavior. When the "creed" of Positivism has been organized the modes of application will be fixed. We shall follow his order of exposition.

THE CREED OF POSITIVISM

Positivism may be defined as the "religion of humanity," the "substitution of the permanent government of humanity for the provisional government of God." [2] The word positivism has no relation to the ordinary use of the term in distinguishing *positive* religions from natural or ethnic faiths. The former refers to Christianity, the latter to Hindu religious forms. The element of supernaturalism which is essential to positive religions, is absent from Comte's list of properties. In his theory the affairs of the world, whether in politics or religion, are in the hands of men directly, not of beings constructed in the likeness of men and temporarily endowed with human attributes. The scheme of faith proposed by him is strictly natural, being traceable to the empirical tendencies of European thought for nearly three hundred years. It therefore possesses an authority that the word of a single person or the uncritical habits of a race cannot by themselves set up.

(a) His first principle is negatively stated—religion cannot be procured by any of the methods hitherto tried. That being true we must study the collective experiences of mankind and deduce the true laws of religious thinking. History, he argues, has passed through three successive periods in the course of its development. These he calls the "law of the three states." The first stage conceived of God as distinct from man yet ap-

---

[1] *August Comte and Positivism*, p. 199.   [2] *Cours de Philosophie Positive*, I, 325.

proachable by him; it is theological in cast and has evoked some of the most beautiful expressions of human feelings. The deity is hidden in the tree or the flashing rivulet and makes his power known through portents and signs. In a later series, God retains his identical forms, though he becomes specialized as tribal divinity in the Greek Pantheon or as the Jehovah of Israel. Still later, reflecting the love of synthesis, Zeus becomes the commander of the Greek gods, while Jehovah asserts his mastery over contending divinities. The second general stage is quite different. Here, personal relations are eclipsed, the anthropomorphisms of earlier systems drop away. In their stead appears an abstract and articulated system of philosophy. Synthesizing the character of Deity follows close upon the synthetic tendencies in the cultivated mind of the Greeks. Concrete conceptions of divinity give place to abstract ideas,—Unity, Cause, Vital principle, Infinity, Eternity. Philosophy, Comte holds, is not the examination of objective data by empirical methods; it is the explanation of facts by means of broad and comprehensive terms. Descartes is at fault here like his predecessors. The passage from polytheism to monotheism was achieved early in the Greek inquiry, mainly through the application of metaphysical concepts. Augustine later used the idea of natural and civil law as the basis for his treatment of divine Will. History clearly shows that Christianity was not the original source of the theory of unity of divine action. The Augustinian dogma which is central to all Christian theology, derives from the study of natural phenomena and the deduction of a common principle of action. Heraclitus was one of the earliest thinkers to adopt this view. Will as equivalent to physical law becomes also equivalent to moral authority in determining the destiny of the human race. This is the essence of Scholasticism.

But the Scholastic stage is only provisional. It cannot be permanent, because it is in essence negative, undetermining. An infinite God, an infinite universe, an immortal soul—what are these but tricks of the fancy palmed off on unsuspecting minds as the foundations of a true religion? Mind requires something positive, constructive, concrete—definitive laws, not abstract terms converted into supersensible substances. Comte, it appears, is the enemy of medieval realism whether in church or state. Political theory revels in such abstract terms as right of private judgment or equality of economic interests, but it issues in greater confusion than was manifest under the regulative government of the Roman Empire. However, we are told, men must not despair; for metaphysical abstractions often embody a "state of anarchy which intervenes between the decay of the old discipline and the formation of new spiritual ties." [3] The new ideas are embodied in the methods and results of the new physical science. Here is

[3] Edward Caird, *The Social Philosophy and Religion of Comte*, p. 14.

something positive. When Newton spoke, metaphysics at once abandoned its right to application in the field of physical law. In due time biology and psychology will reach the same end. Comte did not live long enough to see his most daring hypotheses realized in part, in Darwin, James and Wundt. But his claim for experimental determination of all values was at least the new note of progress in human thinking.

(b) If Science is the last word of authority, why was the world so late in deducing it? His answer is that all knowledge must be systematized with reference to the welfare of mankind. This is the principle with which we began our exposition of his creed. History shows that the order of the development of the sciences is based on logical rules derived from a study of basic human needs. It begins with the simplest, mathematics, whose "truths are true for all things." Thus, arithmetic deals with numbers and geometry with number plus the idea of extension. These studies are highly abstract; we must now bring them in contact with reality. They must be applied first to motion, whose science is called "rational mechanics." No student can understand the meaning of motion without the two primary facts just adduced. At the same time the principle of motion is required for the understanding of the laws of the three dimensions. From this science follow at once astronomy and physics, the theory of gravity and the principle of molecular action. Then, in the process of logical intension, chemistry or the analysis of small substances follows immediately, being directly attached to physics by the nature of the electric current. Furthermore, chemistry must be regarded as one of the most valuable of the sciences, because it satisfies in so many particulars the developing needs of human life. Its expansion may be made the test of human progress. We wonder what remarks Comte would have been inclined to make, could he have seen the uses of this science during the First World War and its successor? The point he insists upon is that scientific research is a matter of the heart not of the head. The mistake of earlier thinkers lies here:— they considered mathematics and physics to be the implements of logic instead of being instruments for the attainment of moral betterment. Experiment is the one criterion of value, and experiment cannot be pursued without regard to the fundamental principles of human behavior. Specifically, at this stage in his discussion, experiment must deal with the phenomena of life. Here, in a most emphatic degree, we adopt the scientific principle of synthesis. Synthesis is always subjective, that is, it expresses the powers of body and functions of mind as united in one personality. Descartes did not understand this mode of thinking; for he separates the body of man completely from its conscious behavior, forgetting that a greater than body was here, namely, the essence of humanity itself; forgetting also that man is associated organically with his animal neighbors, especially with those that have the instinct of procreation and maternity.

We are therefore called upon to recognize a new type of science,—biology, with its subordinate type, psychology. The passage to this science is through the study of organic chemistry, and its purpose is to examine the sources and functions of life, especially the power of life to adapt itself to its physical environment through the processes of instinct and intelligence. Life, for man, is thus a union of brain and consciousness. What appears to be peculiarly true is that behavior is the expression of feeling which has its roots in three physiological properties, the nutritive, the sexual and the maternal. Now, for the first time, the extreme importance of the female principle comes into view, and Comte seizes upon it as the foundation of all the primary laws of human action. It is obvious, however, that the analysis of individual organisms is not enough; they must be studied in their natural and environmental relationships. In fact, this is already demanded by the classification of instincts just mentioned. What is then needed is an additional science which shall collate and appraise the great mass of social phenomena open to every studious mind, a science which holds the individual man to be an abstraction and seeks to know the meaning of the facts of social intercourse. Can we determine certain fixed and regular laws which are, "empirically generalized from history," as Mill says, "and affiliated to the known laws of human nature"? [4] It is true that students of history have for centuries deduced certain provisional principles of action from the movements of races and nations; but, to quote Mill again, "We know not any thinker who, before M. Comte, had penetrated to the philosophy of the matter, and placed the necessity of historical studies as the foundation of sociological speculation, on the true footing." Still it must be with great care that we arrive at just and tenable conclusions. To call the individual an "abstraction" while the human race is itself a stern reality, is to confuse the meaning of terms. The sole object of experiment is the individual; even when reforms are attempted on a large scale and over an extended area, change can be wrought only through the reactions of individual persons.

The study of mass exertions is at bottom a study of individual exertions within the mass. This is admitted by Comte in his recommendations to study the contributions of eminent men in the development of social character. It requires no demonstration to prove that one generation furnishes the ground of the emotional moods of the next. He divides his analysis into two parts, Static and Dynamic; (1) conditions as they exist within a given period of time, e. g., the family, the state, the religious community, the industrial structure, and (2) conditions which develop as men pass

[4] *Op. cit.,* p. 86.

from one social level to another. Comte argues for a form of progress which involves a "social advance towards a definite though never attained destination, by a series of necessarily determined stages." [5] Nothing could be vaguer than this statement, unless it be Spencer's definition of biological evolution. It assumes that an end is foreshadowed in the mind, though the nature of the end is not stated; it affirms that the steps to be taken in reaching it are fixed, though he never cites any principles more definite than liberty, fraternity and order,—the last term being introduced by the Positive philosophy. To be sure, he exhibits an essential sign of advance in his emphasis on the word "Altruism,"—*vivre pour autrui,* and this sign becomes the slogan of the new religion. It seems to have borrowed its meaning from the ethics of Christianity, where "love one another," was the earlier and insistent command; but Comte has metamorphized its content. If the individual as such has no place in the scientific analysis of social facts, it can have no place in man's moral behavior. "Personal calculation," to use his phrases, must be eliminated. The only attention to personal demands should be given to those that contribute to the health of body and mind. The one requisite in the Positive religion was to establish unity of sentiment and action. This can be attained alone through the systematizing of social relations by means of the disciplined behavior of the individual. But such a unity he acknowledged to be impossible "in an existence so complicated as ours"; yet "our happiness and our merit consist especially in approaching as near as possible" to it; and such approach constitutes the true index of "personal and social improvement." [6] In short, the test of virtue and piety lies in our attitude to the demands of Society as the true object of devotion.

(c) We therefore turn to a study of the new object of spiritual worship. It is a recognized fact that men everywhere seek for an object of reverent regard. The historic types of deity Comte has already examined and rejected; they are all fictitious creations of the mind; they are relative, not absolute, as God must be. Even the effort to make the physical universe the object of devotion has proven abortive. The development of the sciences has shown clearly that physics and chemistry can have no value except as interpreters of the nature of man. Hence, the world of matter provides no means for determining religious certitude or moral satisfaction. Where then can the absolute be found? Nowhere, if not in humanity itself. This is Comte's greatest discovery and this is the sure foundation of his religious philosophy. Not only do all sciences inevitably lead up to sociology as their crown and consummation; but a study of their facts, today, show that they must all contribute eventually to human progress; otherwise, they have no meaning. Humanity becomes for him *le grand Être* (the

[5] Levy-Bruehl, *La Philosophie de Auguste Comte,* p. 261.   [6] Mill, *op. cit.,* p. 140.

"Great Being"). Let us not forget that he excludes the individual man, with his defects and actual sins, from consideration. Let us remember, too, that humanity as a present phenomenon is excluded from the synthesis; it does not possess a perfect Form presented for adoration, as certain religions like Christianity have done. Humanity is still in its minority; it must make a long, persistent attempt to realize the subtle ideals which have ever hung before its mental perception. The love of justice, which has inspired noble souls and which poetry, the handmaid of religion, has adorned with the habiliments of divine beauty, is as yet unattained, save in the sacrificial devotion of certain human saints. Individual piety yearns for such attainment and has thus created the dogma of immortality for the enforcement of its hopes. But immortality is not personal, it is social; science is a form of it, since the sentiments and studies and deeds of uncounted generations live again in the latest discovery of genius. Public morality is also one of its forms, the heroic exploits of earlier masters being written boldly upon the actions of the current age. But Positive Religion cannot countenance private persistence; spiritual synthesis is never objective, as in the unlimited continuance of the individual; it is subjective, as in the dominance of great ideas and the development of great projects. "To live with the dead," writes Comte, "is one of our most precious privileges." [7] Death is therefore not an emancipation from pain, it is a positive reward for successful endurance. Hence, the man who approximates most closely to the developed ideals of the community will, in life, be most closely identified with its inner spirit; and in death, most certain to continue his existence in the growing moral sensitiveness of the universal social consciousness. This is the creed of Positivism.

THE PRACTICE OF POSITIVISM

It is generally admitted that a profound change in Comte's point of view took place between the dates of the writing of the two major works, the *Cours* and the *Système*. It is said to be due in large measure to his infatuation for a woman of noteworthy intelligence and thoroughly respectable character. After a year of spiritual acquaintanceship she died, and from that time on Positivism as taught by Comte changed its centre of gravity. For one thing the psychology which he had consistently advocated was deepened; feelings assumed even a higher place in the conduct of life; love took its position at the head of all human endeavors, and scientific deductions must rest their case upon its requirements. It is impossible to change the complexion of the "Great Being" but the feminal factors become inexpressibly more important. Both in sociology proper and in the religious forms which it assumes, maternal love is a relation of in-

---

[7] Levy-Bruehl, *op. cit.*, p. 341.

calculable value, as we shall see later. Thus, in the subjective synthesis, as Comte called it, and in its objective expression which is the structural aspect of society, the influence of women makes a notable contribution to the new system of Positivism. Perhaps more decisively is the influence felt in the application of the religious formulas to external practice. We shall consider two phases of the problem.

(a) It is an accepted rule in the study of religion that creedal statement, whether elaborate or meagre, is invariably followed by an organized system of rites and ceremonies called the *Cultus*. So long as religious ideas remain in their speculative stage we deal only with a philosophy, not with a true type of religion. This has been recognized by scientific experimenters who have as their own purpose the explanation of the spiritual feelings in terms of physical laws, as for instance, Ernst Haeckel, in the *Riddle of the Universe,* 1901. Comte was no exception. In fact, with his insistence upon feeling as the indispensable guide to religion, he could do nought else than provide his worshipers with an objective embodiment of sentiment suited to the moral altruism which he defined as the normal social duty of the citizen. Assuming that humanity *in the large* is the object of veneration, human emotion will not be satisfied without adequate channels for its utterance. Positivism, in its supplemental form, required two different sets of offices, the one private, namely, prayer, the other public, namely, symbolic rituals. It may appear strange that prayer should be found among the duties of the Positive faith; but as Mill shows, prayer does not mean "asking" for benefits but the "outpouring of feeling" quite in accord with the spontaneous emission of emotion on any extraordinary occasion; or, for the matter of that, on any occasion when devotion claims the right to seek expression, as in the adoration of mother or wife. Since religion now takes on the color of attachment to the nature and memory of womanhood—with the subtle reminiscence of Catholicism's exaltation of the Virgin and female saints—we may dutifully regard mother, wife, sweetheart, all noble-minded women in the social group, as *les vrais anges guardiens,*—our guardian angels which exact from us the threefold social sentiments of veneration, attachment and kindness. All this will be elicited from the Positivist worship in the privacy of the chapel or the home.

But the *Cultus* is also public, as the Christian Church for ages had ordained. It consisted of eighty-four celebrations throughout the year, with the glorification of humanity as the one scientific object of human homage; of the several relations in which we stand to our fellowmen; of the slow but growing triumphs of the social mind, and of the four social classes into which a community necessarily divides. Chiefest among the ceremonies are the nine sacraments which commemorate the several critical points in the progress of the social saint: birth, education, marriage, the choice of profession, success, retirement, death or transformation. Celebration of his memory by the social group seven years after decease is a form of collective adoration which may make amends, *in prospectu,* for the loss of the hope of personal immortality. All these forms are prescribed with the utmost minuteness; their intrinsic worth is defined as exemplifying the synthetic unity of society, their practical value to the individual, as the means of coördinating his usual habits and interpreting them in the light of the fundamental needs of humanity. No method must be omitted which will help individual men to know and appreciate their place in the totality of being. Realizing the importance of constant repetition Comte suggests certain formulas as constant *paternosters,*—love as principle, order as ground, and progress as moral end,—three elements which represent the constitutional sentiments of behavior.

(b) But Positivism goes further than this in its desire to systematize the experiences of mankind. It affirms that the social stratification is fixed by nature, not a caste system like the Hindu but wellnigh like the Platonic grouping, with one extraordinary addition, namely woman. There are four divisions in humanity, women, the clergy, the patriciate, and the proletariat. All influences in a *Sociocracy* go back to the love and ministry of women. This being true, the sacredness of the marriage function must be rigorously observed. There can be no divorce, save on one condition,— "when one of the parties has been sentenced to an infamizing punishment, involving loss of civil rights." Comte felt the injustice of this disability, since it happened to be the condition under which his inamorata, Clotilde de Vaux, had to live. Second marriages are not permitted; hence, on the death of one party, the other must take the vow of eternal widowhood. Not only are the chastity of woman and the true succession of physical inheritance thus guaranteed but the solidarity of the race is defended, and the parallel relations of its two independent units, man and woman, fully safeguarded. The sacerdotal class is also carefully delimited. Like women they are to be supported by others, in this case by the State. They are to receive no perquisites, no *stipendia,* for their services; they are to engage in no remunerative occupations, since these would turn their minds from the theoretical part of their labors. Their office is to train the youth in the principles of the Positive science; to minister to the community in the arts of healing; to settle disputes between groups, and if advice fails, to issue writs of excommunication. Hence, the authority of the priests consists in carrying with it the sympathy and aggregated force of the social *masses.* This group, the proletariat, is the last in the series; its members possess no political right, live only by the daily wage, have no education or social prestige, but when summoned by the sacerdotal class will make their force felt in deciding public questions. The third class, the patriciate, is divided into three sub-classes, those who produce, those who transport and those who transform, that is, the manufacturing or industrial section. By virtue of their intellectual vigor and breadth of view, this group tends to associate itself with the learned class, the clergy, and perhaps to attempt to control it and, through it, the proletariat. But the key to the social system lies in the family, in accordance with traditional French philosophy.

Comte does not pretend that the "systematization" thus depicted is the final social state. He does argue that the Great Being has a providential force not unlike the Providence of the Christian Church; but its governing instrument is not faith but knowledge. In his *Picture of the Final Transition* he asserts that men must be governed by the lessons of the past in their contemplation of the future. He seems to have confidence in the wisdom and skill of the scientific class, and expects them to organize a *regime* which shall be as free from the abstractions of metaphysics as from the manoeuvres of the civil politician. Hence, church officialism and legislative assembly are, to him, the survivals of an unenlightened age and must be abolished. In short, the subjective synthesis will be transmuted into an objective synthesis where law both static and dynamic shall exercise its authority over every element in the great society.

CRITICAL COMMENTS

The Definition of Religion

We have now given an abstract of the Positivist conception of religion as fashioned by the hand of its founder. It met in its time an extended and enthusiastic reception. By virtue of its practical implications it caught the fancy of a large group of subtle thinkers in England, among them J. S. Mill, Frederic Harrison, Richard Congreve, Dr. J. H. Bridges and finally Harriet Martineau who translated in condensed form the *Philosophie Positive*. These were prepared for its teachings, because, first, it enabled them to substitute for the formalized idea of religious belief in vogue in British churches an imaginative type of thought which made devotion a matter of solid practice and not a mere sequence of unmeaning words; and because, secondly, it imparted new and living zest to the social formulas which had stirred the interest of cultivated thinkers ever since the days of the industrial revolution. Humanitarian creeds were composed and humanitarian forms of worship set up, both evincing the same fervor that flashed from the words of the original teacher. So deep was the impression on public sentiment that a generation later, in 1889, when a group of distinguished scholars published a series of studies entitled *Lux Mundi,* one of the most penetrating writers could still raise the issue, whether Positivism might be rightly classed as a system of "dogmatic atheism," perpetuating the sting of a bitter controversy which had shaken the church from its smug complacence on all social questions.

But the principal matter at stake was more fundamental; it concerned the definition of religion itself. Mr. Aubrey Moore contended that the "crisis of the present day is a very real one, and that the religious view of God is feeling the change which is modifying our views of the world and man." [8] Biology and sociology had conspired to introduce serious objections to current theological opinion. Darwin proved that the human species was not a spontaneously generated type of animal life but was the end of, or at least a stage in, the continuous evolution of organic bodies. Furthermore, scientific inquiry had shattered the ancient myth of the superior excellence of one stratum in the population; it had endowed the proletariat with capacities and potential rights equal in every respect to those claimed by men who had exercised rule either by political might or intellectual craft. Divinity does not hedge a king; men everywhere possess thoughts and feelings in common, and require only time and discipline to work out their own private and public salvation. Religion, therefore, said Mr. Moore, had to face a new set of social facts; or, to put it bluntly, religion had to meet, under confused conditions, the perennial query— Is the God of religion the same as the God of science and philosophy? "Ideally," he continues, "every one will allow that the religious idea of God and the scientific and philosophical idea of God must be identical; but in actual fact it is not so, and in the earlier stages of the development of both, there is real antagonism." [9] But the author is not willing to agree to a dichotomy as extreme as this. He presents two ways by which it may be avoided; we may either divide the territory between the two segments of thought, faith for one, reason for the other; or by attenuating the definition we may provide a set of basic terms so wide and comprehensive that the event can be but the same, namely, a *compromise* that does not satisfy either party to the controversy.

There is, however, in his argument a suggestion which we cannot disregard. Two different approaches to the subject have been made in the history of thought; Comte distinguishes them and applies appropriate attributes but ultimately rejects both. The first approach is through the isolation of an Object of religious worth ordinarily called God. The Object is first feared, then submitted to, later reverenced and finally loved.

[8] *Lux Mundi* (edited by Charles Gore, 10th Edition, New York: Thomas Whittaker, 1889), p. 49.

[9] *Ibid.,* p. 49.

Fetichism is the elementary form, the objects being totems which enshrine the early instinctive reactions and usually take the shape of visible things in the natural world. In due time, with the assertion of bodily might on the part of a tribal chieftain or successful enemy, the human being himself becomes the object of fear or respect and at length of worship. Or, when the powerful lord has passed to his reward, his memory creates a new type of veneration and pieces of wood or stone are converted into representations of his continuing majesty. Even a group so advanced in the arts of civilized behavior as the Roman public accepts without demurring the deification of its emperors as a principle of statecraft if not of personal adoration. Egypt did not erect its temples and pyramids in vain. In the meantime far beyond the Mesopotamian valley similar evolutions had taken place. Confucius, a profound practical philosopher, undergoes slowly in his own day in the minds of his disciples, a metamorphosis of great moment; he is no longer a teacher, he is a supernal guide; not, to be sure, converted wholly as was Buddha into a reigning diety, but accepted now as the infallible sage whose *Analects* embody the imperial wisdom of the ages. Today, the unmatured mind of Japan bows in reverence before the symbol of Divinity in the person of the Emperor; and who can say that the once self-constituted Teuton "Leader" may not, before many years have passed, turn into a simulated future Jehovah of Hosts, more glamorous than any majesty ever heretofore witnessed by Teutonic eyes? The culmination is reached by the Palestinian spirit under whose direction the object of worship is withdrawn from the perceptive touch completely and lodged in the invisible heavens. Time and space cannot fasten their limitations upon Him. "It is here," says Mr. Moore, "that we reach the point at which we are able to distinguish between the religious and the philosophical ideas of God." [10] "Religion demands a personal object, be the object one or many. It is committed to the belief in a moral relationship between God and man." It is here, too, he is obliged to concede, that philosophy diverges from the religious creed. Philosophy tends to view the religious conception as only an exaggerated form of anthropomorphism. No, says Mr. Moore in effect; we do not propose to anthropomorphize God, but to "theomorphize" man.[11] How this can be done while still maintaining the conceit that God is necesarily a person, hence, moral, the author does not succeed in proving. It should be remembered that to ascribe moral properties to Deity is quite a different proposition from that which holds that belief in God is a sure guaranty against undue submission to moral obliquity. Hume has some justification in his contention that a people without a religion is "but a few degrees removed from brutes." [12] That moral values are espoused by man

10 *Ibid.*, p. 52.   11 *Ibid.*, p. 53.   12 *Ibid.*, p. 54.

does not mean that they have been drawn point for point from the Deity whom men worship. Emulation is not imitation; it is the recognition of sheer goodness in the object chosen by men for their veneration and devoted love.

The second approach to religion is through the medium of first principles; that is, it is analytical. It is just the opposite of the one we have examined, which is strictly synthetical. Synthesis is best expressed in the aesthetic process, especially in the realm of art. All works of beauty have a unity embodied in diversity, as Plato first argued. The drama is directed by a strong and specific *motif* whose dominant terms curb every tangential movement and reduce it to the essential meaning of the Whole. Aeschylus in his *Prometheus Bound* takes the thesis of man's resistance to a divine power which, do what he will, utter what thoughts he may, struggle however violently in the very moment of crisis, as he does, cannot be disowned as his eventual master. Religion as the supreme enouncement of art, registers the same organizing *motif*:—God, the object of reverence, whatever *His* nature, coerces man at length into unqualified submission. The philosophical manner is other than this; it does not depend on subjective adherence but on objective inference. The first principle is that of unity, and it must furnish the leading thought in our entire behavior. The universe for us is a single unit, and the laws that govern there have no exceptions. Hence, the dogma of providence disappears from view. The conduct of man is a single unit, as Aristotle shows; it is in reality a part of physics; not that it is ruled by a drastic and inflexible mechanism, as nature seems to be; but it is itself a unity; the soul, Aristotle argues, is the form of the body, the consummatory idea by which the behavior of human life is expressed. These are the two elements in the metaphysics of experience,—a unitary world and a unitary behavior. Religion can begin its study at no other point.

But religion does not stop there. If there is a unifying law, there are necessarily things which can be unified. Hence, we are obliged to study the relation of things to one another. Historically Pythagoras was the great innovator in the field. He discovered the principle of unity as required for the interpretation of the relation of bodies to one another. Every individual thus became the numerical focus of reality; the cube representing the earth was the sign of solidity, the square the sign of perfect balance, equilibrium in physical things, justice in the deliberations of society. In due time the laws of logic are called into being; for religion, in this theory, is a matter of strict analysis, the determination of exact logical relations. Hence, all the experiences with which men deal must have a specific connection with the principle immediately above them. In this way the world of nature becomes to us a thoroughly organized system, each part in its place, each part performing its duty to the whole. In the same manner what is true of the physical universe will be true also of the universe of social conduct. Unity is the supreme rule.

The next fact is equally important: there is no limit to the world of sense or thought. Space is infinite, time is without end, experience never ceases. Comte remarks that the "noble synthetic aspirations of the mathematicians and astromoners prompted their zeal for analysis," and "metaphysical speculation was detached from scientific investigations which alone sustained it." [13] "It was thus reduced to inherent hollowness and was destitute of all its theoretic coherence." This was, in part, the conclusion of Kant in the *Dialectic*. He saw, for example, that the existence of the human soul cannot be determined by an analysis which depends strictly on sensory perception. We should have nothing but a series of impressions which may be interpreted by the laws of thought but could never be referred openly to a discerned ego. The best we can do is to treat the idea of soul *as if* we have proven its metaphysical existence, and to use the principle of self-consciousness as the instrument for uniting ideas in a logical series. Again, we must treat experiences in the external world in the same manner. These experiences are necessarily without known limit; they are neither finite nor infinite; hence we can never survey the complete magnitude of the world nor pursue our division of a body to its last infinitesimal segment. We must act and think *as if* we had found a universe of infinite reach and divisibility. The rule of causality is a true logical instrument, even though we can do nothing more than trace a necessary connection between two conjoined images regularly repeated. The conjunction in the sense-organ is causal. But when the conceptual judgments are once formed, their contents become our own, and we are at liberty to rearrange the ideas to suit our fancy. This is human freedom, not extended indefinitely, yet going far beyond what the animal mind can produce. Lastly, we cannot prove God to be an existing and rational Being with whom we may have intimate communion. The proofs for his existence are sure to end in a disappointing fallacy; but we have the inveterate and vital idea of God, and we think we can apply it at once to the objective thing. The attempt is vain; still, we cannot rid our mind of the supervisory concept; it means the unity of thought, the essence of reverence, a powerful support to our moral independence.[14]

These are the two approaches to religion; they have their own intrinsic values; they have elicited the suffrage of eminent minds and saintly devotees. Comte rejects them both as partial in content. He rejects the first because human intelligence has no devices by which it can enter into

[13] *Positive Polity*, IV, p. 264.
[14] *Critique of Pure Reason*. Trans. by N. K. Smith, pp. 532–49.

communion with a universal Mind or Will. He rejects it also because he
sees in the common practice of its worshipers a strong tendency to change
the meaning of the object of adoration and ultimately to debase its character. Such deteriorations are evident in the elaborate institutional customs
of the Christian Church. The feudal forms of Catholicism show plainly
how egoistic sentiments have forced wrong and even degrading habits of
behavior upon the adherents of the church. Dishonesty in the fabrication
of official miracles becomes a deliberate stain on the system of morality. The
worship of saints was a challenge to the meaning of Deity. The celibacy of
the clergy was a wanton misinterpretation of one of the most sacred
offices of human nature. The usurpation of the functions of the individual
believer by a supposed vicar of Christ on earth, drove men to an acceptance
of modes of belief which corresponded in no respect either to the canonical
tradition or the demands of the moral conscience. Again, Comte rejected
the second approach because in that way, the mind was divested of its
right to determine for itself matters of the greatest concern to the individual and the social group. Vague and general conceptions rarely lead
to the understanding of concrete situations; men embrace them at times
to escape the sense of utter frustration in face of moral defeat or intellectual indecision. Dogma, however, can never take the place of solid
thought and critical analysis: the one induces spiritual complacence, the
other a stern and often unsuccessful struggle for the apprehension of
truth and duty.

Grand Être as Comtist Deity

Instead of these stereotyped approaches Comte suggests that we adopt
the whole of humanity as our Grand Être, the sole object of reverence.
Religion must in every instance recognize and cultivate the two dominant
qualities of the human mind, namely, the intellectual and the moral. If
we subscribe to the historic approaches separately we shall worship a
truncated Deity. Humanity, on the other hand, presents a complete and
diversified object for consideration. When carefully analyzed it makes a
just demand on the logical powers of the mind, since it stands for the
promotion of order both in (1) the management of thought and (2) the
determination of conduct. (1) The first of these is focussed upon the study
of the five objective sciences, as already noted; indeed, science as an independent pursuit is for the first time in the history of society made a
mandatory part of the curriculum of religious discipline. But it is a mistake to suppose that the physical sciences alone can discover the laws of
the world. By the end of the 18th century biological studies had assumed
the right to interpret certain specific areas of physical phenomena. Not
long afterwards biology was supplemented by the researches of a new

science, sociology, which imposed a different kind of emphasis upon the relations of men to the physical universe and the movements of society. (2) Again, the new type of religion organizes the contents of the second human quality, the impulses and habits of the moral life, especially those tendencies that may be termed "altruistic," the interest in and labor for the good of other men. Many religious creeds mention only the egoistic sentiments; salvation is regarded as a private achievement; spiritual behavior is always a struggle against dangerous and even inimical competitors. Such an attitude is false; it flatly contradicts the essence of religious intention. Man is, by nature, a moral being; Comte rivals even Bishop Butler in his insistence on this point. The true estimate of man's character can be made only in the light of his judgments of his fellows. It would seem, then, that it is right and proper to find in humanity the ideal object of religious veneration as well as the sure guaranty of moral growth. Intellect and morals are united in a common task, which is the exposition of the meaning of humanity and the instilling of obedience to her laws.

The assumption of Comte is unambiguous: there is but one object worthy of religious devotion. The object is real; it is not an hallucination of the fancy nor a logical illusion nor a chance substitute for the old faiths now discredited. Humanity is, for him, a single substantial whole; it is not a collection of imaginary units which the mind, by some quirk of subliminal synthesis, has reduced to a sensible object, as in many of the outworn religions. The French Revolution is a landmark in spiritual evolution; it destroyed the creeds to which uncritical affection had clung for generations; it aimed to place reason on the throne of truth, but it failed to define its terms succinctly and reason fell. Positivism arose to finish the work thus courageously begun. Through many long and busy years Comte developed his thesis and won a considerable number of consenting minds to his standard. But he never really convinced even his most tenacious supporters that he had laid a thoroughly logical foundation for the new faith. The crucial question is, Did he prove conclusively that humanity was vested with the powers of divinity? We shall examine his thesis in the manner followed by Kant, when he overthrew the classical arguments for the existence of God.

In the first place we shall show that the ontological form of the argument is forced to meet the same objections as the other types of religious thought, and that it cannot answer them. The Comtean theory assumes that we have the idea of a complete and total human existence, and that we may at once translate this idea into an equivalent objective substance. The concept includes the properties associated with the career of a civilized race, not merely adult values but images and actions found also in the behavior of children. Comte wrote before the hypothesis of evolution had been proposed; Goethe guessed at some of its possibilities but Darwin and Wallace unfolded its scientific terms. However, humanity, for Comte, is the matured race, not a series of embryos and their promised actualities. It certainly is not a race composed of cultured minds on the one side and on the other, anthropological specimens of stunted or retarded growth. It contains children as we said, for they are essentially "prepotentiated adults"; children are the fecund source of social greatness, and their suitable education is the proper business of the state. In its specific form the humanity which it is proposed to erect into a divinity is a replica of the French nation, with a proud history of many centuries, a long array of great names in statecraft, public service, art and literature, science and philosophy, together with a tradition which confronts the onslaught of political revolution or the criticism of current opinion by men of masterful intelligence, without losing one iota of its essential nobility. Thus, instead of elevating a single person to the position of supreme venerability, as in the case of Christianity, he lifts the race itself to the level, clothing it with the attributes of power and wisdom and "concreting" it into a solitary unit before which the individual citizen bows in reverent awe. This is the nature of the new religion which we are urged to accept as a reality.

We shall centre our criticism on the principle of Unity. Is it true that the human species can be regarded as the complete individual, a Concrete Universal, in the Hegelian sense? Is it true that its powers and properties are such that they are capable of being appraised together at a single and given moment, in the manner in which a particular event in the physical world is taken out of the stream of time and looked upon as a specific whole? The proposition has been stated by Comte in these words:—"The Great Being is composed of all peoples, dead, living or still unborn, who constitute together a *whole,* continuous, unbroken, persistent whole, of beings who converge." [15] He begins his survey with the family, the necessary social unit for him as for most sociologists in the French tradition. The family is indivisible, it is subject to growth, it depends on physical organization, it uses the laws of causality in its adjustments to environment; its instinctive traits, when properly understood, give balance to its behavior and authority to its judgments. The Gallic family is thoroughly coördinated under the control of the father; it is limited in its membership and has a strong attachment to the soil. The family is for Comte the symbol of the larger group, ultimately the state itself. In the latter case, however, new and dissident factors emerge. There is a collision of wills between families, clans and "estates," each fighting to retain

[15] *Op. cit.,* I, 27 sq.

its rights, its physical properties, its political influence. There is, also, a huge mass of separate persons to be absorbed into the hypothetical group, requiring the reconciliation of the conflicting interests of many centuries. Finally, there is the stabilitization of purpose and design in an integrated society which is required to make a thoroughly organized state. All these original types of mind must be united in a common personality to which as the object of supreme worth our formal obeisance must be made.

We reject the assertion that the state is a solid directive will. German Idealism, as a philosophical system, has played dexterously upon this theme. Bosanquet,[16] the English thinker, has taken his cue from the Hegelian tradition, arguing that the state is the objective spirit, the quintessential expression of human reason. The state, he holds, is the embodiment of the ethical ideal; it symbolizes the forms of art in music, painting and sculpture, and the achievements of science in physics, biology and sociology. The particular acts of political genius spring from the intelligence of the great community; hence the individuated man has no volitions of his own but must submit wholly to the decisions of his government. The single man is an abstraction, a sheer phantom, the total state alone is real. The doctrine is peculiarly Teutonic although it has had its repercussions in Anglo-Saxon lands. In America, for example, the Supreme Court has recognized the "personality" of the financial corporation and admitted it to certain rights under the *due process* provision of the Constitution, even though private rights of individuals are thereby contravened. But in general, in the nations holding the British theory of government the citizen is the primary concern of law, the state is secondary. Hobhouse [17] defines the theory clearly:—Individuals created the state by surrendering certain natural modes of action; they reserved to themselves the rights of free thought, individual decision, the privileges of unhindered association, all of which can in no way be curtailed or diverted or annulled except for the common good of the whole community. If the honor or life of the state is placed in jeopardy through external threats or internal rebellion then individual behavior may be restrained in accordance with definite precepts. The unmistakable rule is that the state exists for the citizens, not the citizens for the state. And the reason is plain: the state is the instrument for the making of human character; its values are not intrinsic but contributory; there is no property in the nature of the human being that makes it necessary for him to exist in any particular form of communal

---

[16] B. Bosenquet, *The Philosophical Theory of the State* (London: Macmillan, 1899), Chap. I sq.

[17] L. T. Hobhouse, *The Metaphysical Theory of the State* (New York: Macmillan, 1918), Chap. I.

organization. It is a well-known fact, as Spinoza points out, that true freedom can only be developed under the rubric of law; man may otherwise have license, but he will not have liberty. Gregariousness is an instinctive impulse not a reflective act; it serves to promote the ordinary animal purposes, for instance, protection from cold and enemies. The moment man begins to reason about his needs, he is ready to seek out the means for their fulfillment.

The Teutonic creed is a deduction from the gregarious habits of man; the creed of the Anglo-Saxon is the deliberate assertion of men's right to determine their destiny by free election of mind. For the one the sovereignty of the state is the result of a continued domination of a superior clan; it finds its justification in the theory that "might makes right," a dogma based on the competitive tendencies of the race not on the sentiment of honor and fair dealing which critical thought has woven into the fabric of human motives. For the other, the state has no right to existence if it cannot guarantee the fundamental desires for intellectual development, especially if it cannot organize the ideals of moral character into a system of laws which express not only the simple duties for the preservation of life and limb and property but also the loftier ambitions for purity of thought and correctness of motive. To this should be added the impressive fact that unity built upon the supremacy of military prowess is extremely tenuous; it may abide for a decade or a generation or even longer; it cannot possibly survive the penetrating criticism of a logically trained opposition. Tyrannies raised on conquest or propaganda may be shattered in a night; while governments founded on the rights of the individual seem to endure the crucial shock of international stress, and come out of the conflict stronger in the loyalty of their adherents and finer in their moral determinations.

From the argument which we have just completed we cannot draw the conclusion that the nation is a thoroughly unified group of human beings. Now the nation is the largest associated unit of classified people known to history; if it cannot be regarded as an organic, self-acting community, it is well-nigh hopeless to carry the analogy to the aggregate of humanity and think of it as a concrete individual, with established traits of character and modes of action. To be sure, in these later days we might ask whether the union of national bodies in a League of Nations may or may not represent the form of agreement under which humanity itself should be organized. Still, we are here confronted with the sinister fact that at least one huge corporate state deliberately abstained from joining the League at its inception and steadily declined all advances to participate in any of its official transactions. Furthermore, the later history of the League has reflected the particularistic tendencies afoot in the world; impressing upon the observer the deduction that ideological conflicts invariably interfere with the safe conduct of its normal business. The emergence of a new crisis in human history will alter such an opinion. When ideas which have some persuasive power in them can split in two a union which rational decision had effected, may we expect that sheer instincts embodied in the Caucasian and the Bulu minds or temperaments so different as the dreamy wistfulness of the Slav and the mechanically imitative intelligence of the German, can unite in a common program for the common good? But there is no total unity of mind, and if there be no unity there can be no collective object which men may accept as the basis of submission and worship.

Hence, even if the genius of Comte creates such an appealing reality, it remains but a poetic conceit, it is not a sturdy concept which can be turned into verified fact, amid the stern and brutal realism of common experience. The best Comte could do would be to fashion a series of heroic figures, as the British Positivists actually did; or emulating the Greeks he might erect a pantheon of human virtues, crystallizing each in a symbolic form so beautiful, so convincing that Plato refused to destroy the people's religion, while he pitched his own hopes on an esoteric Good both scientific and aesthetic, which when needed might be translated into an abstract Deity.[18] Thus every phase of the ontological argument runs back to the same stubborn centre, namely, that we have an idea, a mere idea, which always reports *what a God should be* but never allows us to conclude that he necessarily and finally *exists*.

The first of the classical proofs, the ontological, is abortive here; it has no more significance in dealing with Comte's problem than with Anselm's or Descartes'. The cosmological and teleological arguments may be treated in the same manner, and with the same results. We shall pass by this critique and fix our attention on the final proof which in the present system offers greater promise of success. Does the moral sense conceded by Comte to dominate in every segment of human society, lend eminent justification to the claim that humanity is *le grand Être,* the single object of worship for the human spirit?

Nothing is so characteristic of the racial tradition to which we belong as its emphasis on the moral judgment. If then a religion is to be derived from the structure of the human personality it must have as one of its intrinsic purposes the attainment of moral virtue. The Deity itself must possess the power to develop a moral character. Comte appears not to conceive of his *Grand Être* as a finished product; rather he thinks of Being as a continuous process. His attempt to be exact in statement leads him to formulate the principle in the phrase, *Vivre pour autrui* (live for

---

[18] *Supra,* Chap. II.

others). If this phrase were construed in a political sense we should obtain again the Hegelian thesis—a governing political Mind whose every decree we are obliged to accept as ultimate and irresistible. This theory we have rejected; but Comte is thinking of the human race as, so to say, a *domestic unity*. In this opinion he was confirmed after the death of his friend, Mme. Clothilde de Vaux. The virtues of society are to be expounded by the priestly hierarchy, but their practical values are to be communicated by the women members of the household. Reflection shows that the sentiment of altruism is, to all intents and purposes, an ideal, a vibrant hope that one day the sympathetic instincts will resolve themselves into the powerful motives of social experience. Comte is a believer in progress, as he frequently tells us; and progress is an inseparable property of the religious life, and presumably a necessary quality of Deity. Humanity, in fact, is an unfolding process; it follows well-defined laws. The nature of the physical environment, the vital forces at work in each group, such as the intermingling of racial strains in marriage, the reactions of one community upon another in trade, in the exchange of ideas, in the production of the arts with their influence on body and soul, and finally, the genius of individuals, including the emergence of distinguished minds which exercise a magnetic effect on man of inferior or less matured intelligence, —these are factors that cause the curve of progress to veer towards new and untried forms of action. The habits and customs of the social order bear the imprint of the revised ideas. As time goes on and as the interchange of thought becomes more complex, the elementary inductions grow more acute, emotions more subtle, moral character more deliberate in tone. At long last, egoistic pretensions are abandoned and altruism establishes itself as the sole guide to endeavor. "The natural course of human relations would dispose us to cultivate the only instincts which admit of a perfectly universal and almost boundless expansion." [19]

The argument, however, means nothing if we do not understand the nature of his Deity. Is the *Grand Être* a being substantial, real, endowed with unqualified existence, such as the Christian Church insists upon adoring? Or is his Deity in a state of evolution, passing through partial stages of growth, precisely as he expects the human race itself to develop? By hypothesis his *Grand Être* should be complete, beyond the range of addition or substraction; if it be only an appotentiating divinity, how should we distinguish it from the creatures of men's imagination—heroes, demi-gods, saints and intellectual giants? Mythology is full of fantastic figures but we do not call them divine. True, historical philosophy has left a place for a "growing" God, sometimes called a Limited Deity. William James conceived of it as the only spiritual object which the Pragmatic

[19] Comte, *op. cit.*, II, 123.

method could seriously consider. It may be that Comte was thinking of a *Grand* Being, not the *Grandest*. There is no proof of this in his speculations; the *Grand Être* appears as an independent divinity subject to no external forces except, perhaps, the *Ewig Weibliche*. Still, his theory of constant changes in the moral character of the race suggests the undefined image of a changing God to whom man will insensibly conform his own habits of thought and behavior. If such be his doctrine we can easily see how its effectiveness would be enormously increased by the new discoveries of the biological sciences. Here, as we have already noted, the human species perpetuates the fundamental properties of *all* life, not alone the history of a single species. The principles of homogeneity, continuity and diversification are illustrated by the new and pertinent materials of organic evolution. Certainly, the particular principle of altruism or sacrifice is found to be at work in the actions of animals, for example, the lioness' protection of her young at the risk of her own life. The expositor of the Comtean theory has much to support him in his attempt to make humanity a limited divinity, not a full-fledged, self-contained Deity. But even this may not be the final and authentic account of Comte's argument. When his whole field of thought has been canvassed we are forced to ask whether he is not setting up postulates regulating the possible character and activity of the Deity *who is to be,* rather than giving a description of the Being *who already is*. In short, is he not defining the limiting concept which stands at the end of the series of attributes commonly assigned to a creature called man? Must not his Deity, then, be a conceptual Ideal which will be objectified, point by point and by slow degrees, in the unceasing development of the human race?

The subject may be elucidated further by an examination of Kant's analysis of the "Ideal," which he is obliged to regard as a sheer illusion. He tells us that *concepts* of the understanding can in no case represent objective reality; they contain only the "forms of thought," that is, the principles or qualities which belong to an object in the non-mental world, insofar as we have detected them in experience. *Ideas* as contradistinguished from concepts are further removed from the transcendental object, because under no circumstances do we find them presented in the images of the senses; they are logical relations by means of which the mind adjusts its concepts to one another. Again, the *Ideal* is still further removed from reality; it is, for us, a concrete thought which we accept as a mental thing but which we cannot obtain from sensory action. Yet it *seems* to us that if we could proceed far enough in our acquaintance with our inner perceptions, we might come upon a nonempirical manifold, a supreme Object, God, to which we make bold to think it must correspond. This process is common to all attempts to discover the fundamental object of thought. For example, humanity implies at once the "essential qualities belonging to human nature" which I derive by direct sensation; this gives me the concept man. When, however, I observe the highest aims which I associate with the totality of human experience, together with other elements which may in time belong to the character of man, especially the values of moral life, then I reach what Kant calls the "perfect determination of the idea of humanity." [20] But even so intricate an analysis as this does not bring us to a knowledge of the independent object itself. We deal with an idea, only an idea. So far as we may judge this is precisely what Comte has done, and we shall endeavor to prove the truth of the statement in a moment. It is obvious that Kant's argument for the existence of God based on the sense of moral obligation, has no bearing on Comte's discussion. Kant requires, as we know already, the acceptance of two postulates, the immortality of the soul, and the presence, here, of a divine order which can reconcile man's thwarted desire for happiness with the attainment of moral excellence. The latter cannot be reached by the processes of natural law, only by divine intervention in the affairs of men; this implies that God exists; otherwise justice is an insensate dream. Now Comte has no need for this hypothesis, since the *Grand Être,* whether it exist independently or not, is simply the human mind "writ large." The Idea and the Object are completely joined. The Ideal before him is the "idea of the divine mind"—Kant quotes the phrase from Plato; the ideal must be that which is in the process of realization, is itself the very object of adoration and must be consistently accepted as such. We shall show, in the next pages, that Comte mistakes the ideal for the object, when he should have kept its identity with the idea of God, intact and permanent.

Altruism, Spirit of the New Religion

We shall test the validity of his thesis by an examination of the meaning of altruism. Morality, for Comte, was the consummate achievement of human experience. He was profoundly dissatisfied with the decisions of the French Revolution. Men looked upon government as the instrument for the preservation of the social order,—a passive medium of control, a set of prohibitions, a check against trespass upon our political liberties, the maintenance of balance between certain irreconcilable social forces. The whole system was negative whereas it should be positive. He held government to be a constructive agent, "an active function destined to make all special activities work together for one general good." [21] Such an end could not be reached by the imposition of external authority. True liberty

---

[20] *Critique of Pure Reason.* Trans. by Smith, p. 486.

[21] Comte, *Early Essays on Social Philosophy.* Trans. by H. D. Hutton (New York: E. P. Dutton, 1911), p. 318, note.

is the creation of moral character, not a dogmatic formula deduced from abstract reason and hardened into civil law. It is a strange but real fact that morals are the last phase of human behavior to throw off the fetters of metaphysical thought.[22] We assume that the individual will has prescriptive rights and that it cannot be swayed by any judgment but its own. We find, however, by empirical test, that will is a social phenomenon formed and guided by the common needs of the race. This is an important discovery and a permanent contribution to scientific truth. Its value depends on the conjunction of two elementary laws, first, that humanity is a congeries of multitudes of separate wills and secondly, that its essential properties are perpetuated from one generation to another. Society, in fine, is an organism and its behavior is the interaction of all its parts "for the general good." Hence, the ruling principle of conduct must be the law of altruism, a principle now recognized for the first time as the supreme law of social behavior.[23]

So far we have set forth what seems to be the attitude of the Positivist philosophy. It is held to be original, a new theory springing from a new outlook on moral values. This claim we reject and in rejecting it propose to prove (1) that distinguished thinkers have anticipated Comte's conclusions point for point, in many cases far surpassing him in persuasiveness of argument, and (2) that they have applied the results of their researches solely to persons resident in a physical environment, never to an hypostatized humanity whose qualities they could not fully understand.

What do we mean by the term altruism? Comte extracted the word from its Latin sources, stood the ego over against its *alter* and affirmed that moral duty consisted wholly in cultivating the interests of one's neighbor. Modern industry, for instance, implies instant and complete coöperation between capitalist and proletarian worker. He does not take into account the likelihood that the former is sure to demand more altruism of the other than he himself is willing to give.[24] The Positivist principle is infallible; it runs like a flame through all his counsels.[25] It seized upon the imagination of his contemporaries more vigorously than the idea of equality upon the fancy of a preceding age. Humanity, humanitarianism, brotherhood became watchwords of the hour in England as in France. Sir Henry Maine, the noted jurist, writes:—

The notion of what, for want of a better phrase, I must call a moral brotherhood in the whole human race, has been steadily gaining ground during the whole course of history, and we have now a large abstract term answering to this notion—Humanity.[26]

[22] *Ibid.*, p. 234.   [23] A. Comte, *System of Positive Polity*, II, 54 sq.
[24] Levy-Bruehl, *op. cit.*, p. 387.   [25] *System of Positive Polity*, I, 10–11; IV, 366 sq.
[26] *Early Hist. of Institutions.* Quoted by F. E. Marvin, in *Comte, the Founder of Sociology*, p. 189.

The voice of Mazzini in impassioned appeal for Italian independence and the stolid but penetrating invective of Karl Marx against the working-man's serfdom in the ruling economic system, utter the same note of social (not political) equality, in different languages, from different types of experience, but with the same devout fervor—"Let men live for others."

But Altruism as defined by its framer has two meanings, as Levy-Bruehl has well stated: "Once being firmly persuaded that we live *in* humanity and *by* humanity, we shall also convince ourselves that we must live *for* humanity." [27] There is, as Adam Smith argues, a sympathetic induction that belongs to the natural bent of the mind, and the history of mankind confirms its presence and its power. We live by means of society because of a biological decree and we maintain our physical health by obeying the laws of economics and scientific medicine, both of which are social in origin and content. Again, we live *in* society by virtue of our inherited intelligence which enables us to respond to our neighbor's words as well as his muscular behavior by the familiar *contre-coup* or social repercussion. Language and conceptual judgment go hand in hand to make all experience a social procedure. The second meaning introduces the peculiarly moral tone. "Malebranche," writes Levy-Bruehl, "said that God is the seat of intelligence; Comte would say on his side that humanity is the seat of goodwill." It is this aspect of the term that Spencer has adopted. To live for others is something more systematic, more deliberate, than the sudden reaction to another's movement, which may be an imitative response or a gesture of defense as when we shrink back from a threatening object. Resentment and sympathetic advance are both instinctive actions, springing from our relations with our fellows. When these instincts are touched by a specific moral motive they may be properly defined by the terms egoism or altruism. If we say with a writer in the London *Spectator* (May 27, 1938) that "the Germans and Italians are not in Spain for any altruistic reason," we imply that General Franco's foreign aides have sent their battalions and muniments of war not for the purpose of speeding his cause to a coveted victory but because they deem such a victory to be one of the means by which the Fascist creed may fasten its tentacles more firmly upon the body politic of Europe. Altruism is wholly antithetical to Egoism, as Spencer said, and Fascism is a brutal form of Egoism designed to destroy the altruistic principles of a democratic state. This is the second meaning of the term; shall we assume that men did not know its import before Positivism appeared? Let us inspect the evidence.

We begin with the plain unvarnished teachings of David Hume, one of Comte's sponsors. Hume is certain that moral distinctions belong to the original nature of man. If he be invited to give his reasons he will return

[27] *Op. cit.*, p. 386.

in every case to the testimony of experience,—*aposteriori,* as he so frequently says. Truth is always attained by the application of the laws of logical thought; virtue, on the other hand, is determined by the operations of the human sentiments. "Extinguish all the warmer feelings and prepossessions in form of virtue, and all disgust or aversion to vice; render men totally indifferent towards these distinctions, and morality is no longer a practical study, nor has it any tendency to regulate our lives and actions." [28] Nature has provided these "internal" feelings and made them "universal in the whole species." To be sure, in some cases, "nice distinctions must be made, just conclusions drawn, distant comparisons formed, complicated relations examined, and general facts fixed and ascertained"; still the ability to approve the good and reprobate the evil is a function of mind conferred by nature upon the human person, and never extinguished even under extreme circumstances, for example, in confirmed criminals or cynical critics. In his first book, the *Treatise,* Hume defines sympathy as a faculty of the soul on a level with the energy used by man to promote his own interests. In the later book, the *Enquiries,* his exposition takes another turn. Analysis of experience shows that "social virtues" issue from the "circumstance of utility." [29] Skeptics have therefore concluded that moral discriminations are the result of education, "invented and encouraged by the arts of politicians, in order to render men more tractable." But "public affection" is neither a superinduced quality of thought nor a fictitious attitude of behavior; it is the natural approval of agreeable relations with one's neighbor. Sympathy for others is, in the untrained mind, much "fainter than our concern for ourselves," but in cultivated minds the "interests of society" become in time the ordinary incentives to action. In short, friendship, benevolence and the like turn out to be "best supported maxims" of the group. Hence, self-love and regard for others make up together the program of a "complete morality." These are the teachings of David Hume; they refer exclusively to the conduct of a human agent. Hypothetical ideals are excluded; extra-human applications are never mentioned. Comte would have done well to restrict his study of altruism to the society which he personally knew.

Let us test the thesis further by consulting the argument of Immanuel Kant. He is interested primarily in the practical judgment of moral manhood. Morality depends, in no way, upon the operation of the feelings but solely on the exercise of the will, as we have already noted.[30] The one factor in human behavior that can be called *good* is the Good Will. Happiness, a species of feeling, is never an unqualified good; it may and does inspire personal pride, a condition fraught with danger to the moral life;

[28] *Enquiries,* Sec. 1.   [29] *Ibid.,* Sec. 5.   [30] *Supra,* Chap. X.

at times also it generates sheer presumption. Nor are the several sources of happiness certain to produce the desired result, for example, the goods of fortune, power, fame, honor, or the types of temperament such as candor or friendliness, or even the stern moral virtues like self-control or unbounded courage, which may even appear to "constitute the intrinsic worth of a person." A good will is good not because of the favorable consequences its acts may entail but because it embodies the maxim of duty, the express form of the categorical imperative. Duty is the necessity of acting from respect to law, and law is the exact reflection of the judgment of a rational mind. Duty therefore proceeds from the recognition of certain *ends* corresponding to natural laws. Man alone of all natural creatures has the end *in his own person*. Objects which satisfy the ordinary wants of mankind have *market* value only; they serve our needs. Objects which answer to private tastes such as the desire for aesthetic beauty, have a *fancy* value. But that whose value depends on nothing outside it but has a dignity of its own, this is the intrinsic and completely satisfying end, namely, the human self.

It is obvious that rational selves are united by a peculiar bond which Kant proposes to call the Kingdom of Ends. The law which rules in the kingdom may be stated as follows: "So act as to treat humanity, whether in thine own person or in that of any other, in every case as an end withal, never as a means only." Thus, the man who makes a deceitful promise, e. g., a promise to repay a loan though he knows he can never do so, is using a joint member of the kingdom for the borrower's good, and not for the good of the lender. The dignity of his neighbor is seriously invaded; the law of altruistic regard is summarily broken. Neither personal interest nor privileged position can be a true incentive in moral action. For each member of the kingdom is by right a sovereign—he makes the law; but he is also a subject—he must obey the law. Here, surely, is the perfect conjunction of the two principles which guide men in their social intercourse, namely, benevolence and justice. Yet while Kant speaks in one place [31] of the maxims as "Ideals only," he nevertheless insists they represent the only universal application of the principle of duty. Further, while he refers to other intelligent beings "existing as ends in themselves," [32] he is careful to say that we can arrive at the maxim just explained "without quitting the moral knowledge of common human reason." [33] Hence, Comte, even if he were so minded, could not cite the Critical argument in support of his theory that humanity, the supreme object of worship, alone incorporates the attributes of consummate excellence, namely, altruism. Kant is concerned strictly with the lot of man upon the earth.

[31] Abbott, *Kant's Theory of Ethics,* Ed. 6, p. 52.   [32] *Ibid.,* p. 46.   [33] *Ibid.,* p. 20.

There is one last but clinching stroke in the refutation of Comte's thesis. He assumes in his *Polity* that altruism will ultimately be the solitary virtue in human character, and by parity of reasoning the crowning quality in the *Grand Être*. The claim is important and merits close attention. We must distinguish at once between (1) the presence of a single attribute into which all subsidiary qualities have been merged, and (2) the ideal of character, the last term in the series of qualities known to us, the final stage in the development of character, where all the integral qualities are combined into one whole. The first situation is a consolidated fact, the second a noumenal concept, to adopt Kant's phrase. The two situations may be compared, they cannot be indentified.

(1) Is it possible to conceive of a moral self which possesses only a single comprehensive quality? Logic has a convincing answer to the question:— if an object can have but one pervasive color, e. g., *red,* then because there is no other color with which it may be compared and from which it may be distinguished, color as a property of body disappears entirely and the definition of color is canceled. In the same way, if moral agents can develop but one form of virtue, e. g., altruism, the meaning of virtue as a quality of behavior vanishes from view; we are left with a set of psychological reactions and nothing more. Definition is always the conjunction of genus and differentia, the specific form of a given genus. Hence, deductive logic forbids us to follow the course prescribed by the Positivist creed. Again, appeal must be made to inductive experience. Is it true that complementary virtues, egoistic and altruistic, can be eliminated from practical conduct? Spencer has analyzed the situation with rare acumen. In his chapter on *Egoism and Altruism,* he argues, first, that strict attention to the development of his own body and mind enables the individual agent to make himself "the immediate source of happiness to those around him." [34] On the other hand, if men and women suppress the egoistic instincts, they do a direct disservice to their families and professional colleagues, for instance, the self-abnegating mother who injures her health by her undiscriminating care of the children. In many cases the deliberate practice of altruism excites strong egoistic tendencies in the object of regard. Volumes have been written with warnings against a miscalculated benevolence. Ibsen had left us an unforgettable study of wrongs committed in the name of a higher altruism. Pastor Brand with his religious slogan—All or Nothing—sacrificed his mother, his wife and child, the loyalty of his people and his own life. This is a form of unreflecting egoism. Rational egoism, on the contrary, insures a steady development of all our powers, the appreciation of Bishop Butler's teaching that side by side with self-love stands the virtue of benevolence which later he elects to

[34] *Principles of Ethics,* Pt. I, Chap. 13.

identify with conscience. If Comte intends to exclude the former from the supreme Object of adoration, he will have a truncated humanity which he presents as a model to his Positivist followers.

Still more serious are the effects following the elision of egoistic desires on a communal level. Comte assumes that the problems of industry will be settled just as soon as altruism is recognized as the governing principle of action. Employer and employee will adjust their differences by due conciliation on both sides. Unfortunately, here again the acceptance of a noble rule does not insure immediate compliance with its terms. Self-interest asserts its unimpeachable rights for each party to the contract. The man of privilege is opposed by the man of ambition, and neither will yield. Neither *should* yield, if the purposes of mind or body are threatened by the proposed decision. No doubt there is a decision satisfactory to all concerned, if only it could be discovered. It cannot be produced by appealing to the sentimental values of the formula; it must be the result of hard and honest thinking, with compromise here and surrender there. "Living for others" is an ignoble creed, if it requires any man or group of men to contract themselves into economic slavery. So much for affairs within the state. Not different from this is the demand of the totalitarian state that its members submit themselves, body, soul and spirit, to the political hierarchy. Thus, when the issues of war hang in the balance, individual citizens must suffer and sacrifice and die; they have no destiny apart from the destiny of the state. Comte makes no specific pronouncement on the matter of war; he assumed that war was the instrument of an ideology now extinct; hence there was no need to study its effect upon the principle under review. But the facts of experience are against his claim. If altruism rules in human society, war is certainly at an end; but altruism does not rule in any known society, and the conflict of interest is a common phenomenon. Furthermore, the divinity whose nature Comte is unfolding is subject to two unchanging laws, that of order and that of progress. Progress is dynamic, and dynamics is a process leading from a less to a more highly developed status. There will be continued contention between dissimilar ideas; hence, the idea of altruism can only prevail if egoistic instincts are removed. When will that be, and how? Under present conditions the control of interests, sentiments and passions can be instituted in a given group by one method alone, namely, the suppression of individual freedom. It is doubtful whether any intelligent society will long submit to this procedure, or if it should, whether it would retain its intelligence for any length of time.

(2) Turning to the other member of the alternative, we inquire whether the concept of humanity is to be a shadowy hope, an ideal never to be realized, or an historical goal in due time to be attained. It is a

curious incident in the story of English ethics that a mechanical engineer should be the only thinker who attempts to depict an absolute system of moral behavior. The adjective adopted usually refers to those "principles of right conduct that exist out of relation to life as conditioned upon the earth"; they are therefore called "eternal principles" which we can formally conceive but not actually practice. Spencer rejects this interpretation.[35] There are absolutely right actions in every human being's life,—the mother's physical relation to her babe, the father's play with his son. Absolute ethics demands that the "promptings of man's nature should have complete correspondence with the requirements of life as carried on in society." Ideal behavior conforms to the fundamental laws of the physical and biological sciences,[36] precisely as Comte himself taught. Absolute right, then, does not deal with metaphysical rules but with the laws plainly deduced from experimental action. Still, the problems confronting the serious thinker are many. When shall we know that we have acquired the scientific expertness needed for the "absolutely right" actions? Again, if we do arrive at the correct formula of behavior, how shall we stimulate the will to a formal decision with that end in view? "Intellect by itself," says Aristotle, "has no motive power." Furthermore, is moral law in the absolute society the same kind of law that governs in the relative conditions of the present time? Instinctive behavior and habitual patterns will always be the same: how shall we make the necessary adjustments in a totally different environment? Spencer and Comte reach the same impasse. The sole solution rests in a critical analysis of each new situation; we must correct here and eliminate there, until the balance between egoism and altruism grows relatively stable. This is the scientific method open to all men of keen mind and good intentions. Can the Positivist religion yield a more satisfactory program?

[35] *Op. cit.,* Chap. 15.   [36] *Ibid.,* p. 319.

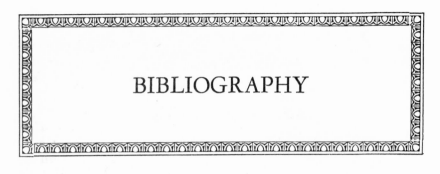

BIBLIOGRAPHY

CHAPTER II: PLATO

Burnet, J. *Greek Philosophy*. Part I. Thales to Plato. London: The Macmillan Co., 1924. x + 360 pp.

Cornford, F. M. *Plato's Cosmology*. London: Kegan, Paul, Trench, Trubner & Co., 1937. xviii + 376 pp.

Hardie, W. F. *A Study of Plato*. Oxford: Clarendon Press, 1936. viii + 171 pp.

Ritter, C. *The Essence of Plato's Philosophy*. Trans. by A. Alles. New York: The Dial Press, 1933. 413 pp.

Robin, Leon. *Platon*. Paris: F. Alcan, 1938. vii + 346 pp.

Stewart, J. A. *Plato's Doctrine of Ideas*. Oxford: Clarendon Press, 1909. 206 pp.

Taylor, A. E. *Plato: the Man and His Work*. London: Methuen & Co., 1926. xi + 522 pp.

Zeller, E. *Plato and the Older Academy*. London: Longmans, Green & Co., 1888. xiii + 629 pp.

CHAPTER III: ARISTOTLE

Aristotle. *Metaphysics*. Trans. by W. D. Ross, 2nd edition, Oxford: Clarendon Press, 1928.

Grote, George. *Aristotle*. London: J. Murray, 2nd edition, 1883. xvi + 687 pp.

Jaeger, Werner. *Aristotle*. Trans. by Richard Robinson. Oxford: Clarendon Press, 1934. 410 pp.

Robin, Leon. *La Morale Antique*. Paris: F. Alcan, 1938. 180 pp.

Ross, W. D. *Aristotle*. London: Methuen & Co., 1923. vii + 300 pp.

—————— *Aristotle's Metaphysics*. Oxford: Clarendon Press, 1924. 2 vols.

Zeller, E. *Aristotle*. English translation. London: Longmans, 1892. 2 vols.

CHAPTER IV: EPICURUS

Bailey, Cyril. *Epicurus: the Extant Remains*. Oxford: Clarendon Press, 1926. 432 pp.

—————— *The Greek Atomists and Epicurus*. Oxford: Clarendon Press, 1928. viii + 619 pp.

Cicero. *De Natura Deorum*. Loeb Classical Library. London: W. Heinemann, 1933. v + 268 pp.

Guyau, J. M. *La Morale d'Epicure*. Paris: F. Alcan, 1910. 292 pp.

Hicks, R. D. *Stoic and Epicurean*. London: Longmans, 1911. xix + 412 pp.
Joyau, E. *Epicure*. Paris: F. Alcan, 1910. ii + 222 pp.
Lucretius. *De Rerum Natura*. English translation by A. J. Munro. London: G. Bell & Son, 1908. xx + 267 pp.

CHAPTER V: MARCUS AURELIUS

Marcus Aurelius. *The Meditation*. Translation and commentary by A. S. L. Farquharson. Oxford: Clarendon Press, 1944. 2 vols.
——— *The Communings with Himself*. Greek text and translation, by C. R. Haines. Loeb Classical Library. London: W. Heinemann, 1916. xxxii + 414 pp.
——— *The Meditations*. Trans by George Long. New York: Lovell, Coryell & Co. n.d. 312 pp.
Loisel, G. *La Vie de Marc-Surele*. Paris: University Press, 1929. viii + 306 pp.
Renan, E. Essay on Marcus Aurelius in *Poetry of Celtic Races, and Other Essays*, London: Scott Publishing Co. n.d. xxxviii + 226 pp.
Sedgwick, M. D. *Marcus Aurelius, a Biography*. New Haven: Yale University Press, 1922. 309 pp.
Taine, M. *Marc-Aurele, in Nouveaux essais de Critique et d'Histoire*. Machette, 1907. 376 pp.

CHAPTER VI: AUGUSTINE

Augustine. *The Confessions*. Translation in *Nicene and Post-Nicene Fathers*, First series, Buffalo, N.Y.: The Christian Literature Co., 1886. Vol. I.
Augustine. *The City of God*. Same, 1887. Vol. II.
Augustine. *The Holy Trinity*. Same, 1887. Vol. III.
Augustine. *De Libero Arbitrio*. Trans. by R. M. McKeon, in *Selections from Medieval Philosophers*. New York: Chas. Scribner's Sons, 1929. Vol. I.
Cochrane, C. N. *Christianity and the Classical Culture*. New York: Oxford University Press. Reprint, 1944. vii + 523 pp.
Gilson, Etienne. *L'Introduction à l'Etude de St. Augustin*. Paris: Vrin, 1929. vii + 352 pp.
Grandgeorge, L. *St. Augustin et le Neo-Platonisme*. Paris: E. Leroux, 1896. 158 pp.
Harnack, A. *History of Dogma*. English translation from 3rd German Ed., Boston: Little, Brown & Co., 1905. Vol. V.
Montgomery, W. *St. Augustine: Aspects of His Life and Thought*. New York: Nodder & Stoughton, 1914. xi + 255 pp.
Nourrison, J. F. *La Philosophie de St. Augustin*. Paris: Didier et Cie, 1865. 2 vols.
Osmun, G. W. *Augustine: the Thinker*. New York: The Abingdon Press. Reprint, 1924. 250 pp.
Warfield, B. B. *Studies in Tertullian and Augustine*. New York: Oxford University Press, 1930. v + 412 pp.

CHAPTER VII: LEIBNIZ

Duncan, G. M. *The Philosophical Works of Leibniz.* New Haven: Tuttle, Morehouse & Taylor Co., 1908. ix + 400 pp.

Langley, A. G. *New Essays of Leibniz.* Chicago: The Open Court Publishing Co., 1916. xiv + 861 pp.

Latta, R. *Leibniz, The Monadology and Other Philosophical Writings.* London: Oxford University Press, 1925. x + 437 pp.

Montgomery, G. M. *Leibniz: The Discourse on Metaphysics, Correspondence with Arnauld and Monadology.* Chicago: The Open Court Publishing Co., 1902. xxi + 272 pp.

Nourrison, J. F. *La Philosophie de Leibniz.* Paris: Machette, 1860. viii + 502 pp.

Russell, B. *Critical Exposition of the Philosophy of Leibniz.* Cambridge: University Press, 1900. xvi + 311 pp.

CHAPTER VIII: SPINOZA

Spinoza, B. *The Ethics,* in *Chief Works of Spinoza.* Trans. by R. M. M. Elwes. London: G. Bell & Son, 1909. 2 vols.

——— *The Correspondence of Spinoza.* Translated and edited by A. Wolf. London: G. Allen & Unwin, 1928. 502 pp.

Brunschvicg, L. *Spinoza.* Paris: F. Alcan. 2nd edition, 1906. 235 pp.

Caird, J. *Spinoza.* Edinburgh: Blackwood & Co., 1888. xv + 315 pp.

Couchou, F. L. *Benoit de Spinoza.* Paris: F. Alcan, 1902. xiv + 365 pp.

Hallett, M. F. *Aeternitas: A Spinozistic Study.* Oxford: Clarendon Press, 1930. xix + 344 pp.

Joachim, M. H. *A Study of the Ethics of Spinoza.* Oxford: Clarendon Press, 1901. xiv + 316 pp.

Martineau, J. *Study of Spinoza.* London: Macmillan & Co., 1882. xi + 371 pp.

Pollock, F. *Spinoza: His Life and Philosophy.* London: Duckworth & Co., 1899. xxiv + 422 pp.

Powell, E. E. *Spinoza and Religion.* Boston: Chapman and Grimes, 1941. xii + 344 pp.

CHAPTER IX: HUME

Hume, David. *Treatise of Human Nature.* Edited by Selby-Bigge. Oxford: Clarendon Press, 1906. xxiv + 432 pp.

——— *Enquiries.* Edited by Selby-Bigge. Oxford: Clarendon Press. 2nd edition, 1902. xl + 371 pp.

——— *Dialogue Concerning Natural Religion.* Edited by W. Kemp Smith. Oxford: Clarendon Press, 1935. 283 pp.

Adamson, R. *Development of Modern Philosophy.* Edinburgh: Blackwood, 1934. viii + 364 pp.

Hendel, C. W. *Studies in the Philosophy of David Hume.* Princeton: University Press, 1925. xiv + 420 pp.

Huxley, T. H. *David Hume.* English Men of Letters series. New York: Harper, 1902. vii + 206 pp.

Laird, J. *Hume's Philosophy of Human Nature.* London: Harrison & Sons, Ltd., 1939. xxxiv + 228 pp.

Orr, James. *David Hume and His Influence on Philosophy and Theology.* New York: Chas. Scribner's Sons, 1903. ix + 246 pp.

Smith, N. Kemp. *The Philosophy of David Hume.* London: Macmillan & Co., Ltd., 1941. xxiv + 568 pp.

Stephen, Leslie. *English Thought in the 18th Century.* New York: G. P. Putnam & Sons, 1927. Vol. I, Ch. 6.

CHAPTER X: IMMANUEL KANT

Kant, Immanuel. *Critique of Pure Reason.* Trans. by N. Kemp Smith. London: Macmillan & Co., 2nd impression, 1933. xiii + 681 pp.

—— *Critique of Practical Reason.* Trans. by T. K. Abbot. London: Longmans, Green & Co. 6th edition, 1923. lx + 368 pp.

—— *Critique of Judgment.* Trans. by J. H. Bernard. London: Macmillan and Co. 2nd edition, revised, 1914. xlvii + 429 pp.

—— *Religion within the Limits of Reason Alone.* Trans. by T. M. Greene and M. M. Hudson. Chicago: The Open Court Publishing Co., 1934. xxxv + 200 pp.

Caird, E. *The Critical Philosophy of Kant.* Glasgow: J. Machlehose & Sons, 1909. 2 vols.

England, F. A. *Kant's Conception of God.* New York: The Dial Press, 1930. 256 pp.

Macmillan, B. A. C. *The Crowning Phase of the Critical Philosophy.* London: Macmillan & Co., Ltd., 1912. xxv + 347 pp.

Smith, N. Kemp. *Commentary to Kant's Critique of Pure Reason,* with Appendix. London: Macmillan & Co. 2nd edition, 1923.

Webb, C. C. J. *Kant's Philosophy of Religion.* Oxford: Clarendon Press, 1926. 218 pp.

CHAPTER XI: COMTE

Comte, Auguste. *Cours de Philosophie Positive.* Paris: Bailliere. 3rd edition, 1809. 6 vols.

—— *The Positive Polity.* London: Longmans, 1875–77. 4 vols.

Martineau, Harriet. *Positive Philosophy, translated and condensed.* New York: Calvin Blanchard, 1855. 838 pp.

Caird, E. *Social Philosophy and Religion of Comte.* Glasgow: Machlehose & Sons, 1893. 210 pp.

Levy-Bruehl, L. *La Philosophie de Auguste Comte.* Paris: F. Alcan, 1900. 417 pp.

Marvin, F. E. *Comte, the Founder of Sociology.* New York: Wiley, 1937. 216 pp.

Milhaud, G. *Le Positivisme et le Progres d'Esprit.* Paris: F. Alcan, 1902. 209 pp.

Mill, J. S. *Auguste Comte and Positivism.* London: Routledge & Sons. n.d. 203 pp.

Roux, Adrien. *La Pensee d'Auguste Comte.* Paris: "Editions et Librairie." E. Chiron, Editeur, 1920. 431 pp.

Whittaker, T. *Comte and Mill.* New York: Dodge (Philosophies ancient and modern) n.d. i + 91 pp.

INDEX